BELLE ISLE TO 8 MILE:
AN INSIDER'S GUIDE TO DETROIT

Editors:
Andy Linn, Emily Linn, and Rob Linn

Authors:
Cassie Basler, Ryan Healy, Andy Linn, Emily Linn, and Rob Linn

Contributing Authors:
Justin Ames, Dan Austin, Matt Beuckelaere, Achille Bianchi, Rachel Harkai, Anna Hipsman-Springer, Greg Lenhoff, Matt Lewis, Diane Linn, Thom Linn, Matt McIntyre, Aaron Mondry, Glen Morren, John Notarianni, Kit Parks, Alison Piech, Matthew Piper, Nicole Rupersburg, Molly Schoen, and Angela Wisniewski

Contributors:
Sara Aldridge, Stephen Austin, Maia Asshaq, D'Marco Ansari, Amy Elliott Bragg, Margaret Cassetto, Aaron Egan, Meagan Elliott, Emily Gail, Emily Lardner, Frank Nemecek, and Alok Sharma

Cover Design and Illustrations by Emily Linn
Design by Angela Fortino
Maps by Rob Linn
Copy Editing by Stephen Bublitz

ISBN: 978-1-4675-5752-8
First Edition

Written, researched, designed, illustrated, edited, and printed in
Detroit, Michigan.

If you discover errors, corrections, or possible additions, please drop
us a line: belleisleto8mile@gmail.com.

Belle Isle to 8 Mile: An Insider's Guide to Detroit is available for
purchase in bulk by institutions and retailers. For information, send
inquiries to Belle Isle to 8 Mile: belleisleto8mile@gmail.com.

This book is dedicated to our parents, Thom and Diane Linn, for teaching us to love Detroit, and to our grandmother, Elizabeth Brunette, for inspiring us with her stories about the city.

ACKNOWLEDGMENTS

We're grateful to Matt Beuckelaere and Alison Piech for their incredible kindness, support, and patience.

Thank you to Dan Austin of HistoricDetroit.org for his knowledge, generosity, and friendship.

This book was made possible in part by support from the Awesome News Taskforce Detroit, Detroit SOUP, and The Next Big Thing presented by Model D.

Special thanks to the following people for their generous support: Lars Abrahamsson, Kendra Arnold, Dan Austin, Richard Bailhe, Kate Baker, William Baker, Melanie Basler, George Basler, Geoffrey Batchelor, Kathy Berghoff, Ben Blackwell, Ken Bloink, Pierre Boulos, Todd Kropp and Darcy Brandel, Elizabeth Brunette, Adrienne Buccella, Nathaniel Burge, Susan Burns, Mary Lorene Carter, Margaret Cassetto, Lisa Charbonneau, William Cole, Fawn Colombatto, Susan Crowell, Denise Dalrymple, Brian Dawson, Marilyn Dickerson, Timothy Dinan, Christopher Dion, Michael Dombrowski, Jocelyn Dombrowski, Matt Drake, Sean Drate, Kenneth Dunn, Shawna Lee and Brendan Fay, Maria Fisher, Nicodemus Ford, Susan A. Fox, Arlene J. Frank, Ryan Frederick, Denny Freitag, Fryar, Erika Fulk, Teresa and Mike Gabry, Carolyn Geck, Sophie George, Stefanie Georges, The Gillard+Blanchard Family, Gary Gillette, Joanne M. Golden, Amy Gore, Adam Grant, Mike Haener, Amy Haimerl, Robert Halford, Chris Hammer, Ann Hanson, The Heap-Hessell Family, Kenny Hemler, Daniel E. Herman, Jane Hoehner, Wendy Hoin, Misty Jensen, Randall Juip, Kellie Kalish, Shellie Kaminski, Chris Kar, Katie, Nycole Kelly, Betty Kennedy, Mike Kirk, Bill & Natalie Klitzke, Renee Paul Knight, Paul and Ellen Koehler, Adam Kramer, Lynda Krupp, Dennis LaVoy, Ondine LeBlanc, Sarah and Greg Lenhoff, Rod Leon, David Lilly, Thom and Diane Linn, Brandon Linton, Stephen Maiseloff, Edward and Roger Maki-Schramm, Nicole Mangis, Elaine and Mark Mardirosian, Adele Martz, Colin McComb, Mike McLaughlin, Joanne McNary, Justin Merrill, Deborah G. Montgomery, Stephanie Newell, Lisa Nowak, Sarah Nowosad, Leroy O'Flynn-Tsang, Jamie Ontiveros, Samuel Patterson, William Phillips, Jeanette Pierce, Emily Raine, Patrick Ranspach, Brendan Ringlever, Brian and Tifani Sadek, Richard Sanders, Hubert Sawyers III, David Schon, Ian Schulz, Jon Schulz, James Serbinski, Arlie Skory, Stacy, Nicole & Andrew Stewart, Eric Szulc, Matthew Terry, Lauren Tolles, David and Veronica Topolewski, Matt Topper, Jordan Twardy, Amanda Van Dusen, Sean Van Wormer,

Alissa Vermeulen, A. Warshaw, Mary Wassel, Kimberly Watts, Lisa Waud, L. Rodger Webb, Mariah Cherem and Jeremy Wheeler, Scott White, Veronica Williams, Kevin Wilson, Christopher R. Wirth, Dave Zabihaylo, Susan Zakrzewski, Christopher Zbrozek, and Brandon Zwagerman.

The following people offered assistance, or support and shared their localized, insider knowledge and invaluable information, tips, and suggestions that made *Belle Isle to 8 Mile* a reality: Todd Abrams, Wayne AJ, D'Marco Ansari, Tina Arcand, Greg Baise, Joe Balistreri, Alana Bartol, Nate Bezanson, Glen Board, Maria Bologna, Mike Brady, Matthew C. Bramlitt, Darcy Brandel, Helen Bratzel, Jonathan Bromberg, Nicholi Brossia, Darrin Brouhard, Caitlin Brown, Gabby Buckay, Dave Bunch, Sarah Burger, Laura Burmann, Jeremy Burr, Sam Butler, Anna Callis, Joe Casey, Lianna Cecil, Stephanie Change, Joe Cialdella, Nanette Clare, Deb Collins, Gail Prohaska Cosgriff, Brian Crane, Julianne Cuneo, Sonia Dedeian, Nikki Desautelle, Gene Diggs, Jan Dijkers, Kristine Diven, Andree Dolan, Eric Dueweke, Pascal Dugay, Erin Ellis, Candace Ellison, Robert Evans, Patty Fedewa, Marni Feldman, Sabrina Fitzwilliams, Ashley Flintoff, Mike Forsythe, Kim Fracassa, Ben Friedman, Hans Fruechtenicht, Karen Gage, Carl Thomas Gladstone, Andy Goddeeris, Francis Grunow, Chris Haag, Evan Hansen, Kat Hartman, Dustin Hayford, Alana Hoey, Brigette Hollis, Greg Holman, LaVern Homan, Sylvia Hubbard, Michael Jackman, Jeffrey Jones, Tom Joseph, Amy Kaherl, Margo & Mark Kempinski, Noam Kimelman, Nicole Klepadlo, Bill & Natalie Klitzke, Emily Kostrzewa, Nick Kovach, Jeffrey Kroow, Mary Beth Langan, Sarah Lapinski, Al Larese, Sarah Lenhoff, Roger Lesinski, Illy Mack, Paul Mardirosian, Mike Maurer, Nicole Messenger, Bradley R. Mock, Sabrina Nelson, Claire Nelson, Sarah Nowosad, Janell O'Keefe, Giuseppe Palazzolo, Crystal Palmer, Gregory Parrish, Jennifer Paull, Lara Pierce, Joe Posch, Kathy Rashid, Kelly Ireland Rembert, Naomi Ruth, John Sauve, Riva Sayegh-McCullen, Ryan Schirmang, David Schon, Jon Schulz, Gary Schwartz, Asra Shaik, Brenda Shea, Shirley Sillars, Suneil Singh, Melissa Smiley, Eric Stephenson, Liz Sutton, Ian Swanson, Rachel & Paul Szlaga, Deborah Thompson, Matthew Tommelein, Geri Trombley, Vito Valdez, Jackie Victor, Michele Walke, Julian Watts, June West, Jeremy Whiting, Sybil Williams, Linda Yellin, Anastasios Zaharopoulos, and Matt Ziolkowski.

CONTENTS

INTRODUCTION

1 DOWNTOWN

2 MIDTOWN

3 EASTERN MARKET

4 CORKTOWN

5 SOUTHWEST

6 NEW CENTER/NORTH END

7 LOWER EAST SIDE

8 UPPER EAST SIDE

9 NEAR WEST SIDE

10 FAR WEST SIDE

11 HAMTRAMCK/HIGHLAND PARK

12 SUBURBS

EVENTS

INDEX

WELCOME
TO DETROIT

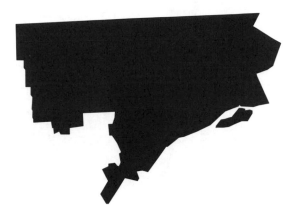

1. Downtown
2. Midtown
3. Eastern Market
4. Corktown
5. Southwest
6. New Center / North End
7. Lower East Side
8. Upper East Side
9. Near West Side
10. Far West Side
11. Hamtramck / Highland Park

WELCOME TO DETROIT

Whether traveling from across the globe or across 8 Mile, visitors to Detroit should come expecting an authentic, resilient city with a rich history and an exciting present. With a past as French as New Orleans, a musical heritage as rich as Nashville's, and a hardscrabble working-class legacy that has earned it the nickname "The Motor City," Detroit offers an unparalleled glimpse at American history through a beauty that can be difficult to capture. Detroit's troubles are well-documented, but it has nothing left to hide. In this city of neighborhoods, each community offers a different angle on the same prism: blue-collar epicureanism, raw art, bootstrap entrepreneurship, moxie-filled residents, and historic architecture. Whether in town for an instant or indefinitely, visitors and residents should look forward to an effusive welcome and numerous opportunities for immersion, inquiry, indulgence, inebriation, and introspection in a city that never misses an opportunity for celebration or inspiration.

HISTORY

1701 to World War II - Founded as a French city in 1701—when New Orleans was just a twinkle in Louis XIV's eye—Detroit embarked on what would become a proud, dynamic history several generations before the United States became a country. Built in the heart of Miami, Huron, and Ottawa tribe territories, city founder Antoine de La Mothe Cadillac named his settlement for the Detroit River—le détroit du Lac Érié—or, the strait of Lake Erie—and helped establish the city's ribbon farms. These long, narrow farms stretched several miles from the river and gave rise to a burgeoning agricultural center. After the Erie Canal opened in 1825, the city quickly became a center of Great Lakes transportation, shipbuilding, and manufacturing, and began its meteoric rise. Between 1820 and 1920, Detroit's population more than doubled nearly every decade, from 1,422 to 993,678 over a century. In 1896, a young Henry Ford built his first automobile, forever altering the city's future. Ford was soon joined by automotive luminaries such as William Durant, James Packard, Louis Chevrolet, Walter Chrysler, David Dunbar Buick, and the Dodge brothers, and Detroit quickly emerged as the center of automobile manufacturing. Attracted by middle class salaries and bountiful single family homes, thousands of residents moved to the city each month until the dawn of World War II.

DETROIT
INTRODUCTION

Post-World War II - Despite a proud, dynamic history for its first 250 years, Detroit is perhaps most associated with its most recent historical chapter. Although it served as the "Arsenal of Democracy" and manufactured material during the war, the end of World War II marked the beginning of a long, challenging time for the city. New manufacturing strategies and postwar trends in single family housing, coupled with plant closures, ill-advised federal policy, suburban sprawl, redlining, highway construction, urban renewal, racism, white flight, contagious abandonment, unemployment, and crime created a perfect storm that perpetuated rapid population loss. Despite promising developments downtown, and tenacious positive action by neighborhood residents and community groups, the city lost a crippling 1,135,791 residents—60% of its population—between 1950 and 2010.

Today - In recent years, the city has developed a renewed energy. In the core neighborhoods especially, new bars, restaurants, shops, and cultural attractions are opening alongside their steadfast, older counterparts. While outlying neighborhoods have traditionally been the most challenged by the city's problems, many are emerging with newfound vitality, as communities discover new, innovative approaches to reactivating vacant spaces and dealing with abandonment. These incremental, positive developments have spurred a change in public perception.

Further Reading - Those looking to learn more about the history, culture, and evolution of Detroit should check out one or more of the following books. Many of these titles are written by local authors and scholars—including Dan Austin, John Gallagher, John Carlisle, Bill McGraw, and Amy Elliott Bragg—who have played an important role in a recent surge in interest in the city's history.

- *313: Life in the Motor City* - John Carlisle
- *American Odyssey* - Robert E. Conot
- *Arc of Justice* - Kevin Boyle
- *Before Motown* - Lars Bjorn, and Jim Gallert
- *Buildings of Detroit, The* - W. Hawkins Ferry
- *Detroit Almanac, The* - Peter Gavrilovich and Bill McGraw
- *Forgotten Landmarks of Detroit* - Dan Austin
- *Grit, Noise, and Revolution* - David Carson
- *Hard Stuff* - Coleman Young and Lonnie Wheeler
- *Hidden History of Detroit* - Amy Elliott Bragg
- *Lafayette Park Detroit* - Charles Waldheim

- *Lost Detroit* - Dan Austin
- *Origins of the Urban Crisis, The* - Thomas J. Sugrue
- *Reimagining Detroit* - John Gallagher

PLANNING YOUR VISIT

Visitor Information Centers - Before arriving in Detroit or once on the ground, visitors and new residents alike should seek out information from one or both of Detroit's information centers, **D:hive** and the **Pure Michigan Detroit Welcome Center.** Though different, both of these resources offer a wealth of advice, answers, and information about visiting the city and the state. For those visiting or moving to the city, D:hive (see separate entry) serves as an exceptional starting point, with renowned tours and information on jobs, housing, and recreational opportunities. For visitors stopping in Detroit before heading for another Michigan city, the Pure Michigan Detroit Welcome Center *(2835 Bagley Ave., (313) 962-2360)* offers a host of information about Detroit and other Michigan cities.

Events - The 1980 Republican National Convention slogan still rings true: "Detroit loves a good party." From the nation's largest local music festival to the nation's second oldest Thanksgiving day parade, Detroiters love having a good time and sharing their city with visitors. Detroit has many parties, parades, festivals and traditions of its own, as well as outstanding celebrations for all of the national holidays. The events section of this book offers more than 75 notable events, and some of the larger events—such as North American International Auto Show in late January, and the Movement Electronic Music Festival in late May—tend to take over the city.

News, Information, and Events Listings - Before visiting the city, visitors can better tailor a trip to Detroit by keeping up with local news, learning about the city's history and architecture, and getting up to speed on the many events, concerts, festivals, and lectures that make Detroit such a lively city. In addition to the events listings and history sections of this book, the following sites offer information help put Detroit in context:

- Crain's Detroit Business - www.crainsdetroit.com
- Deadline Detroit - www.deadlinedetroit.com
- Detroit 1701 - www.detroit1701.org
- Detroit Blog - www.detroitblog.org
- Detroit Free Press - www.freep.com

- Detroit News - www.detroitnews.com
- Detroit Urbex - www.detroiturbex.com
- Detroit Yes - www.detroityes.com
- Forgotten Detroit - www.forgottendetroit.com
- Historic Detroit - www.historicdetroit.org
- Hour Detroit - www.hourdetroit.com
- Metro Times - www.metrotimes.com
- Model D Media - www.modeldmedia.com
- Night Train to Detroit - www.nighttraintodetroit.com
- Radial Logic - www.radial-logic.com
- Real Detroit Weekly - www.realdetroitweekly.com
- Sweet Juniper - www.sweetjuniperinspiration.com
- WDET 101.9 FM - www.wdetfm.org

GETTING HERE

Air - Metro Airport is 20 miles outside of downtown; travelers' options include taxis, car services, car rental, or personal arrangements. A SMART bus route spanning from downtown to the airport is limited to early morning and mid-afternoon service on weekdays.

Bus - Detroit is served by Megabus and Greyhound. Megabus has stops at the Rosa Parks Transit Center *(360 Michigan Ave.)* and Wayne State University *(Cass Ave. and Warren Ave.)*. The Greyhound terminal is located downtown at the Howard Street Station *(1001 Howard St.)*.

Car - If driving in, freeways are usually the fastest option: I-94 from the east/west, I-75 from the north/south, I-96 from the west side of Michigan, and from Canada, either the Ambassador Bridge via I-96, or the centrally-located Detroit Windsor Tunnel. The tunnel is usually the speedier option, but travelers can check ahead for travel times online. *www.dwtunnel.com.*

Rail - Train service into Detroit is restricted to eastbound travelers on Amtrak's Michigan Line, though Amtrak offers service from Toledo by bus. The Amtrak station in Detroit is conveniently located in New Center. *11 West Baltimore Ave.*

LODGING

234 Winder Street Inn - Guests at 234 Winder Street Inn stay in this elegant 1872 Second Empire home in the heart of the Brush

Park historic district. Visitors can enjoy a marble fireplace, antique hardwood furniture, chandeliers, and homemade breakfasts—features that help make 234 Winder an excellent value. Suite options include an expansive 1,800 square foot loft. 234 Winder St., www.234winderstinn.com, (313) 831-4091.

Detroit Marriott at the Renaissance Center - A 73-story hotel on Detroit's riverfront, the Marriott offers comfortable rooms at competitive prices. The nearly 1,300 available rooms feature 37-inch flat-screen televisions, Wi-Fi, and floor-to-ceiling windows for jaw dropping views of the city. There are two restaurants and a fitness center available, and leisure travelers can use the People Mover to conveniently tour downtown. *400 Renaissance Center, (313) 568-8000.*

DoubleTree Suites by Hilton Hotel Detroit Downtown - Fort Shelby - In the heart of Detroit's downtown, the Fort Shelby provides professional accommodations for visiting professionals. Rooms feature HDTVs, ergonomic chairs and desks, high-speed internet access, and include complimentary shuttle and gym access. Prices are higher than local competitors, but its conference capacities make it ideal for business patrons. The hotel is housed in a beautifully restored 1916 Classical Revival hotel. *525 W. Lafayette Blvd., (313) 963-5600.*

Honor & Folly - A small design-focused inn, Honor & Folly is a Corktown treasure. Located on Michigan Avenue above Slows Bar B Q, owner Meghan McEwen's cozy, light-filled bed and breakfast is decorated with charming antiques and Detroit- and Midwest-made goods (many of which are also for sale). There are just two rooms available, and weekends especially book up early, so plan ahead. Not just for out-of-towners, the space can also be rented out for an afternoon or evening for events.
2132 Michigan Ave, www.honorandfolly.com.

Hostel Detroit - A hostel in a simple two-story building in North Corktown, Hostel Detroit provides affordable shared accommodations for travelers. In addition to offering an hour-long orientation aimed at educating visitors about the city, its history, and options for their stay, the hostel also has bikes for rent. Online reservation only (PayPal account required); no walk-ins accepted. *2700 Vermont St., www.hosteldetroit.com, (313) 451-0333.*

The Inn on Ferry Street - Providing refined, comfortable lodging across a range of room types, the Inn on Ferry Street spans four separate late 19th-century Victorian homes and two carriage houses in Detroit's East Ferry Historic District (see separate entry). Each of the rooms—40 in all—offer unique, distinct design schemes, and boast elegant hardwood furnishings and decor. Full personal and business amenities including breakfast, in-room cable and Wi-Fi, and a complimentary shuttle service for greater downtown. Prices are best suited to business travelers and vary by room. *84 East Ferry St., www.innonferrystreet.com, (313) 871-6000.*

The Shorecrest Motor Inn - Located two blocks east of the RiverWalk, The Shorecrest Motor Inn is an upmarket motel suitable for Detroit's pleasure or budget business travelers. Rooms are kept clean, and feature amenities like HBO and Wi-Fi, as well as available room service from its in-house restaurant, the Clique (see separate entry). Free on-site parking and car rental available. *1316 E. Jefferson, www.shorecrestmi.com, (313) 568-3000.*

The Westin Book Cadillac Detroit - Immaculately (and miraculously) restored in 2008, the 453-room Book Cadillac offers a range of comfortable, stately rooms for downtown guests. The historic Italian Renaissance-Style building flawlessly melds comfort and elegance, complete with 42-inch flat-screen televisions, spacious bathrooms, and cloud-like beds. In addition to appropriate business amenities and a swimming pool, there are five bars and restaurants in the building. *1114 Washington Blvd., www.bookcadillacwestin.com, (313) 442-1600.*

GETTING AROUND

Orientation - In the wake of the great fire of 1805, legendary Chief Justice Augustus B. Woodward implemented his Woodward Plan. Inspired by Pierre Charles L'Enfant's plan for Washington D.C., The Woodward Plan established a hexagonal street grid centered on Grand Circus Park and Campus Martius Park. Though the plan was abandoned after only 11 years, and was never fully realized, Woodward's diagonal grid remains intact throughout Downtown and in the city's radial arterial streets. These six arterial streets begin at or near Campus Martius and run far into the suburbs. From Downtown Detroit, Woodward runs north, Grand River northwest, Michigan Avenue west, Fort Street west-southwest, Jefferson Avenue east-northeast, and Gratiot northeast. Beyond Downtown, and the arterial streets, the city assumes a more traditional interlacing east/ west and north/south street grid.

Navigating Detroit - With myriad sudden one-ways, dead ends, and diagonal thoroughfares, finding your way around Detroit can be trickier than Richard Nixon. GPS-less visitors can observe a few rules to avoid getting lost or stuck in traffic.

- Split along Woodward Avenue, the city is essentially divided into an east and west half. Woodward Avenue, is the dividing line for east streets and west streets. Streets perpendicular to Woodward are numbered like different streets on their east and west sides—numbers increase in both directions as you drive away from Woodward. Streets parallel to Woodward are numbered heading north, so numbers increase as you drive or ride away from the river. (Grand Boulevard and Outer Drive both follow horseshoe patterns, and don't follow these rules).

- When lost in Detroit, look for the city's southern star—the light atop the Renaissance Center—that is usually visible across the city. Drive toward it, and you will eventually get downtown. Drive away from it to get to the suburbs. If it is to your left, you're heading west. If it is to your right, you're heading east.

- When on freeways, pay attention to the time of day: rush hours vary depending on where you're headed—into the city in the morning, out of the city in the afternoon.

Buses - Detroit Department of Transportation (DDOT) buses can take you around Detroit, Hamtramck, Highland Park, and few suburban destinations. This system dovetails with SMART, a regional bus agency servicing a few major routes in the city, as well as suburbs in Wayne, Oakland, and Macomb counties. Neither bus gives change, so have surplus silver on hand. *www.smartbus.org*

Car Rentals - Though less common in the city itself, rental agencies are easy to find at the main entry points. For a local car rental, Hertz and Enterprise have offices in the Lower East Side, Downtown, and New Center.

Cycling - Though called the Motor City, Detroit is a cycling paradise. The city is flat, and its surface streets are rarely congested. Cyclists can stow their bike on an outside rack aboard many DDOT buses and all SMART buses for free.

Detroit Bus Company - A small, independent bus/taxi transit company, the Detroit Bus Company is an on-call service that offers bar-centric circuits in Detroit running Friday and Saturday nights. Give them a call to ride in their graffiti-clad buses. *www.thedetroitbus.com, (313) 444-2871.*

Detroit People Mover - Detroit's elevated rail system offers a cheap way to get around downtown quickly, with a truly unique view along the way. The People Mover can get you from Joe Louis Arena to Grand Circus Park, or one of the other eleven stops, for 75 cents in a matter of minutes.

Parking - Though parking is free in most areas, free on-street parking is a rare commodity in greater Downtown. Each area is different, though meters are generally enforced until 10pm Monday-Saturday. Detroit's parking enforcement officers are on the ball, so err on the side of paying fifty cents too much than too little.

Walking - Walking is a good way to get around short distances, and neighborhoods at the heart of the city are closer together than they might seem. For example, Downtown to New Center is 3 ½ miles, about an hour's worth of walking, and ditto Midtown to Southwest.

Zipcar - An international car sharing business, Zipcar allows members to rent a car for a short time, usually a day at most. Zipcars are available in Midtown, but are only available to members, so plan accordingly.

TOURS

Though Detroit is served by a considerable number of tour operators, a few stand out for their knowledgeable tour leaders and unique mode of travel:

D:hive - A highly regarded local non-profit organization serving as a welcome mat for the city, D:hive offers a number of renowned tours. They hold free, public afternoon walking tours of Detroit's downtown and notable buildings weekly on Mondays and Saturdays, an insider's bus tour of Downtown on select Saturdays, and a downtown living tour, as well as a "practically free" bar tour of the greater downtown's watering holes. Private tours available. *www.dhivedetroit.org.*

Detroit Heritage Tours - This series of guided weekly summer architectural and cultural tours of Detroit neighborhoods organized by the local building preservation society, Preservation Detroit. Tours leave Saturdays at 10am at a local landmark for each neighborhood. *www.preservationdetroit.org.*

Detroit Hot Air Balloons - This company provides patrons the opportunity to view Detroit from a new vantage point—hundreds of feet in the air. The gondola allows for only a few people at a time. Must be booked in advance. *www.detroitballoons.com.*

Detroit Tour Connections - With incredibly knowledgeable guides, these tours cover historical Detroit buildings, artwork, and urban development trends, as well as a sampler's tour of Coney Islands, all across different eras in the city each Sunday evening from May to September. *www.detroittourconnections.com.*

Diamond Jack's River Tours - These waterborne tours offer narrated sightseeing tours along the Detroit river from a beautifully maintained vintage 1955 ferry. Tours run Thursday-Sunday all summer, leaving from Rivard Plaza along the Detroit RiverWalk. *www.diamondjack.com.*

Segways2u - This Segway tour company offers two tours, the City Tour, and the Gritty Tour. The City Tour covers Downtown's most significant historic sites and iconic monuments on two wheels. The Gritty Tour, in contrast, focuses on street art and hidden gems. *www.segways2u.com.*

Show Me Detroit Tours - This popular tour operator offers daily guided sightseeing luxury, private, van tours, highlighting the city's landmarks and cultural centers in greater downtown. Tours run for two hours and must be booked in advance. Custom tours available. *www.showmedetroittours.com.*

Wheelhouse Detroit - This beloved bike shop offers wonderful two-wheeled tours spring through fall, on Saturdays and Sundays. The friendly staff hosts a variety of different tour options, with varying ride lengths, difficulties, and tour themes, which can range from automotive history, to architecture, to public art. For a modest additional fee, customers can rent a bike for the tour. *www.wheelhousedetroit.com.*

GETTING IT STRAIT

Talking like a Detroiter - Those looking to talk like locals should begin with the city's street names and the unusual pronunciations Detroiters use. Some of the most unique street name pronunciations in Detroit/De**h**troit/Dee-troit include: Gratiot/Gra**sh**-it; Schoenherr/**Shayner**; Livernois/Liver**noy**/Liver**noyz**; Larned/Lar-**ned**; Cadieux/Ca**djew**; Moross/Mor**aw**ss; Kercheval/Kerchev**ull**; Fenkell/Fink-**el**; Charlevoix/**Shar-levoy**; Chene/**Shane**; Beaubien/**Bowbeon**; Vernor/Ver**ner**; Freud/**Frood**; Goethe/Go**ath**-ee; Lahser/Lah**surr** (also **Lash**er, which will be the same road if you hear it). People who live in or are from Detroit are called De**h**troiters. When visiting Hamtramck/Hamtram**ick** remember these: Dequindre/Dequind**er**; Jos Campau/**Joseph Campo**; Conant/**Con**e-int. Residents of Hamtramck are technically called *Hamtramickans*, but don't be surprised if this sounds strange to them, or you, and if you never actually need to say it.

ABOUT THIS BOOK

Belle Isle to 8 Mile is organized geographically to encourage immersive exploration of Detroit's many neighborhoods. The book begins with Downtown and each successive chapter covers increasingly outlying areas before closing with a brief chapter covering a few suburban highlights. For the purpose of this guide, we have included the two small municipalities completely surrounded by the city—Hamtramck and Highland Park—as a combined chapter. The back of the book includes an extensive events listing and an index of included sites. The bulk of the book, however, is the series of 12 area-specific chapters, each of which is broken into seven sections, listed below. Many businesses that defy ready classification—such as bakeries that serve coffee and could be listed as a shop or a cafe—are placed in the category that seems to most represent their raison d'être. Throughout the book, we have flagged some entries with a double arrow symbol "»" to note destinations that are especially popular with first time visitors, or are particularly unique.

The sections are:

- **Introduction** - A brief history of the area including descriptions of the people, neighborhoods, architecture, and highlights that make it an engaging place to visit.

- **Bars & Restaurants** - The bars, restaurants, cafes, diners, eateries, donut shops, and food trucks that make the area unique. Some bakeries that focus on cafe goods are included in this section.

- **Shopping & Services** - Perhaps the most wide-ranging section of the book, Shopping & Services covers commercial amenities from boutiques to shoe shines, as well as some more resident-oriented enterprises, such as hardware stores.

- **Cultural Attractions** - From basement museums to upscale galleries to one of the nation's finest art museums, the range of these places highlight the city's diverse creativity.

- **Entertainment & Recreation** - A section devoted to the places where Detroiters unwind, Entertainment & Recreation covers casinos, parks, bowling alleys, gyms, concert venues, sports teams, and movie theaters.

- **Sites** - These monuments, curiosities, historic places, architectural masterpieces, historic districts, and cemeteries are the city's finest, most notable attractions, that, although worth seeing, are only a feast for the eyes and generally non-interactive.

- **Points of Interest** - A catchall category for minor attractions such as urban gardens, ghost signs, record labels, miscellaneous graves, murals, curious commercial art, statues, movie scenes, and star homes that a tour guide might point out, but wouldn't stop the bus. These entries are typically brief.

Be a Contributor - We love to hear from residents and travelers. If you encounter something that has changed or something that belongs in a future update of the book, drop us a line *(belleisleto8mile@gmail. com)*, and we'll work to incorporate the change in future editions.

CHAPTER 1
DOWNTOWN

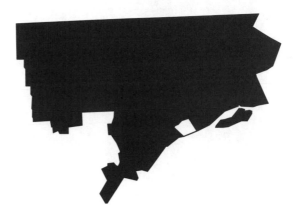

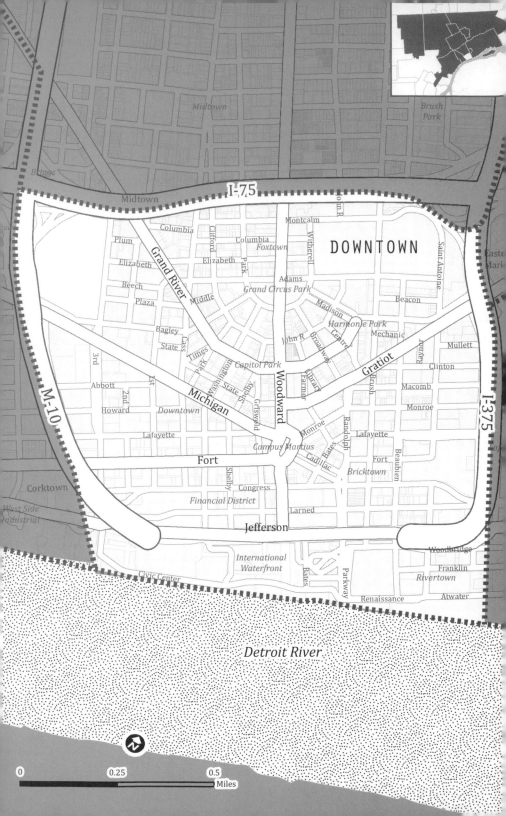

The historic, bustling heart of the city, Downtown is the commercial, entertainment, dining, and public art center of the region, making it the essential starting point of any visit to the city. The area's concentration and mix of elegant eateries, popular bars, historic architecture, and rich entertainment offerings are unparalleled in the region. Downtown, as we define it, is the area bordered by I-375, I-75, M-10, and the Detroit River.

As the oldest section of the city, Downtown's 1.16 square miles are awash with municipal history and reminders of the city's future-shaping past around every corner. Perhaps like no other area of Detroit, Downtown has undergone a continuous—and ongoing—evolution. Downtown's development began with the city's first structure, Antoine de la Mothe Cadillac's Fort Pontchartrain du Detroit, at what is now the corner of Larned Street and Griswold Street. When the city incorporated in 1806, the small heart of Downtown comprised the extent of the city and its 1,650 residents. By 1849, Detroit's burgeoning population had annexed all of what is now Downtown Detroit. In the antebellum period, Downtown became a transportation hub and began its swift population growth and a consequent wave of commercial development. In 1886, the Edison Illuminating Co. began making Downtown Detroit one of the nation's first electrified cities, and the city's network of so-called moonlight towers and rapidly growing collection of Gilded Age architecture led many to refer to Downtown Detroit as the "Paris of the West." The frantic pace of Downtown development accelerated through the first decades of the 20th century, peaking in the late-1920s, when Detroit issued an inflation-adjusted $2.5 billion in building permits in 1926, including 27 for buildings over 20 stories—the most of any U.S. city at the time. During the Great Depression and Second World War, Downtown development was largely stagnant before a revival in the postwar years. During the 1950s and 1960s, Downtown development became increasingly automobile-orientated in an era marked by demolition, freeway development, parking structure construction, and car-centric new buildings such as One Woodward Avenue and Cobo Center. Since this period, development has evolved with mayoral administrations, from marquee civic and commercial projects such as Joe Louis Arena and the Renaissance Center in the 1970s and 1980s, to a preference for catalytic entertainment and recreation development such as MGM Grand Casino, Campus Martius, the Detroit RiverWalk, and Comerica Park in the 1990s and 2000s.

As a commercial area with a relatively small population of nearly 5,000, Downtown is composed more of commercial districts than traditional neighborhoods. These districts—including Bricktown, Campus Martius, Capitol Park, Financial District, Foxtown, Grand Circus Park, Greektown, Harmonie Park, and International Waterfront—draw their identities from their common use or shared anchor. Although each district is distinct from one another, with a unique aesthetic, history, and future, their proximity encourages collective exploration. Together, these areas offer the city's grandest collection of architecture on its distinctive street grid—Judge Woodward's signature baroque hub-and-spoke arterial street system. Keen-eyed architecture observers will spot beautiful examples of many styles among Downtown's eight historic districts, including Art Deco, Art Moderne, Arts and Crafts, Beaux-Arts, Chicago School, Classical Revival, Gothic Revival, International, Italian Renaissance, Modern, Mid-Century Modern, Neo-classical, Neo-Georgian, Tudor Revival, and Victorian.

No trip to Detroit is complete without a visit to Downtown. The area's roster of entertainment offerings, fine eateries, party bars, recreational spaces, and stunning architecture create a diverse, lively destination not to be missed. Although every corner of Downtown offers unique experiences, a few are worth cancelling a flight. Visitors looking to take in live music, theater, or opera should head for Foxtown and Grand Circus Park, which together, anchor Detroit's theater district—the nation's second largest with more than 25,000 seats. Those in search of gourmet cuisine should look no further than the International Waterfront and Financial District areas, where the numerous delicious options include a 72nd-story elegant eatery, and a subterranean steakhouse originally founded 75 years ago. All of Downtown is a sports fan's paradise, being home to all three of the city's major stadiums and a glut of sports bars. Architecture admirers should look no further than Harmonie Park, Grand Circus Park, and the Financial District, which together showcase inspired examples of nearly every architectural style since the Civil War.

BARS & RESTAURANTS

1515 Broadway & Magenta Giraffe Theatre Company - A cafe by day and a live theatre by night, 1515 Broadway is a cozy retreat in the middle of the hustle and clamor of Downtown Detroit. The cafe offers a full line of de rigeur coffee shop fare—coffee drinks, bagels, muffins, fruit, and candy—with an emphasis on homemade, locally sourced, and organic options, alongside a limited menu of entrees, including a host of croissant sandwich options. The massive front windows leave the store awash in natural light and overlook the People Mover, opera house, athletic club, and outdoor chess tables, giving the space an urban, bustling downtown feel. The mix of stylish decor, plush seats, and friendly baristas will have you feeling right at home. Located in the back of the cafe is an intimate theatre that hosts events ranging from poetry slams to interactive workshops and independent plays. It's also home of the Magenta Giraffe Theatre Company, a nonprofit organization committed to enlivening the city's critical civic discourse and theatrical arts culture. *1515 Broadway St., www.magentagiraffe.org, (313) 965-1515.*

1701 Cigar Bar and Lounge - Whether you're a pink lung or a stogie connoisseur, you'll feel at home at this well-appointed Downtown cigar lounge. This two-floor bar is a great place to bump elbows with local powerbrokers. The first floor, which is laden with elegant woodwork, features overstuffed leather furniture, a well-stocked bar, and a walk-in humidor. The large, open, exposed-brick basement hosts a variety of jazz and blues shows on its intimate stage. With the vast array of Claros, Colorados, Maduros, and Oscuros for sale in the on-site humidor, even the most discerning cigar enthusiast will find a suitable nic stick to go along with one of the many fine scotches available. Although nearly impossible to do so, don't miss the t-rex-scale sexy lip smoking sculpture above the bar. Cigar smoking is allowed indoors or on the patio. *140 Cadillac Sq., (313) 223-2626.*

24grille - Paying homage to the year the Book Cadillac Hotel opened, 24grille offers diners an exquisite experience, from the haute cuisine interpretations of classic American dishes highlighting seasonal, regional flavors, to the chichi champagne room (one of the only champagne rooms in the state). Although the menu rarely disappoints, the Thai fried shrimp and mango salad, poutine with pulled pork, truffled mac and cheese, and risotto croquettes stand out. Hand-blown glass baubles, tempered glass panels, exposed structural elements, and a floating "fireplace" give 24grille an edgy sophistication, yet it is still decidedly unstuffy with a wide selection of Michigan craft beers and an affordable happy hour Monday through Friday. Next time you find yourself sporting a Twisted Sister shirt and craving some confit l'orange, fear not - 24grille has no dress code. *204 Michigan Ave., (313) 964-3821.*

Al's Paradise Cafe - This unassuming and delicious Middle Eastern breakfast and lunch spot is as famous for its shawarma platters, fresh juice bar, delectable Middle Eastern breakfast fare, and mujadra spinach melts as it is for affable owner and cook Ahlan "Al" Wasahlan's jovial stories. Offering dine-in, carryout, and delivery, Al's is a great option for a quick bite before a Downtown show or game. *218 E. Grand River Ave., www.alsparadisecafe.com, (313) 962-4498.*

» American Coney Island - An authentic Detroit institution—and one of the world's first two Coney Island restaurants—American Coney Island has been a Mecca for the city's Coney fans since 1917. With its metallic ceiling, white and black-checkered floor, dinette tables and staff in paper soda jerk hats, the restaurant's retro diner atmosphere is an integral part of its position as a cherished city tradition. Though American offers a full menu—including Greek salads, tuna salad sandwiches, gyro platters and baklava—the real draw are the Coney dogs. The Coneys begin with a warm steamed bun, with a specially seasoned natural-skin casing Dearborn Sausage wiener, the restaurant's signature spicy chili sauce, topped with a line of mustard and sweet Vidalia onions. For a classic Detroit experience, sit in the Flatiron-like acute corner, and watch traffic and bustle pass as you scarf down tradition. Check out the bitter rival next door, Lafayette Coney Island, and pick your favorite. Open 24/365. *114 W. Lafayette Blvd., www.americanconeyisland.com, (313) 961-7758.*

Anchor Bar - The crinkled, yellowing photos of long-gone journalists set the scene at this Downtown watering hole. Nestled between the headquarters of The Detroit News, Detroit Free Press, the WDIV studios, and city hall, The Anchor Bar is Detroit's de-facto muckraker drinking spot. In the old days, beat reporters would stop in for a beer and a shot on their way to cover city council. More recently, much of the reporting that led to Kwame Kilpatrick's resignation was unfurled in booth three. Open 7am–2:30am, 364 days a year, it's also an off-hours hotspot for many of Downtown's midnight shift workers. Slide in at 7am on a Saturday, and you might find yourself surrounded by a gaggle of stagehands, or even a hundred postal workers. *450 W. Fort St. (313) 964-9127.*

Andiamo Detroit Riverfront - Andiamo and the Riverfront are a perfect pair. With excellent views of the river and superb cuisine, this location of the small regional chain is the definitive Andiamo experience. White-coated waiters observe classical restaurant service techniques, setting and resetting your table with each course. Located just off the Winter Garden, the dining rooms of Andiamo are open and large, yet feel intimate. A full menu of Italian favorites is beautifully presented—from simple pasta dishes to elegant entrées, including some dishes prepared with a healthier approach. Try the gnocchi or the veal marsala and be sure to dine on the waterfront patio when weather permits. *400 Renaissance Center, www.andiamoitalia.com/ detroit, (313) 567-6700.*

» **Angelina Italian Bistro** - Located in a renovated former theater, this upscale Italian eatery, arguably Downtown's finest Italian restaurant, offers a relaxed atmosphere and an innovative menu. The contemporary, airy interior is laid back yet makes no aesthetic compromises. With massive walls of accordion windows overlooking Grand Circus Park, the generous amount of ambient light highlights the beauty of the simple wooden tables, wrap around bar, open kitchen, and decorative flourishes, including a large black metal reed sculpture. The menu offers modern interpretations on classic dishes—from Italy and elsewhere—that highlight Angelina's outstanding ingredients, including fresh-made pasta, organic pork, free-range poultry, house-smoked fish, and its signature mozzarella, which is made on site. Among the restaurant's many fine offerings, the sweet potato gnocchi, grilled swordfish, and squid ink fettuccine standout, though our favorite is the roasted butternut squash ravioli. The menu thoughtfully denotes the many vegetarian and gluten free options. Dinner only. *1565 Broadway St., www.angelinadetroit.com, (313) 962-1355.*

» **Astoria Bakery** - Opened in 1971, this beloved old-timey bakery in Greektown has been a local favorite for more than 40 years. Inside, under the gorgeous tin ceiling and antique hanging lights, patrons pick their pleasure from the seemingly endless bakery counter and sit at the cozy cafe tables. The bakery offers 120 decadent homemade European sweets, chocolates, cakes, and pies, as well as more than 20 varieties of ice cream, and house-roasted coffee and cappuccino. Though the cafe setting can be a relaxing respite from the bustle of the neighborhood, Astoria can box any of its baked delights and offers cones for the road. The bakery is open until midnight on weekdays and 1am on weekends to best serve the sometimes revelous Greektown crowds. *541 Monroe St., www.astoriapastryshop.com, (313) 963-9603.*

Baltimore Bar & Grill - To call the Baltimore pretty might be a stretch, but what the dimly lit Downtown dive lacks in aesthetic appeal, it makes up for with a surprisingly healthy booze selection and tasty grease-heavy bar food that's worth writing home about. In the larger front room, the joint serves breakfast, lunch, and dinner and offers a billiards table. On weekends, the otherwise quiet, speakeasy-style back room hosts dance-friendly DJs and serves free-flowing shots that bring shoulder-to-shoulder crowds. While the Baltimore claims to cook the best burger in town and it's a solid choice, we suggest its grilled cheese or patty melt, which are both tasty enough to compete with the best out of your grandma's kitchen. *1234 Randolph St., (313) 964-2728.*

Bangkok Crossing - Got the shakes for some larb? Renowned for its speed, outstanding service, and tasty food, this unassuming Thai spot is popular among residents who need to grab some gang gai on the go. Although Bangkok Crossing specializes in mild Thai dishes, try some of the more authentic options like the Pad Ma Kher or Pad Prik Khing after digging into the complimentary shrimp chips and soup. While there is always ample seating in this spare, utilitarian restaurant, Bangkok Crossing offers lightning-fast carryout. Although the vegetarian and vegan selection is minimal, the staff and cooks are very accommodating. *620 Woodward Ave., www.bangkokcrossingthaifood.com, (313) 961-3861.*

Ben & Jerry's - Yearning for ice cream, but worried about the calorie-induced guilt? At the Ben & Jerry's Scoop Shop in Downtown Detroit, you can justify your craving by knowing that the proceeds from each frozen confection directly benefit the community. That's because the licensed franchise is independently owned and operated by the Goodwill Industries of Greater Detroit, as part of Ben & Jerry's Partnershop program. The store is located just a block north of Campus Martius park, making it a perfect stop during any trip downtown. With ice cream that not only tastes good, but also actually does good, there's no reason not to indulge. *1014 Woodward Ave., www.benjerry.com, (313) 964-2185.*

Bucharest Grill - A cheap, fast, outrageously delicious carryout counter in the tradition of Romanian street food (an amalgamation of Middle Eastern and German cuisine) with a healthy dose of greasy American bar fare thrown in for good measure, the Bucharest serves shawarma, hummus, loaded knockwurst, sliders, curly fries, and pretty much anything else that goes well with pickles, cabbage, or garlic. Popular favorites include the signature Bucharest (chicken) and Vegetarian shawarmas—the latter of which is known lovingly as the "french fry sandwich," The Detroiter—a $4.50 knockwurst coney that's worth every penny, and traditional Romanian dishes like the stuffed pepper. Take advantage of cheap carryout or delivery to your door or, if you prefer to have a beer with your food, Bucharest will bring your order to your table at the adjoining Park Bar. Open until 2am every night except for Sunday and Monday when it closes at midnight. *2040 Park Ave., www.bucharestgrill.com, (313) 965-3111.*

The Buhl Bar - Flanked by the majestic Guardian Building, the Buhl Bar is a refined, iconic establishment that revives the business-class happy hour tradition of Detroit's heyday. Though a relative newcomer to the Financial District, the Buhl Bar exudes old-school class, with a clean, dark setting highlighted by the large wood bar that makes it a natural habitat for Downtown executives and movers and shakers—and those who want to feel like one. Open from 3pm to 8pm on weekdays, the Buhl serves up generous pours and martinis, as well as a selection of aperitifs, including meats, cheeses, and bar mixes that complement the drinks, atmosphere, and clientele. An ideal setting to make an impression or a deal with your next business partner or persuade the opposition with drinks, become a regular or just get gussied up and join the crowd. *535 Griswold St., (313) 963-6118.*

» Cafe D'Mongo's Speakeasy - A great place to see and be seen, D'Mongo's is an essential stop during a stay in Detroit. The destination has become famous for being a quirky bar and soul food joint that feels like a combination of an antique store and your grandmother's living room. The emerald green walls are clad with photos of famous jazzmen and infamous mobsters, gold-painted accents, classic advertisements, old-timey photos, musical instruments, and "gold" records signed by regulars. The comfy, tufted gold velvet furniture is a sight for sore thighs that contributes to the homespun DIY glamour of the atmosphere. The bar is full of character, as well as characters, and none is more charming than the personable proprietor, Larry Mongo, a tall drink of water who loves greeting customers with a tall glass of whisky or a tall tale. At the bar, guests can get a full line of cocktails—including Larry's signature Vernor's and Canadian Club "Detroit Brown"—and bottled beer. Come early and catch the popular, albeit limited, soul food menu, featuring ribs and barbecued chicken, black-eyed peas, cornbread, and mac and cheese. An extremely varied docket of live music is common—don't miss George, the bluesman on the piano with an eye for the ladies. The bar is open Fridays and some Saturdays. *1439 Griswold St., www.cafedmongos.com.*

Carmine's Pizza Kitchen - The newest entrant into a competitive Downtown pizza market, Carmine's Pizza Kitchen is a laid-back lunch and dinner spot with a reputation for moderate prices and quality food. The open kitchen and bright, contemporary decor make the space breezy and inviting, yet unassuming. Carmine's specializes in Neapolitan-style pizza with crispy, flaky crusts, and a perfect balance between sauce and cheese. In addition to its considerable stable of 29 toppings, they also offer some distinct specialty pizzas including the enjoyable Steak Supreme, Greek, and Pesto Primavera. Carmine's also offers calzones, subs, and salads—all of which are tasty choices. Delivery, dine-in, and carryout available. *107 Monroe St., www.carminesdetroit.com, (313) 496-1111.*

Centaur Bar - Distinguished by the "life-sized" silver sculpture of a centaur leaping from the facade, this three-story drinkery in Foxtown overflows with modern luxury and swank. Offering three stories of class—that sometimes veer into lounge territory—a color scheme of onyx and magenta pervade throughout. Bar and traditional high- and low-top table seating are available on the first and third floors, while the mezzanine offers plush couches and contemporary murals in an Art Deco style. Patrons are treated to a relatively pantheonic selection at the bar, with myriad draft beers and bottled wines available, as well as a regular cocktail and martini menu that includes palatable seasonal offerings alongside standards—many of which are just $5 during happy hour. Paired well with the beverage menu, Centaur offers a bevy of affordable small plates such as scallops, petite chops, mahi tacos, and caviar. A moderate dress code is enforced. *2233 Park Ave., www.centaurbar.com, (313) 963-4040.*

Checker Bar - In the heart of the Financial District is a perfect burger 'n' beer bar. Founded in 1955 and still family-owned and operated, Checker Bar has earned a reputation for its hearty, generous, well-cooked burgers. The place takes pride in using fresh ingredients, including the Amish chicken wings. The shotgun-style eatery is decked with Reagan-era wood paneling and has tables fit for any chess fan. Checker Bar's hours cater to the Downtown crowd—the kitchen closes at 7:30pm and the bar is closes by 9pm. The second floor is available for private events. *124 Cadillac Sq., (313) 961-9249.*

CK Mediterranean Grille & Catering - Located on the ground level of the Compuware Building, CK Mediterranean Grille is a concept born out of the popular suburban restaurant Mr. Kabob. Known for its fresh, healthy Mediterranean food, the family behind Mr. Kabob launched a small chain of Café Kabob (CK) Mediterranean Grilles in 2008 and continues to be a leader in providing fast, fresh, healthy food in a casual environment. The stylish cafeteria setting of the Detroit location is buzzing with workers from the many nearby corporate offices all throughout the week and is easily one of the best spots downtown to get a flavorful, homemade, healthy Mediterranean meal on the go. *119 Monroe St., www.ckgrille.com, (313) 496-6666.*

» Cliff Bell's - Named for founder John Clifford Bell, Cliff Bell's is a fully restored 1930s Art Deco nightclub, featuring beautiful murals and woodwork, live music, and elegant cocktails. After a storied history, the bar was abandoned in 1956. In 2006, it underwent a thoughtful and thorough restoration by owners Paul Howard, Scott Lowell, and Carolyn Howard, and today the space looks just as it did after prohibition, with floor-to-ceiling Art Deco woodwork, period murals, ornate backlit bar, original mosaics, antique mirrors, and bartenders in sleeve garters. The food complements the atmosphere, and is as inspired as the space. The menu, with its subtle French influences, melds traditional and contemporary with an emphasis on local ingredients—including locally raised beef, herbs and vegetables from Brother Nature, and Michigan wines. Those looking for a three-martini (rather than a three-course) meal, won't be disappointed by the well-appointed liquor selection and highly regarded wine and beer list. However, surpassing the ambiance and the flavors is the music. The bar hosts one of the city's finest rosters of live jazz, with shows almost every night, many of which don't have a cover. Though the schedule favors traditional and big band music that's appropriate for the setting, look for a variety of musical acts on the stage. Also look for WDET's The Moth story series and Open City small business panels that are hosted at the venue. *2030 Park Ave., www.cliffbells.com, (313) 961-2543.*

Coach Insignia - Soaring 72 stories above Downtown and the riverfront, Coach Insignia is a dazzling experience that marries the city's most breathtaking view with some of its finest cuisine. Not for those with trepidation about heights, the scenic experience begins with the glass-walled private elevator ride to the two-story dining room. As if further aesthetic incentive was necessary, the contemporary restaurant is tastefully decorated with automotive memorabilia related to the building's major tenant—General Motors. A Matt Prentis restaurant, guests are treated to a varied menu that runs the gamut from the indulgent Lobster Corndogs to the extravagant Rabbit and Foie Gras Risotto and boasts a 26-page wine list. If you're a budget conscious consumer leery of 72nd story prices, the view can be enjoyed for the price of a craft cocktail or a decadent dessert (try the mousse-laden chocolate torte). *100 Renaissance Center, www.theepicureangroup.com/coachinsignia.html, (313) 567-2622.*

COLORS - With rich, innovative flavors and an ethical business design, this worker-owned eatery is not only a destination for quality cuisine but is also beneficial to the well being of the city it serves. Located in the basement of the historically German Harmonie Club, patrons dine at long, communal tables or sit at small bistro tables in the reserved, white-walled setting highlighted by hardwood floors and antique lighting. Serving lunch and dinner out of the open kitchen, the eatery offers a limited but varied vegetarian-friendly menu of refined food at reasonable prices. Though everything is made with quality, locally sourced ingredients, favorites include the Moroccan Meatballs (made with succulent lamb), perfectly prepared Sweet Potato Wontons, the flavorful portabella club, and burgers with uncommon add-ons like fried egg and bacon jelly. While the caliber of the food should be inspiration enough to visit COLORS, a foundation of the establishment is that every employee has a share in the company, collaborating with and training each other to bring each meal to the table, so that you can satisfy not only your stomach but also your conscience. *311 E. Grand River Ave., www.colors-detroit.com, (313) 962-5020.*

Da Edoardo Foxtown Grille - A sister restaurant to a Grosse Pointe predecessor, this ristorante in Detroit's entertainment epicenter has plenty to distinguish itself as an in-demand venue for lunch, dinner, or drinks. Da Edoardo Foxtown is housed in a massive mocha-colored space adjacent to the Fox Theater, with flowing vine-like lamps, intimate views of Woodward from floor-to-ceiling windows, hardwood tables and chairs, and an intricate mural of an Italian plaza. Gourmands should enjoy offerings of northern Italian cuisine, including freshly made pastas, generously portioned meat entrees, rustic pizzas, upscale versions of American fare, and refined simplicities like delicately hearty house minestrone. Though the bar is not extensive, it does feature Birra Moretti and grappa digestifs. Reservations are recommended. *2203 Woodward Ave., www.daedoardo.com, (313) 471-3500.*

Detroit Beer Company - Any restaurant with "beer" in its name is doing something right, but "The Brewery on Broadway" goes all the way with a full menu of food and house-brewed beers and an inviting atmosphere. Inside, guests are treated to a bi-level space with high ceilings and a warm, rich atmosphere highlighted by dark woodwork, exposed brick, and the focal point of the space, the visible fermentation tanks. The establishment offers an eclectic menu that goes far beyond usual pub fare, with a wide selection of brick-oven pizzas, jambalaya, fish tacos, shepherd's pie, and bread-bowl soups. However, as the name would suggest, beer is the main event, with more than two-dozen house brews on tap. We're especially fans of the Detroit Dwarf beer, in homage to one of our favorite Detroit legends and neighborhood parades, the Marche du Nain Rouge! Don't miss the awesome patio, and don't forget to pick up some beer to go on your way out. *1529 Broadway St., www.detroitbeerco.com, (313) 962-1529.*

Detroit Seafood Market - This spacious, elegantly designed restaurant and full bar in Harmonie Park, just minutes away from stadiums and theaters, gives customers satisfying, succulent, balanced meals and a wide-range of seafood choices, including swordfish, flounder, snapper, and crab cakes in a comfortable, warm setting. Macaroni and cheese enthusiasts should try the restaurant's popular Lobster Mac 'n' Cheese for a decadent take on a homemade classic. Check out the generous Sunday brunch buffet. Reservations recommended. *1435 Randolph St., www.thedetroitseafoodmarket.com, (313) 962-4180.*

Detroiter Bar - The bar that the city was named for—or was it the other way around? Our grandfathers probably drank here, and the bar hasn't changed much since. With its tin ceiling, old-timey patio lights, creaking wood floor, and worn bar, this neighborhood sports dive seems to ooze history. At the same time, the bar is no stranger to some modern amenities, including a multiplicity of TVs and a contemporary beer selection. The Detroiter offers regular bar fare along with some novel additions inspired by its Greektown neighbors, including saganaki, flaming sausage, and gyros. The bar is usually quiet but gets rowdy on game nights. *655 Beaubien St., (313) 963-3355.*

Detroit's Cheesecake Bistro - Providing a soul food and contemporary American counterpoint to the titular cuisine of Greektown is infamous restaurateur La-Van Hawkins' sleek, glossy new establishment at the corner of Brush and Monroe. The digs are upscale but relaxed, with onyx pieces and pastel tones, frayed bell-form lighting at the bar, glittery mosaic floor inlays, simple black wood furniture and floor-to-ceiling windows rounding out the atmosphere. The menu runs the gamut from decadent breakfasts (like crab and shrimp eggs benedict, lemon ricotta pancakes, or chicken and waffles), to reasonably priced lunches (like half-pound loaded burgers, a steak sandwich with fried egg and ham, or robust and hearty gumbo), and dinners touching on high-end modern American favorites (like surf and turf, rack of lamb, and veal, all served with buttery honey-glazed biscuits). The eponymous dessert is made in-house in a rotating set of varieties, including red velvet, blueberry, Oreo, and more. *1045 Brush St., www.detroitscheesecakebistro.com, (313) 962-4061.*

El Guapo Grill - On the forefront of the city's food truck scene, El Guapo features Mexican-fusion creations available at various locations throughout the city and special events (check the website for location updates). Although the jovial staff takes an irreverent tone with menu titles—some of which are inspired by the film Three Amigos—it is made up of serious culinarians who emphasize fresh ingredients and a well-seasoned, California take on Mexican food. Though the entire menu is worth exploration, our favorites are the pork belly confit burritos, sweet potato burritos, Ned Nederlander burrito, and Korean Beef tacos. Completely equipped with veggie options—including fried tofu—as well as Faygo, there's something for everyone in this mobile-sensation. Food truck aficionados should also look for popular alternatives **Dago Joe's** and the **Mac Shack**, which are also delicious but are downtown less frequently than El Guapo. *www.elguapogrill.com, (313) 720-0360.*

Elwood Bar & Grill - Named for its original location at Elizabeth Street and Woodward Avenue (El and Wood), the Elwood Bar and Grill was opened in 1926 and designed by noted Art Deco architect Charles Noble. In 1997, this small architectural treasure—and the nearby Gem and Century Theaters—were moved several blocks by owner Chuck Forbes to make way for the Tigers' new home, Comerica Park. At the time of the move, the entire structure was authentically restored to its original splendor, the highlight of which is the glistening white enameled-steel exterior. During games, the place is packed with sports fans sipping on 16-ounce beers. "Off" hours provide a quieter atmosphere at which time the honest, reasonably priced burger-coney-fries menu is yours to savor. *300 E. Adams St., www.elwoodgrill.com, (313) 962-2337.*

Fishbone's Rhythm Kitchen Cafe - A lively Louisiana-themed, gas-lit restaurant in a restored, timbered 19th-century manufacturing building, Fishbone's has been a center of Cajun and Creole cuisine in the city since 1989. The restaurant has a bright, loft-esque interior littered with a collection of tchotchkes and exposed brick walls, contemporary woodwork, and a variety of seating options at spacious hardwood tables. Though the menu offers a mix of Japanese, American, and Louisianian fare, the sushi and Cajun items seem more distinguished than the typical American fare. Undecided visitors should try the crawfish etoufee, snapper beausoleil, lobster po' boy, or Italian muffuletta, all of which are tasty. *400 Monroe St., www.fishbonesusa.com, (313) 965-4600.*

Flood's Bar and Grille - Occupying the first floor of the historic Detroit Cornice and Slate Building is this refined bar. Regulars mingle either at the impressive central island bar, on the dance floor (with a smaller bar itself), or while dining in view of one of the many flat screen televisions. Ambient highlights include an exposed brick interior, the scarlet painted industrial ductwork, and architectural holdovers like outsize wood molding—but most importantly, a focused and refined selection of music: live jazz, soul, contemporary R&B, and dance-oriented DJs. The menu at Flood's is upmarket pub food, with preference toward refined southern and soul. Cover charges and minimums apply for live music events and an unimposing dress code applies on all nights. *731 St. Antoine St., www.floodsdetroit.com, 313) 963-1090.*

» Foran's Grand Trunk Pub - Want to try a Michigan beer? Or forty? Grand Trunk boasts an almost-unbelievable beer menu, with 14 taps dedicated exclusively to Michigan brews and more than 30 other locally brewed bottles. Though converted to a bar in 1935, this beautiful 1879 building was originally a jeweler's shop and the Grand Trunk Railway ticket office, and Foran's preserves many of these gorgeous historic features, including 25-foot vaulted ceilings, a hardwood bar, intricate woodwork, and massive chandeliers. Try a bite from the delicious, locally sourced menu of pub-centric comfort food including fish 'n' chips, Jameson Meatloaf, shepherd's pie, and the stellar McGee sandwich—shaved turkey, roasted red pepper, avocado, romaine, monterey jack, and mayo on sourdough. *612 Woodward Ave., www.grandtrunkpub.com, (313) 961-3043.*

Fountain Bistro - Located in the heart of Downtown Detroit's Campus Martius, Fountain Bistro is an elegant little place with incredible views of the city. In the winter, you can watch ice skaters glide past while cozying up with a hot chocolate; in the summer, try sitting on the shaded terrace with a glass or five of house chardonnay—it's as tasty as it is affordable. The menu is full of French cuisine, mostly soups, salads, and sandwiches, with some entrees. Fountain Bistro has a full bar, and with a happy hour from 4pm to 7pm, it's the perfect spot for an after-work drink. *800 Woodward Ave., www.fountainbistro.com, (313) 237-7778.*

Golden Fleece Restaurant - As one of the last mainstays of Greek cuisine in Greektown, the Golden Fleece has a colorful history dating back to 1971 when it was opened by the Dionysopoulos family. An old-timey establishment with a light, unassuming air, guests sit at blue-and-white checked tablecloths under a trellis of charmingly synthetic greenery (you might wonder how that greenery avoids going up in flames at each and every "OPA!" but somehow it survives). Though the casual place offers a full menu of classic, tasty favorites— from house-made spanakopita, to shish kebabs, and saganaki—the tender lamb gyros are the stars, with meat carved to order right off the spit spinning prominently in the front of the restaurant. To round out the menu, Golden Fleece offers a wide selection of Greek beer and wine, as well as a chilled Ouzo machine, serving up the anise-flavored liqueur. Open until 3am, The Fleece can keep every demographic of the Greektown set satified—from family diners to post-bar frenziers. On Monday nights during the summer, don't miss Exodus, the lush rooftop club that transforms into the city's most serene jazz venue this one magical evening every week. *525 Monroe St., (313) 962-7093.*

Greenroom Salads - A compact corner eatery in the ground floor of the historic Ford Building, Downtown professionals on the go frequent this carryout soup and salad bar for fast and healthy lunches. Paying by the pound, visitors craft their own salad from a wide selection of greens, veggies, fresh and dried fruits, cheeses, dressings, croutons—and even less common ingredients like wasabi peas. Add a cup full of one of Greenroom's nine delicious soups for under three dollars, or opt for a more filling—yet still healthy—pre-made, fresh sandwich from the cooler, complements of the popular Lunchbox Deli in suburban Grosse Pointe. The Greenroom caters to the waistline-minded office worker set, so it's only open 11am to 3pm for lunch. *120 W. Congress St., (313) 963-9565.*

Greenwich Time Pub - Red, yellow, and chestnut stained glass windows cast a warm glow on the ample wooden seating and freshly whitewashed walls of the Greenwich Time Pub, named for the owner's wife's fondness of London. Clocks behind the bar display the time for cities all over the world and antique pictures of Detroit and London decorate the walls. The wrap-around bar snakes around the beer tap to the hot grill, where cooks serve up the best fresh burgers for the price—big juicy cheeseburgers run under $7. If the bar seating isn't for you, follow the winding weathered wooden staircase up to a lunch dining and private banquet area surrounded by tall windows. There, take one of the popular window seats and enjoy the view that's been a Downtown favorite since 1952. *130 Cadillac Sq., (313) 961-7885.*

Ham Shop Cafe - As the name would suggest, the Ham Shop specializes in serving up a plethora of delicious dishes centered around thick, juicy cuts of the eponymous meat delivered fresh from Dearborn Ham. From ham-sprinkled split-pea soup to the ham-heavy Hungryman breakfast of bacon, ham, sausage, eggs, and spuds, there's plenty to keep pork lovers happy. However, the Ham Shop Cafe also features deli sandwiches (though many feature ham, there is some variety), soul food specials such as broasted chicken, and a variety of affordable vegetarian breakfast and lunch deals. Carryout is a primary component of the spot, but there are plenty of tables inviting visitors to dine in for breakfast or lunch and enjoy the nice view of Greektown's main drag. *330 Monroe St., www.hamshopcafe.com, (313) 965-0088.*

Harbor House - A relative newcomer to the neighborhood, Harbor House is the Downtown iteration of a classic mainstay of the eastern suburbs. In a low-key but refined setting punctuated by finished woodwork and exposed brick, guests sit at one of the many round tables or the stunning 50-foot bar. Though the menu covers wide, meat-centric territory, the foci are steaks, ribs, and—above all—seafood. Popular favorites include the lobster macaroni and cheese and the crab legs, though those looking for a reason to loosen their belt might prefer the all-you-can-eat concept that's also available. Sports fans should be sure to check out the inexpensive brunch before Lions' games. *440 Clinton St., www.harborhousemi.com, (313) 967-9900.*

Hot Taco - With its sleek, modern design, the taqueria with the dirty name is a lunchtime and late night—they're open until 2am—post-bar favorite. Behind the stainless steel counter, the formidable crew slings Baja style Mexican fare. While it offers a plethora of burritos, its tacos, which are mostly $3 each or three for $6, are our weapons of choice. Three favorites are the tilapia, veggie, and marinated chicken tacos (a house-specialty), which are all especially tasty, and go well with one of the many imported sodas. *2233 Park Ave., www. hottacodetroit.com, (313) 963-4545.*

The Hudson Cafe - For breakfast, brunch, and brinner in Downtown Detroit, hit up the Hudson Cafe. Located in the central business district across from the former site of the storied J. L. Hudson department store, Hudson Cafe offers modern twists on classic breakfast and lunch items from classically French-trained Chef Tom Teknos in a bright, airy space with soaring ceilings and a contemporary vibe. Everything is made from scratch, including the house-made buttery biscuits, corned beef hash, buttermilk fried chicken, and the signature red velvet pancakes with cream cheese drizzle. Enjoy your hearty breakfast with some fresh-squeezed orange juice, or if you're in a hurry, step right up to the coffee bar in the lobby where you can grab a specialty coffee drink to go. You can also make a selection from the Hudson's homemade baked goods display, order an express breakfast sandwich, or pick up carryout orders from the cafe bar. Because of its focus on breakfast foods, the place closes at 3pm on weekdays and 4pm on weekends. *1241 Woodward Ave., www.hudson-cafe.com, (313) 237-1000.*

Jacoby's German Biergarten - One of the oldest establishments in Detroit, Jacoby's has been serving authentic German food and beer since 1904. The stunning old-world two-story tavern is decked out with historic woodwork, antique light fixtures, exposed brick, and character at every turn. In addition to a rotating selection of drafts, the classic night spot offers a mind boggling 100—and often more—varieties of bottled beer that complement the extensive menu of American pub fare and German favorites like spatzle, potato pancakes, sausage, and a variety of schnitzels. On weekdays, Jacoby's is popular with lawyers, politicians, and other nine-to-fivers working Downtown, while on nights and weekends the destination favorite draws an eclectic mix of sports fans and music lovers of many stripes. The upstairs bar occasionally hosts live local music on weekends, and it can also be rented out for private functions. *624 Brush St., www.jacobysdetroit.com, (313) 962-7067.*

Joe Muer Seafood - This iconic—even legendary—Detroit restaurant was recently reborn under restaurateur Joe Vicari of the family of Andiamo restaurants. Joe Muer himself is a partner in the business, and this new incarnation of Joe Muer Seafood—located on the third floor of the Renaissance Center with sweeping vistas of the Detroit River—is every bit as decadent as the original (which shuttered in 1991), right down to architect Ron Rea's dramatic modern design. It is a classic American seafood and steakhouse with heavy French influence, so expect lots of succulent dishes stuffed with crab and smothered in meuniére sauce. The prices reflect the haute cuisine, so be sure you plan on a splurge during your visit. *400 Renaissance Center, www.joemuerseafood.com, (313) 567-6837.*

La Casa De La Habana - Set across from a quiet park, the flagship location for this local collection of cigar lounges offers visitors a mellow, relaxing alternative to the urban grind. Housed in the former Harmonie Studios building, made of orange brick with subtly beautiful tile work, La Casa de La Habana has three distinct facets dedicated to giving aficionados a posh, laid-back experience: a retail cigar shop, a lounge and martini bar, and a paid membership VIP space. Both initiates and beginners can enjoy La Casa's shop—the walk-in humidor housing more than 100 varieties of stogies is staffed by sales people knowledgeable in cigar manufacture, taste, aroma, and differentiation, sells high-end cigar paraphernalia like cutters, lighters, cases, chemicals for home humidors, and offers $5 shoe shines in an antique wooden chair. Smokers can light up at the separate lounge—a classy, moodily lit den with red and black leather sofas, flat screen TVs, ornate original wooden molding, a dark wood bar with a brass rail, and crimson and white wall decoration reminiscent of a finely marbled steak. The vibe is unapologetically comfy, drawing patrons for after-work cocktails from its practically exhaustive bar—a selection of high-end scotches, bourbons, vodkas, and go-to import lagers are points of emphasis. First-timers will see a fair share of suits worn by a chatty crowd of regulars, but no uniform is required. Live music is offered gratis twice weekly. Upstairs is the club—a leather and wood seclusion spot with Wi-Fi, flat screens, conference space, and personal humidors. True connoisseurs may take advantage of La Casa's roll-to-order service—offering choice Central American tobacco rolled expertly by expat Cubans. *1502 Randolph St., www.lacasadelahabana.com, (313) 285-8332.*

» **Lafayette Coney Island -** With its original cash register, photo-clad white tile walls, retro all-chrome fixtures, mint green accents, and charmingly gruff staff in paper garrison caps, the shotgun-style diner has been a Coney cathedral since 1917. This small, always-packed counter joint features limited table seating, which makes it an eavesdropper's paradise and beautifully reminiscent of pre-war diners. Along with next-door archrival American Coney Island, Lafayette is one of two originators of the Coney Island dog and is perhaps generally favored by purists. The backbone of the restaurant's limited menu is its coveted Coney concoctions: naturally cased Dearborn Sausage franks wrapped in gooey, steamed buns, smothered in its distinctive, flavorful, beefy chili topped with minced Spanish onions and mustard. This tubesteakhouse is firmly carnivore country, though—fries and pies round out the vegetarian portion of the 15-item menu. Open 24 hours a day, 7 days a week. *118 W. Lafayette Blvd., (313) 964-8198.*

Loco's Tex-Mex Grille - As you might expect, the most authentic Mexican food in the city isn't found in Greektown at Loco, but it's a solid late-night Coney-alternative. Loco's boasts huge portions and stays open 'til 2am on weekdays and 4am on weekends—and it's within stumbling distance of many of Downtown's attractions and bars, to boot! They have a pleasant, lively, spacious dining room, and offer a generous menu of traditional Mexican fare and a selection of Mexican beers and Margaritas. Check out the $1 Taco Tuesdays! *454 E. Lafayette St., www.locobarandgrill.net, (313) 965-3737.*

London Chop House - After a storied 53-year existence, the London Chop house closed in 1991 before a celebrated reopening in 2012 in the same basement location that reigned over the Detroit restaurant scene for decades. This elegant, recently re-established Detroit tradition looks and feels much the same as when the founders ran the place, and features the same circular red leather booths, iron-and-hardwood tables, mirrored oak bar, dark woodwork, and even the original phone number. This mignon minster is a verified sanctuary of sirloin and is not the place for a quick meal. It is rather an exquisite, dignified destination for rare scotch and generous portions of aged stakes and rich food fit for the auto barons. The menu boasts delectable takes on American cuisine, with an emphasis on traditional techniques, and the finest, freshest ingredients, with everything made from scratch, in-house. Though every item on the succinct lunch and dinner menus is exceptional, the steak tartare, veal chop oscar, seared ahi tuna, New York strip, and baby arugula and roasted beet salad stand out. The well-appointed bar offers an unparalleled selection of fine liquors and a thoughtful beer list. The restaurant also offers a separate cigar bar and small stage, with quiet live music. Limited vegetarian offerings. *155 W. Congress St., www.thelondonchophouse.com, (313) 962-0277.*

Luci & Ethel's Diner - For those looking for a respite from an oversaturation of post-bar Coney fever—and incredible people watching—breakfast and well-rounded American fare are served all day (and many nights) at this greasy-spoon diner. With decor installed during the Eisenhower administration and 24-hour service on the weekends, this is a perfect spot for an old-fashioned omelet, breakfast sandwich, low-tech burger, or grilled cheese. Throw in bottomless coffee and wall to wall windows that pour in sunlight (or moonlight), and this is quite the Downtown oasis. Though the style is retro, they do have the modern amenity of wireless internet. *400 Bagley St., (313) 962-2300.*

Lunchtime Global - Located in the stately and historic First National Building, the asynchronously modern Lunchtime Global—with floor-to-ceiling views of Cadillac Square—offers a rotating menu of eight tasty soups made fresh each morning. Other lunch specials are wrapped and ready in the cold case for customers craving affordable items like the $3 pesto pasta salad, but the main event here—and

the real gem—is the soup selection, with a wide-variety of crowd-pleasers like broccoli cheese, split pea, dill pickle, and chicken chili made with locally sourced ingredients. Though meatatarians will be more than satisfied, there's also always a well-rounded stable of vegan and vegetarian options, too. If you're on the go, enter directly off of Congress Street. However, if you have some time on your hands, take a stroll through the sky lit Woodward Avenue lobby of this elegant historic building and meander through the marble interior. Be sure to check online for the latest list of soups and specials, and try to visit just before noon to ensure the daily special hasn't run out! *660 Woodward Ave., www.lunchtimeglobal.com, (313) 963-4871.*

Monroe St. Steakhouse - A staple of its Greektown neighborhood, this steakhouse is a popular and well-recommended sanctuary for carnivorous diners in need of filling, attentively prepared eats. The masthead offerings at Monroe St. are all Chairman's Reserve cuts—USDA Choice or higher—cooked to order, counterweighted with select seafood, barbecue, and pasta entrees. The subdued atmosphere creates an inviting experience—Monroe St. is well lit and cozy, with exposed brick, a teak ceiling, and numerous symbols of Detroit pride. Service is knowledgeable and attentive without being overzealous, and the Greektown digs mean casual dress works and spontaneous revelers are welcome. Full bar. *561 Monroe St., www.monroeststeakhouse.com, (313) 961-3636.*

Motor Bar - This contemporary lounge-style bar oasis is tucked away on the second floor of the elegant Westin Book Cadillac Hotel. Temporary home to hotel and dinner guests, and sometimes the in-town Hollywood crew, this comfortable lobby area has enough space for large groups but, with its subdued lighting, is cozy enough for intimate conversations. A rare reliable non-casino option for a respectable scotch before last call, the Motor Bar is a true late night option with a touch of class. The lounge has a relaxing atmosphere that blends well with the unobtrusive and sleek surroundings. Cap off a meal or take in a nightcap and discover a specialty cocktail or one of many martinis, including the signature Book Cadillac Side Car. *1114 Washington Blvd., www.bookcadillacwestin.com/detroit-bar-motor-bar, (313) 442-1600.*

» Motor City Wine - Whether you're looking for an intimate after-dinner date spot, a cozy place Downtown to throw a party, or just somewhere to drop in and pick up a delicious but reasonably priced bottle of wine, Motor City Wine has you covered. Your hosts are both knowledgeable and unpretentious, gladly helping everyone from experts to novices find the perfect wine for their particular budget and occasion. Monthly tastings provide the opportunity to learn the difference between tannins and teinturier, but if wine's not really your thing, check out the weekly jazz concerts and disco dance parties. *608 Woodward Ave., www.motorcitywine.com, (313) 483-7283.*

» New Parthenon - One of the area's last Greek restaurants, New Parthenon is a Greektown tradition that boasts old-world character with a homey, unassuming, charm and a tasty, traditional Greek menu. Its signature "art-Greco" interior features sculptures of Greek gods, a two-story mural, stone walls, charming mint upholstery, and a massive bank of windows and skylights that keep the space awash in natural light. The mezzanine dining area is typically quiet and private, while the lower level dining room is more bustling, particularly before closing at 3am. The menu features a handful of Italian and American favorites alongside an impressive roster of remarkable, traditional Greek dishes. Although it is hard to miss with the seafood-heavy Greek portion of menu, the most popular options are the moussaka, yiaprakia (stuffed grape leaves), spanakotiropita (spinach cheese pie), lemon rice soup, and beef taskebab (veal in tomato wine sauce over rice). Don't forget to order saganaki—OPA! *547 Monroe St., (313) 963-8888.*

Nick's Gaslight - Formerly the home of a four-star restaurant, Nick's Gaslight was a burnt-out shell as recently as 1984 when the current owners rebuilt the bar (their previous restaurant, now a People Mover stop, fell to eminent domain). Inside, not much appears to have changed since then (one notable exception: a poster-sized photograph of Janet Jackson's infamous Superbowl "wardrobe malfunction"). Today, the bar draws an eclectic mix of Polish union workers, Greek suburbanites, and curious Downtown partygoers. Perhaps the only bar in Detroit that hosts live Greek music (the first Saturday of the month all winter long), where you can still get treated to a rousing rendition of "Who Stole The Kishka" by a Polish union boss during the afternoon. *441 Grand River Ave., (313) 963-9191.*

Niki's Pizza - With its waxed mustachioed mascot, Niki's has been a Detroit-style pizza institution since 1980. Located near the Greektown People Mover stop, this Downtown classic greets customers with a warm, loft-aesthetic of exposed brick, oak structural beams, and hardwood floors—all remnants of the building's historical use as a warehouse. The extensive menu offers a number of variations on the square, Detroit-style deep dish pizza that the establishment is known for, including several less common Greek toppings, like lamb and feta, though the most popular varieties remain the standards. In addition, patrons are treated to a bevy of traditional Greek dishes like saganaki, moussaka, lamb kababs, and spanakopita. In the summer months, diners can enjoy the street-side patio, which is the ideal environment for the beer-and-pizza experience. Don't miss half-price pizza on Wednesdays. *735 Beaubien St., www.nikispizza.com, (313) 961-4303.*

The Old Shillelagh - Nestled in Greektown's nightlife center rather than the historically Irish Corktown, The Old Shillelagh is the Downtown mega-pub for Detroiters whose Irish roots go as deep as the volume of Guinness and Jameson they can slug. With three floors (including a rooftop deck) and an outdoor bar that's open for game days, the Old Shillelagh knows how to pack 'em in. And, with a St. Patty's day following that's 10,000 drinkers strong, you can bet those towers of plastic cups behind the bar aren't just for show. During the day, the wood and brick interior accurately evokes the nostalgia of an authentic neighborhood Irish Pub, but on weekends, before ballgames, or during any Downtown drinking holiday, you'll likely be too cramped (and "spirited") to notice. *349 Monroe St., www.oldshillelagh.com, (313) 964-0007.*

Orchid Thai - The power-lunch establishment for the Thai connoisseur, this efficient restaurant has a wide variety of delicious cuisine and generous portions. With cream-colored walls and Spartan Thai decor, the bright yet unassuming space places more emphasis on flavor than ambiance. Though Orchid Thai offers well-balanced takes on classic favorites such as Pad Thai, the most popular dishes are the spiciest curries, tangy noodles, and hot fried rice dishes, all of which are offered with beef, chicken, shrimp, and tofu options. Truly vegetarian friendly, the accommodating staff is happy to hold the fish sauce or substitute tofu. This joint is serious about spice—so be careful how you order. ¡Thai, caramba! In the summer months, get carryout and head for Campus Martius, up the block. *115 Monroe St., (313) 962-0225.*

» Park Bar - Head to this popular Downtown hangout spot for a large selection of local microbrew drafts in an unassuming, beautifully modern space. The industrial, loft-like interior offers exposed brick and ductwork, hardwood floors, contemporary stools and booths, and enough windows to make a greenhouse jealous. Grab a spot at one of the window-side booths to bask in the natural light and practice people watching, or snag a seat at the large circular bar to rub elbows with locals or bend elbows with local brews. The beer list features 17 local brews from nine local breweries, alongside an impressive roster of other microbrews and better-known imported and domestic offerings. For those through with brew, the Park Bar also offers a fine selection of liquor and cocktails behind the bar. Though the bar does not offer food, it is connected to the Bucharest Grill, and serves as its dining room. The space hosts occasional live music and Doggy Style, a fun monthly co-hosted by Supergay Detroit and Canine to Five. Those looking for live music should check listings for the **Elizabeth Theater,** a beautiful second floor theater offering live theater and music. *2040 Park Ave., www.parkbardetroit.com, (313) 962-2933.*

Pegasus Taverna - Open since the 1980s, Pegasus is a stronghold of old Greektown and a reminder of a time when the neighborhood was not just a late-night destination but an epicenter of Greek culture and food. With an animated neon sign depicting the flapping wings of the mythical flying creature from which the restaurant takes its name, Pegasus offers guests always-packed table, booth, and U-shaped bar seating in a refined Grecian garden setting. With a comprehensive menu of delicious, authentic, and generously portioned Greek cuisine churned out of the gigantic open kitchen, lucky diners can choose from favorites like spanikopita, moussaka, lemon rice soup, pastitsio (blasphemously best described as Greek lasagna), lamb in dozens of preparations, and essential, crowd-pleasing saganaki. In keeping with Greektown hours, the restaurant is open until 3am on weeknights and 4am on weekends. If you're looking for delights to take home, check out the deli counter where you can purchases cheeses, sweets, and pastries for later. And, Honey, don't forget the baklava! *558 Monroe St., www.pegasustavernas.com, (313) 964-6800.*

Pizza Papalis - Founded in Detroit in 1986, Pizza Papalis has perfected the famous Chicago-style round-deep-dish-sauce-on-top pie, producing distinctive pies with rich, buttery, flakey crust, a two-inch-thick pile of dough, cheese, sauce, and toppings, and slightly spicy yet tangy sauce. The Greektown Taverna location keeps things fresh with a large Italian menu and an even larger open-seating area with towering brick archways, tall wooden booths, and a full-service bar flanked by flat screens. Picky eaters can find options from chicken fingers to salads (and yes, even thin-crust pizza). But since the Spinach Special pizza is so popular that it gets shipped half-frozen to fans across the country, why bother ordering anything else? Stop by for affordable lunch specials that are anything but "junior" sized, or look online for the latest coupon deals on large pies—perfect for sharing with family and friends! *553 Monroe St., www.pizzapapalis.com, (313) 961-8020.*

Plaka Cafe - Nestled on a bustling block, Plaka is an unassuming Grecian spoon joint with lightning fast service, offering Coney-style Greek fare in a contemporary diner atmosphere. The space features white tiled floor and walls, comfortable booths and tables, an open kitchen, and walls clad in impressive murals of Greek gods flying by Detroit landmarks. The diner menu offers a mixture of American and Greek options, including fries, conies, and breakfast all day, alongside baklava, lamb kebabs, gyro sandwiches, and saganaki, though unafraid locals go with a cheese feast: saganaki, grilled cheese, cheese sticks, and cheese fries. Though this 24-hour joint is usually fairly quiet, things become a bit more raucous after last call at the nearby bars. *535 Monroe St., (313) 962-4687.*

Presto Gourmet Deli - Tucked next to parent restaurant Andiamo in the Renaissance Center, Presto provides a tasty and affordable breakfast and lunch, Monday through Friday between 9am and 3pm. Known throughout the RenCen for its enticing full-pasta lunch, black bean burger with special habanero sauce, juicy sirloin burgers on pretzel buns, and some of the best cookies around, Presto has something for everyone. The $6 pre-prepared salads offer a quick lunch on the go (opt for the house made creamy garlic dressing). With Italian espresso machines, friendly staff, and a frequent diner rewards card, it pays to be a regular. *400 Renaissance Center, (313) 567-6700.*

Red Smoke - Since bursting onto Detroit's packed barbecue stage in 2010, Red Smoke has been winning accolades and devotees for its contemporary industrial atmosphere, attentive staff and exemplary wood-smoked barbecue fare. The 120-year-old building has been beautifully renovated and updated, featuring a full mezzanine, exposed brick, a massive pig chandelier, and 30-foot ceilings. Don't be fooled, though—owners Michael and Tasso Teftsis' team are as gifted in the kitchen as they are with architecture. While offering a full menu with yummy takes on all the usual suspects—Amish chicken, pulled pork, and ribs—its specialties are the ultra-tender brisket and the delicious green beans with fried leeks. Both would medal in any Detroit barbecue Olympics. Red Smoke has a bevy of appetizers, such as the fried pickles, jalapeno cornbread skillet, and catfish bites that shouldn't be overlooked, despite the linebacker-sized entree portions. *573 Monroe St., www.redsmokebarbeque.com, (313) 962-2100.*

» Roast - Roast is one of Detroit's most high-profile restaurants and with good reason. Situated on the bottom floor of the beautifully renovated Westin Book Cadillac, a historic skyscraper that was a beacon of luxury during the earlier days of Detroit's prominence and home to more celebrity stories than People magazine, Roast is quite possibly the crowning achievement of this pivotal rehabilitation project. With celebrated chef Michael Symon (of Iron Chef and The Chew fame) behind it, Roast is a celebration of all things meat—right down to the "roast beast" cooking on a spit in full view of the dining room (but vegetarians are also welcome, and in fact the vegetarian-friendly dishes are some of the best things on the menu—try the macaroni and cheese). From beef cheek pierogi to roasted marrow served on sawed bone, Roast consistently impresses. With an exceptional wine selection, classically inspired craft cocktails and an extensive craft beer list, Roast is known nearly as well for its bar as it is for its food and atmosphere. Its happy hour is the best in town. *1128 Washington Blvd., www.roastdetroit.com, (313) 961-2500.*

» Rowland Cafe - Though Detroit boasts some fierce coffee shops, none offers surroundings as awe-inspiring as the Rowland Cafe. Situated in the center of the stately Aztec-inspired Art Deco lobby of the Guardian Building—and named for its architect, Wirt C. Rowland, the cafe manages to maintain an unexpected level of intimacy and European charm. Serving Italian-made Illy coffee, the seasoned baristas sling cups of coffee, tea, and espresso drinks. In addition to the caffeinated offerings and free Wi-Fi, Rowland offers a selection of moderately priced juices, sodas, cold sandwiches, and locally sourced pastries and baked goods. For a wider selection of lunch items and hot baked goods, check out the smaller Stella International Cafe located adjacent to the building's north entrance. *500 Griswold St., www.therowlandcafe.com, (313) 964-1928.*

Santorini Estiatorio - Named for a Greek island in the Aegean Sea, this estiatorio—formerly the Mosaic restaurant, but under the same ownership—is decorated patriotically with azure and white flourishes, including a pair of mock schooners, amid light brown undertones such as wicker chandeliers and decorative raw wood in a warm, amber-lit space. Some vestiges of the old restaurant remain—recessed mosaic tile ceiling inlays, mammoth ornamental glasswork over the horseshoe bar, and nautical compass insignias, but Santorini is distinguished far beyond its legacy. Authentically prepared modern and traditional Greek cuisine comprise the menu, including succulent lamb, mild and creamy avgolemono soup, attentively made versions of Greek classics like moussaka, dolmathakia, and Greek preparations of fish, cuts of beef, and chicken. Out of regard for purity and creative control, lamb and beef are butchered in-house and even the house bread is specially made. A full bar including Mythos lager, Skinos liqueur (recommended), Metaxa, and a menu of unique Mediterranean cocktails is available. *501 Monroe St., www.santorinidetroit.com, (313) 962-9366.*

Small Plates - Recently under new ownership and management with a street-style facelift to go with it courtesy of local artist Antonio "Shades" Agee and Motor City Denim, Small Plates lays claim to be the first restaurant of its kind in the country with a federally trademarked name and concept. In the tradition of Spanish tapas and Italian antipasti, Small Plates serves a melting pot of American cuisine with a particular Detroit flare—dishes are inspired from ethnic cuisines prominent in Detroit, like Mediterranean and Mexican, and Small Plates also offers an interpretation of the coney dog. Michigan beers abound and they also serve a Sunday brunch. *1521 Broadway St., www.smallplates.com, (313) 963-0702.*

Steve's Place - The din that emanates from Saint Andrew's Hall next door accentuates the taciturn nature of Steve's place. Owned and operated by Steve Francis and his wife Sophia for more than 40 years, the bar exudes a ghostly poetic calm that is simultaneously post-apocalyptic and gently welcoming. With its green and blue roller rink hues, mid-century lunch boxes above the bar, and a cigarette machine that sells brands that have been off of shelves for years, the bar looks as if it has seen few updates since its grand opening in 1970. However, though these eccentricities add to the bar's curious charm, it's the elderly owners behind the counter that make the place such a wonder. Greek immigrants, Steve and his wife speak in soft aged voices as they regale their guests with stories about Greece during the Second World War and Detroit in the 1960s. Don't be surprised if Steve slips you a complimentary shot of schnapps in between tales. "It's good for the breath, good for kissing," he says. If you're lucky, you'll catch Travelin' Blues, a grizzled regular who plucks through blues standards and plays almost nightly (and accepts tips). Open every day except Christmas. *439 E. Congress St., (313) 961-5559.*

Sweetwater Tavern - Tucked inside a beautiful, quaint, 1941 brick building, Sweetwater Tavern is an upscale bar and restaurant catering to the city's young urban professionals. Beyond its impressive liquor selection and small but well-curated beer list, Sweetwater is a sacred site for wing worshipers, selling 600 pounds a day. Sweetwater's wings are brought in fresh from Eastern Market each day, marinated for 24 hours, dredged in a delicious spice blend, and fried as you order. Known for its distinctive, tangy, mildly spicy flavor and crispy exterior, these outstanding wings are served with celery and bleu cheese. Not a one-trick pony, the menu also offers succulent breaded catfish and perfect reuben sandwiches. Sweetwater keeps the kitchen open until 2am and offers a free shuttle to the stadiums, making it a great pregame option. Don't stop here on the way to the hospital—the place is usually packed, and the service is on the slow side. *400 E. Congress St., www.sweetwatertavern.net, (313) 962-2210.*

Tom's Oyster Bar - A favorite among critics and Downtown professionals alike, Tom's Oyster Bar has been a destination for shellfish seekers and recovered ostraconophobics since 1985. The restaurant is reminiscent of a New England chowder house, with cherry walls, blue-checkered tablecloths, vintage tile floors, large front windows, a tin ceiling, and walls adorned with a bounty of nautical prints. In the warmer seasons, the rooftop seating is a grand place for a beer, as it offers patrons a generous view of Downtown. In addition to its outstanding, signature selection of six types of oysters—served with its distinctive mignonette or zesty habanero vinaigrette, the wide-ranging seasonal menu offers an array of chowders, salads, sandwiches, steaks, and seafood. Those looking beyond bivalves will enjoy the Mackinac smoked whitefish sausage, po' boys, pulled pork sandwich, sushi, or Black Angus flat iron steak. *519 E. Jefferson Ave., www.tomsoysterbar.com, (313) 964-4010.*

Tommy's Detroit Bar & Grill - The view of the Joe should tell you lots—this Downtown bar caters heavily to Detroit sports fans, particularly those who bleed red in winter. Tommy's is a comfy, welcoming place to get a quick lunch of house-dredged wings or cheap, fresh burgers cooked deliciously well-done, as well as a spot to take in a game from one of five flat screens while tipping back a few. Tommy's also offers a slice of history: its red brick building originating in 1840 still features hidden underground rooms, from the building's role in the Underground Railroad. The rich, woody interior is warm and cozy, and made to resemble the inside sling of a schooner's hull. A game room with pool, darts, and video poker and a small street-side patio round things out. *624 3rd St., www.tommysdetroit.com, (313) 965-2269.*

The Town Pump Tavern - A contemporary, laid back spot in an airy, handsome space, the Town Pump has been a Downtown destination since 1996. Located in the Park Avenue House, an old-school apartment hotel, the bar offers a modern reflection of the historic building, with a forest worth of contemporary wood paneling, antique brass lights, and tin ceiling. With its convenient location steps from the stadiums, the bar is popular with rowdy sports fans celebrating Tigers triumphs and drowning sorrows after Lions losses. The bar offers 18 drafts alongside a roster of international and domestic bottles, and a menu of hearty pub fare. Though the belles of the ball on the menu are the cheese-laden, hand-tossed pizzas, the tavern also offers tasty sandwiches, salads, sides, and hamburgers, including the popular Atlantic cod po' boy. Local DJs spin on weekends and attract large crowds to late night watering hole. *100 W. Montcalm St., www.thetownpumptavern.com, (313) 961-1929.*

UDetroit Cafe - Equal parts bar, restaurant, radio booth and television studio, this lively space from local music veterans, Mark and Brian Pastoria, allows guests to interact with the internet radio and television stations—UDetroit Radio and UDetroit TV—that broadcast live from the dining room. This cafe is a physical manifestation of the music, news, and sports webcasts. The recording stage is set up right at the storefront, so patrons can soak up discussions and live performances while they enjoy the Detroit-music-inspired menu items, such as The Detroit House salad, Funk Bros Cappuccino, or the Lose Yourself Martini. Got a story to tell? The bartender might be listening, but so are the radio hosts. You might just make it on the air! *427 Randolph St., www.udetroit.com, (313) 962-0660.*

» Vicente's Cuban Cuisine - A little piece of Havana in Detroit, Vicente's Cuban Cuisine is renowned for its signature Cuban food and handsome, contemporary space. It serves authentic Spanish-style tapas ranging in Latin influences from traditional Cuban flavors to more Spanish and South American styles from the influence of well-traveled Chilean chef Roberto Caceres. Its extensive menu also includes popular paellas, pressed sandwiches on genuine Cuban bread made with lard, and a variety of Spanish wines, flavored mojitos, and sangria. The refined dining room features elegant tables with bud vases, a bright color palette, wood floors, and an open ceiling, as well as a sweeping hardwood dance floor. On weekend nights, the dance floor supplants the food as the primary attraction, with free salsa lessons, salsa dancing, live bands, and DJs. Vicente's is the full-on Latin supper club experience in Detroit's central business district, perfect for business lunches as much as date nights. *1250 Library St., www.vicente.us, (313) 962-8800.*

Wah-Hoo - This recent addition to Downtown's lunch and dinner scene has a captive audience for anyone craving Asian cuisine. Decor at this sleek, modern space is understated—visitors dine at polished hardwood tables under elevated ceilings, at the marble wraparound bar backed with flat screens, or at a small sushi bar with an intimate view of Wah-Hoo's open kitchen. The Pan-Asian cuisine emphasizes fresh ingredients—Chinese offerings include house-made wontons, while food across the sea uses delicate, market-fresh fish for sushi; brown rice is also available. Drinking at Wah-Hoo can be adventurous—a selection of sakes and Asahi and Sapporo beer highlight the imports, but footnoting its cocktail menu are 30- and 50-ounce "fishbowls" starting at $10 and $20, respectively. Carryout is available. *536 Shelby St., www.wah-hoo.net, (313) 324-8700.*

WaLa - With an impressive roster of hearty, flavorful sandwiches, and a name stemming from its location at Washington and Lafayette, WaLa has become a destination for hungry Detroiters in the market for an outstanding sandwich or ballad-worthy salad since opening in 2012. With contemporary prints adorning the walls, all-chrome chairs, and a street-corner patio, this unassuming space gives off a lively, character-full ambiance to match the food. The menu offers tasty takes on sandwich staples with fresh, local ingredients—including breads from On the Rise Bakery (see separate entry). The shrimp po' boy, mile-high Italian, and Lizzy—panko breaded tilapia and slaw—are standouts. *1010 Washington Blvd., www.waladetroit.com, (313) 963-5450.*

The Well - It's an easy bet that most patrons going to the Well are too busy chatting over basement priced drinks and spotting a game from of The Well's flat screens or big screen to pay mind to the decoration, but The Well is no slouch for environs. This mellow-lit joint features exposed brick, a long hardwood bar, wood tables and chairs, and a monogrammed glass entrance. There's no need to be bored simply conversing with regulars, but those who want to can enjoy the game room in the rear. Patio seating available. *1228 Randolph St.,* *www.thewellbars.com/detroit, (313) 964-0776.*

Wolfgang Puck Pizzeria & Cucina - Inside MGM Grand Casino is a recently launched upscale Italian eatery designed by famed chef and restaurateur Wolfgang Puck. Since it's in a casino, no expense was spared on the comfortable and opulent interior—from the marble horseshoe bar with marble, to the leather furniture, massive brass-plated ringed chandeliers suspended from the 20-foot ceiling, and the twin glass cases on the dining room floor displaying hundreds of bottles of fine red wines. The food emphasizes control of preparation and quality of ingredients—all pasta is made in-house, the amply sized pizzas (totally shareable) are stone-fired, and updated versions of traditional Italian dishes round out the high-end cuisine. Aside from the copious wine selection, drinks include bottles of unusual artisanal Italian beers, a succinct cocktail menu of classic Italian favorites, and an aggressive selection of top-shelf scotches. First-timers to a casino should be prepared for highly attentive, professional service. Open for dinner only. *1777 3rd St., www.mgmgranddetroit.com/restaurants, (877) 888-2121.*

SHOPPING & SERVICES

Blumz - This floral shop makes a bold and beautiful statement as much as it provides convenience, being centrally located downtown. With a wide-ranging variety of reasonable price-points and classic, modern, and seasonal arrangements, Blumz can accommodate any well-wish, romantic, or birthday need. Though the small shop abounds with baskets, bouquets, and planters, the store is most renowned for its vibrant, inexpensive, grab-and-go arrangements. Friendly and knowledgeable staff can expertly craft a comprehensive floral design plan for events and weddings, dealing with even the most prickly of customers or thorny situations. *1260 Library St., www.blumz.com, (313) 964-5777.*

The Broadway - Offering brand name fashions at firesale prices, The Broadway has been a dapper Downtown destination for more than a generation. Fellas looking to look sharp will find a large showroom of fully tailored high-end Moschino and Versace suits for $200–$15,000. The shop carries a number of designer shirts by Luchiano Visconti, Pelle Pelle leather jackets, and the latest in men's sportswear from lines such as Sean Jean. Ladies will appreciate the small—but growing—selection of women's designer jeans, and casual tops.

Gentlemen will find the perfect finishing touch to any outfit from The Broadway's selection of men's shoes, ties, and cufflinks. If you're looking for suits or jeans and are on a tighter budget, stop by J L Stone Co. (1231 Broadway St.) a few doors away.
1247 Broadway St., www.shopthebroadway.com, (313) 963-2171.

City Slicker Shoes - A formal footwear destination since 1977, City Slicker Shoes is the world's largest supplier of men's alligator and crocodile footwear. With rows upon rows of exotic-skin shoes— think ostrich, pony, gator, croc, fox, sting ray, eel, lizard, and goat— in every color and hue under the rainbow, the store has a bright, vibrant atmosphere. Wayne, the manager, has a passion for helping customers select from among the shop's diverse selection of Mauri, Pajar, Mezian, and Lacoste shoes, as well as helping visitors create custom kicks. Don't miss the photos of famous customers, including Michael Jackson, who have visited over the years. *164 Monroe St., www.cityslickershoes.com, (313) 963-1963.*

» D:hive - Every visit to the city should begin at the D:hive. As a welcome mat for those interested in engaging with or living, working, and playing in the city, this nonprofit has quickly developed a reputation for selling visitors on Detroit with renowned tours and information on jobs, housing, and recreational opportunities. The Downtown Welcome Center offers a contemporary aesthetic, with wooden fixtures and a bright color palette. Inside the space, visitors are greeted by a retail store with local Detroit art and clothing, and an outgoing team of on-staff liaisons who can help guests find a restaurant, concert, job, or apartment. Since merging with Inside Detroit, the D:Hive has begun offering jovial Jeanette Pierce's bevy of bus and walking tours, including the Insider's Walking Tour of Downtown, Downtown Living Tour, Insider's Bus Tour of Greater Downtown, and our favorite, the bi-weekly Bar Tours. Those looking to hang their shingle should consider the BUILD Classes, which use a nationally recognized curriculum to assist and support the city's existing and aspiring entrepreneurs. No matter how you'd like to engage with Detroit, make a deeline for the D:hive.
1253 Woodward Ave., www.dhivedetroit.org, (313) 962-4590.

Djenne Beads & Art - If the beautifully handcrafted African textiles hanging in the window do not draw you in from the streets of Greektown, the rich aromas of Egyptian perfumes will. Djenne Beads founder and glass craftsman Mahamadou Sumareh specializes in authentic imported African artifacts, clothing, jewelry, fabric, baskets, drums, and body oils. Visit him at the International Building, and you might get a crash course in the history of African trade beads. Whether you're a collector of ancient African glass beads, a jewelry lover with a flair for custom-made pieces, or a craft enthusiast looking for a unique gift, Djenne Beads has you covered. *1045 Beaubien St., (313) 965-6620.*

» DSE @ Grand – The name is an acronym for "Definitive Style Exclusive." James Morris opened this store in 2008 in Harmonie Park—a neighborhood that his grandmother, artist and gallerist Dell Pryor, helped reinvigorate. Compact but packed, DSE is part of a block of Downtown with an uncommonly lively density of small boutiques that have established themselves as a local retail destination. Here, Morris's iconic, reasonably priced lines of Support Detroit, Detroit Love, and Union DSE tees, tote bags, hats, sweatshirts, and sweaters grace the walls and are displayed on the shop's honey-colored wooden shelves lined with sleek black trim. In addition to his own line, Morris offers a collection of local artwork, earrings, eyewear, and small home accessories. *202 E. Grand River Ave., www.dsedetroit.com, (313) 963-0533.*

» DuMouchelle's Art Galleries - A creaky walk through this glittering treasure trove is truly an eyeful. Open to the public, the two-story gallery is wall-to-wall, floor-to-ceiling antique furniture, jewelry, rugs, paintings, tapestries, books, fine china, silverware, sculptures, and other dazzling decorative objects for your petite maison or mansion. Visit during the monthly auction to be hypnotized by one of the droll auctioneers and raise your paddle for a deal on a carousel horse, Civil War–era bayonet, or marquise diamond ring. The detritus from suburban estate liquidations occasionally brings to light a Warhol, Picasso, or fabulous taxidermy lot and auction previews are conducted at the gallery for one full week prior to the sale. Wondering if your uncle's collection of antique snuff bottles is worth anything? DuMouchelle's offers free verbal appraisals on Wednesdays and Saturdays from 1pm to 4pm. With complementary entry, valet parking, coffee, tea, and the occasional platter of snacks, there is no reason not to stop in for an auction during the third weekend of every month. Beware: It's easy to get caught up in the excitement so when the gavel drops, you may find yourself the unwitting owner of a rare Steinway piano or Wildebeest mount. *409 E. Jefferson Ave., www.dumouchelle.com, (313) 963-6255.*

Gents By D'Mongo's Salon - Tucked away in a second-level corner near the Sky Bridge that connects the Renaissance and Millender Centers is just one of the D'Mongo locations about town—part of the salon dynasty of well known Canadian Detroiter, Dianne Mongo. Offering barber services, haircuts, perms, colors, beard trims, lines, and eyebrow waxing, this one-stop shop is popular with Downtown professionals and is efficient and affordable so you can get back to business quickly. The salon also offers manicure services (for men and women) by Christine—from full polish and French manicures to a simple, natural buff, she'll have you shaped up and shipped out in a half hour. With her warm nature and affable personality—and since she knows everyone in town—you're bound to make a new friend or two as you exit with sparkling fingertips. Appointments suggested, walk-ins upon availability. *333 E. Jefferson Ave., Ste. 220, (313) 222-0733.*

Good People Popcorn - Upon entering the charming historic brick building that houses this family-owned establishment, customers will receive a friendly greeting as they are invited to sample the 12 taste-tempting varieties of popcorn made fresh throughout the day. The shop offers classics like buttered popcorn and caramel corn, but first-timers would be remiss not to try some of the more esoteric flavors, like bacon-cheddar, caramel apple pie, chili-cheese, white-cheddar salsa, or the decadent caramel chocolate drizzle. Thirsty patrons can grab a glass of fresh-squeezed lemonade or one of the store's special seasonal beverages. *633 Beaubien St., www.goodpeoplepopcorn.com, (313) 963-2499.*

» Henry the Hatter - A Detroit tradition since 1893, Henry the Hatter is a beloved haberdashery and Downtown Detroit icon. Once past the old-timey neon sign above the door, visitors will find a beautiful, long, narrow shotgun-style store with mint-colored shelves and antique racks bursting with caps. Whether you are in the market for a bowler, derby, fedora, homburg, driving cap, or any other variety of formal

headwear, you are bound to find a number of options among the large selection of hats from respected brands, including Bailey, Biltmore, Borsalino, Dobbs, Giorgio Cellini, Henschel, Kangol, Selentino, Stetson, and Tilden. Dwight D. Eisenhower's inauguration hat was from this shop, and contemporary customers include LL Cool J, Run DMC, and Kid Rock. *1307 Broadway St., www.henrythehatterdetroit.com, (313) 962-0970.*

Hot Sam's - Open since 1921, Hot Sam's is a choice Downtown locale for classic men's professional and casual wear. Catering to the office set, the Detroit staple offers a diverse selection of suits, hats, khakis, polos, ties, fedoras, button-ups, and other items that belong in any self-respecting man's wardrobe. The store's selection of fitted items is friendly for any body type, as Hot Sam's offers a wide-variety of big and tall items. Customers can also take advantage of comprehensive tailoring services and free alterations on the store's antique belt-driven sewing machine. *127 Monroe St., www.hotsams.net, (313) 961-6779.*

Little Foxes Fine Gifts - On the south side of the Fox Theater complex lies Little Foxes Fine Gifts, a classic high-end gift and collectible shop with three rooms of elegant housewares, home decor, and accessories. Although the space is brightly painted with aqua walls and features tin ceilings, baroque gold moldings, elaborately detailed floors, and an indoor fountain, the store is dominated by the numerous resplendent displays and fixtures brimming with colorful merchandise. Customers in the market for a lady's gift will find an impressive selection of purses, cards, keepsakes, MacKenzie-Childs furniture, Waterford crystal, Emma Bridgewater pottery, Heron porcelain, and other trinkets. *2211 Woodward Ave., www.littlefoxes.com, (866) 983-6202.*

Lott Anter Tailoring and Cleaning - Since 1919, the Anter family has led Detroit in expert tailoring. Despite an unassuming shop tucked in the drab Murphy-Telegraph building, Clark Anter gets every kind of job done with the help of his antique 1909 sewing machine. Locally and nationally known for repairing almost 100 American flags for free each year, Clark "honors his dad, grandfather, and country in one easy swoop." With dependable, affordable, and eco-friendly dry cleaning, fixed-while-you-wait buttons, zippers, and hems, and hand-perfected vintage wear or modern tuxedos, Clark and his wife are in the business of making sure you're ready for business. *151 W. Congress St., (313) 282-2684.*

The Natural Hair Market - This all-natural organic beauty supply store opened in 2012 in a little shop space fitted with wooden shelves stocked with luxurious products. Owner Victoria Roby creates the moisturizing bath soak and lip balm but also vends locally produced body lotions and soaps, heavenly scented candles, and hair products. Environmentally conscious shoppers can pick up one of the graphic market bags sporting The Natural Hair Market curly-Q logo, which are screen-printed right next door at DSE. *204 E. Grand River Ave., (313) 638-2551.*

PenzDetroiT - Don't let the "z" in the name fool you—PenzDetroiT is serious about fine writing instruments, quality paper, and premium luggage. The owner, Alex Lebarre, is a self-proclaimed collector who can recommend the perfect writing utensil and notepad for your budget. Connoisseurs will find limited edition fountain pens for hundreds to thousands of dollars, and the rest of us can get fine writing utensils for about 15 bucks. Best of all, Alex is happy to let visitors take a pen out for a test-scribble. *333 W. Fort St., www.penzdetroit.com, (313) 961-7474.*

Pete's Barber Shop - Located within another store front, Pete's Barber Shop is an affordable place to get a respectable haircut. Open since 1962, the shop is an old fashioned space with mint green and exposed-brick walls, vintage fixtures, and classic photos of customers and friends. Ask Pete (known locally as Pete the Greek) the story behind any of the many photos on his wall and you'll be entertained. You can browse a vintage Playboy while the barber gives you the straight razor treatment around the ears and finishes off the trim with a splash of hair tonic—you'll leave a new man. Not necessarily for mixed company. *438 Macomb St., (313) 964-7200*

Pure Detroit - What began as a small T-shirt company and shop in the David Whitney Building in 1998 has grown into a thriving Detroit business and a beloved local brand. Though its flagship store is in New Center (see separate entry), Pure Detroit's other two storefronts are in iconic buildings downtown—the Guardian Building and a smaller outlet in the Renaissance Center. The Guardian Building location, especially, offers an elegant shopping experience in a contemporary space with glass walls that allow full view of the building's incredible lobby. At all three locations, visitors will find Pure Detroit's signature designs on tees, totes, sweatshirts, magnets, undies, and pet leashes, as well as Detroit gifts such as Sanders treats, delicious McClure's pickles, and Faygo pop. Additionally, the Guardian location offers the largest selection of books and artwork of the three. Pure Detroit has become a destination for visitors and locals alike looking to stock up on some Detroit swag. 500 Griswold St., www. puredetroit.com, (313) 963-1440. Second location in GM Renaissance Center: *100 Renaissance Center, (313) 259-5100.*

RAGS - High-end Detroit fashion lives at RAGS, a beautiful shop on a bustling corner in Harmonie Park. With its loft-like interior, polished cement floors, hidden granite bar, and spiral staircase, this sleek and contemporary space makes shopping a pleasure. The peach-painted walls in the front of the store showcase women's designer dresses and silken tops, while the Spartan white walls of the back room highlight men's designer jackets, jeans, and belts. The shop offers pieces for men and women who craft their own unique style. Don't expect to see any of RAGS' Evisu Japanese jeans with hand-embellished Swarovski crystals elsewhere. *1376 Broadway St., (313) 623-6158.*

Serman's - For generations, Serman's has been dressing Detroit's men and boys in classic suits, contemporary outerwear, sportswear, slacks, and hats. The shop carries an almost unparalleled selection of suits, with more than 1,000 styles across 13 sizes—36 to 62. Those looking for a seasonal ensemble will find suits in every color—from white to gold to hot pink—and in an array of materials, such as rayon, sharkskin, and wool. Serman's offers full tailoring services, a wide shoe selection, and an ongoing buy one suit, get two free, deal. As owner Steven Ross likes to say, "short or tall, fat or thin, Serman's has the suits to put you in!" Open since 1917, the shop is said to be the oldest men's retailer in the area. *1238 Randolph St., www. sermansclothes.com, (313) 964-1335.*

Simmons & Clark Jewelers - This is where Detroiters buy jewelry— Simmons & Clark has been a good friend to those looking to buy a girl's best friend since 1925. The façade features a beautifully restored black Vitrolite and tall, open storefront windows, Visitors will notice Simmons' respect for the past and pride in old-school quality service as they admire the glass case of black and white photographs and newspaper clippings detailing the store's history and browse the selection with owner Michael Simmons. The shop stocks an array of pieces in gold, silver, stainless steel, and platinum in classical and contemporary styles, with special attention to wedding, engagement, anniversary, and religious jewelry. Free validated parking in the Detroit Opera House garage. *1535 Broadway St.,* *www.simmonsandclark.com, (313) 963-2284.*

Spectacles - A Harmonie Park staple for more than a generation, Spectacles is a destination for contemporary apparel and accessories and a focused selection of books and local hip hop, R&B, and electronic albums. Owner Zana Smith is a knowledgeable, bespectacled woman who's hip to the current and historical goings-on in Detroit's music and fashion scenes. Smith keeps her contemporary, loft-like boutique stocked with her signature Detroit Soul shirts, modern jewelry, vintage military caps, aviators, camouflage outerwear, Schott jackets, books such as Butch Jones' autobiography, and a diverse, constantly changing selection of albums from artists like rapper Phat Kat and soulstress Monica Blaire. This boutique becomes a lively venue every Friday when local DJs spin until close. *230 E. Grand River Ave., www.spectaclesdetroit.com, (313) 963-6886.*

Tip Toe Shoe Repair - This classic, brass tacks shop has been repairing and shining shoes for a generation out of its small, unassuming space. With its amber walls and red tile floor, retro two-seater shoe shine stand, and jovial staff, the modest storefront is reminiscent of old-school Detroit. Whether you've got trouble with wingtips, loafers, pumps, boots, heels, or oxfords, Tip Toe can save your sole with new stitching, soles, heels, buffing, laces, grommets, or a simple shine. The shop also offers a limited selection of new men's shoes, belts, hats, umbrellas, and other accessories. *127 Michigan Ave., (313) 961-0066.*

CULTURAL ATTRACTIONS

» Detroit Opera House / Michigan Opera Theatre - The magnificent C. Howard Crane masterpiece now known as the Detroit Opera House debuted as The Capitol Theatre in 1922 and was one of the five largest theaters in the world when it was completed. The entertainment palace hosted jazz legends like Louis Armstrong and Duke Ellington before taking a turn as the home of the Detroit Symphony Orchestra, but it ultimately devolved into an illicit movie house. Though the building fell into disrepair and closed in 1985, it was purchased by Michigan Opera Theatre in 1988, and the organization completed an extensive historic restoration of the structure. The stunning beauty of the building is belied by the relatively reserved exterior—inside, patrons are treated to an opulent architectural feast of ornate details and elegant crystal chandeliers that wrap the stately 2,700 seat auditorium, which offers main floor, balcony, and private box seating. Since the grand opening of the Detroit Opera House in 1996, Michigan Opera Theatre has programmed the storied venue. The company stages four operas annually during the season, hosts dance companies from around the world, and offers elaborate shows and productions ranging from Broadway to comedy. A highlight of the activities also includes one of Detroit's best dress-up parties: BravoBravo, an annual benefit to support the Opera House. Dedicated to education and enrichment, dress-rehearsal seating is available on the cheap for pre-paid groups of students and seniors. *1526 Broadway St., www.michiganopera.org, (313) 237-7464.*

Isaac Agree Downtown Synagogue - Founded in 1921, the Isaac Agree Downtown Synagogue moved into its current, four-story historic home in the early 1960s—you can't miss the rainbow-colored windows along the long sides the Flatiron-shaped building. Its principal mission was to address the unmet needs of the Jewish community, for those who worked downtown or were visiting the city, by providing a traditional, Conservative presence in the heart of Detroit. As it stands, the institution is currently the only Synagogue in the city of Detroit, and over the past several years, it has seen a revival through its committed young and old members alike. In addition to the expected Shabbat services, Torah studies, and High Holiday Services, the Synagogue has become a community hub and gathering place, hosting neighborhood events such as book clubs, concerts, film nights, and renowned well-attended dance parties to which all are welcome. *1457 Griswold St., www.downtownsynagogue.org, (313) 962-4047.*

Library Street Collective - A reimagination of the Long-Sharp/ Curis Gallery that opened with a splash in 2011, the Library Street Collective has established itself as a destination to view exquisite works by prominent names. The gallery is elegantly utilitarian— exhibition space is divided into an oblong 1,200 square foot whitewashed ground level with unfinished wood floors and an expansive second floor—a cavernous setting with stark industrial columns. The aesthetic of this bi-level space suits the modern and contemporary work emphasized at the gallery, which (under the two names it has held, both abbreviated as LSC) has shown work by marquee 20th century artists such as Roy Lichtenstein and Andy

Warhol. Exhibitions are often paired with educational components such as talks, films, or demonstrations. *1260 Library St., www.lscgallery.com, (313) 600-7443.*

Rose and Robert Skillman Branch, Detroit Public Library - Built in 1932, the DPL's beautiful, two-story neoclassical Downtown branch houses an important public archive (the National Automotive History Collection), a circulating collection of popular materials, an internet cafe, and an auditorium. Clad in limestone, bronze, and copper, with a grand rotunda and marble floors, the Skillman Branch is a stirring, well-preserved example of monumental 20th century library architecture. It's also a busy branch, boasting the second largest children's room in the DPL system after the Main Library. The century-old Automotive History Collection, actually a distinct entity within the library, houses more than 600,000 items of particular interest to automotive enthusiasts, journalists, and historians, and includes photographs, service manuals, periodicals, and advertising literature, among much more. *121 Gratiot Ave., www.detroitpubliclibrary.org/branch/skillman, (313) 481-1850.*

Sam's Barbershop - Having held court across three different floors throughout 58 years in Detroit's landmark Dime Building, Sam's is an in-demand spot for members of Downtown's professional fraternity looking to get an expert haircut, shave, or shoe shine at a reasonable price. Its current second-floor home has interior floor-to-ceiling windows that look out on the Corinthian columns and ornamentation of the Dime's lobby. Inside, Sam's is strictly business: the equipment is all recent and well maintained—including a hairdresser's vacuum to keep any trace of your locks from getting inside your Oxford— with some accidentally vintage furniture and accent pieces (see the decades-old hairdresser's chairs and wood furniture) thrown in for good measure. Sam knows his customers well—some as long as he's been open—and is in enough demand to make appointments required. *719 Griswold (Dime Building), Suite 220 (313) 961-7373.*

START Gallery - START grew out of its owner's dedication to providing new and under-recognized artists a venue to exhibit their work in a professional, dynamic space. This beautiful, modern gallery, occupying 2,300 square feet on a second floor at the corner of Grand River Avenue and Broadway Street, achieves just that. The interior of the gallery is a beautiful, raw, Spartan space with obsidian floors, track lighting, and a cavernous layout that accommodates the mobile divider walls and modular stage. Many artists incorporate the space into their installations, covering the walls and ceilings with many murals. Exhibitions at START change quickly—some months feature multiple shows, so visitors should inquire about upcoming openings. A small store in the rear sells a sampling of previous exhibited work, as well as the owner's proprietary "Defend Detroit" clothing. *206 E. Grand River Ave., www.startgallery.net, (313) 909-2845.*

Virgil H. Carr Cultural Center - This 20,000 square foot Downtown arts center is the home of the Arts League of Michigan, an organization devoted to preserving and presenting the work of African and African-American artists in a wide variety of media. The beautiful, recently restored 1895 Beaux Arts building was originally used as a gathering place and concert hall by Detroit's German immigrant population. Today it's a busy arts hub, holding multicultural art exhibitions, performances, readings, fashion shows, lectures, and parties, in addition to numerous art classes and workshops for students of all ages. Stop by the Paradise Valley Gift Gallery while you're there, a shop dedicated to Detroit's historic African-American arts community, featuring books, art, CDs, clothing, and more. *311 E. Grand River Ave., (313) 965-8430.*

ENTERTAINMENT & RECREATION

Boll Family YMCA - With its beautiful and modern building, 53 cardio machines, 34 weight machines, basketball court, two pools, indoor 3-lane 100-meter track, rock-climbing wall, friendly staff, and welcoming atmosphere, the Boll Family YMCA is a great choice for exercisers of all stripes, from novice to veteran. For visitors seeking a more structured routine, the Boll also offers a wide variety of exercise classes and experienced personal trainers. For those looking to exercise their minds instead of their bodies, the YMCA also offers art classes and theater productions open to the public. Though the gym is private, visitors can purchase multiday guest passes for $15. *1401 Broadway St., www.ymcadetroit.org, (313) 309-9622.*

» Campus Martius Park - Campus Martius Park, known as "Detroit's Gathering Place," is an award-winning park steeped in local history. Though recently re-established, the park was originally conceived by Judge Augustus B. Woodward as the starting point for Detroit's street system, following the Fire of 1805. Under Woodward's plan, Campus Martius—"military ground" in Latin—serves as the hub of the city's arterial streets, and the point of origin for the region's mile roads. As automotive traffic increased in the city, the park was demolished, but was redevelopment and re-opened in 2004. Today, Campus Martius is a vibrant, beautiful urban plaza, complete with fountains, sculptures, a bar and café, a games pavilion, two stages, and even a seasonal ice-skating rink which spans 7,200 square feet and is patterned after the rink at New York's Rockefeller Center, with capacity for 200 skaters. The park is home to a variety of events, from the Winter Blast in February (see separate entry in events), to movie screenings in summer, and the Christmas tree lighting in November. The southern end of the park is anchored by the 60-foot-tall bronze and granite **Michigan Soldiers' and Sailors' Monument,** dedicated to the memory to Michigan's fallen soldiers and sailors. Erected in 1872, this stunning memorial is topped by an 11-foot bronze female warrior with a raised sword. The periphery of the octagonal granite base includes four bronze female figures symbolizing victory, history, emancipation, and union, and four male figures depicting an infantryman, a sailor, a cavalryman, and an artilleryman. Between the figures, visitors will find smaller bronze bas-relief plaques honoring President Lincoln, General Sherman, General Grant, and Admiral Farragut. *800 Woodward Ave., www.campusmartiuspark.org, (313) 962-0101.*

» **Comerica Park / Detroit Tigers -** A titan in Major League Baseball's American League Central Division, the Detroit Tigers are one of the nation's most popular and successful baseball clubs. Founded in 1894, Detroit is the oldest single-name, single-city team in the American League, and one of the league's charter members. The team has had 11 MVPs, 40 Gold Glove recipients, 11 American League pennants, and four World Series victories. All of this success has made them a beloved fixture in city culture—Detroit has been the only American League team to draw one million fans each year since 1964. The Tigers currently play in Comerica Park. Opened in 2000, the park is a fairly new stadium, but is packed with nostalgia for Tigers of yore. Along the lower concourse are museum-style chronological displays full of artifacts from the Detroit Tigers' 115-year history, as well as statues of key figures in the team's past, from the legendary Ty Cobb to beloved broadcaster Ernie Harwell. The stadium features large fountains, fireworks displays, a 6,000 square foot scoreboard, a Ferris wheel, and a merry-go-round. Our favorite seats are in sections 138–143 by third base, although seats in sections 321–345 offer the best views of Downtown. *2100 Woodward Ave., detroit.tigers.mlb.com, (313) 944-4141.*

Detroit Athletic Club - Housed in one of the many Detroit buildings designed by famed architect Albert Kahn, this private club has maintained a tradition of regional class and ambassadorship for more than a century. Members—numbering more than 4,000—take advantage of this preeminent athletic club for activities like boxing, fencing, squash, and swimming, socialize at one of the DAC's eateries (including separate kitchens for both the men's and women's locker rooms), and share a collective history that has seen visits from presidents and royalty and members including iconic Detroiters such as Ty Cobb. Facilities include swimming pools, ballrooms, squash and basketball courts, full service exercise rooms, guest rooms, and a venue for a distinguished league of underground bowlers. In addition, the club is home to a considerable collection of fine art, including two pieces by Frederic Remington. On game days, the roof of the parking deck offers better sightlines than some seats in the stadium. The club is private and open only to members and their guests. *241 Madison St., www.thedac.com, (313) 442-1017.*

Detroit Princess Riverboat - Quietly parked along the city's scenic riverfront, the Detroit Princess could easily be mistaken for a vestige of Mark Twain's time but was originally a gulf-area riverboat casino that came to Detroit via the St. Lawrence Seaway since it was too large to travel up the Mississippi. With a full commercial kitchen and four decks available for guests, the Princess has become a sought-after ticket for floating dinner with concerts or theater, as well as a rental for private parties. Cruise tickets may be purchased in advance online. *201 Civic Center Dr., www.detroitprincess.com, (877) 338-2628.*

» Detroit RiverWalk - Developed in 2007, this celebrated 3.5 mile walkway connects a host of waterfront attractions and has become a destination in its own right. The beautiful walk connects a series of parks, plazas, and pavilions with a brick-paved path dotted with public art, ornamental gardens, and educational installations. Except for a short stretch by the Stroh River Place, the RiverWalk is a continuous path that stretches from Joe Louis Arena to Mt. Elliott Park (near Belle Isle) and offers unique up-close views of Detroit landmarks such as Joe Louis Arena, the Renaissance Center, the Chene Park amphitheater, and Hart Plaza, as well as a relaxing and enjoyable walk or bicycle ride along the Detroit River. **Rivard Plaza** is the focal point of the span, located roughly in the middle of the East Riverfront segment, and includes a pavilion housing a café, Wheelhouse Detroit (see separate entry), and restroom facilities. A playground built in 2011 and the Cullen Carousel—with seats made of whimsical depictions of native local wildlife—offer fun for children. The plaza features gardens, fountains, a granite inlay map of the Detroit River, and an ornate glass depiction of the St. Lawrence Seaway. The carousel and café hours vary seasonally. Though the RiverWalk is best accessed by bicycle from the Dequindre Cut or Hart Plaza, parking is available at Rivard Plaza for four-wheeled visitors. *1340 Atwater St., www.detroitriverfront.org, (313) 877-8057.*

The Fillmore Detroit - Located in the heart of the entertainment district, The Fillmore Detroit—previously the State Theater—and the attached twelve-story-tall Francis Palms Building were completed in 1925 and designed by legendary architect C. Howard Crane. The highlight of the ornate terracotta-sheathed Renaissance Revival complex is the breathtaking six-story theater and lobby dotted with Beaux-Arts ornamentation. Though, originally, the theater had seating for nearly 3,000 patrons, today, under the management of Live Nation, the venue can accommodate 2,200 concertgoers between the main floor, mezzanine, and balcony. Due to the flexibility of the space—it can be adjusted to allow for either terraced cabaret seating or a hardwood dance floor—entertainment at the venue is widely varied, often highlighting national popular acts, as well as The Detroit Music Awards, which are held annually at the venue every April. The adjoining **State Bar & Grill,** which has a classy sports bar atmosphere and a full menu of pub food, has its own entrance and is open independent of the venue's schedule. *2115 Woodward Ave., www.thefillmoredetroit.com, (313) 961-5451.*

Ford Field / Detroit Lions - Lions loyalty emblematizes the dedication of Detroiters. Almost all Lions fans remember the team's electrifying former running back, Barry Sanders, one of only three players in NFL history to rush for more than 2,000 yards in a season. Most are also strong enough to forget many of the Lion's most infamous seasons. Though the team has had only one playoff victory in the past half-century, many pundits believe the Lions' better days are near on the horizon. Ford Field, an indoor stadium located downtown, has been home to the Detroit Lions since August 2002. It seats 65,000 for football games and more than 80,000 for other events. In 2006, it hosted Super Bowl XL, features the annual MAC championship game, and also offers the annual Little Caesar's Pizza Bowl. Ford Field pioneered hosting basketball events in large-capacity arenas in 2003 when MSU played Kentucky in an NCAA men's basketball game, and was later home to the 2009 NCAA Men's Final Four. The stadium occasionally hosts concerts and other large-draw events. *2000 Brush St., www.detroitlions.com, (313) 262-2012.*

Fort Street Presbyterian Church - Constructed in the years leading up to the Civil War, this impressive sanctuary has come to define the street from which it drew its name. Built in a Decorated Gothic style, its design elements include a 265-foot spire and intricate flourishes—ornamental finials, flying buttresses, carved limestone faces, and patinaed copper elements intended to recall foliage. The church's interior is a nuanced balance of majestic scale and delicate detail—the soaring sanctuary seats 1,200 parishioners on its main floor and crescent balcony and boasts a more-than-3,200-pipe organ, but this awe-inspiring scale is matched in aesthetic power by subtle refinements like tile work by Pewabic Pottery founder Mary Chase Stratton, 13th century style Grisaille stained glass windows, and a Caen stone baptismal font with Mexican onyx pillars. *631 W. Fort St., www.fortstreet.org, (313) 961-4533.*

» Fox Theatre - The anchor of the surrounding Foxtown district, The Fox Theatre is as resplendent as it is historic. The theater, which was restored in 1988, is the largest surviving Fox Theater and is one of the most opulent remaining 1920s movie palaces in the United States. You needn't look far to find it—the enormous winged foxes and Art Deco sign light up Woodward Avenue for blocks. The interior is an extravagant amalgamation of Burmese, Chinese, Indian, and Persian motifs in lavish gold and vivid colors that provide a stunning backdrop for any live performance or event. The first movie theater in the world constructed with built-in sound equipment for "talkies," and one of the few that retains its original custom organ, the Fox continues to be the crown jewel of Detroit's entertainment district. Live shows range from the Rockettes to Bob Dylan, Sigur Rós to the family-friendly Sesame Street Live. *2211 Woodward Ave., www. olympiaentertainment.com, (313) 471-3200.*

Gem and Century Theatres - The Gem and Century Theatres are two separate theatres housed in the same elegant brick building with carved-stone ornamentation. Originally simply the Century Theatre, a cabaret-style venue established in 1903, the complex grew during a Spanish Revival–themed renovation in 1928 to include a new, smaller theater known under six different names before its ultimate rechristening as the Gem. In 1997, the entire facility was trucked on wheels to its current location 563 meters away from its original site (a record for a building its size) to make way for Comerica Park. Both venues currently offer live theater, though Century typically offers comedies, while the Gem runs dramas. The Century offers rowed seating, but the Gem is composed of seated tables, permitting patrons to bring bar drinks inside. The interior of the complex exudes staid elegance in an atmosphere of incandescent warmth, and there is a recently completed garden patio outside. Dressing the part is appreciated but not required. The Gem and Century are available for weddings and other events. *333 Madison St., www.gemtheatre.com, (313) 963-8000.*

Greektown Casino - Centrally located in the center of Greektown, this neon-clad casino offers gamblers a contemporary, classically styled atmosphere, with casino-opulence reminiscent of Las Vegas. Easily accessible by car, People Mover, or foot, this 24/7 destination offers three restaurants, a bar, a 400-room hotel, and 2,700 slot and video games and 62 table game tables across its 100,000 square foot gaming floor. This casino is easily the best for nonsmokers, offering 12 nonsmoking tables in its elegant poker room, which also boasts TVs, complimentary snacks, and attentive bar service. Greektown also offers rotating minimum bets on common table games like baccarat, blackjack, three-card poker, craps, roulette as well as less common offerings such as Pai Gow Poker, and Mississippi Stud. Those looking to enjoy a weekend downtown or to try their luck in the morning can stay in the casino's luxurious Greektown Casino–Hotel and stay fed at one the casino's many dining options, such as Shotz and Bistro 555. Bring your ID as you have to be 21 to enter. *555 E. Lafayette Ave., www.greektowncasino.com, (888) 771-4386.*

Hart Plaza - In a city in which buildings and spaces often reflect a curiously Sci-Fi aesthetic, Hart Plaza—a popular Downtown gathering place that hosts the city's largest outdoor festivals—looks like it might be the landing pad for the mothership. Designed by internationally noted artist, landscape architect, and designer Isamu Noguchi and built in 1976, the plaza, named for U.S. Senator Philip Hart, is an expansive 14-acre public square along the riverfront that hosts the Movement electronic music festival, the African World Festival, and the Motor City Pride Festival, among many other major events. While it boasts several singular subterranean spaces, including an amphitheater and dance floor, aboveground, the concrete landscape plays host to an abundance of public art, including the 120-foot stainless steel Pylon (1973) by Isamu Noguchi, the at once representational and abstract Transcending (2001) by David Barr and Sergio De Giusti, and a monuments to the Underground Railroad (see separate entry) and city-founder Antoine Cadillac. The most renowned installation in the plaza is the Noguchi-designed **Horace E. Dodge and Son Memorial Fountain,** erected in 1978 with a $1,000,000 gift from Dodge's widow, Anna Thompson. The stainless steel fountain is composed of two angled arms extending up 30 feet over a black granite pool and topped by a ring with 300 water jets that spray down into the pool. While Hart Plaza is best known for hosting jam-packed events, it's a lovely spot during quieter moments, too, affording a commanding view of Downtown and Windsor across the river, plenty of space to roam, and easy access to the Riverwalk. *1 Washington Blvd.*

Joe Louis Arena / Detroit Red Wings - One of the greatest hockey franchises in history with eleven Stanley Cup Championships and a legendary roster of Hall-of-Famers such as Gordie Howe (the NHL all-time points leader), Ted Lindsay, and "The Captain" Steve Yzerman, the Detroit Red Wings' popularity in Detroit is well justified. This tradition of success has continued in recent years, one marker of which is the Wings' NHL-record 23-game home winning streak. Though the well-worn Joe Louis Arena—known simply as "the Joe"— is beloved by fans for its utility more than its beauty (as well as its lax security for smuggling in playoff octopi), it remains a centerpiece of Detroit's Downtown. The inside of the Joe is home to unique action statues of famous Wings, banners, and memorabilia. Aside from hockey, the Joe hosts concerts, events, and was home to the 1980 Republican National Convention. The Wings' days at the Joe are certainly numbered, but until the ice melts for good, the glory of the Joe lives on. *600 Civic Center Dr., redwings.nhl.com, (313) 396-7000.*

Leland City Club - This edgy little dungeon club is a good destination if you're dressed to the nines in fishnets and have a slight fetish for electrical tape. Existing in the underbelly of the Leland Hotel at Bagley Street and Grand River Avenue, City Club is a dark after-hours spot that pumps industrial music onto a huge dance floor filled with members of the rivet-clad industrial scene. The club has been open since 1983 and formerly was The Leland's Grand Ballroom, which hosted parties for the city's elite in its heyday in the 1920s. This supposedly haunted nightclub, hosts many MEMF events and other raucous after parties. If you need a little party fuel, visit Luci & Ethel's diner upstairs for some bacon and pancakes (see separate entry). *400 Bagley St., www.lelandcityclub.net, (313) 962-2300.*

MGM Grand Detroit - The first of the city's three casinos, the MGM Grand offers the city's gamblers a taste of authentic Las Vegas gaming, and deals a healthy hand of Vegas-style opulence. The casino has a massive, 100,000 square foot, glittering gaming floor, clad in flashing lights, contemporary decor and luxurious furnishings. With 24 table games across 115 tables and more than 4,000 slot and video machines, the casino has the most diverse offerings of the city's casinos, including all of the de rigueur table game offerings—baccarat, Spanish 21, Texas Hold 'Em—as well as less common games—Mississippi Stud Poker, Two-Way Monte, Pai Gow Poker, and Double Exposure Blackjack—at values beginning at $1. The gaming experience is complemented by the plentiful bar service, numerous complimentary pop/coffee bars, video poker bar, and a five-restaurant food court. If you'd like to make a weekend of it, try the attached luxury hotel, spa, Starbucks, and upscale dining options such as Wolfgang Puck Pizzeria & Cucina (see separate entry). Don't forget your ID—the casino is only for the 21+ crowd. Although MGM allows smoking, nonsmoking gamers can enjoy the smoke-free slot room. Good luck! *1777 3rd St., www.mgmgranddetroit.com, (888) 646-3387.*

Music Hall Center for the Performing Arts - Since Matilda Dodge Wilson opened Music Hall's doors in 1928, the intimate Downtown venue has been a significant player in Detroit's performing arts sector. Originally named the Wilson Theater, it was designed in the Art Deco style and the Madison Street facade is flush with decorative orange and tan brick as well as Pewabic tile and stone accents. The Music Hall is the only Detroit venue built for the primary purpose of presenting live performances. Though the theater has served as the home of the Detroit Symphony Orchestra, Michigan Opera Theatre, and a Cinerama screen in the past, today, the hall provides accessible music, theater, dance, and performances from travelling and local acts. The Jazz Cafe, a modern addition, offers an intimate bar and performance space for the everyday music lover with an ongoing series that highlights many of Detroit's great native artists from such as Luis Resto and Kimmie Horne. *349 Madison St., www.musichall.org, (313) 887-8500.*

PuppetART - Founded in 1998 by a group of puppeteers and artists trained in the former Soviet Union, the heart of the PuppetART Center is its intimate 70-person puppet theater which houses magical performances—ranging from miniature finger and rod puppets to shadow, marionette, and life-sized puppets. PuppetART offers a

repertoire of eight shows for kids and adults from cultures around the world scheduled on Saturday afternoons and Thursday mornings. Each performance includes a tour of the organization's puppet museum and studio workshops. *25 E. Grand River Ave., www.puppetart.org, (313) 961-7777.*

Ren Cen 4 - To see a first-run Hollywood film, try this small aptly named four-screen movie theater inside the Renaissance Center. The 680-seat theater offers a comfortable, contemporary atmosphere with plenty of legroom. The concession counter offers more than typical theater fare, with welcomed additions such as pizza, beer, and flavored popcorn. Crowds often add colorful commentary that, depending on the film, can be a boon. Matinee prices available. *200 Renaissance Center, www.riverfront4.com, (313) 259-2370.*

Saint Andrew's Hall / The Shelter - Built in 1907 as the mammoth clubhouse for the St. Andrews Scottish Society of Detroit, Saint Andrew's Hall has served as a popular venue for rock, punk, hip hop, and EDM acts since 1982. The classical brick building is home to three venues—the Main Ballroom, a wood-floored balcony-lined 1,000-person space with a 35-foot bar, **The Shelter,** a subterranean 400-seat venue with cabaret-seating and a small stage, and **The Burns Room,** a small, intimate space with chandeliers, hardwood floors, lounge furniture, and elegant windows overlooking Congress Street. While all three venues offer full bars with several dozen liquors and more than 80 domestic and imported beers, The Shelter also offers a limited food menu and is typically open during shows in the other two spaces. Together, many renowned acts have taken the stage at the three venues, including Eminem, Iggy Pop, Bob Dylan, Paul Simon, and Nirvana. *431 E. Congress St., www. saintandrewsdetroit.com, (313) 961-8961.*

SITES

Book Cadillac and Book Tower - Successful sibling entrepreneurs the Book brothers—James Burgess, Herbert, and Frank—wanted to make Washington Boulevard an elegant commercial district, hoping to create a "Fifth Avenue of the West." Central to this goal were two buildings, the Book Cadillac, which, at the time of its construction in 1924, was the largest and tallest hotel in the world, and the 38-story Book Tower, which was the tallest building in the city when it was completed in 1926. Designed by Louis Kamper, the Neo-Renaissance

Book Cadillac had 1,136 rooms across 29 floors, and featured Corinthian pilasters, a marble staircase, and grand chandeliers in the elegant Venetian-style lobby and ornate Florentine-style ballroom. The exquisite facade still features statues of important figures in Detroit history, including Antoine de la Mothe Cadillac. After an extended vacancy, the hotel was beautifully restored and has served as the Westin Book Cadillac Hotel since 2008. Though begun in 1916, the construction of the neighboring Book Tower was stalled for a decade due to material shortages during World War I. Louis Kamper's elegant Italian Renaissance–style design features intricate Corinthian columns, crests, florets, caryatids, and a cartouche by sculptor Corrado Parducci, all of which are reminiscent of the Academic Classicism style. Unlike the beloved Book Cadillac, the Book Tower's design has been derided by critics as clumsily garish, with many impracticalities, such as the lack of an interior evacuation route—necessitating the nation's tallest fire escape—and the limestone facade, which absorbs pollutants and cannot be readily cleaned. In 2009, the last tenant left, and as of 2012, the building is awaiting redevelopment and stands as one of the world's tallest abandoned buildings. *1114 Washington Blvd. (Book Cadillac) and 1265 Washington Blvd. (Book Tower).*

Capitol Park - "Do you think there's a dead body in there?" Actually, yes. The State of Michigan's first governor—and the youngest governor in United States' history, is interred in the base of a Capitol Park statue commemorating his life. Stevens T. Mason became territorial governor in 1834 at the age of 22 and shepherded Michigan to its 1837 statehood, lobbying successfully for the Upper Peninsula. A state financial crisis drove Mason from power and he died in 1842. A curious relic of the Woodward Plan of 1805, Capital Park itself is an old-world grassless urban gathering place paved with bricks and tightly bordered on all sides by 17 historic buildings varying in condition. Historically, Capitol Park was the last stop on the Underground Railroad—escaped slaves, bound for Canada, stayed at Seymour Finney's barn-turned-tavern, though the structure has long since been demolished. Though, in the past, the park has been known to be a little rough around the edges, in 2009, it was endowed with a $1.1 million grant and repairs were undertaken, including the addition of lighting and other amenities. During the 1990s, the space was known as an epicenter of Detroit's electronic music scene and a destination for late-night raves. Today, the park is a popular daytime hangout for locals, but at night it becomes the perfect backdrop for

skateboarders and in-line skaters who take over to grind and ollie by the moonlight. *Bordered by State St., Griswold St., and Shelby St.*

Central United Methodist Church - A Methodist congregation that has served as a wellspring of social justice and progressivism for almost two centuries, Central United Methodist has earned the title "the Conscience of a City." Though the congregation has had several homes since it was founded in 1822, its current house of worship was completed in 1867. The elaborate gray limestone building is designed in a mix of Tudor and Gothic styles and features a series of spires and gables that cap resplendent stonework and old world details. Inside, an enormous 70-rank pipe organ, 30-foot-tall white oak reredos, ascendant mural of the apostles, and beautiful stained glass windows add to the stature of the nave, which frames its altar between ornate banners of "Peace" and "Justice." Central United's reputation for causes of human dignity is exemplified from the outcry over an 1830 execution that took place in front of the church. Parishioners immediately launched efforts to ban execution in Michigan, making it the first English-speaking democracy to do so. The church leads events such as rallies and marches, including the annual MLK day march, and has held concerts for social activist performers such as Janis Ian. The church is also home to a peace center and art gallery, **Swords Into Plowshares,** which hosts rotating exhibits and offers limited hours. *23 E. Adams St., www.centralumchurch.com, (313) 965-5422.*

Cobo Center - Though most well-known for hosting the world-famous North American International Auto Show each January, Cobo Center hosts scores of conventions and events each year and has played an important role in the city's history. Named for former Mayor Albert E. Cobo, the hall was built in 1960 at the end of Jefferson along the river. Designed by noted stadium architect Gino Rossetti, Cobo retains many of its original design elements—such as the geometric facade and utilitarian aesthetic—despite a considerable remodeling and expansion project in 1989, and larger, ongoing renovation work. Today, this modern facility boasts 722,000 square feet of exhibit space—625,000 of it contiguous, besting the equivalent of ten football fields. Inside, the center has a 12-foot bronze statue of Joe Louis and displays one of the boxing gloves Joe Louis wore when he beat Max Schmeling in a rematch symbolic of the fight against Nazism, the glove bronzed for posterity. The center is popular among local historians both because it was built on the

same ground that Antoine de la Mothe Cadillac landed upon in 1701, and because Cobo witnessed Martin Luther King, Jr. address a crowd of 25,000 Civil Rights activists at the end of the Detroit Freedom Walk in 1963, where he began to articulate his "I Have A Dream" speech. Aside from Dr. King, Cobo has hosted many notable speakers, including every sitting U.S. President since Eisenhower, who gave the keynote address at the center's inaugural convention.
1 Washington Blvd., www.cobocenter.com, (313) 877-8777.

Daniel Burnham Architecture - As Burnham once said, "make no little plans; they have no magic to stir men's blood." Though he's not a Detroiter (nobody's perfect), Daniel Burnham is regarded as one of the greatest American architects. With a laundry list of achievements—including being a co-author of the city-shaping Chicago Plan of 1909, a founder of the Chicago school of architecture, the chief coordinating architect of the "white city" at the 1893 Columbian Exposition, and the architect of New York's Flatiron Building—Burnham has been called a father of the skyscraper and one of the most influential minds behind early 20th century architecture. During his career, Burnham designed four buildings in Detroit. One, the Majestic Building, which was built in 1896 and demolished in 1961, has been lost, but fortunately, three remain. In 1909, the architect completed his first structure in Detroit, the **Ford Building** (no, not that Ford—the Edward Ford Plate Glass Co.) At 18-stories, the structure, a shining example of the refined elegance of the Chicago school, towered over the burgeoning city and was hailed by the Free Press as Detroit's "first real skyscraper." In 1912, Burnham completed a more ornate Neoclassical masterpiece dubbed the **Dime Building,** for the bank that once occupied its floors. Connected to the Ford Building with a secret underground tunnel, the 23-story Dime is similarly a trademark Burnham, clad in white terracotta. Undergoing renovation after lying fallow since 2001, the true masterpiece of Burnham's remaining buildings in Detroit is the **David Whitney Building.** A sentinel standing guard over Grand Circus Park, the mundane exterior of the 19-story building—which was "modernized" in the 1950s—belies the breathtaking Beaux Arts interior which features a dramatic skylight-covered, four-story atrium lobby decked throughout in terracotta and marble. If you are able to peek inside, it's worth the trouble. *615 Griswold St., (Ford Building), 719 Griswold St (Dime Building), and 1553 Woodward Ave. (David Whitney Building).*

Grand Army of the Republic Building - Towering over the corner of Grand River Avenue and Cass Avenue, the turrets and battlements of Detroit's castle make it look like an ancient fort built to defend the city from Ohioan invaders. However, the historic, imposing, and distinctive building, designed by architect Julius Hess in the Richardsonian Romanesque style (read: castle style), opened in 1900 as a place for local Civil War veterans to congregate—the design selected because the stone fortress was said to look as strong as the republic the boys in blue had fought to preserve. However, by 1934, most of the gray-bearded veterans had died and the ground floor retail tenants could no-longer cover operating costs for the building. The City converted it into a public space and operated it as the GAR Recreation Center until it was finally closed in 1982 due to budget constraints and lack of use. The GAR was left abandoned until 2011, when the building was sold to local creative studio Mindfield, which plans to complete a $3 million renovation of the infamous castle ruin by the end of 2013. *1942 Grand River Ave.*

Grand Circus Park - A five-acre semicircular green space anchored by the iconic buildings that surround it, Grand Circus Park, which is bisected by Woodward Avenue, connects the city's theater and financial districts. Though planned as a component of Augustus Woodward's radial street plan following the city's catastrophic 1805 fire, the park wasn't established until 1850. In a compact but bucolic setting, the grounds include antique statuary and fountains, the most notable of which is the **Hazen S. Pingree Memorial**. Pingree, now considered one of the greatest Mayors in United States History, was simultaneously Mayor of Detroit (elected 1889) and Governor of Michigan (elected 1896) until he was forced to resign his Mayoral post by the Michigan Supreme Court as it was deemed unacceptable to hold both posts simultaneously. The noted King Edward VII lookalike fought privatized monopolies, advocated for public transit, encouraged urban farming through his "Potato Patch Plan," exposed corruption, expanded public welfare programs, and created public works projects for the unemployed. Beloved by his constituents, his monument decries that he is "The Idol of the People." Across Woodward Avenue sits the **William Cotter Maybury Monument** that was built by the city's business leaders to honor Pingree's conservative rival and Mayoral successor—though Maybury's statue doesn't say "Idol" on it. The park is also home to the Russell A. Alger Memorial Fountain, named for a major lumber baron who settled in Detroit after the Civil War, and the Millenium Bell (created by artists

Chris Turner and Matt Blake), which was commissioned by the city in 2000 and is rung every New Year. With its storied landmarks and historic urban surroundings, Grand Circus Park is a fabulous place to enjoy a carryout lunch or take a romantic late-night stroll. *1601 Woodward Ave.*

» Guardian Building - Known as Detroit's Cathedral of Finance, the lavish, incredibly beautiful facade of the Guardian Building boasts the city's most intricate ornamentation, a theme continued on the grander interior. Opened in 1929, this Wirt Rowland masterpiece emerged during the height of Art Deco architecture and used the finest materials to create the city's grandest example of the style. The 36-story main structure is topped by two spires, one of which extends four stories, reaching 632 feet. The ornate orange-tan brick facade features stunning pink granite banding, Mankato stone, vibrantly glazed Pewabic tile mosaics, and terracotta details around entrances—the building's signature Aztec theme. The interior of the structure continues the motif, with a three-story lobby clad in Pewabic and Rockwood tile that features a multi-story mural of Michigan's people and enterprises with solid gold leaf detail by Anthony Eugenio. The lobby features Italian Travertine marble columns, Belgian marble bases, and red Numidian marble details. *500 Griswold St.*

Joe Louis Fist Sculpture - In addition to being one of the greatest heavyweight boxers of all time, with a 140-month, 27-fight championship reign, the Brown Bomber crossed color lines and became an American hero when he defeated Nazi symbol Max Schmeling in 1938. This 24-foot-long bronze fist was commissioned by Sports Illustrated Magazine to honor the Detroit native who became a national icon. Designed by Robert Graham, the sculpture was completed in 1986 and is suspended from a steel harness looming over the intersection of Jefferson Avenue and Woodward Avenue, just north of Hart Plaza. *E. Jefferson Ave. and Woodward Ave.*

Lafayette Greens - Built in 2011 on the site of the Lafayette Building, a singular but neglected 1927 C. Howard Crane high rise demolished in 2009, Lafayette Greens is a Downtown demonstration garden owned by Compuware and maintained by its employees (who work just a few blocks away). With fruit trees, a children's garden, and 35 raised beds overflowing with a multitude of flowers, vegetables, and fruit, this half-acre urban oasis is a masterful burst of color, fragrance, biodiversity, and geometry in the heart of the business district. The

garden is open to the public during the week and makes for a perfect spot to eat lunch, read a book, or stroll among the greenery. *142 W. Lafayette Ave., (313) 227-5555.*

Mariners' Church of Detroit - At the foot of Randolph Street lies the oldest stone church in Michigan and the state's only church incorporated by legislative act. Mariners' Church, a national historic site, has served as a non-diocesan parish for sailors since it was founded in 1842. The church is a nautical temple—the Gothic Revival structure sports an insignia of an anchor on its bell tower, there is a nautical compass rose window, and marine-themed stained glass windows overlook its sanctuary. Inside the building, marine artifacts such as anchors, bells, and a collection of paintings from local 19th century artist Robert Hopkin cement the church's maritime legacy. The church building was physically relocated to its current location in the 1950s—a move that revealed a secret basement chamber evidencing the church's role in the Underground Railroad. In 1975, the church was immortalized in Gordon Lightfoot's "Wreck of the Edmund Fitzgerald," which tells of how the Mariners' bell "chimed 'til it rang 29 times" for each man who perished. To this day, the church holds an annual memorial service every November for all brave seafarers, with Lightfoot himself having performed the song at the ten-year remembrance. Mariners' has been used prominently by other music icons—it hosted the 1980 wedding of punk's high couple of cool, Patti and the late Fred "Sonic" Smith. *170 E. Jefferson Ave., www.marinerschurchofdetroit.org, (313) 259-2206.*

Michigan Theatre Parking Garage - Once one of the world's most exquisite entertainment venues, today it is the world's most exquisite, heartbreaking, and curious parking facility. Built on the site of Henry Ford's original workshop, the building was completed in 1926. With a capacity of 4,050, the jaw-dropping theater, which featured ten-foot chandeliers and a gilded four-story lobby, was described by the Detroit Free Press as "beyond the dreams of loveliness; entering, you pass into another world." However, by 1976, the theater's popularity had waned, and it closed. Though plans eventually surfaced to demolish the structure, they were halted when engineers discovered that such action would destabilize the attached office building next door. Consequently, the majestic interior space was gutted and retrofitted with a 160 car parking structure built within the shell. Many remnants of the glorious renaissance-style structure remain intact, and hint at its past greatness. Consequently, the facility has become a popular legal urban exploration site, explorable from the safety of your car—as long as you pay for parking. *220 Bagley St.*

One Detroit Center - The work of celebrated post-modernist architects John Burgee and Philip Johnson, One Detroit Center, formally known as Comerica Tower, was constructed between 1991 and 1993. Michigan's second tallest building after the Renaissance Center a few blocks away, the 619-foot, 43-story skyscraper is noted for its juxtaposition of postmodern architectural design with Flemish-inspired neo-gothic accents, which simultaneously contrast with and complement the city's historic skyline. Originally intended to be one of two towers, Two Detroit Center, which was to be directly east of the current structure, was never built. *500 Woodward Ave.*

One Woodward Avenue - Designed by Minoru Yamasaki, a preeminent architect of the 20th century and a master practitioner of New Formalism, this 32-story, 430-foot-tall high-rise was completed in 1963. As Yamasaki's first skyscraper, the building introduces elements such as a pre-cast concrete exterior, narrow windows, Gothic arches, decorative tracery, and sculptural gardens that would become the architect's signature motifs. For this reason, the building has been called the forerunner to the architect's iconic World Trade Center in New York. One Woodward Avenue was commissioned by

the Michigan Consolidated Gas Company and features a delicate lattice of narrow, 12-inch-wide windows set in a mixture of pre-cast concrete and marble chips, which gives the building a stark brilliance. This minimalist motif, which begins on the second floor, is offset by the incredible gravity-defying glass lobby and loggia, upon which the building seems to effortlessly float. The uppermost floors, which are inset and conceal the building's mechanical systems, are illuminated at night with seasonally appropriate colors. Don't miss the graceful sculpture Passo di Danza (Step of the Dance) that was created by Italian sculptor Giacomo Manzù. *1 Woodward Ave.*

Penobscot Building - The 47-story Penobscot Building and its iconic red orb have dominated the city's skyline since its construction in 1928. Detroit's tallest building until the completion of the Renaissance Center in 1977, the opulent Art Deco masterpiece soars 566 feet into the air and is the Indiana limestone-clad anchor of the Financial District historic. Designed by noted local architect Wirt C. Rowland, the limestone and granite structure features intricate architectural relief sculptures by Corrado Parducci. The building's name and ornamentation were chosen by the original owner and lumber baron, Simon Murphy, who chose the Penobscot Tribe of his home state of Maine as the inspiration for the building's name and elaborate carved Native American motifs. *645 Griswold St.*

People Mover Station Art - Opened in 1987, the Detroit People Mover is a 2.9 mile automated monorail system that circles Downtown. Though the system only averages 7,083 daily riders, and its utility as a mode of transportation is sometimes debated—it runs one-way in a loop and the subsequent phases that would have connected the system to the city's residents were never built—it is superbly clean and well-maintained and serves as a colorful (climate controlled) top-down tour of Downtown. The People Mover stations themselves are a special visual treat. From 1984 to 1987, fifteen different artists were commissioned to install large-scale decorative works in each of the 13 stations, resulting in a wide variety of colors, textures, and visually immersive sites for riders. Complimentary tours for groups of 10 to 30 are available by appointment during the week from May to October. Although all of the stations are visually engaging, favorites include the Times Square and Cadillac Center stations, with three elaborate mosaic works made from locally legendary Pewabic tile; the Cobo Center Station with Cavalcade of Cars, a celebration of the Big Three in Venetian glass mosaic; Siberian Ram by Spirit of Detroit sculptor Marshall Fredericks at the

Renaissance Center Station; the eponymous Las Vegas flair of Neon for the Greektown Station; The Blue Nile, a Noah's Ark themed mural in a traditional African style by celebrated local artist Charles McGee at the Broadway Station; and Catching Up in the Grand Circus Park Station, a bronze statue that depicts a man reading the paper and often causes passersby to double take. *The stations dot Downtown, but a convenient place to pick up the train is the Times Square Station at Grand River Ave. and Park Pl., www.thepeoplemover.com, (313) 224-2160.*

Renaissance Center - A massive, unmistakable complex of seven buildings along the river that forever changed Detroit's skyline, this city within a city was originally built by Ford between 1977 and 1981 as an urban renewal project. It is currently owned by GM and serves as that company's world headquarters. The central, cylindrical, 73-story tower is home to the Detroit Marriott hotel and is the tallest all-hotel tower in the Western hemisphere. Designed by John Portman with a Modernist's emphasis on glass and a Brutalist's penchant for concrete, the complex aroused the ire of urbanists in the years after its construction for being essentially walled off from the rest of Detroit, as well as difficult to navigate. A recent $500 million renovation by GM mitigated these concerns with the addition of a lighted glass walkway and two glass atria, one opening to Jefferson Avenue and the other, the soaring Wintergarden, connecting the complex to the Riverwalk. With the circular design, new walkway, atria, and all that glass and concrete (including towering columns, unexpected alcoves, and numerous pod-like balconies), it's a strange, spectacular, self-contained world that still feels futuristic. Complimentary tours of the architectural icon are available twice daily, Monday to Friday at 12pm and 2pm and depart from the Pure Detroit store (see separate entry) in the building.
1 Renaissance Center, www.gmrencen.com, (313) 568-5624.

Second Baptist Church of Detroit - Founded in 1837, the historic Second Baptist Church is the oldest African-American congregation in the Midwest. This large red brick house of worship stretches across nearly a whole block of Monroe Street, lining the sidewalk with panes of turquoise, blue, and yellow stained glass windows and large oak doors. But the real marvels of this church are hidden in the walls of historic sepia-toned photographs, newspaper clippings, murals, and church archives that document visits from Frederick Douglass and Dr. Martin Luther King Jr. The attached bookstore conducts tours of the church, which detail the history of Detroit's African-American community through the church's history as the last stop before Canada in the Underground Railroad and a center for Civil Rights leadership. Historic tours run for a $5 suggested donation on Wednesday, Friday, and Saturday at 10am, 11:30am, and 1:30pm. Call to schedule a special appointment. Visitors also enjoy free parking at the casino lot near Fishbone's restaurant. *441 Monroe St., www.secondbaptistdetroit.org, (313) 961-0352.*

Spirit of Detroit - Located at the foot of the Coleman A. Young Municipal Center, the Spirit of Detroit is a 26-foot-tall oxidized green bronze statue of a man holding a gilded bronze family in one hand and a sun in the other. Though never named by the sculptor, residents have taken to calling it the Spirit of Detroit thanks to a quote on a wall to its rear from 2 Corinthians: "Now the Lord is that Spirit: and where the Spirit of the Lord is, there is liberty." The sculpture was crafted in Oslo, Norway, where sculptor Marshall Fredericks waived his fee for the project and absorbed some of the costs personally. The statue is the largest cast bronze statue created since the Renaissance. The Spirit instantly became emblematic for the city, and, in recent years, has donned oversized sports jerseys to support Detroit teams playing in respective championships. *2 Woodward Ave.*

Wayne County Building - Designed by Detroiter John Scott, this five story Roman Baroque style edifice features elements of Beaux Arts Classicism that was popular at the time of its completion in 1902. The incredibly ornate pink granite and sandstone facade features numerous sculptures by Edward Wagner and John Massey Rhind, including two stunning bronze allegorical works depicting female figures driving chariots representing Victory and Progress, and four smaller female statues representing Law, Commerce, Agriculture, and Mechanics. The elegant structure is dominated by a sweeping flight of stairs, a portico of Corinthian columns, an ornate balustrade above the third floor, and a dome-topped tower and spire that stands at 247-feet tall. Although Wayne County no longer occupies the building, the name remains. *600 Randolph St.*

POINTS OF INTEREST

Abraham Lincoln Statue - First designed as a way of promoting a freeway stretching from the Atlantic to the Pacific, to be named after President Lincoln, this statue sits comfortably in front of the Skillman

Branch of the Detroit Public Library, the inscription reading, "Let Man Be Free." *121 Gratiot Ave.*

ATAC International Records - In this landmark tower, R&B singer Gino Washington opened his record label in 1970, releasing many of his own tracks. *65 Cadillac Sq.*

Bagley Fountain - Modeled after a ciborium in St. Mark's Basilica in Venice by architect Henry Hobson Richardson, this 21-foot-tall fountain—which was the city's first drinking fountain—seems to have found a permanent home in Cadillac Square, having endured a couple of moves since its dedication in 1887. *Cadillac Sq. and Bates St.*

Birthplace of Kiwanis - The international service organization was born in this building in 1914, when businessmen Allen S. Browne and Joseph G. Prance came up with idea of banding like-minded individuals and businesses together.
Griswold St. and Grand River Ave.

Black Bottom and Paradise Valley - In the early 20th Century, these neighborhoods with a shared boundary jointly served as the epicenter of African-American culture, commerce, and life. Black Bottom, which was developed earlier, began at Gratiot Avenue and

extended as far south as the Detroit River between Brush Street and the Dequindre Cut and served primarily as a housing center for the city's African-American population. Paradise Valley extended north from Gratiot Avenue, along the same corridor and was a dense district full of cultural amenities and scores of renowned African-American–owned businesses. The two neighborhoods developed in response to discriminatory housing policies in the prewar period and were tragically and systematically erased under the banner of postwar urban renewal programs. *Gratiot Ave. and Brush St.*

Blue Cross Blue Shield Campus Art - The Downtown campus of the health insurance giant contains a number of important sculptures including "Dancing Hands" by Robert Sestok, "Urban Stele" by Sergio De Giusti, and "The Procession (A Family)" by John Nick Pappas, the last being one of the largest bronze statuary ensembles in the United States. *600 E. Lafayette St.*

Christopher Columbus - This larger-than-life bust of the famous explorer, sculpted by Italian artist Augusto Rivalta in 1910, gazes out atop an ornate travertine pedestal. *E. Jefferson Ave. and Randolph St.*

Color Cubes - This colorful mural located on the side of the Julian C. Madison building was designed by artist David Rubello to appear to shift its forms depending on which part of the piece the viewer focuses. *1420 Washington Blvd.*

David Broderick Tower - A 1928 project designed by Louis Kamper, the Broderick Tower is a distinctively simple towering 35-story example of neo-classical Chicago-school architecture. In 1997, local artist Robert Wyland painted Whale Tower, a 108-foot mural of three humpback whales on the eastern wall of the then-abandoned building that was beautifully redeveloped for apartments in 2012. *10 Witherell St.*

Emily's Across the Street - In the 1970s and 1980s, when the city's morale was at an all-time low, dynamic and charismatic Detroit super-booster Emily Gail worked to shift the paradigm through her beloved, legendary shop in this space, where she encouraged everyone to "Say Nice Things About Detroit." *161 W. Congress St.*

Father Gomidas Armenian Memorial - This striking black figure depicts the Armenian priest and composer who was imprisoned by Turkish forces in 1915 and, after being released, died a broken man in Paris. The statue, by Canadian sculptor Arto Tchakmakchian, was funded by local Armenian groups as way of commemorating

the genocide of 1.5 million Armenians at the hands of the Turkish government between 1915 and 1923.
W. Jefferson Ave. and Woodward Ave.

Finney Barn Site Historic Marker - A barn owned by Detroit abolitionist Seymour Finney once sat on this site and acted as an important passenger depot along the Underground Railroad, often as a last stop for escaping slaves as they made their way across the river into Canada. *State St. and Griswold St.*

First National Building - Opened in 1930, this Albert Kahn designed skyscraper uses a unique "Z" shape to expose most of the offices inside to natural light. The hair salon in the lobby was featured in 2011 George Clooney film "The Ides of March." *660 Woodward Ave.*

Garrick Theater Site - Although the Garrick Theater is now gone, it was on this site that Harry Houdini performed for the final time before dying a few days later in Detroit's Old Grace Hospital. *1120 Griswold St.*

Gateway to Freedom International Memorial to the Underground Railroad - A masterpiece by sculptor Ed Dwight, the memorial includes two larger-than-life-size granite and bronze sculptures across the Detroit River from one another. The profoundly moving U.S. sculpture depicts a family of escaped Canada-bound slaves. The Canadian sculpture depicts the family's arrival. *Detroit RiverWalk at Hart Plaza.*

General Alexander Macomb Statue - This dashing figure, executed by sculptor Adolph Alexander Weinman in 1908, commemorates the accomplishments of a man who earned his fame during the War of 1812 and whose family once owned Belle Isle, Grosse Ile, and most of what we now know as Macomb County. *Washington Blvd. and Michigan Ave.*

General Thaddeus Kosciuszko Statue - A gift from the people of Krakow, Poland, to the city on the occasion of the American Bicentennial in 1976, this huge statue of the Polish and American Revolutionary hero sits confidently on his horse watching the procession of cars and pedestrians down Michigan Avenue. *Michigan Ave. and 3rd St.*

George Washington Statue - Presented to the city in 1966 by the Masons of Michigan, this Donald DeLue bronze statue depicts Washington in the regalia of the Freemason Order. *170 E. Jefferson Ave.*

Ghetto Recorders - The eye of the garage rock hurricane that exploded out of Detroit in the late 1990s and early 2000s, producer (and former Dirtbombs bassist) Jim Diamond recorded many of the most significant Detroit bands of the era (including The White Stripes, The Von Bondies, The Dirtbombs, and countless others) on his vintage analog equipment in this studio with "all the amenities of a prison." Bands still travel from around the world to record with the veteran producer. *58 W. Elizabeth.*

Goodrich Tire Ghost Sign - Although the service station no longer exists, this beautiful old hand-painted advertisement remains. *524 E. Larned St.*

The Hand of God, Memorial to Frank Murphy - This towering sculpture, designed by Cranbrook artist Carl Milles, was dedicated to famous Detroit politician and eventual Supreme Court Justice Frank Murphy. The piece consists of a newly created man standing on the fingers of a huge hand, both sitting somewhat precariously atop a 26-foot-tall granite shaft. *St. Antoine St. and Gratiot Ave.*

Harmonie Park - This beautiful little park is home to a handful of sculptures, including "The Entrance" by John Piet, and "Hard Edge Soft Edge" by Hanna Stiebel, both of which were installed in the mid-1970s. *Randolph St. and Centre St.*

Henry Ford Workshop Site - The small workshop, which sat behind his modest home, where Henry Ford built his first car was demolished to make room for the Michigan Theater. You can, however, see a reconstruction of the building at Greenfield Village. *58 Bagley St.*

Invictus Records - The Cadillac Tower was home to this record label starting in 1969 when the Motown songwriting team Holland-Dozier-Holland, responsible for many of that label's biggest hits, left the pop giant and started their own label. Parliament's first record, "Osmium," was an Invictus release. *65 Cadillac Sq.*

Kern's Clock - Built in 1929 to advertise the Kern's Department Store, this oversized clock has been a handy point of reference for Detroiters ever since: Meet me at the Kern's Clock! *Woodward Ave. and State St.*

Old Plum Street - In space now entirely occupied by the MGM Grand Casino, Plum Street was once Detroit's hangout for hippies in the late 1960s. At its peak, 43 shops graced the district. *Plum St. between 4th St. and 5th St.*

Old St. Mary's Church - Founded in 1834, this church is the third oldest parish in the city. The edifice of the massive, striking church combines elements of Pisan Romanesque and Venetian Renaissance. Inside, it is spacious and grand, with enormous stained glass windows, beautifully detailed stations of the cross, an altar bathed in cool blue colors, and an elegantly intricate apse above the transept. One of the three Sunday Liturgies is still held in Latin. *646 Monroe St.*

Plum Street Greenhouse - A production-focused greenhouse and site for many educational farming programs located, surprisingly, in between a handful of skyscrapers. *2228 3rd St.*

Saints Peter and Paul Jesuit Church - Despite the relatively plain exterior, this Catholic church, completed in 1848, is the oldest standing church of any denomination in the city. The architectural highlight of the structure is the subdued and refined interior with stately columns and an incredible vaulted ceiling. *438 St. Antoine St.*

Second Baptist Church - A congregation formed by 13 former slaves in 1836, the original church building housed a secret chamber that served as a stop on the Underground Railroad to 5,000 escaped slaves on their way to Canada. Unfortunately, the original church was destroyed by a fire and was replaced by this reserved limestone church building with Gothic influences in 1914. Additions were added east and west of the church in 1926 and 1986, respectively. *441 Monroe St.*

Site of 1805 Fire - In 1805, ashes from the pipe of local baker John Harvey inadvertently caught fire to a barn located at this site. The flames spread quickly and decimated the largely wooden city. In response to the city's destruction Judge Augustus Woodward proposed reinventing the city with the "Woodward Plan" of radial spokes fanning out from the city's center—the essence of which remain today. *W. Jefferson Ave. and Wayne St.*

St. Aloysius Church - Part of the tight Washington Boulevard streetwall, this church is curiously sandwiched between the surrounding commercial structures. Completed in 1930, the broad planes of limestone on the exterior are dotted with ornate carved flourishes. Though the interior is relatively aesthetically reserved, the three-story atrium and unusual tiered seating make it one of Downtown's great spaces. *1209 Washington Blvd.*

St. John's Church - Built in 1859, this ornate Victorian Gothic style Episcopalian church boasts a limestone facade with sandstone trim and beautiful buttresses. The single bell tower stands 105 feet tall, overlooking the intricate, decorative gargoyles that dot roof. Checkout the Michigan historic marker facing Woodward. *50 E. Fisher Fwy.*

Stearns Telephone Plaque - On September 22, 1887, a Bell telephone, the first in the city, was installed in the drugstore run on this site by Frederick Stearns, connecting the store to the Stearns laboratory half a mile away. *511 Woodward Ave.*

United States District Court 7th Floor Marble - Dubbed "the million dollar courtroom" at the time of its construction, this beautiful space, which was originally located in another building finished in 1896 and then disassembled and rebuilt inside of this 1934 building, contains over 30 kinds of marble, East Indian Mahogany, and unique sculptural work. *231 W. Lafayette Blvd.*

Waterfront Ziggurat - Though ziggurats are technically square, this curious, secluded conical spiral pyramid has earned the nickname and is a popular choice for a quiet late night date or hang out by the water. *Detroit RiverWalk and Steve Yzerman Dr.*

Wish Tree for Detroit - Slightly relocated from its original location to make room for the Rosa Parks Transit Center, this "living sculpture," which was dedicated in 2000, consists of a gingko tree, a granite rock, and a bronze plaque inviting visitors to "Whisper your wish/ to the bark of the tree." *Grand River Ave. and Park Pl.*

Woodward Windows - The many vacant storefronts on this quiet stretch of Woodward Avenue have been reinvented as a public display platform for artists who have filled the storefronts with installations that often reflect on their settings with commentary, observation, and humor. *Woodward Ave. between Park Ave. and Gratiot Ave.*

Wurlitzer Building - Namesake of the organ manufacturing company, this 14-story abandoned building is a favorite among architecture buffs and once contained display space for the company's musical products, a salesroom, instructional studios, soundproofed audition booths, a 400-seat auditorium, and more. That the beautiful structure could accommodate these varied functions in such a narrow footprint is a testament to the work of architect Robert Finn. *1509 Broadway St.*

CHAPTER 2
MIDTOWN

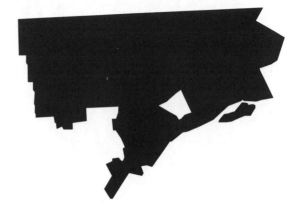

Come tour museums, visit galleries, admire architecture, catch movies, browse boutiques, enjoy eateries, and hunt for antiques in the bustling commercial, cultural, and geographic heart of the city. Every trip to Detroit should include a visit to Midtown, home to regional assets such as the Detroit Institute of Arts, Museum of Contemporary Art Detroit, Detroit Main Library, Detroit Symphony Orchestra, Detroit Historical Museum, and the Charles H. Wright Museum of African American History. Become one of the two million annual visitors who explore the city's most popular cultural amenities, most diverse architecture, and some of its densest shopping and dining districts.

As defined for this guide, Midtown spans 2.9 square miles, is bounded by I-94, I-75, and Grand River Avenue, and encompasses a number of neighborhoods, including Art Center, Brush Park, Cass Corridor, Cultural Center, Jeffries, Medical Center, Sugar Hill, the Wayne State University Campus, and Woodbridge. Collectively, these distinct communities showcase an array of physical forms and styles and are home to the city's most diverse group of residents.

As one of the oldest sections of the city—Midtown was annexed between 1815 and 1875—the area was initially built piecemeal, before the city's automotive renaissance. The neighborhood first developed as a mix of stately mansions and retail along Woodward Avenue, gradually expanding east toward John R. Street and west towards Cass Avenue as development pushed north. Over time, the eastern portion of Midtown became home to a large tract of Paradise Valley—a renowned, vibrant, early African-American neighborhood, as well as one of the city's first Jewish enclaves surrounding the old Temple Beth-El. Although Midtown fell victim to repeated waves of urban renewal—which spurred widespread demolition of the earliest structures, and these historic communities—the area remains one of the city's oldest, since most existing buildings date between 1875 and 1931. Before the advent of more spacious worker housing fueled by Ford's $5 days, Midtown's proximity to one of the city's first streetcar lines and nearby factory work led to the development of the area's signature elegant brick mid-rise apartment buildings for neighborhood workers.

Home to fourteen of the city's forty historic districts, the elegant apartment buildings, remaining stately homes, historic churches, and impressive Wayne State University campus architecture collectively create one of the city's finest, most diverse collections of historic architecture. Architectural historians will notice beautiful examples of the Art Deco, Modern, Italianate, Romanesque revival, Neo-Byzantine, Beaux-Arts, Neo-Renaissance, International, French Châteauesque, Queen Anne, Shingle, Second Empire, American Four Square, Craftsman, Tudor Revival, and Italian Renaissance styles. The district offers a beautiful urban fabric to match—parts of Midtown feature elegant parks, tree-lined streets, and a tight street-wall, creating a lively, walkable environment.

Today, Midtown's neighborhoods continue their long traditions of constant evolution. Drawn by the central location, proximity to Wayne State University and the Cultural Center, and beautiful architecture, Midtown has attracted scores of younger and cr2eative newcomers, who've joined existing residents in opening new businesses and redeveloping large swaths of the area. Today, Midtown is home to 19,406 inhabitants, with many areas growing rapidly. Between those drawn to the architecture and culture, and the students, researchers, faculty, and medical professionals moving to be near the universities and hospitals, the neighborhood is becoming younger and increasingly diverse, with many residents hailing from other parts of the region and country.

While nearly every corner of Midtown offers something to visitors, a few areas offer the greatest concentration of destinations. Those looking to enjoy unparalleled cultural and recreational amenities and fine architecture should spend a day along the Woodward Avenue corridor. Visitors interested in shopping should head for the burgeoning retail district on and between Canfield Street and Willis Street at Cass Avenue. If looking to soak in some of Detroit's finest dive bar culture, visitors should start with bars in the Cass Corridor neighborhood.

BARS & RESTAURANTS

» Atlas Global Bistro - Want to show off your cultured palate to out-of-town guests or dress your best for a date? Atlas is your destination, featuring creative, contemporary American and International cuisine with an emphasis on outstanding presentation. The restaurant is set in a refined, subtle atmosphere highlighted by the Art Deco wood bar and floor-to-ceiling vistas of Woodward Avenue. Guests are treated to seasonal brunch, lunch, and dinner menus, which offer innovative dishes and complex flavors. House dinner specialties include pheasant breast, lamb shank, and pork medallions, while brunch and lunch menus skew towards improvements on traditional favorites, such as Vanilla Bean Pancakes and Smoked Michigan Whitefish Salad, respectively. Be sure to check out the rotating list of signature cocktails—Atlas' mixologists make their own syrups, mixers, infusions, and bitters. If you're worried about having only a student-sized budget, check out 50% off martini Mondays and grab an appetizer as an accompaniment. *3111 Woodward Ave., www.atlasglobalbistro.com, (313) 831-2241.*

» **Avalon International Breads** - Founded by Ann Perrault and Jackie Victor in 1997, Avalon was an early anchor of recent retail development in the Cass Corridor and remains a beloved, wildly popular Detroit institution to this day. Customers pack the cafe tables inside and out—and often line up out the door for the incredible baked goods and treats—if you're able to snag a seat and sit there long enough, you'll probably see everyone you know in Detroit! The bakery serves up hearty, flavorful, freshly baked, organic bread, a broad selection of sweet and savory treats (including a bevy of yummy vegan options), a full menu of coffee drinks, and a great selection of packaged local and regional coffees, teas, chocolates, and jams. At lunchtime, check out the coolers for prepared sandwiches (the Garden Works is essential) and salads, or get a made-to-order hot sandwich at the counter. Sealing the deal on the experience is the lively and colorful, character-rich space highlighted by the whimsical hand-drawn signs that feature friendly anthropomorphic baked goods offering up the monthly specials. In addition to using all organic flour and mainly organic ingredients, Avalon donates generously to the community, so you'll have no problem adhering to its motto—"Eat Well. Do good."—when you buy the bread with cred. Don't leave without a sea salt chocolate chip cookie! *422 W. Willis St. (although moving to the 400 block of Canfield St. in early 2013), www.avalonbreads.net, (313) 832-0008.*

The Bottom Line Coffee House - With fine coffee and a handsome interior to match, this quaint subterranean coffee shop has won the hearts of many in the neighborhood since opening in summer 2012. The bright and lively interior features exposed brick walls, vintage and topical prints, and contemporary woodwork. The gorgeous interior, soft music, aroma of fresh ground beans, and friendly student customers all contribute to the charming neighborhood hangout atmosphere. Owners Al and Pat Harris have good taste in food and coffee, using Intelligentsia beans from Chicago, locally roasted coffee from Righteous Bean, and baked treats from Traffic Jam and Snug. All of the drinks on the menu—from espresso drinks including cafe con panna and macchiato, to a variety of hot teas—are nectarous and priced to sell. *4474 3rd St., www.tblcoffeehouse.com, (313) 638-2759.*

» **The Bronx Bar** - A beloved, straightforward shot-and-a-beer stronghold in the heart of the Cass Corridor, The Bronx Bar is known as a stalwart destination for those looking for a pint of beer without an ounce of pretension. This popular firewatering hole is known for its bright, vintage neon-basted exterior with its wrap-around deck, and its dark interior dominated by classic arcade machines, a pool table, a drink board, and a handful of gewgaw antiques atop the beautiful antique bar. Without TVs and with everything from Etta James to LCD Soundsystem pouring from the two jukeboxes— perfectly curated by bartenders and regulars—the bar has a mellow atmosphere made for conversation. Customers can get both noshed and sloshed, thanks to a full line of liquor, a solid stable of drafts and bottles, and one of the city's tastiest assortments of bar fare— including the outstanding Bronx Burger, black bean burger, and the "Veggie Machine," all served on incredible butter-grilled Iraqi bread. Conscientious owners Paul Howard and Scott Lowell have a personable staff, including affable cocktailian Chris and Charlene, a dry-witted charm school dropout. Although recently renovated, the bar stays true to tradition, and remains a place where working class and brunching class rub elbows. *4476 2nd Ave., (313) 832-8464.*

Byblos Cafe and Grill - Named for a city along the Mediterranean Sea, though this neighborhood classic looks a little reserved on the outside, step inside to be transported to another land by way of walls covered with kitschy hand-painted Mediterranean scenes and faux stone arches. Specializing in authentic Middle Eastern, Lebanese, and African cuisine, the restaurant offers tasty renditions of popular favorites such as shawarma, falafel, and mujadara, as well as lesser-known dishes like sambousek (fried dough and cheese). Though it's an economical destination for vegetarian and omnivore fans of Mediterranean food, less adventurous palates will be more at home with available diner fare. Patrons hoping for an option a little further south will enjoy the sleek and modern satellite location (4830 Cass Avenue)—a perfect place for affordable take-out or dine-in meals. *87 W. Palmer Ave., www.bybloscafeandgrill.com, (313) 831-4420.*

» Cass Cafe - A hub for artists, students, and neighborhood folks of all stripes, the Cass Cafe is a casual bar and restaurant in an informal, contemporary gallery setting. Showcasing prominent and up-and-coming local artists through monthly art exhibitions, the rotating artwork that fills the expansive walls of the restaurant inform the atmosphere of the understated, unpretentious industrial theme. Offering a thoughtful, vegetarian-friendly menu with daily specials, favorites include the Monterey turkey burger, curried-lentil soup, and the killer lentil walnut burger. Of course, all options are best augmented with the "love basket"—a crowd-pleasing mix of fries and onion rings. The full bar offers a selection of local brews and some of the neighborhood's best nightly drink specials, including $3 margaritas and $1 beers. Look for regular DJ nights, music, and spoken word performances. *4620 Cass Ave., www.casscafe.com, (313) 831-1400.*

Circa 1890 Saloon - Owner Stephan Zantheas' Circa Saloon is a great bar for a cold, cheap bottle of Schlitz or Black Label after a long day of work or class. Frequented by Wayne State students and a stable of regulars, Circa is a low-key bar without pretension. The exterior features a 1970s marshmallow awning, while the lively interior is littered with old timey bric-a-brac that may or may not be reminiscent of the 1890s. Shoot pool or darts in the back, watch the game, or just shoot the breeze while downing some of the renowned wing dings, a veggie reuben, or one of the hand-tossed pizzas. *5474 Cass Ave., (313) 831-1122.*

Comet Bar - "Karokee & Sports T.V." reads the sign for Detroit's Comet Bar. Correct spelling be damned, this is a dive bar, after all, where you'll sit in a plastic folding chair and drink from a plastic cup. But where the Comet Bar may have cut corners in decor and glassware, they've compensated by way of cheap drinks (including $7 pitchers). The place is revered for its Friday and Saturday night karaoke, which has just about the most supportive crowd you can imagine. In summer, the bar's backyard opens for volleyball and horseshoe games. Don't miss sampling an incredible sweet or savory slice from **Dangerously Delicious Pies**, based out of the kitchen of the bar. *128 Henry St., (313) 963-6763.*

Fourteen East - Just a few yards from the triumphant stone steps of the Detroit Institute of Arts stands Fourteen East, a coffee bar dedicated to perfecting the art of coffee in an aesthetically pleasing atmosphere. Order a cup of Michigan-roasted Chazzano Coffee (you can choose from drip, French press, or vacuum siphon methods of preparation) and be sure to try a few of the French macarons. The walls of local art, custom-made light fixtures, and beautiful molded-plywood seating invite you to leisurely sip your beverage and take in the thoughtful, contemporary decor. *15 E. Kirby St., www.14eastcafe.com, (313) 871-0500.*

» Good Girls Go to Paris Crepes - A delicious reminder of Detroit's French heritage, Good Girls Go to Paris is a bustling Midtown crepêrie and cafe located in the historic Park Shelton. With more than 50 crêpes on the menu, divided into "Left Bank" (savory) and "Right Bank" (sweet), the hard part is choosing your pleasure. Better just get a savory and split one of the delectable, generously portioned dessert crêpes with a friend. Decorated with brilliant, oversized subway posters from the French cinema, affable owner Torya Blanchard's beautiful shop is a great place to relax before or after a trip to the DIA or Detroit Film Theatre, both located just across the street. *15 E. Kirby St., www.goodgirlsgotopariscrepes.com, (877) 727-4727.*

» Goodwells Natural Foods Market - With the mission of being a "good well in the city," Goodwells is equal parts boutique health food store and vegan-friendly carryout destination. Occupying two connected storefronts on West Willis Street, the "grocery side" of the small store is packed with a variety of fresh produce, organic foods, frozen food, and canned goods that cater to nearly every dietary restriction. However, it's the carryout counter, which attracts a seemingly endless line, that has most put this place on the map.

Most renowned for its insanely addictive "Famous Pita Pocket Sandwich"—a delightful sandwich packed with a soy patty, a slew of greens and vegetables, a super secret sauce, and optional cheese and avocado—the counter also offers yummy samosas, a handful of daily soup specials, delicious salads (try the kale!), and other hot and cold options. Because of the pita pocket's popularity, we recommend calling ahead for carryout. *418 W. Willis St., (313) 831-2130.*

» Great Lakes Coffee - Self described as an Institute for Advanced Drinking, owner James Cadariu takes coffee—roasted nearby under the Great Lakes label—as seriously as he does imported wine, craft beer, and fine cocktails. Inviting patrons to hydrate, caffeinate, and inebriate, Great Lakes offers a wide selection of gourmet coffee—including cold-press on tap in the summer—and espresso drinks, as well as an exceptional, curated bar, with innovative offerings, many of which incorporate java and booze. Though Great Lakes doesn't offer a full menu, its sweets, baked goods, and cheese plates—including a vegan "better than cheese" plate, which is a highlight—are delicious ways to stave off hunger. Located in a beautifully renovated historic building, the design of the stunning 2,000 square foot interior innovatively incorporates exposed brick, reclaimed wood from demolished homes in Detroit, and adapted industrial components. Those who prefer outdoor refreshment can enjoy the covered street side patio. *3965 Woodward Ave., www.greatlakescoffee.com, (313) 831-9627.*

Harmonie Garden - Nestled in the digs of a former bar, Harmonie Garden is a Middle Eastern restaurant committed to serving affordably priced, healthy, diverse cuisine with plenty of vegetarian and vegan options. Classics like falafel, homemade lentil soup and shawarma are popular options, but the menu also offers a unique spin on classics, such as beet hummus, fruit and nut fattoush, and a category of "Special Falafel Ideas" which includes the amazing Falamankoush (veggies, falafel, and Syrian cheese between two pieces of grilled zatar bread) and "Flobby Joe." Patrons dine casually along the carved wooden bar with matching wood overhang, or sit at cozy tables or booths under hanging lamps. With an impressively large weekend breakfast buffet, Middle Eastern coffee and fresh juice round out the reasons why so many people have become fans of the new, quirky neighborhood staple. *4704 Anthony Wayne Dr., www.harmoniegarden.com, (313) 638-2345.*

Harry's Detroit Bar and Restaurant - Harry's is a comfortable, modern bar on the edge of Foxtown offering quality food and a well-stocked drink selection. The interior is open, spacious, and clean, but sports fans—Harry's main clientele—will appreciate the eight HD televisions ringing the first floor, with four more on the upstairs patio (open on Tigers and Lions home game days). Harry's has daily food and drink specials, and those working downtown can enjoy happy hour specials anytime. Darts available. *2482 Clifford St., www. harrysdetroit.com, (313) 964-1575.*

» Honest John's Bar and No Grill - No matter what day of the week, if it's 1am and you find yourself craving dinner, a 40-oz Black Label, and some sweet Motown jams, get thee to Honest John's. Well known and dearly loved for its stellar juke box and for serving food every night until 2am, Honest John's is an indispensable Cass Corridor neighborhood bar with a generous menu and booths (almost literally) the size of Buicks. The food—pleasing for both vegetarians and omnivores alike—ranges from the deliciously greasy (deep fried, battered macaroni and cheese triangles and the coleslaw reuben called the Eastsider) to the less detrimental but still delicious (hearty vegetarian chili and the veggie and feta pita called the Pocket of Joy). Be sure not to miss breakfast, featuring the famous smothered hash and served 'til 5pm on weekends for the hangover set. *488 Selden St., www.honestjohnsdetroit.com, (313) 832-5646.*

Hot Spokes - The savior of the hungry and pressed-for-time, Hot Spokes offers daily bicycle delivery from 11am to 4pm and covers Corktown, Downtown, Midtown, New Center, and Woodbridge. For a base charge of $3, Shane O'Keefe will deliver piping hot vittles from participating restaurants—even during the coldest winter days. Simply place your order directly through the restaurant of your choice and request delivery through the service. Tips accepted. Currently, participating restaurants include: Cass Cafe (313) 831-1400, Shangri-La (313) 974-7669, Slows To Go (877) 569-7246, Goodwells (313) 831-2130, PJs Lager House (313) 961-4668, Seva Detroit (313) 974-6661, Avalon International Breads (313) 832-0008, Louisiana Creole Gumbo (313) 962-1982. *www.facebook.com/HotSpokes, (313) 831-1400.*

International Institute of Metropolitan Detroit - Since 1919, the International Institute has helped welcome immigrants to the Detroit area by offering English language courses and guidance on the path to American citizenship, and cultivating understanding among the

city's many ethnicities and cultures. Highlights of the facility include an auditorium with a display of flags from more than 80 countries, an expansive collection of dolls modeling traditional clothing of world nations, and a large collection of models of historic ships that brought immigrants to the United States. However, the institute's most popular feature is the International Cafe, which offers an expansive, delicious, and affordable menu of traditional Indian, Italian, Mediterranean, Mexican, and American dishes. Welcoming diners every weekday from 11am to 2:30pm, the cafe allows visitors the rare opportunity to inauthentically pair tasty authentic dishes (would you like samosas and hummus with your quesadilla?).
111 E. Kirby St., www.iimd.org, (313) 871-8600.

Jumbo's Bar - A beloved, classic neighborhood dive, Jumbo's is an oasis in the southern Cass Corridor desert. On an otherwise pretty barren stretch of 3rd Street (save for Third Avenue Hardware), windowless Jumbo's always looks as though it might be closed, but it isn't. Step into the front door (or park in the lot and walk in the back door where you'll find smokers huddled), and you'll be greeted by a warm, brass-tacks interior, a pool table, several tables with chairs, ephemera from the bar's history, and a pair of killer touch-screen machines at the bar. Family owned, you can find sisters Holly and Stephanie tending bar most nights. Sassy, friendly, and down-to-earth, they'll fix you a stiff drink (and the occasional shot on the house if you're a regular) or pour you a $2 beer while you strike up a conversation with an unexpected array of neighborhood folks. Spend the warmer months outside on their cozy patio or playing horseshoes. Saturdays year-round find Jumbo's hosting an extremely popular karaoke night; be on the lookout for other regular events including a favorite long-standing biweekly Thursday DJ night. Have a dog or a bike with you? Walk or wheel 'er right on in.
3736 3rd St., (313) 831-8949.

Lefty's Lounge - Owner Dave Marcon—a retired lefty major league pitcher and Blue Jays draftee—hit it out of the park with this baseball-centric sports bar. Opened in 2008, the contemporary interior is clad in breweriana and vintage sports paraphernalia, and offers sixteen 50-inch TVs, darts, and arcade machines. Aside from the impressive beer list—including 21 beers on tap and a few local brews—Lefty's offers a solid menu of baseball-inspired dude food, including tasty pizza, half-pound burgers, ribs, BLTs, and calzones with names like "Stolen Base," and "Bull Pen." In warmer months, sit at the outdoor veranda, overlooking an Art Deco swimming pool. *5440 Cass Ave., www.leftysloungedetroit.com, (313) 831-5338.*

Majestic Café - A part of the Majestic Theater Complex, the Majestic Café offers a refined, raw setting with hip appeal. Inside, patrons are greeted by the warmth of wood floors and exposed brick walls that, on a rotating basis, highlight works by local artists. The menu features an eclectic mix of international flavors, but skews towards Middle Eastern and Italian cuisine, as well as thoughtful American fare, with highlights being the savory pastas and burgers (including a three-grain veggie option) with seemingly endless potential for customization with gourmet toppings and condiments. At the bar, look for a wide-selection of beer, wine, and liquor, with a specialty in Michigan-made varieties. Though the stage has been relatively quiet in recent years, it's a wonderful setting for an intimate acoustic performance. The Majestic also serves a stellar brunch. *4120 Woodward Ave., www.majesticdetroit.com, (313) 833-9700.*

Mario's Italian Restaurant - A Cass Corridor icon since 1948, Mario's is an upscale, Italian restaurant and supper club. The traditional interior, dignified ambience, and fine woodwork contribute to an old-school charm that feels untouched by time. Despite the elegance, the mood is unpretentious and laid back. The cuisine is no different—the decadent offerings, including the renowned Scaloppine Siciliana, Tournedos Maison, and Chicken Cacciatore, are served unassumingly. The diverse menu offers a host of hearty options and comprehensive beer, wine, and liquor menus. The six or seven course meals—bread, antipasto, soup, salad, pasta, and main course—and other amenities—such as tableside cooking— take time, so plan accordingly. As a supper club, Mario's offers live music and ballroom dancing on weekend nights. *4222 2nd Ave., www.mariosdetroit.com, (313) 832-1616.*

Mitch's On The River - Named not for the Detroit River, but for its site on the shores of Grand River Avenue, Mitch's is down the road from the casino, but hardly a casino bar. An enduring social scene made great by its regulars, Mitch's primes the pump on weekends by offering live DJs for those enjoying the ample dance floor. The weekdays are a little more subdued, giving patrons a chance to enjoy a stretch into this deep bar, housed in a raw red brick building that is more than a century old. Patrons are welcomed by a clipper ship carved into the wooden door, and greeted inside by a laid-back atmosphere of rich wood paneling, exposed brick, windows with stained glass flourishes and a mile-long bar with a vintage brass cash register at its back. The bar offers a limited selection of tasty pub fare. *2549 Grand River Ave., (313) 965-4542.*

» **Motor City Brewing Works** - Since 1994, the small but mighty Motor City Brewing Works has made a name for itself as one of Michigan's finest microbreweries, and in this beer-rich state, that's saying something. Serving out of its constantly packed taproom dotted with locally designed tile mosaics and metalwork, owners John Linardos and Dan Scarsella offer a stable of handcrafted beers anchored by the signature Ghettoblaster, "the beer you can hear." Flanked by seasonal varieties such as Pumpkin Ale and the popular Summer Ale (best with an orange wedge), tasty house-made sodas, and locally made wines, the brewery has a beverage for every palate. If the beverages weren't enough, the neighborhood institution also boasts delectable thin-crust brick-oven pizza made with locally grown ingredients from the Bronx Bomber (cheese and meat heaven) to Roasted Pear and Fig. Visit on Wednesday nights for the popular This Week in Art one-night art shows. Bottled brews are distributed regionally, and growlers of soda and beer are available to take home. *470 W. Canfield St., www.motorcitybeer.com, (313) 832-2700.*

» **The Old Miami** - Officially a veterans bar ("Miami" is short for Missing in Action Michigan), this grade-A dive is welcoming to everyone and draws a diverse crowd of streetwise veterans, Cass Corridor old timers, and discerning 20- and 30-somethings who know a quality juice joint when they see one. The back bar and walls are covered with a thousand relics that tell as many stories, from vintage firearms, to a cheery painting of (controversial) Mayor Coleman Young, and a stuffed beaver that's more often used as a beer stand than admired. Though in colder months, patrons congregate around the pool table, and sit in the mismatched comfy chairs, a highlight of the place is the exterior greenery. When weather permits, guests spill out into the gargantuan back yard, which is decked out with Vietnam paraphernalia (Missile? Check! Sign directing you to Saigon? Check!), a cozy bonfire pit, dozens of lawn chairs, and a koi pond. On select nights, the stages (there's one inside and one outside) play host to indie, punk, and metal bands, as well as local DJs (check out Nothing Elegant to shake it down). *3930 Cass Ave., (313) 831-3830.*

Olympic Grill - Located on the southern edge of Wayne's campus, this popular student hangout serves patrons fast, affordable meals from a menu of the usual suspects: coneys, wraps, grilled sandwiches, and burgers—with a few specials like saganaki and yogurt smoothies thrown in. Fare is filling and tasty, served in a clean, comfy, and welcoming setting—padded cloth and vinyl booths, hardwood tables, a few lamps, checkered-tile pillars and an open kitchen. Hours are based around the university crowd: open early and closed before the very last classes let out. *119 W. Warren Ave., (313) 832-5809.*

The Potato Place - Starch lovers, here's your haven. Offering crazy three-pound potatoes the size of a small child, pile your spud with your choice of toppings (broccoli to taco), cheese, and butter, and watch the calories roll in. The loaded, perfectly textured, and creamy potatoes go down easy but are nearly impossible to finish in one sitting—though you'll likely try. While the focus of the place is obviously on everybody's favorite tuber, you can opt to substitute your tater for a heaping plate of pasta smothered with your selection of vices. Don't have the appetite for a three-pound potato? Split a spud with a friend or try the salads, house-made soups, baked goods, and award-winning ice cream. Keep in mind that "this is not a fast food restaurant" (as the sign by the register reminds patrons), so call ahead if you're in need of a quick fix. *107 W. Warren Ave., www.thepotatoplace.com, (313) 833-8948.*

» **Rodin** - This brand new entrant to Midtown's dining scene is a thoughtful play on classical French cuisine. Occupying a large corner space in the first floor of the Park Shelton, Rodin is an elemental mix of refinement, high style, and French heritage—crimson drapes hang beneath an exposed concrete ceiling in front of historic windows; repurposed wooden pews bathed in mellow lights line the dining corridor by a poured concrete bar; and French film subway posters add to the allure. The menu—emphasizing locally sourced ingredients—consists of canonical French dishes reimagined as contemporary small plates—coq au vin avec champignon becomes a wing battered in brown rice & Porcini flour while lamb navarin is reinvented as a pulled-lamb stew over brioche with fennel. The French aren't known for cocktails, but a liquor menu including top-shelf French liqueurs, European (as well as local) beers, and a selection of refined yet affordable French wines is available. *15 E Kirby St., www.rodindetroit.com, (313) 285-9218.*

Salad 101 - Health-conscious Wayne State students and faculty appreciate this fresh to-go salad bar joint, which also offers homemade soups, pita wraps, and grilled panini sandwiches for under $6. The newly built storefront is spare, bright, white, and clean with tile floors and a few simple cafe tables set around the main centerpiece of the room: a long salad bar counter decked out with all the fixings from arugula to pine nuts. Like any freshman intro class, finding healthy eating at Salad 101 is a no-brainer. *5122 Anthony Wayne Dr., www.salad101online.com, (313) 833-0000.*

» Seva Detroit - To the delight of vegetarians (and everyone else), Seva—based out of nearby Ann Arbor since 1973—opened a Detroit outpost in 2011. Attached to the N'Namdi Center for Contemporary Art, Seva offers patrons two dining rooms that feature a refined, industrially oriented contemporary gallery setting with concrete floors, exposed ceilings, floor-to-ceiling windows, and artwork that colorfully fills the walls. The expansive and versatile menu offers a wide range of vegetarian and vegan cuisine, with options that will satisfy even the heartiest appetite or the most particular palate. Highlights among the many appetizers, sandwiches, salads, and entrees include the indulgent deep-fried goodness of General Tso's cauliflower, a solid cilantro peanut stir-fry, a yummy club sandwich (amazing smoked-coconut pinch hits for bacon), and a rotating menu of flavorful and filling salads. Also offering a full bar backlit by a glowing white wall, the beverage menu itself is four pages long, offering homemade sodas, fresh juice combos, signature cocktails, and a slew of local beers and wines. Don't miss the daily happy hour food and drink specials (yes, gouda tots are as good as they sound) and a weekly Sunday brunch. *66 E. Forest Ave., www.sevarestaurant.com, (313) 974-6661.*

Sgt. Pepperoni's Pizzeria & Deli - Although most popular at 2am when three sheets and looking for treats, the speedy service and tasty slices will leave customers of any blood alcohol level saluting the Sergeant for a job well done. Complementing the golden crust and gooey cheese, the rich sauce offers a distinct, slightly spicy and slightly tangy, piquant flavor, making all of the signature thin-crust pies pretty tasty. While the individual slices are celebrated by the inebriated, Sgt. Pepperoni's offers whole pies, alongside a stable of salads, and sandwiches—including the yummy grilled veggie reuben and baked Italian sub. Although the toppings mostly remain in familiar territory, visitors can opt for vegan cheese, blue cheese, or chevre. Open late. Limited delivery available. *4120 Woodward Ave., www.majesticdetroit.com/sgt-pepperonis-detroit, (313) 833-7272.*

Shangri-La - Since opening in 2009, Shangri-La has quickly become a destination for authentic Cantonese cuisine in the city. An open, bi-level, contemporary space, Shangri-La is an inviting and lively setting featuring a wealth of Eastern decorations. While owner Cholada Chan is renowned for her innovative, flavorful, and delectable Dim Sum, the other dishes available, from sushi to massaman curry are also notable. Shangri-La offers a full bar, with an impressive selection of potables, including sake, Asian wines and beers, as well as all the usual suspects. *4710 Cass Ave., www.midtownshangri-la.com, (313) 974-7669.*

Slows To Go - With each clamshell container offering a delectable, sapid homage to the deep south, Slows To Go follows in the footsteps of its revered Corktown parent, Slows Bar B Q. Housed in a 1926 building that has variously been a bank and storefront church, the interior of the beautiful restaurant features high ceilings, contemporary wood paneling, and engaging artwork on the brightly colored walls. Slows To Go offers Midtown Slows Bar B Q's renowned, toothsome entrees, such as the pulled pork, ribs, wings, as well as Slows signature sandwiches, such as the ambrosial Amish chicken and mushroom Yard Bird, and the incredible TVP and slaw Genius—alongside its own tacos and turkey offerings. If able to spare the stomach space, visitors should indulge in one of the revered sides, such as the rich, creamy Mac and Cheese, or the sweet, tangy pit-smoked baked beans. Although primarily a carryout location, visitors can dine in the relaxed lobby or picnic al fresco at the tables located to the south. The Old Miami—just up the block—makes a great place to enjoy Slows To Go over a cold brewski. Internet ordering available. *4107 Cass Ave. www.slowstogo.com, (877) 569-7246.*

Socra Tea - With a name that's a playful nod to ancient Greek philosopher Socrates, Socra Tea—Detroit's only dedicated tea shop—is located on the garden level of 71 Garfield. Offering a space built out with materials garnished from a demolished home in Hamtramck, the shop, which opened in 2012, sets a new standard for how reclaimed materials can be used to artfully reinvent a space, from the counter built with lathe and discarded marble floors to the leaded glass windows incorporated into the free-standing wall that separates patrons from the kitchen. However, proprietor Meg Jones has put as much thought into her product as her decor. In addition to an inspired selection of more than 50 organic gourmet loose teas, from soothing classics like Earl Gray, to less common blends like O'Connor's Cream (which has delicate whiskey notes) and Bossa Nova (with enough zip to satisfy the coffee drinking set), the shop also offers fresh cookies, muffins, and scones. Guests can enjoy hot tea by the cup or pot, or can purchase bags of loose-leaf tea to take home. *71 Garfield St., Ste. 50, www.socrateadetroit.com, (313) 833-7100.*

Temple Bar - Visit the Temple Bar and meet the owner, George—Detroit's most opinionated, whimsical, mercurial, and charming bartender. The bar has been in George's family since the 1920s (and holds one of city's first 100 liquor licenses), but it's hard to imagine the joint without its modern day, larger-than-life proprietor. While the Temple Bar is pretty much the last business on this stretch of Cass Avenue, and the area is a little rough, you'd never know it once you get buzzed in the front door. This charmingly tarnished jewel of an Art Deco bar was a haven for African-Americans in the 1920s and interracial couples in the 1970s, before attracting its current mix of grizzled Corridor residents, drag queens, and hipsters. Today, its disco-ball-adorned dance floor is home to some of the city's best see-and-be-scene dance nights, from Haute To Death to the newly minted Menergy. To top it all off, the liquid courage doled out from behind the bar is stupid cheap. Dollar drafts? Eight-dollar microbrew pitchers? That's what we're talking about. But go quickly: word on the street is that a local magnate has been buying up all the property nearby for a "future project" (a new stadium?) and George says he expects to get booted from his own bar by 2014. Which is a damn shame, because they don't build local color like this anymore. *2906 Cass Ave., (313) 832-2822.*

Third Street Bar - Though it bills itself as a "rustic urban oasis," Third Street is a hip, tastefully decorated haven of hooch. With a gorgeous wood-laden, high-ceilinged interior illuminated by muted Edison-bulb lighting, the roomy bar features historic tin ceilings in the restroom, a wood-burning fireplace, and a hand-hewn bar and tables to match. The bar gives off a laid-back, mountain lodge atmosphere, complete with shuffleboard, darts, internet jukebox, and old-school movies on the TV above the bar. Though Third Street is a full bar with 30 imported and domestic beers in bottles, the bar offers only three drafts, and liquors are limited to favored call mixers. In the summer, patrons can eat or drink al fresco on the patio. Free Wi-Fi. *701 W. Forest Ave., (313) 833-0603.*

» Traffic Jam & Snug - A Detroit institution since 1965, the Traffic Jam is famous for its eccentric decor and quality American fare. Bedecked with old school pieces of Americana, the beautiful interior boasts exposed brick, classic red tile, knotty pine woodwork, and a laidback atmosphere. The diverse menu approaches American cuisine with an emphasis on fresh, local ingredients, and an innovative eye. Although the menu is mostly strikes and no gutters, a few options shouldn't be missed, including the Portobello mushroom soup, the Tex-Mex lentil burger, the madras meatloaf, the vegetarian lasagna, the Traverse City dried cherry and pecan salad, and the house-brewed dopplebock braised beef brisket panini. The fine restaurant is also home to an in-house brewery, dairy, and bakery, and visitors can pick up some of these fresh treats near the entrance. Those looking to drink their meal should visit the Snug, the attached, cozy bi-level bar, which offers new house brews, mixed drinks, and ice cream to go. *511 W. Canfield St., www.trafficjamdetroit.com, (313) 831-9470.*

Union Street - Signaled by the iconic retro neon sign, Union Street has been a staple of the neighborhood dining experience since the 1970s. Offering patrons an elegant but casual Art Deco dining experience, the establishment features a stunning atmosphere highlighted by mirrored walls, lush red lighting, and historic dark wood fixtures, the touchstone of which is the simple yet incredible, curvy Deco bar. The moderately priced menu runs the gamut of sandwiches, pastas, and a bevy of classic entrees in the American tradition—a favorite of which is the Union Street Jambalaya (thick, meaty Creole stew over rice). The bar, which is often lined with thirsty customers, offers an astonishing 15 beers on tap and 100 in bottles, in addition to a full line of wines, liquors, and craft cocktails.

Don't miss the popular Sunday brunch. *4145 Woodward Ave., www.unionstreetdetroit.com, (313) 831-3965.*

Wasabi Korean & Japanese Cuisine - Korean and Japanese restaurants are hard to come by in Detroit, but Wasabi's dual menu serves up a solid version of both cuisines. On the Korean side, the Dolsot Bibimbab is especially tasty (including the delectable vegetarian tofu variation), and the Japanese menu features a full range of sushi and traditional noodle dishes, along with a selection of sakes. Nestled in the ground floor of the Park Shelton, the interior is cozy, clean, and modern. If you find yourself visiting day after day, it might be worth your while to invest in one of the prepaid meal plans, from $150 for 17 lunches, to $1300 for 100 lunches and dinners. *15 E. Kirby St., www.wasabidetroit.com, (313) 638-1272.*

» The Whitney - A romantic restaurant set in a mansion of unparalleled extravagance and sophistication, the Whitney is a highlight on any culinary—or architectural—tour of Detroit. Once described as "one of the most elaborate houses in the west," the Romanesque revival residence, which was built by lumber baron David Whitney Jr. in 1894 and converted to a restaurant in 1986, is indeed magnificent. From the stately exterior, to the 52 exquisitely appointed rooms, to the Tiffany glass windows, the restaurant offers surroundings that do its food justice. The menu, which changes seasonally, covers wide gastronomic terrain, but favors succulent and savory American flavors, with exceptional fowl, fish, and steak. Oenophiles will be equally pleased by the wine cellar, which offers a generous selection of local and international varieties. In addition, the Whitney offers a buffet-style Sunday Brunch and a rotating lineup of entertainers in its garden and at the Ghost Bar on the third floor. Though they have no formal dress code, business casual attire is recommended at a minimum. *4421 Woodward Ave., www.thewhitney.com, (313) 832-5700.*

» Woodbridge Pub - Featuring vintage touches like antique tin ceilings, salvaged leaded glass, gorgeous historic paneling, and a reconstituted 1890s oak bar, this beautiful pub and neighborhood gem offers an eclectic, locally sourced menu reflective of the seasons. Although personable owner Jim Geary's menu features a stable of palate-pleasers, the Stevers McFever black bean burger (with zing from a balsamic reduction), buffal-pho, toasted pumpkin ravioli, and Trumbull ham pot pie are not to be missed. The pub boasts an impressive selection of beers including rotating Michigan-brewed selections and a full line of liquors. On Sunday mornings, make a beeline for Woodbridge for the special brunch menu and bottomless mimosas. The pub plays host to a fun roster of weekly events, including Pie-Sci—a specialty pizza feast—on Sundays, pub trivia on Wednesdays, and a slow jam night each Monday. *5169 Trumbull Ave., www.woodbridgepub.com, (313) 833-2701.*

SHOPPING & SERVICES

Architectural Salvage Warehouse of Detroit - As the answer to the question "where can I purchase gently used 2x4s, a working refrigerator, antique corbels, and ornamental balustrades," the Architectural Salvage Warehouse is Detroit's reigning king of architectural salvage. Though active in advocacy and education, the backbone of the organization—and what it is best known for—is its successful (and legitimate) deconstruction and architectural salvage operation. All of the components that the facility collects and saves from landfills—from the historic to the mundane—are organized by type and laid to bare (and priced to sell) in the organization's massive two-story disposition center. Though its website is fairly comprehensive, it's not always completely up-to-date, so phone inquiries or in-person visits are recommended. *4885 15th St., www.aswdetroit.org, (313) 896-8333.*

The Black Dress - A women's clothing boutique, The Black Dress is stocked with contemporary wardrobe essentials to outfit you from career to cocktails. Owned and operated by mother-daughter duo Sandra Allen and Missy Lewis, The Black Dress has become a local dress-tination for the classy, sassy 30-and-up crowd on the hunt for fun printed separates, sleek cocktail dresses, chic pullover ponchos, unique handbags, accessories, jewelry, and more. Although they carry a full range of sizes, The Black Dress specializes in larger sizes up to 5X. If you love a garment but would love it more if altered to your personal measurements, simply ask Sandra, a seamstress at heart. *113 E. Canfield St., www.theblackdressonline.com, (313) 833-7795.*

Bob's Classic Kicks - Don't let the "classic" in the name fool you, BCK is Detroit's best place to find old-school and new school sneaks. With its colorful murals, high ceilings, and open and airy feel, the hip, tightly curated boutique slings whatever stylin' Reebok, Adidas, and Nike kicks your feet desire—whether you're looking for classic, cutting edge, or locally designed foot fashions. In addition to quality footwear, the boutique also stocks a selection of flat-brim hats and locally designed tees. On the last Saturday of every month, Bob's hosts The Air UP There, an intimate hip hop performance and party. *4717 Woodward Ave., www.bobsclassickicks.com, (313) 832-7513.*

Canine to Five - If dog is a man's best friend, Canine to Five is a close second. A necessity for any busy dog owner, gregarious storeowner Liz Blondy's charming shop has been offering doggy daycare since 2005 in the heart of the Cass Corridor. If your pup is in need of a babysitter, walk, new hairdo, sleepover, or fun play date, head for this impressive, recently renovated operation which boasts 4,500 square feet of cage-free indoor play space, 8,000 square feet of secured outdoor play space, and designated areas for puppies, small dogs, and quiet time. With monthly dog-friendly special events, dog-care supplies, grooming, and boarding, the business seeks to support all types of canine needs. Located inside is **Woofbridge Feed and Supply**, a shop dedicated to helping keep your animal well fed and healthy. They are happy to consult on the best nutrition plan for your dog and even order your favorite supplies as you need them! *3443 Cass Ave., www.caninetofivedetroit.com, (313) 831-3647.*

» City Bird - In 2009, Andy and Emily Linn opened this shop featuring their own Detroit-themed goods and work by more than 200 other local artists, designers, and crafters. They began making their distinctive city-branded products in 2005, which run the gamut from hand-engraved Detroit neighborhood rocks glasses, to Detroit map soap, silkscreened notebooks, T-shirts, prints, jewelry, housewares, cards, and other Detroit souvenirs for Detroiters—all celebrating the city. These products, along with a wide range of goods from other local makers and artists, are displayed in the warm, friendly, sun-drenched shop with antique wooden fixtures and artful displays. City Bird is especially popular for its affordable jewelry by independent designers, its revolving selection of specialty Detroit T-shirts, and a bevy of great gifts at any price point. To top it off, with more than 400 unique illustrated, letterpressed, silkscreened, embossed, or lasercut, designs, their greeting card selection is something to write home about. *460 W. Canfield St., www.citybirddetroit.com, (313) 831-9146.*

Curl Up & Dye - Open since 2008, Curl Up & Dye is a beautiful, airy, stylish, and sassy full-service salon. Through its focus on organic personal care, you'll leave with more than just a new hair-do, fresh face, or well groomed eyebrows: you'll have a whole new attitude. As they say, they can "cut, dread, chop, thread, highlight, perm, wash, relax, trim, blow out, wax, curl up & dye all types of hair." The prices are reasonable considering the top-of-the-line organic products that are used every step of each process—check out the house line of nontoxic skin, hair, and body care products, Cass Brand Organics, which are created by salon owner Jennifer Willemson and are available for purchase. Call ahead to schedule an appointment—walk-ins are hard to come by. *4215 Cass Ave., www.curlupanddyedetroit.com, (313) 833-5006.*

» Detroit Antique Mall / Senate Resale - Though, depending on the sign, it's alternately known as the Detroit Antique Mall or Senate Resale, by either name, the 12,000 square foot shop is one of Detroit's largest and finest antique stores. Boasting 12 vendors spread over two gigantic floors, the neatly compartmentalized antique mini-mall is organized by vendor—each of which specializes in a unique area of antique and vintage expertise. Once buzzed in, customers are greeted by a relatively neatly ordered and wide selection of Art Deco, Mid-Century Modern, Arts and Crafts, Victorian and Mission furniture and decor, architectural salvage, 1950s and 1960s collectables, lighting, jewelry, periodicals, and numerous other facets of the antique experience, making it hard to walk out of the large emporium without finding a treasure. *828 W. Fisher Fwy., (313) 963-5252.*

Detroit Community Acupuncture - Practicing a centuries-old relaxing and painless method proven to help alleviate numerous ailments, Detroit Community Acupuncture is dedicated to bringing affordable acupuncture treatment to the community. To the tune of peaceful, ethereal music, patients sit together in comfortable reclining chairs as they await or receive treatment in the large, shared open space, emphasizing camaraderie and togetherness. Dedicated to bringing healing to the community, the office accepts both appointments and walk-ins, and charges only $15–$35 on a sliding scale, based on how much patients can afford to pay. *4100 Woodward Ave., www.detroitcommunityacupuncture.com, (313) 831-3222.*

» Flo Boutique - In Felicia Patrick's cozy, lively, eclectic clothing boutique you'll find a collection of effortless style and soul. Think feminine dresses, comfy cotton separates, patchwork denim skirts, and all the right accessories to go with them from wooden bracelets to fashionable fedoras, leather wallets, and fabulous shoes. Alongside the goods for women, Flo carries a smart collection of gear for men, all artfully displayed in her inviting shop with vintage and natural accents. Named for her mother, Patrick's store is the fulfillment of her lifelong dream of opening a shop and her love of fashion. Don't forget to take a whiff of one of the fragrant essential oils and grab a chic envelope clutch made from upcycled jute coffee bean sacks. *404 W. Willis St., www.flowingflava.com, (313) 831-4901.*

Fred's Key Shop & Locksmith - Two parts expert locksmiths, one part wisecracking comedians, these doctors of deadbolts, maestros of mortises, connoisseurs of cylinders, and teachers of tumblers have been a Cass Corridor institution since 1962. Owner Fred "Sarge" Knoche and his four smart aleck brothers are expert locksmiths and bring a sense of fun and sophistication to their craft. Between telling off-color jokes, the endearing staff offer comprehensive locksmithing services, key-cutting, safe sales and services, and auto alarm, remote starter, and kill switch installation. The small, unassuming shop offers a small waiting area, a pop machine, and chuckle-worthy banter coming from behind the counter. Don't get comfortable in the waiting area, though, in addition to being incredibly honest and affordable, the Knoche brothers are lightning-fast. *3470 2nd Ave., www.fredskeyshopandlocksmith.com, (313) 831-5770.*

» Goods - Founded by College for Creative Studies Alumna Karry Brook, Goods is a T-shirt Bakery and gift shop with a DIY attitude. Upon entering the clean, contemporary shop, customers can peruse the quality selection of Michigan-made T-shirts, accessories, bath products, and artwork, but the highlight of the store is the inspired "bakery" counter. Conceive of your concept (your text, your image, or an on-hand graphic), pick your medium and color from the wall of apparel (T-shirts, hoodies, baby onesies, and totes are available), and watch as your custom creation is produced before your eyes. For those designing T-shirts for an upcoming event, Goods also advises on and processes bulk orders. *15 E. Kirby St., www.goodsdetroit.com, (313) 703-7754.*

Grace Harper Florist - Owner John Kewish's popular shop has been a Woodward staple since 1918. The old-timey interior features a beautifully utilitarian wood counter, rows of coolers bursting with a massive inventory of vibrant blooms, and a showroom brimming with elegant centerpieces, wreaths, bouquets, terrariums, corsages, boutonnieres, and bouquets. Kewish and his capable staff create both traditional and contemporary arrangements, full of color and cheer. In addition to flowers, Grace Harper also offers gourmet fruit baskets, balloons, stuffed animals, and greeting cards. Same day delivery available. *4135 Woodward Ave., www.graceharperflorist.com, (313) 831-1164.*

» The Hub of Detroit - Greetings from the land of used vintage bicycles! The Hub is Detroit's cyclery with a conscience and home to perhaps the state's largest selection of used bicycles in various states of repair. This lively unpolished shop is known for its friendly staff, very affordable repair services, and its unparalleled collection of used parts—from Italian threaded bottom brackets to indicator spindles. The Hub stays true to the values of its nonprofit roots, and works to train local youth in bike repair, help them earn bikes, and offers them jobs in the shop. If you know your way around a cone wrench and chain whip—or want to learn—you can take classes and volunteer at the affiliated nonprofit Back Alley Bikes on the second floor. The Hub also hosts Fender Bender, a mechanic training program for women and LGBT cyclists. The Hub accepts donated bicycles. *3611 Cass Ave., www.thehubofdetroit.org, (313) 879-5073.*

» Hugh - Born as a retail pop-up "happening" in 2010, after 65,000 votes were cast, owner Joe Posch emerged the popular victor in the first annual Hatch Detroit retail competition, granting him the startup capital needed to make his store a permanent fixture on the Detroit retail scene. The first business to open in Midtown's new Auburn building, Hugh is an enthusiastic celebration of classic 1950s and 1960s bachelor pad style. Impeccably decorated in a manner that would make Don Draper proud, the store's stunning midcentury wood fixtures display a wide-selection of classic barware, men's accessories, smoking accoutrements, and new and vintage glassware and home decor. Patrons will find flasks (including one tastefully concealed in a book), myriad cocktail shakers, stylish cufflinks, artful ashtrays, and even a selection of vintage Playboy magazines. Offering items at a wide range of price-points, Posch, with his stunning taste and advice, can help every man—or the man in everyone's life—be outfitted in timeless style. Thank Hugh. *4240 Cass Ave., www.lovehughlongtime.com, (313) 887-0900.*

Little Asia Mart - Follow the fragrant aromas of radhuni, chutney, anise seeds, curry, and asafoetida, and let your nose lead you to Little Asia Mart. This south and mideast Asian grocery caters to Wayne State's substantial international student population, but its items, such as naan bread, dumplings, frozen fish, and an array spices, are popular among those from both Bangalore and Boston-Edison. With its clean, bright interior, lime green flooring, and welcoming staff, it's a great place to load up on ingredients for a curried feast, or a quick snack of vegetable rolls and samosas from the counter. Check out the considerable display of Bollywood DVDs. *5110 Anthony Wayne Dr., (313) 833-0618.*

Mantra - Stepping into Mantra in old Chinatown is something like exploring your grandfather's basement—if your grandfather was a 1960s, 1970s, and 1980s swingin' bachelor and a little bit of a packrat. Though the vintage and antique shop isn't heavy on organization, it's brimming with trinkets and treasures and covers wide territory. From mod lamps, to velvet paintings, to space-age bar sets, to kitsch-en items, if you're willing to explore a little, enjoy searching for diamonds in the rough, and don't mind a little dust, owner Greg Sobieraj's eclectic collection will be right up your alley. *3401 Cass Ave., (313) 657-0728.*

Marwil Bookstore - Located on the campus of Wayne State University since 1948, Marwil is the independent option for Wayne State students looking to buy textbooks, but it's also a great browse for the general bibliophile. Students will find textbooks well organized in the relatively tight quarters, and if you can't find what you're looking for, the experienced staff will helpfully point you in the right direction. Customers who aren't in the market for school books will find a surprisingly ample and diverse collection of other materials to peruse: popular and niche fiction, nonfiction, local interest, and one of the best selections of magazines in the city, especially rich in political and lifestyle publications. *4870 Cass Ave., www.marwilbookstore.com, (313) 832-3078.*

Motor City Party Supply - Any party, birthday, or fun occasion is a good excuse to visit Motor City Party Supply (formally called Zakoor Novelty), and it never disappoints. Even though it moved around the corner from its original location a couple years back and did a lot of cleaning out, the store still has lots of old and new treasures of the celebratory variety to be found in this party-supply mecca. Monstrously huge bag of confetti? Check! Metallic letter balloons? Check! Deadstock inflatable clown masks? Check! Life-sized cowboy cardboard cutout? Check! And of course it stocks a good supply of all the basics: balloons, streamers, party hats, raffle tickets, gift bags, and everything you'd need for any party theme imaginable. It's right across the street from a high school, so try to avoid going at around 3pm as the street gets pretty backed up. *40 Selden St., (313) 831-6969.*

» Nest - Brought to Detroit by the brother-sister duo behind City Bird next door, this shop opened in 2011 and features housewares and gifts with a design focus. With a long wall of 1920s oak library shelves rescued from a demolished Detroit high school, 1920s rolling shelves from a shoe factory, a meticulously restored general store counter, and nearly floor-to-ceiling windows, the warm, light-filled, wood and brick interior of this former industrial space is the perfect backdrop for the interesting glass and barware, terrariums and air plants, linens and blankets, stationery, home office accoutrements, fine soaps, old-timey toys, gifts for pets, local foods, and home decor. It's an ideal spot to find a Michigan-themed gift, too, including Michigan cookie cutters, ice cube trays, plates, and glasses. *460 W. Canfield St., www.nestdetroit.com, (313) 831-9776.*

» Nora - Born out of a collaboration between local entrepreneurs Liz Boone, Toby Barlow, and Joe Posch, Nora—a complement to Posch's bachelor lifestyle store Hugh next door—is a stunning design shop. The airy, white space with natural open wooden shelves is punctuated by the artfully displayed products that are the store's focal point. Part of Midtown's emerging shopping district—the bright, light-filled space has a gallery feel and specializes in thoughtful, contemporary design from a wide-range of influences, including a well-curated selection of Scandinavian housewares, Japanese ceramics, and work by select local designers, in addition to textiles and decor items. *4240 Cass, Ave., www.noramodern.com, (313) 831-4845*

Pauline's Closet - Tucked inside a charming brightly painted house nestled between two restaurants, Pauline's Closet is a tidy, colorful consignment shop packed with quality contemporary used clothing, with the occasional vintage pieces. The prices are very reasonable, and although the shop mainly features women's clothing, accessories, and shoes, there are a few treasures for men as well. Just let owner Donna Arnell know what you're looking for, and she'll help you find perfect new duds that won't break the bank. *4246 2nd Ave, (313) 832-4711.*

» The Peacock Room - Shopping at the Peacock Room is an elegant experience for distinguished ladies and gentlemen. Bringing together new, consignment, and vintage clothing, as well as an eclectic array of accessories—from earrings featuring Frida Kahlo portraits and feather fascinators to men's ties and scarves—this beautiful boutique covers all the bases. The merchandise is not the only reason to take a look—the shop is located in the gorgeous former formal dining room of the historic Park Shelton, which was built as a hotel in the 1920s and is known for having hosted the likes of Diego Rivera and Bob Hope. Peacock Room owner Rachel Lutz discovered the original

molding and plaster detail hidden behind drywall as she began to build out the space before opening. Now uncovered, this architecture creates the perfect atmosphere for upscale, affordable shopping. *15 E. Kirby St., (313) 559-5500.*

» People's Records - Detroit's most storied and lauded record store, People's is an incredible destination used vinyl venue spread through two former guest suites (on two floors) of a repurposed motel. Hailed as one of America's top 50 record shops by Rolling Stone Magazine in 2011, fans travel from around the globe (yes, literally) to tap into down-to-Earth owner Brad Hales' encyclopedic music knowledge and peruse the store's music collection. The first floor offers a comprehensive selection of LPs and 45s, from blues to country and rock to hip hop, but it's upstairs—piled to the ceiling with an ungodly number of funk and soul 45s sorted by label, style, and artist, as appropriate—where the store's specialty comes to the fore. With records coming in daily from a forgotten box in grandma's attic or grandpa's garage, People's is the place to score extremely rare limited pressings from obscure Detroit artists of the 1960s and 1970s. Check out the amazing signage by Detroit legend Hermon Weems and the killer dollar bin. In addition to running his shop, Brad is also one of Detroit's most popular DJs and holds regular soul and funk nights around town. *4100 Woodward Ave., (313) 831-0864.*

Showcase Collectables - The teal and bubble-gum pink Showcase Collectables offers an approachable and organized take on the treasure-hunting experience. Customers are greeted by friendly, wandering store dogs and the amicable, chatty owners who enjoy their social time in the shop. The large, one-story vintage and antique mini mall is divided into vendor booths, cabinets, bookcases, and display cases that are crammed (neatly) with a wide-range of collectables and antiques, from military and sports ephemera, to glass bottles and jars, costume jewelry, housewares, furniture pieces, trinkets, electronics, record albums, signs, advertisements, printed matter, and hundreds of other small curiosities. While the majority of the store's most intriguing items are found in the many cases and cabinets that line the walls and circular checkout counter of the large main room, in the rear of the store, customers can find a series of connected individual booths that form a horseshoe pattern. Each room flows naturally into the next, with the exception of one booth concealed by a mysterious black curtain that hides the "Adults Only" collection of vintage adult videos and nudie magazines. The articles are fantastic. *3409 Cass Ave., (313) 831-6397.*

Showtime Detroit - Once you step foot into the 5,100 square foot Rock 'n' Roll/Goth/Glam/Industrial wear Mecca that is Showtime, you're in for something, well, different. Holding true to his duty of "dressing Detroit bands and entertainers since 1989," Showtime host proprietor Dan Tatarian keeps his warehouse of rock stocked with men's and women's garb from the grunge to the glitz. Shop everything from deadstock Doc Martens, creepers and sparkly stilettos, skintight jeans, brocade coats, tough leather jackets and paisley print suits, to ornate silver jewelry in shapes of dragons and skulls, slinky club wear, and locally branded T-shirts. Tatarian has outfitted everyone from local aspiring rock gods (side note: Showtime is one of the only places to buy guitar strings in the city) to the well-known including the likes of the MC5, The Romantics, Alice Cooper, Nickelback, and more. *5708 Woodward Ave., www.showtimedetroit.com, (313) 875-9280.*

Sole Sisters - Sole Sisters boutique keeps Detroit's women strutting in style down the sidewalk, catwalk, or RiverWalk! With corrugated sheet metal walls and sleek glass showcases, the interior reflects the urban-chic vibe of the merchandise. A selection of unique shoes ranging from $17 to $130 leaves just the right pair for any fashion taste, from sporty to bohemian. The wide selection of dresses and blouses hang eye level above the footwear, tempting shoppers to revamp their look from head to toe. An array of distinctive jewelry and bags keeps the focus on quality design and fashion-forward looks. *87 E. Canfield St., www.solesistersdetroit.com, (313) 831-9013*

» **Spiral Collective:** Dell Pryor Gallery, Source Booksellers, and Tulani Rose - Detroit artist Dell Pryor opened this Cass Corridor space in 2002 as a supportive community for female entrepreneurs and a venue to promote African-American artists. When you enter the cozy, open space, expect to be greeted with soothing, earthy scents and friendly smiles that will invite you to stay the whole afternoon. While several businesses have been a part of the collective over the years, it currently houses three:

- **Dell Pryor Gallery** - Dell Pryor is an institution of the Detroit art scene. An interior designer herself, she has been promoting and showing work by African-American artists in Detroit since the 1970s. First located in Eastern Market, she moved her gallery to Greektown and then Harmonie Park before founding this collective. In addition to varied relevant exhibitions, the gallery hosts artist talks, lectures, readings, and other special events.

- **Source Booksellers** - With a focused inventory specializing in history and culture, health and wellbeing, books about women, and the metaphysical and spiritual, owner Janet Jones' community-oriented bookstore showcases her authoritative knowledge and passion for her specialty subject areas. Be sure to visit on Saturdays for a rotating schedule of yoga, tai chi, qi gong, and belly dancing classes. Look for Source to move to a new space across the street on Cass in 2013.

- **Tulani Rose** - A charming lifestyle gift boutique, owner Sharon Pryor first opened her shop in Harmonie Park in 1997, before moving to this collective on Cass when it was founded by her mother. The perfect place to find thoughtful gifts such as fine soaps, candles, decorative notebooks, scarves, Detroit tote bags, and jewelry, Pryor's warm personality, taste, and knowledge of the neighborhood always makes it a pleasure to visit.

4201 Cass Ave., www.dellpryorgalleries.com, (313) 833-6990 (Dell Pryor Gallery), www.sourcebooksdetroit.com (313) 832-1155 (Source Booksellers), (313) 832-2477 (Tulani Rose).

Textures by Nefertiti - Offering a full-service holistic spa experience at her Cass Avenue salon, Nefertiti draws on her deep knowledge of natural hair care, fashion, yoga, and meditation. From all kinds of braids and weaves, to locs, sister locks, interlocks, dreads and more, Nefertiti specializes in natural hair styles and treatments for African-American women and men, and massages, manicures, pedicures, waxing, and an array of massage therapy services for everyone. Visit Textures to recharge and relax or get a new look in the calming atmosphere of this inviting and serene salon. Be on the lookout for poetry open mics and other events. *4147 Cass Ave., www.texturesbynef.com, (313) 831-4771.*

Third Avenue Hardware - Like a good guidebook review, Third Avenue Hardware is incredibly charming, small, and offers everything you need. Although owner "Gorgeous" George Sultana's shop crams an array of inventory into tall, loosely organized shelves, the knowledgeable staff love to play cicerone for customers by providing home repair advice and helping find ballcocks, rivet guns, rakes, epoxies, and the other essentials in stock. In addition to a tailored inventory of hardware, electrical supplies, plumbing parts, paint, landscaping tools, the shop also offers key cutting services and an impressive selection of used bicycles. Available year round, the bikes—mostly 1950s and 1960s domestic cruisers—are well tuned, adjusted, and ready to roll. *3645 3rd St., (313) 832-7241.*

University Foods - A favorite among Woodbridge and the Midtown/ Wayne State area residents since 1979, owner Edward Yaldoo's University Foods is an outstanding neighborhood grocery store that offers an assortment of fresh meat, produce, dairy, frozen foods, baked goods, organic foods, and a selection of vegetarian fare. In addition to standard grocery items, University Foods carries many local products like Calder's Ice Cream, Faygo, and microbrews from across the state. The lunch counter is a great place to pick up sandwiches and pizza at a good price. *1131 W. Warren Ave., www.universityfoodsmidtown.com, (313) 833-0815.*

Utrecht Art Supplies - Yes, it's a national chain, but prior iterations of this store have served Cass Corridor students and artists for generations—and it's the only dedicated art supply store within the city limits. For artists—or those with artistic aspirations—working in nearly any media, this is the go-to place. In addition to supplies,

Utrecht offers full framing services, an informative educational blog, an online learning center, class supply lists for WSU and CCS students, and an extremely helpful staff. *4501 Woodward Ave., www.utrechtart.com, (313) 833-9616.*

Wayne State University Farmers Market - Founded by an Urban Planning professor at the school, the Wayne State University Farmers Market is a small but mighty open-air market in front of Wayne's Business School Building, a modernist gem designed by Minoru Yamasaki. The market boasts one- to two-dozen vendors every week, including farmers, horticulturists, local bakeries, and restaurants. Though it's relatively new to the neighborhood, it's become a popular lunchtime destination during the sunnier months. The Market is open from 11am to 4pm on Wednesdays from June to October. *Cass Ave. between W. Kirby St. and Putnam St. www.clas.wayne.edu/seedwayne.*

Ye Olde Butcher Shoppe - Opened in 2012 by brothers Michael and Peter Solaka, Ye Olde Butcher Shoppe is a comely, upscale grocery in Midtown's Brush Park neighborhood. The store's Art Deco sign and facade contrast beautifully with the exposed brick, red floor, high open ceilings, and contemporary aesthetic of the 8,100-square-foot interior. The store offers a diverse selection of fresh meat, spices, dry goods, dairy, produce, frozen foods, baked goods, organic options, cleaning supplies, and kitchen sundries, and an outstanding wine selection. The full deli butcher counter is unparalleled among area grocers, offering numerous varieties of turkey, ham, sausage, smoked fish, fresh lox, free-range and Amish chicken, and grass-fed bison, all cut to order. The two wine aisles are thoughtfully organized by origin, including dozens of Michigan varieties among the extensive selection. Though the store skews towards gourmet—including Lavazza coffee, Calder dairy, and San Marzano tomatoes—shoppers of any persuasion will leave with a bulging buggy. *3100 Woodward Ave., www.yeoldebutchershoppedetroit.com, (313) 974-7356.*

CULTURAL ATTRACTIONS

The Contemporary Art Institute of Detroit - Founded as a nomadic arts entity by a group of prominent Detroit artists in 1979, CAID has been based in its present location—a space previously occupied by a related arts organization, the Detroit Contemporary—since 2004. In addition the Detroit Contemporary space, CAID is an umbrella organization for Whitdel Arts (see separate entry) in

Southwest Detroit, the Detroit Broadcasting Company based in the main building, and a variety of other smaller arts endeavors. Now a community-based nonprofit organization, CAID uses its bi-level gallery space, stage, and spacious yard to host interesting community-based exhibitions, performances, shows, lectures, conversations, educational programs, artist residencies and raucous dance parties. *5141 Rosa Parks Blvd., www.thecaid.org.*

Center Galleries - Since 1997, the College for Creative Studies has enriched Detroit's cultural scene with inspiring art exhibitions, literary readings, artist forums, and film screenings through Center Galleries, a cluster of four modern spaces housed in the Manoogian Visual Resource Center. The building itself stands as a work of art, featuring geometric orange metal ornamentation atop its contemporary cement-slab roof. Inside, the lobby features student art exhibitions, which leads to the Alumni and Faculty Hall, the College's Permanent Collection Gallery, and the Main Gallery. Each space hosts rotating exhibitions and special events—check the website for upcoming happenings. When in the building, check out the Manoogian Visual Resource Center Library, which holds more than 40,000 art and design books and 250 periodicals. Only CCS students can check out library materials, but the public is welcome to browse its fantastic collection of hard-to-find magazine titles. Main gallery closed in the summer months. *301 Frederick Douglass Ave., www.collegeforcreativestudies.edu/center_galleries, (313) 664-7800.*

» Charles H. Wright Museum of African American History - Originally founded in 1965 by its namesake physician, the Charles H. Wright Museum has grown to become the largest institution dedicated to African-American history in the world. The monumental, Sims-Varner-designed structure features a beautiful 100-foot-in-diameter stained glass dome, and a contemporary, minimalist facade adorned with aluminum and gold ornamentation by artist Richard Bennett crafted in the style of Malian Bambara masks. The 120,000-square-foot museum houses a permanent collection of more than 30,000 artifacts and archival materials, seven exhibition areas, a 317-seat theater, the Latimer Cafe refreshments area, as well as a four research repositories and historical collections. In addition to rotating special exhibits, the museum offers a 22,000-square-foot core exhibition, "And Still We Rise: Our Journey Through African American History and Culture," which uses interactive installations to chronicle African American history from prehistory to present. The stunning Ford Freedom Rotunda—the Ring of Genealogy, a 37-foot-wide terrazzo tile mosaic by local artist Hubert Massey—shouldn't be missed. *315 E. Warren Ave., www.thewright.org, (313) 494-5800.*

College for Creative Studies - This Midtown anchor arts college offers undergraduate and graduate degree programs in its varied, highly regarded programs from automotive design to crafts, industrial design, photography, and illustration. Members of the public can attend CCS' Toyota Lecture Series on art and design, featuring acclaimed artists and designers like Stefen Sagmeister and Ken Walker. Additionally, CCS offers a comprehensive, affordable summer and semester-long continuing education courses in a wide array of art and design disciplines for adults and youth in ten-week, three-week, and workshop formats. *201 E. Kirby St., www.collegeforcreativestudies. edu, (313) 664-7400.*

» Detroit Artists Market - A nonprofit contemporary gallery, the Detroit Artists Market was founded in the 1930s by a group of local art patrons as a venue for young Detroit artists to exhibit and sell their work. Within a few years, the gallery grew to exhibit emerging and established artists of all ages. These days, DAM continues to do wonderful work in the city, featuring contemporary work from Detroit and the region in creative and thought-provoking exhibitions installed in its gorgeous, modern gallery space. The gallery shop carries a wonderful assortment of smaller artwork, jewelry, and paper goods year round and expands into the whole gallery during the holidays, making it a favorite destination to shop for affordable smaller art and crafts for gift giving. The annual design show is a highlight of the year. *4719 Woodward Ave., www.detroitartistsmarket.org, (313) 832-8540.*

» Detroit Historical Museum - Since its founding in 1928, the Detroit Historical Museum has grown to become one of the nation's largest museums dedicated to metropolitan history, attracting 100,000 visitors each year. In 2012, the museum underwent a $20 million renovation and modernized its beautiful 78,000-square-foot space. The museum's impressive collection spans 250,000 items, including a Ty Cobb game bat, a Purple Gang Tommy gun, an Art Deco fountain from Detroit's Hudson's, and one of Bob Seger's guitars. Strolling through the exhibits, visitors can experience Detroit's 300+ year history, evolving from a French trading post, to the Motor City, to Motown, to present-day Detroit. Among the museum's many offerings, our favorites include:

- **Streets of Old Detroit** - This life-size exhibit puts you in a recreated vision of 19th-century Detroit, complete with brick streets and period storefronts, including a blacksmith, barber shop, bicycle shop, pharmacy, Sander's confectionary, and more.

- **Kid Rock Music Lab** - As an homage to the city's music legends and their contributions to rock, gospel, jazz, soul, techno, and funk, this interactive exhibit features original photos and posters, historical memorabilia, videos, countless artifacts such as Kevin Saunderson's mixing board, and an interactive kiosk which allows visitors to mix songs.

- **Detroit: The Arsenal of Democracy** - This new exhibit highlights the city's contribution to WWII war efforts, and the conflict's effect on Detroit, through thoughtful installations of ephemera, historic documents, photos, and interactive displays. The exhibit is organized into three focus areas: the factory, the community, and the home.

- **Doorway to Freedom** – Detroit and the Underground Railroad - To better understand the city's role in the network of safe houses and abolitionists that comprised the antebellum Underground Railroad, visitors follow an interactive, experiential, information-packed, trail illustrative of those taken by Canada-bound slaves.

- **Legends Plaza** - An outdoor plaza featuring the handprints and signatures in cement of dozens of notable Detroiters, including Thomas Hearns, Sam Raimi, Elmore Leonard, Juan Atkins, Dave Bind, Alice Cooper, and Al Kaline.

5401 Woodward Ave., www.detroithistorical.org, (313) 833-1805.

» Detroit Institute of Arts - One of the finest art museums in the country, the DIA is an essential stop not only for art lovers but for any visitor to the city. Its encyclopedic collection, consisting of more than 65,000 works, includes art from around the world and from prehistory to today. The breadth and quality of their collection—on view in more than 100 galleries—is what sets it apart, and there is an abundance of extraordinary work in every collection, from Ancient Egyptian to Contemporary. Of particular note:

- The astonishing, 27-panel Detroit Industry fresco cycle by Diego Rivera, painted between 1932 and 1933. Commissioned by Edsel Ford and museum Director William Valentiner, Rivera considered these frescoes to be his best work.

- Large-scale outdoor works by notable artists, including August Rodin's The Thinker, Alexander Calder's Jeune Fille et sa Suite, and a 30-ton, 27-foot tall geometric 1961 Tony Smith sculpture, Gracehoper.

- The DIA's African art collection (which is one of the finest in the country) including works from nearly 100 cultures. A highlight is a masterpiece 19th century Kongo Nail Figure sculpture.

- The American galleries in general, and specifically John Singleton Copley's Watson and the Shark, Frederic Edwin Church's Cotopaxi, James Abbott McNeill Whistler's Nocturne in Black and Gold: The Falling Rocket, John Singer Sargent's Mosquito Nets, and John Sloan's McSorley's Bar.

- The colorful brick Dragon from the Ishtar Gate at Babylon (604–562 B.C.E.).

- The Asian galleries including the popular Reeds and Cranes screens by Suzuki Kiitsu.

- An incredible 15th century Qur'an written on colored Chinese papers.

- Exquisite Native American textiles and beadwork.

- Small but popular galleries exhibiting Egyptian mummies and artifacts.

- The awe-inspiring Great Hall off of the Woodward entrance, lined with suits of armor.

- The European art collection, which is one of the largest and most distinguished in the country, was founded with a gift of 100 Old Master paintings from newspaper magnate James Scripps in 1889, and features a broad range of media from across the continent spanning periods from Ancient Greece to modern works from first half of the 20th century. Notable artists include Pieter Bruegel the Elder, Giovanni Bellini, Titian, Rembrandt van Rijn, Andrea and Luca Della Robbia, Edgar Degas, Paul Cézanne, Georges Seurat, Caravaggio, Peter Paul Rubens, Auguste Rodin, Vincent Van Gogh, Pablo Picasso, Henri Matisse, and many, many others. The German Expressionist collection is one of the museum's strengths, and the DIA was the first American museum to collect a painting by Van Gogh—Self-Portrait with Straw Hat, from 1887.

- The Department of Prints and Graphics is one of the museum's most diverse collections, with about 35,000 prints, drawings, photographs, watercolors, posters and artists' books from the 16th century to the present including studies by Michelangelo for the Sistine Chapel and prints by Albrecht Durer.

- The museum's GM Center for African American Art was one of the first curatorial departments dedicated to African-American art at any museum. Established in 2000, highlights of the collection include works by Benny Andrews, Romare Bearden, Jacob Lawrence, Martin Puryear, Lorna Simpson, and Carrie Mae Weems.

- The James Pearson Duffy Department of Contemporary Art collection, which spans the period from the mid-20th century to the present day, including notable works by Willem de Kooning, Donald Judd, Andy Warhol, Eva Hesse, Alberto Giacometti, Claes Oldenburg, Judy Pfaff, Francis Bacon, and many others including numerous younger contemporary artists.

Founded in 1885, the DIA moved to its current location 1927, an incredible, stately Beaux-Arts building designed by Paul Cret. Two wings were added in the 1960s and 1970s, and a major renovation and expansion was completed in 2007 making the museum its current 658,000 square feet. The DIA hosts crowd-pleasing special exhibitions, regular Friday night music performances that are free with admission, and a variety of special events, including free art-making workshops every Friday, Saturday, and Sunday and lectures by important contemporary artists, designers, and critics. It also houses the **Detroit Film Theatre** (see separate entry), an elegant cafeteria, a great gift shop, a 380-seat lecture hall, a coffee shop housed in an astounding formerly open-air courtyard, a state-of-the-art conservation laboratory, and a research library holding a quarter million volumes. In 2012, three Southeastern Michigan counties (Wayne, Oakland, and Macomb) came together to pass a millage to support the museum, in a reassuring show of regional support for this incredible cultural jewel. As a result, residents of these counties have free unlimited general museum admission and access to expanded programs. If you happen not to be an art lover already, the DIA is the place to become one—the information-rich interpretive displays don't assume that every viewer is an expert, and curators and educators take time to contextualize the work for a broad audience. *5300 Woodward Ave., www.dia.org, (313) 833-7900.*

» Detroit Main Library - This treasure-trove is the anchor of the massive 4.2 million-volume Detroit Public Library system, which, after the University of Michigan's collection, is the second largest in Michigan. Within the walls of the building—completed in 1921 and designed by US Supreme Court architect Cass Gilbert—the library's vast collection includes books, vinyl records, and contemporary media. Of special interest are:

- The massive Burton Historical Collection of Detroit historical documents, which is a boundless and essential resource for genealogists and historians where visitors can peruse and touch authentic maps, photographs, records, and histories from the past 300 years.

- The Ernie Harwell Collection, seeded by a donation from the legendary sportscaster in 1966, consists of books, team annuals, media guides, programs, scorecards, baseball cards, clippings, photographs, recordings, and artifacts from the city's rich sports history.

- The E. Azalia Hackley Collection of African Americans in the Performing Arts, which opened in 1943, includes books, manuscripts, and historic documents, with dance, blues, jazz, soul, and electronic music well represented, documents from Motown Records are a special highlight.

- The Rare Book Collection, which opened in 1948, includes a Babylonian tablet, a Gutenberg Bible, original manuscripts to the Little House on the Prairie, Tom Sawyer, and Huckleberry Finn, an irreplaceable facsimile copy of Handel's original Messiah score (complete with cross-outs and droplets of perspiration), as well as thousands of other priceless first editions and other printed artifacts.

- The media libraries which, in addition to sizeable CD and DVD offerings, still lend from their incredible library of vinyl records.

- A Microfilm library of historic American newspapers, including the Detroit Free Press, Detroit News, and New York Times dating back to 1873—as well as digital access to even older materials.

201 Woodward Ave., www.detroit.lib.mi.us/branch/main, (313) 481-1300.

Elaine L. Jacob Gallery - This beautiful, bi-level gallery on the campus of Wayne State University presents work by contemporary regional, national, and international artists across media. It opened in 1997 as part of a mid-1990s addition to **Old Main**, the 1897 architectural symbol of the university. Its clean design, elegant spiral staircase, and abundant light provided by a dramatic 20-foot by 40-foot wall of windows make it an exquisite space in which to encounter a variety of exceptional work. *480 W. Hancock St., www.art.wayne.edu/jacob_gallery.php, (313) 993-7813.*

Gordon L. Grosscup Museum of Anthropology - Named for famed Wayne State University archaeologist Gordon Grosscup, The Grosscup museum is a small, well-curated 1,500-square-foot museum featuring an array of permanent and travelling exhibits. Although it offers exhibits on a range of topics—from Congolese fetish figures to Anishnabeg artifacts—some of its most compelling installations draw from Wayne State's long work performing archaeological digs at major downtown development sites. The artifacts extracted from sites such as Kennedy Square, 150 West Jefferson, the Hotel Pontchartrain, and the Renaissance Center tell fascinating stories about Detroit's earliest residents and contemporary development projects. The incredibly friendly and knowledgeable staff can help you use the impressive research equipment, including binocular and polarizing microscopes, thin-sectioning equipment, and a kiln. *4841 Cass Ave., 1st floor Old Main, www.clas.wayne.edu/anthromuseum, (313) 577-2598.*

» G. R. N'Namdi Gallery - The G. R. N'Namdi Gallery is the focus of the spectacular N'Namdi Center for Contemporary Art, housed in a vast 16,000-square-foot facility punctuated by a cobalt blue facade. Prominent local collector George N'Namdi founded the gallery in Harmonie Park in 1981, and after several moves, found a home in this renovated former auto garage in 2010, as a cultural anchor of the recently resurrected historic Sugar Hill Arts District. The interior, with its soaring open ceilings and warm reclaimed wooden floors, houses four exhibition spaces as well as a performance space called the Black Box. Originally intended to showcase N'Namdi's extensive collection of African-American art (including works by the likes of Benny Andrews, Romare Bearden, Chakaia Booker, Jacob Lawrence, and Hughie Lee-Smith), the gallery's focus has broadened to include an exciting exhibition schedule of work in a range of styles and media by local, national, and international artists. *52 E. Forest Ave., www.nnamdicenter.org, (313) 831-8700.*

Hellenic Museum of Michigan - A fledgling institution celebrating Greeks and their contribution to Detroit, the Hellenic Museum of Michigan opened its doors for preview events in 2010. While the nonprofit organization—which is housed in the exquisite historic Sherer Mansion (notably the birthplace of the gel capsule)—is still growing its scope, it aspires to be a "mouseion"—a "house of muses"—where visitors can learn about Hellenic culture through exhibitions, workshops, lectures, and cultural events. Currently, the museum exhibits a selection of ephemera from Greece and the golden age of Greek Detroit and holds a smattering of regular events, including a series of film screenings and social hours. Look for event listings on their web and Facebook pages. *67 E. Kirby St., www.hellenicmi.org, (313) 871-4100.*

Josephine F. Ford Sculpture Garden - Built in 2005 in a collaboration between Cultural Center behemoths the DIA and CCS with funds from Josephine Ford (granddaughter of Henry), this majestic sculpture garden is the only one of its kind in the city. Stop here to take a break or have a picnic lunch while basking in the presence of nine large-scale jaw-dropping works from the DIA's collection including pieces from 20th-century art-world heavy-hitters Richard Serra, Beverly Pepper, and Alexander Calder. In addition to the art, the two-acre garden features an elliptical walkway that connects CCS buildings, benches along the walk, and a variety of trees and plantings. Open to the public 24 hours a day. *John R. St. and E. Kirby St.*

» Michigan Science Center - The Michigan née Detroit Science Center has existed to provide youthful and inquisitive minds a venue to engage and explore scientific concepts since opening in 1970. Now the 10th largest science museum in the country, the original storefront science center has been expanded repeatedly over the years, becoming a polished and modern facility that provides hundreds of hands-on exhibits ideal for families, groups, or simply the curious. The science center boasts the largest movie screen in Michigan and a domed IMAX, in addition to a planetarium, a theater for examining electromagnetism at play, and rotating exhibits. Science education can be stereotyped for being too dry or abstract—but the Science Center's method of using colorful, stimulating, and educational activities guarantees this won't be a problem. The Michigan Science Center has been on a hiatus, and was not open at the time of publication of this guide, but is expected to be open for

regular hours in 2013. *5020 John R. St.,*
www.michigansciencecenter.net, (313) 577-8400.

» Museum of Contemporary Art Detroit - Located in the Sugar Hill
Arts District, The Museum of Contemporary Art Detroit presents
art at the forefront of contemporary culture. The Museum opened
its doors in late 2006 and has featured work by internationally
renowned contemporary artists like Barry McGee, Kara Walker, Alex
Melamid, Martin Creed, Yona Friedman, Hans Schabus, Mike Kelley,
and Fischli/Weiss along with local favorites like Design 99, Ben Hall,
and Gordon Newton. The raw and industrial 22,000-square-foot
former auto dealership transforms every three months to showcase
a new temporary exhibition. Each exhibition is accompanied by a
series of public programs that include musical performances, films,
readings, lectures, creative and family workshops, gallery tours,
and sometimes raucous dance parties. The Museum also houses the
MOCAD Store, which features art and design books, art objects and
other hard-to-find goods. Except for openings and special events,
admission is free. Guided tours take place on Wednesdays at 1pm and
Saturdays at 1pm and 4pm. *4454 Woodward Ave.,*
www.mocadetroit.org, (313) 832-6622.

» Re:View Contemporary Gallery - One of the few galleries in
Detroit proper that actively represents local artists (in addition to
providing them space), Re:View Contemporary works hard to exhibit
great work, connect it to an interested public, and sell it at affordable
rates. Under founder and director Simone DeSousa, Re:View has a
mission to make art accessible and personally meaningful to metro-
Detroiters. The gallery space usually houses work by one or two
artists at a time (including the occasional performance piece) and is
adjacent to a design store where you can see and purchase work by
all 15 represented artists, including some of Detroit's best-known
talents. *444 W. Willis St., www.reviewcontemporary.com,*
(313) 833-9000.

Scarab Club - Founded in 1907 by a group of artists, the venerable Scarab Club built this Italian Renaissance building in 1928 to serve as its clubhouse. The interior features exquisite tile work from Pewabic Pottery, warm woodwork, a bright gallery space, and a charming outdoor brick-walled garden. Walk upstairs to visit the six gorgeous artist studios and the cozy upstairs lounge with ceiling beams signed by acclaimed artists who have visited, including Diego Rivera, Marcel Duchamp, Norman Rockwell, Marshall Fredericks, and John Sinclair. In the club's early years, its annual costume balls were the most important social occasion in the city—Life magazine even published a two-page spread of photos of the 1937 "Scarabean Cruise" ball. Today, the club maintains its identity as a lively club for working artists with a full exhibition schedule and classes, workshops, and events for members and the public. The space is available for private events. *217 Farnsworth St., www.scarabclub.org, (313) 831-1250.*

Sugar Hill Clay - Opened in 2011 by Ernie Zachary and Diane Van Buren, two of the visionary developers behind the resurgent Sugar Hill Arts District—and many of the individual development projects that have formed the district—Sugar Hill Clay is a full-service ceramic studio and classroom space on the Garden Level of 71 Garfield. With five instructors on staff, the community-oriented space offers assisted open-studio time and a wide range of classes and workshops for children and adults, including courses in foundational skills, hand building, vessels, and wheel throwing. For the tepidly curious, the $30 one-night walk-in classes can be an opportunity to explore the medium. Sugar Hill Clay also offers private studio rental and a sales gallery in adjacent SocraTea that features work by the instructors, some of whom are also affiliated with the legendary Pewabic Pottery (see separate entry). *71 Garfield St., www.sugarhillclay.com.*

Walter P. Reuther Library - Located on the Wayne State University campus, the Walter P. Reuther Library is a contemporary four-story concrete and glass building that has the distinction of being North America's largest archive dedicated to labor and urban affairs. With a mission "to collect, preserve and provide access to the documentary and visual heritage of the American labor movement," the library boasts more than 2000 distinct collections related to labor, with topics ranging from the history of mainstream organizing, to minorities in the labor movement, to radical splinter initiatives. In addition, the library also contains healthy archives of historical information related to the city of Detroit, social welfare, health care, politics, civil rights, women's rights, Detroit's regional social communities, and Wayne State University's history and development. In recent years, the institution has made efforts to increase accessibility through digitization of documents and artifacts, some of which date to the 1800s. Generally, an appointment is needed for access to the archives. *5401 Cass Ave., www.reuther.wayne.edu, (313) 577-4024.*

Wayne State University Art Department Gallery - Since 1956, Wayne State University has featured artwork by prominent Michigan artists and WSU students and faculty in this gallery, where tall windows stretch floor to ceiling along one long side of the space creating a light-filled clean, white setting that is perfect to showcase the work. Highlights of the annual exhibition schedule are the WSU Undergraduate, MFA thesis, and faculty exhibitions. Since this gallery caters to students, it is closed on weekends and has more limited summer hours—check the website before going. *5400 Gullen Mall, www.art.wayne.edu/communityarts_gallery.php, (313) 993-7813.*

Wayne State University Planetarium - A longtime favorite among children, stargazers, and guidebook writers alike, the Wayne State University Planetarium is a large, state of the art digital projection facility. This 59-seat planetarium hosts weekly 90-minute events on Friday nights. While every event includes interactive demonstrations and current night sky presentations, all conclude with one of its many full dome films, from the scientific documentary Black Hole: The Other Side of Infinity, to the children's animated adventure video Zula Patrol: Down to Earth. To ensure a seat, planetarium-hounds typically come 15–20 minutes early. Visit their website for schedules. *4841 Cass Ave., www.planetarium.wayne.edu, Room 0209, (313) 577-2107.*

Work: Detroit - A companion gallery to Work: Ann Arbor, Work: Detroit is an extension of the University of Michigan's School of Art & Design. Intended to foster connections between U-M and the city of Detroit, the gallery is located inside U-M's Detroit Center at Orchestra Place. It's particularly notable for exhibiting art and design work by a remarkable range of makers and thinkers, from Detroit public school kids to U-M students and faculty to local artists and internationally known designers. *3663 Woodward Ave., www.art-design.umich.edu/exhibitions/work_detroit, (313) 593-0940.*

ENTERTAINMENT & RECREATION

Be Nice Yoga - With classes seven days a week in its convenient Midtown location, Be Nice Yoga makes it easy to unwind, de-stress, and re-energize all over again. The location's certified instructors are patient and attentive, providing a personalized, pressure-free environment for all students. Classes include slower-paced sessions such as the Slow Flow class, and Vinyasa classes of a sweatier variety. Scheduling and payment are just as flexible as the yoga instructors themselves: visitors and new students can try Be Nice free for a week, with the option of buying a discounted two month membership afterwards. Classes are held in a gorgeous, soothing space, featuring natural wood flooring, warm colors, and beautiful natural light. *4100 Woodward Ave., www.yogaindetroit.com, (313) 544-9787.*

Bill's Recreation - The last of an old breed, Bill's is strictly a pool hall—there's no alcohol or gambling, just pool played by a contingent of a few dozen regulars, mostly older men who come to play specialty skill games like bank or one-pocket for a modest hourly rate. Built in 1921, the hall itself is a den of staid utility. The lamps are low-slung fluorescent tubes, small black chalkboards used to keep score are tacked to the building's columns, old strands of beads used to score straight pool are slung over tables, and the solid wood tables—estimated to be more than 60 years old—are set with wood racks. The hall was used as a filming location for the recent movie Sparkle, which paid for all the tables to be resurfaced. Newcomers are welcome but should arrive with the necessary chops to keep up. Bottled G-rated drinks and snacks available. *3525 3rd St., (313) 833-4238.*

Bonstelle Theater - One of two landmark theaters owned by Wayne State University featuring student actors, the Bonstelle is housed in a century-old Beaux-Arts neoclassical building that emulates the Pantheon. Originally the Temple Beth-El Synagogue, the theater was designed by Albert Kahn and C. Howard Crane and completed in 1902. Unfortunately, the Bonstelle had to shed its front columns when Woodward was expanded in the 1930s, but the sizable auditorium, with its ample apron, is still striking and comfortably seats 1,200 patrons for its regular live performances and Broadway-style plays. The players at Bonstelle—WSU undergraduates—perform dramas, comedies, musicals, and show pieces, with full-run shows running four times per year. *3424 Woodward Ave., www.bonstelle.com, (313) 577-2960.*

Cass City Cinema - Out of the ashes of the beloved Burton Theater (now reborn as the Corktown Cinema, see separate entry), the Cass City Cinema opened in 2011, and offers an eclectic mix of recent major Hollywood releases on delay, independent and art-house movies, vintage favorites, and movies that feature Detroit or Michigan prominently. Cass City Cinema, built in a former public elementary school, is comfortable, and committed to providing a great viewing experience. The theater seats 130, and shows films twice a day Thursday through Saturday. Seats for the upstairs theater are from the Fillmore Theater, and its chandeliers are authentic Catholic church heirlooms. Cass City Cinema uses both 35mm professional analog projectors and new digital projectors for its movies, and all audio is Dolby 5.1 8-channel surround. Admission, snacks, and drinks are priced to sell. *3420 Cass Ave., www.casscitycinema.com, (313) 281-8301.*

Detroit City Football Club - Get ready for celebratory smoke bombs, brilliant chants, dedicated fans, intense rivalries, a jean-short cannon (catch the shorts and win free refreshments), and riveting soccer. With a name honoring the city's French heritage, Le Rouge is Detroit's beloved National Premier Soccer League soccer team. On game days, Cass Tech High School field—where games are held—has a friendly, electric atmosphere that brings out the hooligan in all of us. By mid-match, you'll know all the chants, including our favorite, "Allez Allez! Allez Allo! Detroit City, we love you so!" Although all the games are fun to watch, the vuvuzelas are a little louder, and the flags wave a little faster during games against Midwest Division arch rivals FC Buffalo and AFC Cleveland. Tickets are always available at the door. Come hungry—the taco truck concessions are top notch. *2501 2nd Ave., www.detcityfc.com.*

Detroit Derby Girls - Roller derby is a competitive, full-contact extravaganza played on a flat track in which each team of five roller skaters attempts to help their offensive player, or "jammer," lap members of the opposing team by any means necessary. The Detroit Derby Girls (DDG) first introduced the Motor City to the sport in 2005. Comprised of five all-female home teams—with names like the Detroit Pistoffs and the Grand Prix Madonnas—that regularly battle one another, the DDG also fields three All-Star teams that take on challengers nationwide. DDG bouts are bound to please, with halftime rock bands, glammed-out referees, and punk cheerleaders ensuring that every outing is a spectacle. Don't be intimidated by the brawling lasses. Though they have pseudonyms like VeroniKILL (#187), Rocky Brawlboa (#I-V), and Princess Die (#4:20), they come out and sign autographs after games. The regular season runs from November to June, with most home games at the Detroit Masonic Temple. *www.detroitderbygirls.com.*

» Detroit Film Theatre - Attached to the Detroit Institute of Arts, the Detroit Film Theatre is where local cinephiles go to see movies they aren't likely to find anywhere else in metro-Detroit. Specializing in art films, documentaries, and international and classic cinema, the DFT is also known for its outstanding special programs, including live film accompaniment, lectures by noted filmmakers, and themed series. (Recurring programs of note include Academy Award–nominated short films, an animation showcase, HD opera broadcasts, and annual performances by silent film accompanists The Alloy Orchestra.) Every DFT season is a carefully curated treasure trove of new and classic cinema that brings the wide world of film art to Detroit. And the grand 1927 theatre itself, with its resplendent architectural detail, is nothing to sneeze at; in the age of the multiplex, it remains a true movie palace. Before screenings, enjoy a snack and a glass of wine in the second-floor Crystal Gallery Cafe. *5200 Woodward Ave., www.dia.org/dft, (313) 833-7900.*

Detroit Masonic Temple - As the largest Masonic Temple in the world, this Neo-Gothic limestone giant is a sight to behold. Designed by renowned architect George D. Mason, the cornerstone of the building was laid in 1922—with the same trowel used by George Washington to ceremonially start construction of the United States Capitol—but the gargantuan structure was not completed until 1926. The icon, which towers over the lower Cass Corridor, is ornately decorated inside and out, with beautifully carved marble, sweeping staircases, and floor upon floor of tile mosaics, making the building one of the most opulent in Detroit. The temple is a labyrinth of hallways, corridors, and passageways, and boasts 1,000 rooms, including numerous ballrooms, sanctuaries, theaters, a Cathedral, a drill hall, and a signature seven-story auditorium. Since the day it opened, the Masonic Temple has hosted a variety of events, shows, and organizations, a tradition which continues today, as visitors come weekly for fairs, elaborate parties, a wide-range of concerts, theatrical performances, Broadway shows, and the Detroit Derby Girls (see separate entry) who are based out of the venue. Come for an event or a tour and try not to get lost. It's purported that the temple is haunted! *500 Temple St., www.themasonic.com, (313) 832-7100.*

» Detroit Symphony Orchestra / Orchestra Hall / Max M. Fisher Music Center - A major anchor of Midtown, the 2,014 seat historic Orchestra Hall, designed by C. Howard Crane in 1919, and famous for its perfect acoustics, is home to the world-renowned Detroit Symphony Orchestra (DSO). Though the Symphony was founded in 1914, it was during the 1920s, on the back of the booming automobile industry that the DSO became one of the most prominent orchestras in the country, performing with spectacular guest artists such as Enrico Caruso, Igor Stravinsky, Richard Strauss, Marian Anderson, Sergei Rachmaninoff, Isadora Duncan, Anna Pavlova, Jascha Heifetz, Pablo Casals, and others. Due to the strain of the Great Depression, the symphony was forced to leave its home in 1939, and though the Hall enjoyed a stint as a jazz venue called the Paradise Theater—hosting greats such as Count Basie, Billie Holliday, Ella Fitzgerald, and Duke Ellington—and then became a church, it was scheduled for demolition in 1970. However, after a dedicated preservation effort, the Hall was saved and was beautifully restored and reoccupied by the symphony in 1989. In 2003, a massive expansion was undertaken and the facility became known as the new Max M. Fisher Music Center. Today, under Music Director Leonard Slatkin, the DSO enjoys a reputation as one of the top ten orchestras in the United States. Regular offerings include a variety of concert programs for every age and taste, including classical, jazz, movie music, big band, seasonal performances, and more. *3711 Woodward Ave., www.detroitsymphony.com, (313) 576-5111.*

» Garden Bowl - A part of the Majestic Theater Complex and in business since 1913, the Garden Bowl is America's oldest continually operating bowling alley. Though it offers a full bar, it boasts a family-friendly environment during the day and is perfect for birthday parties or field trips. At night, the black lights come on, and the illuminated lanes lend a spacey, campy feel and the party starts. A variety of DJs keep the atmosphere upbeat, spinning anything from classic R&B to lo-fi punk rock. In addition to the regular revelry, the alley occasionally hosts concerts, with a stage suspended above the lanes, so one can quite literally "rock 'n' bowl." *4120 Woodward Ave., www.majesticdetroit.com, (313) 833-9700.*

Hilberry Theater - The repertory theater for Wayne State University's competitive graduate theater program, Hilberry productions leave crowds mesmerized and coming back. The theater is based out of the former First Church of Christ Scientist building which was completed in 1917 in a neoclassical style with eight ionic columns set off by compound ramps greeting visitors from its Cass Avenue entrance. The Hilberry became Wayne's graduate repertory theater in 1964, after the building was remodeled to feature an intimate, 500-seat theater with an oval, open stage. The season offers six to nine shows per year featuring canonical and contemporary comedies and dramas by MA and MFA students. Recently added to the basement is the Studio Theatre, an intimate 100-seat space for experimental works. *4743 Cass Ave., www.hilberry.com, (313) 577-2972.*

Magic Stick / Alley Deck - Located above the Garden Bowl, the Magic Stick, a vital part of the Majestic Theater Complex, served as a backbone to Detroit's explosive garage rock revival in the late 1990s and early 2000s. Bands such as The White Stripes, The Von Bondies, The Detroit Cobras, The Dirtbombs, and more played here before touring the rest of the world, fuzz pedals and cigarettes in tow. Nowadays, the venue is consistently booked with local bands and national-touring acts, primarily of the indie rock variety, but with sizeable proportions of hip-hop, reggae, metal, and electronic as well. With a standing capacity of about 250, the venue is spacious enough to relax by the bar and get a beer, yet intimate enough to catch the sweat dripping off of whatever sultry lead singer you're eying from the front row. Open seasonally, the Alley Deck is a second-story outdoor bar and patio located just outside of the Magic Stick, which subs in for an almost tropical getaway, complete with torch lighting and tiki decorations. Every Sunday morning, weather permitting, the Alley Deck is home to Bloody Marys, mimosas, cinnamon rolls, and other goodies guaranteed to stop a hangover—or at least delay its onset. *4120 Woodward Ave., www.majesticdetroit.com, (313) 833-9700.*

Majestic Theater - At the time it was originally built in 1915, it was the largest movie-only theatre in the world. Undergoing numerous transformations through the years, including the addition of a glorious Art Deco façade prompted by the expansion of Woodward Avenue and requisite demolition of the original, historic frontage in the 1930s, the space became a live music venue in 1987. With the largest capacity of any venue in the Majestic Theater Complex, the venue plays host to everything from successful independent acts like Yo La Tengo, to world beat and hip hop groups, and Juggalo gatherings. Note that the venue offers no seating aside from the bar, so plan to stand. *4120 Woodward Ave., www.majesticdetroit.com, (313) 833-9700.*

Midtown Yoga Shelter - Edgier than most yoga outlets (class names like "Xflowsion" speak volumes), the Midtown Yoga Shelter provides both traditional yoga classes, as well as some cardio-infused hybrids. Beginners might want to start out with the Slow Flow or Foundations classes, which focus on strength and breathing. For the more adventurous, there's the heated Yoga Rocks class, Yin Yoga, which incorporates holding poses for extended lengths of time, and the aforementioned Xflowsion, which integrates Yoga, Martial Arts, and Dance. The background music played during each 45- to 75-minute session varies by instructor and class type. Expect anything from top 40 to rock to ambient to silence. Thoughtfully designed by local firm M1/DTW, the gorgeous, contemporary space emphasizes the clean lines of stacked plywood fixtures and bamboo flooring, as well as warm hues and natural materials to create an incredibly alluring and soothing studio. Drop-in rates available. *69 W. Forest Ave., www.yogashelter.com, (313) 831-9642.*

The Trumbullplex - Established in 1993, the Trumbullplex is an anarchist collective that sprawls over two slightly disheveled turn-of-the-century Victorian mansions, an enviable vegetable garden, a chicken coop, a campfire pit, a large indoor performance venue, and a huge swath of green space. While the complex is not public per se, as it is home to at least a dozen residents at any given time, members of the collective are very welcoming to passersby, especially like-minded allies of activism. The performance venue between the Victorian homes is a popular punk, metal, and folk venue for both local and indie touring acts. Additionally, among other offerings, the Tplex hosts parties, potlucks, and public open hours in its expansive zine library. An up-to-date schedule of events and hours can be found on the Trumbullplex website. *4210 Trumbull St., www.trumbullplex.org.*

Wayne State Warriors Football - Rah-Rah-Rah-Cis-Boom-Bah! Since 1918, the Warriors, who until 1999 were known as the fighting Tartars, have graced the gridiron at Wayne State University. Though the NCAA Division II team has historically been an underdog, they've been on fire in recent years, coming off of a competitive championship run in 2011 and bolstering its respectable 91-year-record of 317-444-29. As an additional incentive to spectate, the team plays with heart and determination that is frequently missing from pro ball. While the team's home, Tom Adams Field, only seats 6,000, tickets are a bargain at just $8. Be sure to dress warmly in colder months. *5101 John C. Lodge Expy., www.wsuathletics.com, (313) 577-0241.*

SITES

Brush Park - In 1825, the completion of the Erie Canal enabled immigrants and industry to travel to Detroit by ship, spurring the growth of new development and opportunity in the city. In the early 1850s, enterprising developer Edmund Brush (son of the city's second Mayor, Elijah Brush) began developing his grandparents' ribbon farm into a stately neighborhood for the city's burgeoning contingent of wealthy residents. His development grew to encompass 300 two- and three-story homes across 24 blocks, and, to this day, boasts magnificent brick homes built in the Second Empire, Gilded Age, Queen Anne, French Renaissance Revival, Romanesque, and other Victorian styles. The structures showcase the skill and craftsmanship of the period, with mansard slate roofs, Romanesque columns, and cornices with intricate dentition. The streets in the area still carry the names he chose, including Adelaide for his mother, Alfred for his brother, Edmund for himself, Brush for his family, and Winder for his friend Colonel John Winder. However, a century after the neighborhood's meteoric rise, it began a long descent, with population loss and demolition taking heavy tolls. Although some blocks remain relatively intact, many are sparse—with just two or three remaining structures—only hinting at their former grandeur. The Woodward East Historic District—which encompasses the earliest, grandest, and most central portions of the neighborhood— has been hit the hardest. Although many stunning mansions have been lovingly restored, just as many remain dilapidated and sit in a pastoral setting alongside fields of tall weeds—a jarring juxtaposition that creates a beautiful, stirring landscape. The neighborhood's simultaneous deterioration and revivification has been a focal point for works by renowned urban observer Camilo Jose Vergara. *Bounded by Mack Ave., Woodward Ave., Beaubien St., and Fisher Fwy.*

Cathedral Church of St. Paul - This reserved architectural gem is one of the first examples of the Late Gothic Revival style perfected by architect Ralph Adams Cram, who designed the century-old building. Though the church itself was completed in 1908, the parish dates to 1824, making it the oldest Episcopalian parish in the state. For the design of the building, Cram forewent contemporary steel

framework, favoring medieval construction techniques, so that the limestone structure is supported only by its own weight, and is an authentic representation of the period it emulates. The highlights of the relatively understated exterior of the cathedral are the towering pillars, pointed arches, and vermillion doors, while the interior is more ostentatious, with wide expanses of richly colored stained glass artwork done in 13th and 14th century English styles—some of which were imported from a medieval Spanish cathedral, distinct Pewabic tile floor inlays, and an intricate wood reredos which is representative of the elaborate woodwork throughout the cathedral. The building's impregnable stone construction creates the impression of a cloistered fortress for worshippers, but the parish of St. Paul— the home to the Episcopalian diocese of Michigan—is extremely active in community outreach. *4800 Woodward Ave., www.detroitcathedral.org, (313) 831-5000.*

East Ferry Street Historic District - Historically an upper class Jewish and then black enclave, the neighborhood, comprised of East Ferry Street between Woodward Avenue and Brush Street is a national historic district, primarily featuring homes in the Late Victorian, Romanesque, and Queen Anne styles. The neighborhood was established when local farmer D.M. Ferry—founder of what is now the Ferry-Morse Seed Company—began to subdivide his farm in the 1880s. Though the neighborhood was built out with elaborate residences by the 1890s, it became a destination for ascendant Jewish professionals before the First World War. In the 1920s, a second demographic shift took hold, and the neighborhood became an upper-class extension of the vibrant, primarily African-American, Paradise Valley neighborhood, as white-collar black families began to move into the mansions that comprise the area. Today, anchored by The Inn on Ferry Street and Wayne State University, the neighborhood is a stable—largely institutional—scenic destination for architecture aficionados. Though the East Ferry Historic District features an inspired array of stately homes from the end of the 19th century along the vernal stretch of closely-plotted residences, notable highlights include:

- **The Charles Lang Freer House:** A Queen Anne residence by architect Louis Kamper built of blue limestone. *71 E. Ferry St.*

- **The Col. Frank J. Hecker House:** A distinct, awe-inspiring, Chateauesque design with stone turrets. *5510 Woodward Ave.*

- **The Inn on Ferry Street:** A four-home complex comprised of a mix of stately, well preserved Victorian mansions. *84 E. Ferry St.*

- **The Lewis College of Business:** A Colonial Revival residence now the home of the Detroit Association of Women's Clubs. *5450 John R. St.*

- **Omega Psi Phi Fraternity:** A converted Romanesque Revival mansion. *235 East Ferry St.*

First Congregational Church - Originally located on the Detroit river when the parish was founded in 1844, First Congregational moved to its present location, a temple of impressive red limestone, in 1890. The building was designed in a mix of Romanesque and Byzantine styles by architect J. L. Faxon, featuring a campanile tower topped with an eight-foot green copper statue of archangel Uriel. The church has a sanctuary and chapel resplendently decorated with ornate woodwork gilded with quotes from scripture. Visitors are treated to rose windows, cruciform brass chandeliers, an imposing organ installed over its wood foyer, and a domed ceiling ornamented with hagiographic paintings of the four Gospelers. The church considers itself a living museum, and so is open to the public to view its architecture, examine exhibits about the history

and culture of the church, and visit the Underground Railroad Living Museum, a theatrical program of a tour and narrative storytelling about the underground railroad, including First Congregational's role in sheltering escaped slaves in the original church's basement while they awaited final transit to Windsor (charges apply, must be arranged in advance). *33 E. Forest Ave., www.friendsoffirst.com, (313) 831-4080.*

The Green Garage and Cass Farms Green Alley - Housed in a sustainably renovated, 12,000-square-foot former Model T showroom originally built in 1920, the Green Garage is many things: an incubator for environmentally conscious small businesses, a co-working community, a demonstration center for sustainable building design and operations in Detroit, and the home of a cutting-edge library committed to helping Detroiters live more sustainably. It's also a staggeringly beautiful place—expansive, soulful, and consummately designed. You can feel the history in the reclaimed and locally sourced materials, and see the future in the work that's done there every day. To learn more in person, pack a lunch and visit on any Friday at noon for a welcoming community meal and engaging conversation. Don't miss the **Cass Farms Green Alley** adjacent to the facility. Paved with permeable reclaimed materials and populated with native plants, the pedestrian walkway is an inspiring and inviting example of what public space can be. *4444 2nd Ave., www.greengaragedetroit.com, (313) 444-4054.*

Old Main of Wayne State University - A gargantuan icon of Midtown, Old Main—with its unmistakable clock tower, pitched roofs, and yellow bricks—is the most recognizable structure on Wayne State's campus. Originally Detroit's Central High School, the sprawling yellow brick building hosted 2,000 students when classes began in 1896, the building's inaugural year. In 1917, after four years of offering college level courses, the College of the City of Detroit began operating as a two-year college in the building. By 1925, the college, which eventually grew into Wayne State University, was the third largest in the state. Today, Old Main houses the College of Liberal Arts and Sciences as well as classes for students in the dance, visual arts, music, and geology programs. The building houses the William Grosscup Geology Museum, The Wayne State University Planetarium, and the Elaine L. Jacob Gallery, which are public, but have their own separate entries. *4841 Cass Ave.*

St. Josaphat Catholic Church - Constructed in the Victorian Romanesque style with Gothic and Baroque flourishes, St. Josaphat—established to accommodate Detroit's growing community of Polish immigrants—became the city's third Polish-speaking church in 1889. The exterior is comprised of red brick, carved sandstone, and a triad of steeples, sheltering an interior featuring Polish-style stained glass windows—produced in 1903 by Detroit Stained Glass—ornate religious statuary, and elaborate murals beneath a vaulted ceiling. The nave is spectacular, and illuminated by a galaxy of small lights, evidence of the historical fascination with the electric light bulb—a technology that was en vogue when the building was completed more than 100 years ago. Additionally, there are five decorative altars, as well as murals with liturgical paintings above the confessionals. For travelers on southbound I-75, the church is one of the city's most popular architectural curiosities, as the three spires of the landmark line up perfectly with the towers of Downtown's Renaissance Center. Traditional Tridentine Latin Mass is offered every Sunday morning. *691 E. Canfield St., www.historicstjosaphat.org, (313) 831-6659.*

West Canfield Historic District - A beautiful, stunningly preserved block of houses occupies Canfield Street, between Second and Third Avenues. In 1869, sisters Matilda Cass Ledyard and Mary Cass Canfield, daughters of Territorial Governor Lewis Cass, subdivided the block from their property and named Canfield Avenue after Mary Cass's late husband, Captain Augustus Canfield. The first homeowners of the neighborhood were prominent attorneys, architects, doctors, and dentists, and by the 1880s, the area became known as Piety Hill, owing to the alleged moral and social character of its inhabitants. The resulting, decadent two- and three-story residences followed between 1870 and 1890 and feature a variety of styles, including Gothic Revival, Italianate, Second Empire, and Queen Anne. To this day, the intricately preserved mansions offer sightseers slate shingles, metal cresting, and ornate wooden trims, painted in era-appropriate colors. The West Canfield Historic District became Detroit's first local historic district in 1970, and it was listed on the Natural Register of Historic Places in 1971. Any visitor to Midtown should consider a stroll along the one-block historic street, which affords sightseers a picture-perfect cobblestone road, Victorian-style streetlamps, and tall, shady trees to complement the beautiful homes. *Canfield St. between 3rd St. and 2nd Ave.*

Woodbridge - Thanks to a strong, active community, Woodbridge, which is known for block after block of historic homes, was relatively unscathed by Detroit's historical penchant for demolition and redevelopment in the area. The neighborhood, which features houses and duplexes in the Victorian, Queen Anne, Colonial Revival, and Georgian Revival styles, was named for Michigan's second governor, William Woodbridge, who owned much of the property on which the neighborhood sits today. Housing demand created by the advent of the automobile industry and active streetcar lines on Trumbull Street and Grand River Avenue positioned the neighborhood as an early white-collar bedroom community for downtown office workers, and the area exploded between 1900 and 1920. However, after World War II, the population and stability of Woodbridge began to decline, as a countrywide trend of suburban migration took hold. In a misguided response to the neighborhood's perceived instability, in the 1960s, the City of Detroit and Wayne State University began an aggressive "urban renewal" campaign and razed as much as one fifth of the neighborhood—mostly east of Trumbull—to make way for public housing and the expansion of the University. Fortunately, the dynamic neighborhood community responded with a formidable preservation effort, and the destructive attack was halted. Today, the Woodbridge area is a stable mix of families and students and boasts a strong sense of community and renewal. Neighborhood gardens have taken root in formerly vacant lots, and, recently, brightly hued art installations have popped up throughout the neighborhood. While nearly every home in the shady tree-lined neighborhood is stately, yet reserved, highlights include:

- **Northwood-Hunter House:** An inordinately elaborate French Renaissance mansion, most recently the Woodbridge Star Bed & Breakfast. *3985 Trumbull Ave.*

- **The Phoenix Group Building:** A sprawling, stunning mansion in the French Châteauesque and French Renaissance styles that served for a time as the Eighth Precinct Police Station. *4150 Grand River Ave.*

- **The Ty Cobb Duplex:** The modest historic home of legendary Detroit Tiger Tyrus Cobb from 1913 to 1915. *4115 Commonwealth St.*

The remaining historic portion of the neighborhood is bounded by I-94 to the north, Lincoln St. to the east, Grand River Ave. to the south, and Avery St. to the west.

Yamasaki Architecture on the WSU Campus - One of the 20th century's most prominent architects, in 1957, Minoru Yamasaki was hired by Wayne State University to develop a master plan that grew to include many of the features that define the campus today, including the streets closed to automotive traffic and the large internal courts and pathways. However, his greatest contributions to the campus were the four buildings that he designed for the university after he completed the plan. These gifts to the city's architectural landscape are small masterpieces that demonstrate Yamasaki's reserved brilliance while retaining an approachability not demonstrated in the skyscrapers he designed later in his career. Among them, our favorite is **The McGregor Memorial Conference Center,** which is arguably both the crown jewel of the campus and Yamasaki's most beautiful and intricate structure. Completed in 1958, the two-story building is constructed with travertine marble and Mankato stone and features a triangular glass motif that brilliantly weds Western modernism with Eastern traditionalism. Though the exterior is wrapped by a recently renovated reflecting pool and sunken sculpture garden, the interior atrium, with its soaring tessellated glass skylight, marble floors, and Mies van der Rohe furniture is the highlight of the structure. Steps away lies the four-story **College of Education Building** which, built in 1960, features narrow windows and a light pre-cast concrete exoskeleton that stylistically foreshadows Yamasaki's later work. Southeast of these buildings lies **Prentis Hall,** which was completed in 1964 and defies nature with a vertical, angular pre-cast concrete motif which appears to float above an airy glass first-story. Adjacent to Prentis Hall and designed to harmonize with it, is the **Helen L. DeRoy Auditorium.** Built concurrently with Prentis Hall, and connected by an underground tunnel, the auditorium is curvy, yet monolithic and windowless, with an empty reflecting pool that now serves as a moat and makes the building a fascinating oppositional complement to the architect's other nearby works. All of the buildings are generally open to curious—and courteous—visitors and are within a short walk from one another. *The McGregor Memorial Conference Center is located at 495 Ferry Mall, the College of Education Building at 5425 Gullen Mall, Prentis Hall at 5201 Cass Ave., and the Helen L. Deroy Auditorium behind it to the west at 5203 Cass Ave.*

POINTS OF INTEREST

Art Center Community Garden - Founded in 2010, this raised-bed community garden is managed by the University Cultural Center Association. Neighbors pay an annual fee to grow vegetables and plants in their own dedicated bed. *John R. St. and Palmer St.*

Automotive Mural - This 6-foot by 40-foot mural, originally finished in 1941 by artist William Gropper for placement in a Detroit post office that has since been demolished, is striking in its explicit references to Diego Rivera's "Detroit Industry" mural at the DIA. Whereas Rivera was concerned with the intersection of technology and life, Gropper's work seems to place emphasis on the power of labor. *Anthony Wayne Dr. and W. Palmer Ave.*

Brewster-Douglass Housing Projects - A name ascribed to four low- and high-rise public housing developments completed between 1942 and 1952 the Brewsters were a flagship urban renewal project. While there was great promise surrounding its development— Eleanor Roosevelt attended the groundbreaking in 1935—it is largely viewed as a failed measure of urban development. Abandoned since 2007, demolition was announced in 2012. Notable residents included all three founding members of the Supremes as well as actress Lily Tomlin. *2700 St. Antoine St.*

Brush Park Community Garden - Once occupied by regal residential structures, these vacant lots are now home to this well-kept raised-bed community garden. *John R. St. and Alfred St.*

Casey Kasem Home - The famous Top 40 host spent his early years in Detroit in this brick Midtown apartment building. *454 W. Alexandrine St.*

Charles Lindbergh Home - Though the original structure, a historic single-family home, is long gone, it was the birthplace of this legendary pilot and American folk hero. *1120 W. Forest Ave.*

Chase Scene from Beverly Hills Cop - The action-packed post–drug bust chase scene in the 1984 film Beverly Hills Cop—that starred Eddie Murphy as hardscrabble Detroit detective Axel Foley— incongruously skips around the city, including a romp through this intersection. *Henry St. and Park Ave.*

Former Translve Energies Site - Now the site of a strip mall, this location was the late 1960s headquarters for counterculture luminaries John Sinclair, the MC5, and other self-proclaimed "hippies." *4857 John C. Lodge Fwy.*

Fortune Records - This vacant lot was once home to Jack and Devora Brown's label that, in its run from 1946 to 1995, recorded artists ranging from John Lee Hooker and Nathaniel Mayer to doo-wop artist Nolan Strong and The Diablos. *3942 3rd St.*

Fourth Street Garden - A testament to the hard work of area residents, this lovely neighborhood community garden features raised-bed planters and brick-lined beds in whimsical shapes. *4055 4th St.*

Gold Dollar - Right in the heart of the Cass Corridor, this shuttered club was once the beating heart of late 1990s Detroit rock, helping to launch the White Stripes, among others, to stardom. *3129 Cass Ave.*

Hygienic Dress League Wheat Pastes – This series of wheat pastes—one of the most recent works by local artists Steve and Dorota Coy—continues the artists' exploration of the pervasiveness of marketing in American culture though their prolific promotion of the anonymous, mysterious, and ominous Hygienic Dress League brand. Look for their elaborate and intriguing wheat pastes, murals, and installations throughout the city. *70 W. Alexandrine St.*

Marquette, LaSalle, Cadillac, and Richard Sculptures - Originally made for display in Detroit's 1871 city hall, these sandstone sculptures depicting four of the city's most important French pioneers were saved from the wrecking ball that brought down the city hall building in 1961. The figures, sculpted by artist Julius Melchers in 1874, were moved to their current location in 1974. *Anthony Wayne Dr. and W. Warren Ave.*

Mike Wallace Home - While he was working for WXYZ radio in the early 1940s, the "60 Minutes" mainstay lived in this apartment building just south of Wayne State University. *4863 2nd Ave.*

North Cass Community Garden - Created in 2009, this community garden turned a blighted piece of land into a place where the residents of the Cass Corridor could try their hands at gardening in individual raised beds. *611 W. Willis St.*

Peck Park - This lovely little park tucked behind the College for Creative Studies features play sets for kids and often features outdoor movie screenings in the summer. Across the street, visitors will see "Patterns of Detroit," a multicolored glazed tile installation celebrating the area's diversity, created by artist Hubert Massey. *E. Kirby St. and Brush St.*

Robert Burns Sculpture - This George Lawson sculpture, dedicated in 1921 with help from Detroit's Burns Club, catches the young Scottish poet in a moment of seeming contemplation.
2nd Ave. and Temple St.

Scripps Park Sensory Garden - Inspired by the nearby Douglass Branch of the Detroit Public Library, equipped to serve blind and other physically impaired Detroiters, the garden located in this park is specially designed to excite all five senses of its visitors.
3717 Trumbull St.

Warrior Demonstration Garden and St. Andrew's Allotment Garden - Located on the campus of Wayne State University, these gardens are designed to let students get involved in the growing urban gardening movement in the city. The gardens' produce ends up in student meals, sold at the campus farmer's market, or is donated to charitable organizations. *656 W. Kirby St. and 5105 3rd St.*

Welcome to Woodbridge Mural - This huge colorful giraffe mural—created by Summer in the City—presides over the southern end of Woodbridge, a piece that gets a lot of views thanks to the city's slowest traffic light at the nearby intersection. *3530 Grand River Ave.*

Woodbridge Bikes Art Installation - Sponsored by local developer Larry John, this vibrant public art installation features sculptures of colorful, abstracted bicycles, and murals. *5086 Commonwealth St.*

Woodbridge Community Garden - Art projects, shows, and community meetings all find a common space here amidst heirloom vegetables, herb patches, and apple trees. Run by volunteers, the garden is maintained through regular weekly workdays and is a pleasant place to sit and enjoy some sunshine, to meet a friendly neighbor, or to get your hands dirty pulling weeds.
Merrick St. and Trumbull St.

CHAPTER 3
EASTERN MARKET

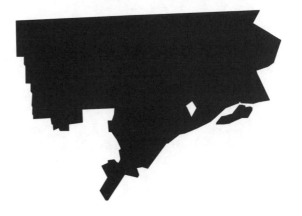

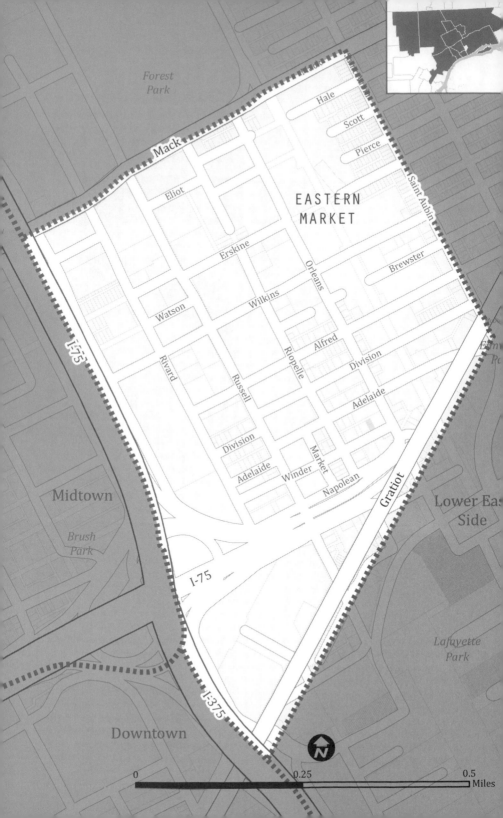

Forest
Park

Mack

Hale

Scott

Pierce

Eliot

EASTERN
MARKET

Saint Aubin

Erskine

Orleans

Brewster

Wilkins

Watson

I-75

Alfred

Rivard

Riopelle

Division

Russell

Adelaide

Division

Midtown

Adelaide

Market

Brush
Park

Adelaide

Winder

Napolean

Gratiot

Lower East
Side

I-75

Elm
Po

Lafayette
Park

I-375

Downtown

N

0   0.25   0.5
                              Miles

Come soak in the sights, sounds, smells, and tastes of the largest and oldest historic public market district in the United States, and enjoy the delicious bounty of farms from across Michigan, Ohio, and Ontario. A venerable Detroit landmark since 1891, Eastern Market attracts more than two million visitors each year to its lively, charming open-air markets.

Although geographically the smallest neighborhood in this guide, Eastern Market is a dense historic commercial district anchored by the market itself, which has been in continuous operation as an outdoor market space since 1850. Located about a mile northeast of the city's central business district, as defined for this book, the neighborhood is bounded by Mack Avenue to the north, St. Aubin Street to the east, Gratiot Avenue to the south, and I-75 (the Chrysler Freeway) to the west.

In the 1850s, Eastern Market was just one of three large-scale outdoor markets in the city, the others being Western Market on the site of Tiger Stadium in Corktown, and Central Market in Cadillac Square downtown. However, in 1891, the three markets were consolidated, and Eastern Market was designated as the region's primary public market area. In the following decades, Eastern Market grew substantially. During the 1920s, the public market area grew as sheds were added. In the late 1940s, the market cemented its position as the hub of the regional wholesale food distribution industry, as a substantial number of wholesalers and food processors moved into the area. The public market area was overseen by the city until 2006, when a public-private partnership was forged, and administration and development of the area was ceded to the Eastern Market Corporation. This newly formed organization has overseen substantial improvements of the market, including the restoration of the historic sheds, the addition of the Tuesday market day, the transition of the neighborhood into an active, mixed-use district, and the planned construction of new facilities.

While the outdoor farmers market is open on Tuesdays and Saturdays and hosts nearly 300 vendors and 45,000 visitors every weekend, its neighborhood is home to more than 100 permanent specialty wholesalers, retailers, and restaurants, which make it a vibrant destination all week. Dotted with quaint historic brick commercial buildings, Eastern Market is not only a destination for produce, poultry, livestock, spices, flowers, and other fresh products but is also one of Detroit's most active districts.

Please note that most businesses in Eastern Market are closed on Sundays and Mondays and some have more limited hours—be sure to call before visiting. On football Sundays, Lions fans take over the market to tailgate for $45 per car.

THE MARKET

The primary commercial and cultural anchor of its namesake neighborhood, the market spans five sheds across five city blocks and is home to more than 300 independent vendors and merchants who sell fresh fruit, vegetables, dairy, baked goods, fresh-cut flowers, cider, honey, jam, syrup, grass-fed meat, plants, prepared foods, and an eclectic mix of home goods. Open year round, the market's specialties follow the seasons from affordable flats of perennials in the spring, to fresh seasonal produce all summer long, and from Michigan apples and squash in the fall, to Christmas trees and wreaths in the winter. The Saturday markets are a vibrant urban experience, an authentic Detroit tradition, and a destination for shoppers looking for incredibly fresh produce at bargain prices. The months from July to October bring additional, smaller market days on Tuesdays.

First time visitors should come on Saturday to experience the widest array of vendors. Although the market is open from 7am to 4pm, the best selection is available in the morning. However, to sell out their stock, vendors gradually lower their prices in the afternoon. Depending on the length of their shopping list, veteran shoppers bring tote bags, wagons, or carts with them, as many vendors don't offer bags. Eastern Market is not credit card territory, so be sure to bring cash.

Most visitors begin their trip at the southernmost shed, Shed 2, which is located at the corner of Russell Street and Winder Street, and gradually work their way north, toward Shed 6, where goods become increasingly specialized. Enjoy the interstitial space between the sheds, where historic architecture, buskers, and the smell of barbecue offer a delightful complement to the commercial commotion of the sheds. Visit the Welcome Center at 1445 Adelaide, to get a map to plan your visit or to find an ATM.

In addition to the regular markets, Eastern Market is home to a number of annual and seasonal events. Our favorite events are Flower Day in May, the Harvest Festival in October, the Detroit Fall Beer Festival in October, and the monthly Summer Eastern Market Truck Stop food truck rallies. *www.detroiteasternmarket.com.*

BARS & RESTAURANTS

Al's Fish, Seafood & Chicken - One of Detroit's many "you buy, we fry" locations, Al's Fish Market stands apart from the rest because of its large selection of fresh fish, seafood and chicken and giant selection of spices and batters. To the left, shelves of bulk spices, rice, and condiments line up next to a mountain of cardboard boxes that are ready to be filled with large to-go fish orders. To the right, a long glass counter full of catfish, perch fillets, shrimp, prawns, and crab legs lines the wall. In the back, to-go cooks fry up battered shrimp, chicken, and fish in affordable lunch specials or by-the-pound prices. Just grab a number, grab a seat on a red vinyl chair, and watch your fish fry. *2925 Russell St., (313) 393-1722.*

Bert's Market Place - Anyone who has visited Eastern Market on a Saturday has probably been enticed by the smoky flavors wafting from Bert's outdoor metal barrel grill and the grooves emanating from the raucous karaoke patio party. While we recommend Bert's delicious barbecued ribs and chicken any Saturday, we also recommend getting a taste of slow-cooked soul food and cheap, strong drinks at Bert's Thursday jazz night. Every Thursday from 9pm to 12:30am, talented improvisational musicians, poets, and singers rock the house for less than a $5 cover charge. *2727 Russell St., (313) 567-2030.*

Cutter's Bar & Grille - Located on the periphery of the market, this neighborhood dive serves pub grub, including one of the freshest and most admired hamburgers in the city. If its eight-ounce "slider" isn't enough for you, consider upgrading to the 16-ounce version—as long as, hunger permitting, you don't rule out buying the two-pounder. For looks, Cutter's is a hole-in-the-wall, but it's always hopping, domestics are cheap, and cocktails are generous. Known as a destination after-work eatery and sippery, Cutter's may wind up getting some patrons to stay longer than they anticipated. Closed Sundays except for Lions games. *2638 Orleans St., www.cuttersdetroit.com, (313) 393-0960.*

Eastern Market Seafood Co. - Yes, the Eastern Market Seafood Co. specializes in seafood and slings a wide array of relatively inexpensive fresh and frozen seafood, from standard fare to delicacies like king crab legs, alligator, and the largest, mutant-size jumbo shrimp you've ever seen. However, the real attraction—especially on Saturdays, when it often draws a line out the door—is its three-sausage pita sandwich. Your choice of three sausage varieties (the options include everything from bratwurst to Cajun andouille) are diced and laid out over lettuce, tomato, and onion and then smothered in mustard, which makes the $3 sandwich a steal. *2456 Market St., (313) 567-8359.*

Farmer's Restaurant - Open at 5am on Saturdays for hungry farmers traveling from afar, Farmer's Restaurant is one of Eastern Market's premier diners, serving up a hearty portion of hotcakes and sausages. Most of its ingredients must come from the market, because its omelets are always fresh and its hash browns always delectable. Located just east of Shed 3, next to the Cultivation Station, Farmer's Restaurant is one of the only places in Detroit to get a good omelet and great service for the early breakfast set. Be forewarned that you'll most likely need a box for your leftovers—it's like two meals for the cheap, cheap price of one. *2542 Market St., (313) 259-8230.*

» Germack Coffee and Tea Shop - Under the same roof as the storied Germack Pistachio Company, the Germack Coffee and Tea Shop is a wonderful new addition to the market. Amid a thoughtful atmosphere of wood floors, exposed brick, sliding industrial doors, and antique accent pieces, Germack offers a full selection of espresso drinks, drip coffee, cold brew, and teas. It uses a wide variety of beans roasted on site and you can even sneak a peek of the roasting process in the back! In addition, it sells its own coffee roasts by the bag, fresh spices by the ounce, and a curated selection of pantry items and caffeinated-beverage-related housewares to facilitate your addiction. *2509 Russell St., www.germack.com, (313) 556-0062.*

Louie's Ham and Corned Beef - A little thing most people don't know about Detroit: It's corned beef country, and Eastern Market is the hub. At Louie's Ham and Corned Beef, breakfast is served any time, and that includes its selection of 18 massive three-egg omelets (in fact, all portion sizes at Louie's are massive, so be sure to come extra hungry.). The menu is vast, and it has a wide variety of Detroit-area diner specialties. But the name says it all: When you go to Louie's, you get the ham or the corned beef. The corned beef comes from the infamous Wigley's, also located in Eastern Market. For the holidays, order a whole ham from Louie's (from Dearborn Ham Co.) or satisfy your craving with a mound of meat stuffed between two slices of rye. There's even an improbable (but somehow completely reliable) drive-through. *3570 Riopelle St., www.louieseasternmarket.com, (313) 831-1800.*

Mike's Pita & Grill - Coated inside and out with sunny yellow paint, this cozy coney island offers hot pita sandwiches, hot dogs, hot soups, and warm welcomes to visitors. Because of the affordable lunch specials, Mike's gets hopping around noon. Sit-down diners might have to wait for a space during the lunch or dinner rush, since there's just enough room for a grill top, black cushioned stools at the counter, and a few tables and chairs—but that all adds to the cozy coney experience. If hurrying through a lunch break, call ahead for extra-snappy carryout that's easy on the wallet. *2719 Russell St., (313) 259-8151.*

Milano Bakery & Cafe - Conveniently located on the northern edge of the market near Midtown, Milano is a solid bakery with a large selection of affordable classic cakes, cookies, pastries, coffee cakes, Kosher breads, rolls, and breadsticks. The space is airy, spare, and clean, and service is usually quick and friendly. While many of the cakes are quite basic, the carrot, pineapple-upside down, German chocolate, and red velvet are especially tasty and a good value. Order ahead or take your chances and choose from the case—though not extensive, there is usually a selection of small and large pre-made layer cakes to choose from, and employees will happily add a custom message on the top. Milano also offers a nice menu of salads, soups, sandwiches, and pizza—with large portions for a reasonable price—available for carryout or dining-in in the pleasant, bright cafeteria-type setting. *3500 Russell St., www.milanobakerydetroit.com, (313) 833-3500.*

Mootown Creamery and More - Open since 2011, Mootown's delicious frosty treats have been a welcome addition to the market for the hoards of summertime market shoppers. It specializes in classic Michigan products, including Faygo soda, Vernors ginger ale, Sanders fudge, Better Made chips, and delicious Hudsonville ice cream. Ice cream flavors range from classic favorites (like chocolate or butter pecan) to state-themed varieties (such as Grand Traverse Bay Cherry Fudge, Sleeping Bear Dunes Bear Hug, or Michigan Deer Traxx). Prices are reasonable, and the yummy scoops are generous. *2641 Russell St., www.mymootown.com, (313) 393-6016.*

» Roma Café - Known as Detroit's oldest restaurant, and identified by the cheerful red-and-white striped awning outside, this historic business began life as a boarding house for local farmers but became an eatery in 1890. Owned by the Sossi family since 1934, the café's esteemed recipes and traditions have been in good hands. This is old-school Italian in the most charming of settings: dimly lit romantic interior, all-male servers in tuxedos, and all of the traditional Italian fare. House specialties include succulent veal in the classic variations from cacciatore to picanti, fried calamari, homemade potato gnocchi, a thick minestrone soup, and stupendous, crisp cannoli. As one would expect, Roma offers a healthy selection of wines and a full bar. On Mondays, don't miss the all-you-can-eat, diet-destroying buffet of nearly every Italian dish ever invented for $15. Sports fans should note that Roma is a popular post-practice pit stop for the Detroit Red Wings, who are often spotted dining at the restaurant. *3401 Riopelle St., www.romacafe.com, (313) 831-5940.*

» Russell Street Deli - This popular deli serves up some of Detroit's tastiest eats for carnivores and vegans alike in a clean, contemporary setting. From classic deli sandwiches like the BLT (made with double-smoked hickory bacon) and reubens stuffed with corned beef, to hearty vegetarian options such as the Avocado Melt and the TLT (tofu, lettuce, and tomato), all of Russell's sandwiches hit it out of the park. If sandwiches aren't your bag, RSD is known for tasty salads and the best soups in town, offering five or six options each day, made from scratch in-house with all-natural, local ingredients. Try our favorites—black-eyed pea with collard greens, Tuscan potato, or Moroccan chickpea—or just flip a coin. They don't disappoint! In the summer, RSD's mint iced tea or fresh lemonade are a must. Expect a long wait for Saturday breakfast and note that all the deli's tables seat six, so be prepared to share a table if you come with a smaller group or split up if you have a larger party. Open for only breakfast and lunch. *2465 Russell St., www.russellstreetdeli.com, (313) 567-2900.*

» Sala Thai - An antidote for coney fever, Sala Thai serves up some of the city's finest Thai food from its home in a retired 1888 firehouse. The menu offers all of the de rigueur Thai options—like pad Thai, pad prik, pad khing, and gaeng phanaeng—alongside more adventurous options, such as shrimp-and-mussels-stuffed squid—all of which are equally delectable. Although the menu is almost exclusively Thai, it includes a diverse selection of fresh, visually stunning sushi, including octopus, white tuna, red snapper, and eel. Setting the right mood for diners, Sala Thai eschews the Thaikea ambiance of other Thai restaurants in favor of a more authentic feel, including bamboo-thatched booths, door gods, and beautiful murals and sculptures. In addition to the food offerings, Sala Thai offers a full bar, with a superior selection of sakes, plum wines, and Asian beers like Sapporo and Tsingtao. Vegetarians beware: There are few non-fish sauce options available, although the veggie sushi is popular. *3400 Russell St., www.salathaidetroit.com, (313) 831-1302.*

» Supino Pizzeria - Believe the hype: Supino serves up some of the best thin-crust brick oven pies in Metro Detroit. Inspired by relatives in the village of Supino, Italy, owner and maestro Dave Mancini painstakingly honed his craft before he opened up shop in 2008. Melding balanced, rich, traditional flavors with perfectly textured New York-style crusts, Supino's enormous pies are delights that never disappoint. Though there are dozens of options, adventurous meat-eaters should try the Bismarck: homemade red sauce, fresh mozzarella, and salty prosciutto, with an egg cracked in the middle, blending brilliantly with the tomato and cheese. Vegetarians (and anyone who likes delicious food) shouldn't miss the Supino: homemade red sauce, fresh mozzarella, sublimely roasted whole garlic cloves, olives, and fresh ricotta. Though Supino does a steady carryout business, the cozy dining room, charmingly decorated with reclaimed wood doors and salvaged institutional tables, adds to the experience. As an added bonus, you can watch a master hand toss pies in the open kitchen while you wait. *2457 Russell St., www.supinopizzeria.com, (313) 567-7879.*

Vivio's - Vivio's has been an Eastern Market tradition for more than 40 years. Whether tailgating before a Lions game on Sundays, enjoying a boozy Saturday brunch, or savoring the succulent burgers or mussels on just any old day, Vivio's is a Detroit favorite. Known best for its signature Bloody Mary—made with a house mix and served in a pint glass with a beer chaser—Vivio's is a popular spot centrally located in the Eastern Market district. The first floor is a quaintly decorated bar space with historic decor and cozy booths, while the upstairs has a more relaxed atmosphere with comfortable couches. Though the menu is specialized, the friendly staff is extremely knowledgeable and accommodating. Vivio's offers a complimentary shuttle bus for Tigers, Red Wings, and Lions Games, making it a popular pre-game destination. If you haven't finished scratching your Bloody Mary itch by last call, pick up some of the bottled house-made mix on your way out. *2460 Market St., www. viviosbloodymary.com, (313) 393-1711.*

Zeff's Coney Island - A mainstay of the market's Russell Street restaurant strip, Zeff's has been around longer than neighbors Russell Street Deli, Supino Pizzeria, and Mootown Creamery combined. The food is great, the staff is friendly, the huge portions are relatively inexpensive, and its charming classic diner counter and airy front windows make dining-in a pleasure. At first glance the menu seems pretty standard as far as coney islands (there are basic coney dogs, hot dogs, loose burger, and the coney taco down to a science), but Zeff's uses quality, market-fresh ingredients, including Wigley's corned beef (which is as delicious as it is famous). Its coffee is tasty and employees will happily keep it full, especially if you've brought your laptop and are grinding away the hours working on their free Wi-Fi—just don't expect to be able to sit with your computer all day on a Saturday, because you'll barely be able to get a table. *2469 Russell St., (313) 259-4705.*

SHOPPING & SERVICES

Busy Bee Hardware - Located in an old bank building covered in colorful happy bee murals on the edge of the market, Busy Bee Hardware is an old-fashioned hardware store with charming worn wooden floors, cluttered shelves, and friendly, knowledgeable service. Family-owned for four generations, Busy Bee staffers are well-versed in historic home repairs and construction projects and are happy to offer cheerful, sage advice about the minutia of your complicated and obscure home repair job. The store carries a bevy of difficult-to-find specialty items and also makes keys, fix screens, and replace glass, along with providing a lot of other handy services. *1401 Gratiot Ave., (313) 567-0785.*

Capital Poultry - Nested near the end of Riopelle Street, just before the I-75 service drive, is Capital Poultry. Don't expect to hear any chickens clucking here: This establishment welcomes customers into the walk-in cooler to choose from pre-plucked poultry. Enter through the hammered steel door—it will stay open, don't worry about getting locked in!—and chat with poultry chefs. Order a chicken whole, cut up any which way, or request certain cuts bagged-and-bought-by-the-pound. Exit the chilly cooler with your bag full of freshly cut Amish chickens, special Pekin ducks, or a dozen fresh brown or white farm eggs, and cash out with the friendly counter clerk in the main lobby. Closed Sunday and Monday. *2456 Riopelle St., (313) 567-0800.*

Cheap Charlies - Need a rug, work boots, gently used work shirt, socks, shopping cart, underwear, utensil, pocketknife, stockpot, lucky rabbit foot, or oversize piggy bank? If you need any of these items—or pretty much anything else for that matter—Cheap Charlies probably has it for you, packed into its pleasantly cluttered heaping displays. The sign above the door reads "THE WORKING MAN'S STORE," and it doesn't lie: in addition to a healthy stock of every type of work-related apparel, its goods are priced to sell, and it's hard to step foot inside without picking up a steal. *1461 Gratiot Ave., (313) 567-7788.*

» Cost Plus Wine Shoppe - This family-owned and operated wine shop boasts a fabulous variety of more than a thousand wines at reasonable prices. A market institution since it opened on St. Patrick's Day in 1986, the selection is also well-curated. Enjoy reading the descriptive signs and perusing the bottles sold from boxes stacked high on the worn wooden floors, or ask for advice—the staff members really knows their stuff and have a knack for helping to select the perfect variety for your menu and budget, whether you are an oenophile or just turned 21. The store sells a nice selection of Michigan wines—from labels like Chateau Grand Traverse, Black Star Farms, and Peninsula Cellars—and also carries a great selection of specialty, Michigan, and imported beers. *2448 Market St., (313) 259-3845.*

» The Detroit Mercantile Co. - Part of a recent boom of new business in the area, this shop, located just a little north of the main drag of the market, opened in 2012. Watched over by its stuffed mascot, Coleman the Buffalo, this beautifully merchandised shop features a broad range of old-timey takes on classic household items, from hand-built bicycles to cloth-covered extension cords, as well as a curated, but healthy, selection of high-end antiques and a wide assortment of topical T-shirts from Detroit Manufacturing. Many of the antiques offered are truly special and Detroit-centric—such as an awe-inspiring vintage pull-down map of Detroit. If you're looking for an event space, check out the spacious area behind the store that is available to rent for special occasions. *3434 Russell St., www.detroitmercantile.com, (313) 831-9000.*

Detroit Wholesale Produce - Geared toward restaurant owners and individuals alike, any shopper can come here to enjoy wholesale prices. The front room is lined with a wall of refrigerated dairy products and refreshments, while crates of produce for individual sale populate the main floor. Visitors are also welcome to walk through the clear vinyl curtain strips to the six refrigerated backrooms (which make Detroit Wholesale Produce a nice place to cool off on a hot day as the temperature is kept to a cool 48 degrees). There, a cornucopia of fresh produce is available, including many varieties of potatoes, strawberries, onions, and pineapple—anything available at a gourmet grocery store but by the 10-pound crate. *2614 Riopelle St., (313) 309-1000.*

» DeVries & Co. 1887 - Founded by Rudolf Hirt Jr. in 1887, and still family-owned, an incarnation of this shop has been an Eastern Market staple for generations. The only cheese shop in the city, with its high ceilings, worn wooden floors, and friendly counter service, shopping here is a charming experience from another time. The knowledgeable staff will happily recommend a cheese to suit your fancy, and tastes are encouraged. In addition to its vast array of cheeses, this fine specialty foods shop carries an impressive array of imported dry goods including European mustards, shortbreads, jams, chocolates, crackers, local dairy products, and teas. The shop's recent facelift left it cleaner and airier than before. *2468 Market St., (313) 568-7777.*

Discount Candles - Whether you're spiritual, superstitious, or just plain into candles, this place offers all the herbs, roots, scented oils, incense cones, colorful waxes, tarot cards, lucky candles, and religious votives you could hope for. Open for more than 80 years, business still bustles inside, where lemon yellow walls adorned with blue waves and spiral script surround energized shoppers as they browse shelf after shelf of products. Conveniently, Discount Candles offers free parking in the church parking lot on the nearest side street, so visitors won't need to worry about trying to parallel park on Gratiot during rush hour. *1400 Gratiot Ave., (313) 566-0092.*

» Division Street Boutique - Known for its ever-popular apparel emblazoned with the phrases "Detroit Hustles Harder" and "RUN DET," the Division Street Boutique is the home base of Aptemal Clothing, the company that hand-prints everything in-house, up the stairs on the second floor. When the store's open, the large garage door opens up to the street, just off of the market's main drag, to show off all the goods and welcome visitors. Though it's a small store, it's brimming with awesome, hip apparel and accessories for gents and ladies, too. While Aptemal Clothing is also available elsewhere, this is the company's flagship location and is the best place to find the entire line. Insider tip: Keep your ear out for parties that happen after close. They're not to be missed. *1353 Division St., www.divisionstreetboutique.com, (313) 412-3337.*

Eastern Market Antiques - Eastern Market Antiques glows with the light of glass saloon bar lamps, vintage chandeliers, and modern light fixtures that drape above the entire first floor showroom. The extra lighting illuminates collectibles from more than 15 vendors selling vintage aprons, secondhand furniture, 1990s computer games, comics, posters, wall hangings, typewriters, tools, even Detroit salvage pieces, such as theater seats. Upstairs, it's all about the rarer things: 1950s postcards from each of the 50 states, designer turn-of-the-century hats and dresses, and even taxidermy animals. *2530 Market St., www.easternmarketantiques.com, (313) 259-0600.*

Embassy Foods - With many a wholesale retailer at Eastern Market, customers might find it hard to differentiate between one meat market and the next, but Embassy Foods makes a name for itself with its top-notch customer service. Here, the staff welcomes visitors through the clear vinyl cooling barrier curtain like they're welcoming a long-lost relative into their living room. That might be because Embassy has been family-owned for three generations and caters to three generations of loyal customers—half the people there might as well be related to the owner! Customers range from coney island restaurant owners to family cooks. Freshly trimmed chicken legs by the pound-bag, frozen breaded shrimp, rib tips—you name it, Embassy has it. Browse their large product books for party dish ideas, or ask for advice and specials. *2478 Riopelle St., (313) 259-2100.*

Ftoni Wholesale Meats - Eastern Market shoppers can't miss Ftoni Meats—mostly because the beet-red facade of the large brick building features a brightly colored mural of plump farm animals grazing under a red Pistons basketball sun. Inside, the store features tall wire racks full of bulk batters, oils, condiments, and a variety of pre-prepared cakes. Snake a grocery cart through the wholesale items to the back of the store, where Ftoni's famous meat counter showcases freshly ground beef and pork, fish, and poultry. *2800 Riopelle St., (313) 832-3770.*

Gabriel Importing Co. - Family-owned in Eastern Market since 1914, almost any Lebanese specialty can be found here: seasoned and baked pita breads, fresh fattoush and tabouli salad, goat cheeses, dry goods, hummus, and a huge selection uniquely brined olives. If you aren't sure what to get, you're in luck, because free samples abound. To complement the wonderful selection, the prices are competitive and the customer service is fantastic. If you love fresh, homemade Mediterranean food, you will love this store, but even if Mediterranean food isn't your thing, you will probably still love Gabriel Importing Co. for its charming and affordable shopping experience! *2534 Market St., (313) 567-2890.*

Germack Pistachio Company - Long a staple in Detroit and a household name throughout Michigan, the Germack Pistachio Company has been roasting pistachios since 1924, which makes it the oldest roaster in America. Since the early days, their product line has grown substantially. Today, in small batches, Germack roasts and manufactures a wide variety of nuts, seeds, dried fruits, spices, coffees, chocolates, nostalgic candies, and other items, selling them wholesale and out of their Eastern Market shop. Though it only recently migrated to its new, more central location in the core of the market, the store, which was opened in tandem with its coffee shop next door, feels as if it has been there for a century. With beautiful wood floors, exposed brick, and heavy industrial doors, the building is a perfect fit for such a storied business—and a perfect place to buy old-timey treats and pantry items, both in bulk and in consumer quantities. *2509 Russell St., www.germack.com, (313) 393-2000.*

Gratiot Central Market - Just a short walk over the pedestrian bridge from the main drag of the market is this meat heaven. From steak to sausage to rabbit, options abound for the shopper who loves fresh cuts at great prices. Originally built in 1915, this meat house has seen two serious fires, a new highway, and hundreds of thousands of happy customers. If meat isn't on your menu, make sure to check out the bakery, cheese counter, and health food store tucked in the back hallway. Gratiot Central Market is worth a stop, if not just to see the trademark Bulls' heads hanging over the door. *1429 Gratiot Ave., (313) 259-4486.*

Kap's Wholesale Meats - Though not for vegetarians or the squeamish, Kap's Wholesale Meats serves everyone from restaurant chefs to the beginner barbecuer. New customers may appreciate the helpful posters of the pig, cow, and bird that decorate the entrance to Kap's, which outline every cut available. Done admiring the posters? Then get ready to walk through the large metal doors to the meat cooler, where whole pigs hang sliced down the middle, chilling upside down on meat hooks in the center of the room. Surrounding the porky centerpieces are racks of condiments, barbecue spice rubs, coolers of cheese products, and a glass meat counter that wraps around the perimeter of the room. Though the whole pigs are the most popular selling items, on Saturdays, customers will also find individual cuts of steak, pork chops, and Amish turkey and chicken. For first time bulk meat buyers, Kap's butchers can suggest the best cut of meat for a desired dish and the right amount of food for a party. *2630 Riopelle St., www.kapswholesale.com, (313) 832-2300.*

Kay Foods - Kay Foods is a friendly, family-owned wholesale foods distributor that caters to everyone from coney island restaurants and local churches to general shoppers. The caring folks at Kay are the real gems here, ready to help customers decide how many pounds of potato salad to feed their family at a reunion, or how many gallons of beverage syrup to purchase for a church's holiday fruit punch. Kay employees help customers tour the main showroom, which is filled with fully stocked shelves of take-out boxes, frozen meats, pre-cut veggies, disposable tableware, and more. The large selection of tablecloths and napkins makes Kay Foods a go-to location for party preparations. Although Kay welcomes visitors throughout the workweek, market goers will want to come by early, because Kay closes at noon on Saturdays. *1352 Division St., (313) 833-6133.*

» Rocky Peanut Company - In the produce-delivery and peanut-roasting business since 1931, the Russo family's enterprise became a Detroit institution when brothers Dominic and Rocco—aka Rocky—opened their brick-and-mortar location in Eastern Market in 1971. Though the eastside classic offers a mind-blowing selection of sweet and savory seeds, nuts, and peanuts, they also offer a completist's selection of pantry items, including bulk options, such as fine coffee, dried beans, spices, flour, sugar, dried fruit, and old timey candies. Though we're always suckers for the chocolate-covered nuts, Rocky's fresh honey-roasted almonds are conveniently located by the register, so they're hard to pass up. *2489 Russell St., www.rockypeanut.com, (313) 567-6871.*

Saad Wholesale - On market Saturdays, the Saad Wholesale meat locker bustles with white-coated butchers filling customers' red-orange shopping carts full of fine halal meats. Among the first zabiha halal (lawful slaughter) meat distributors in the United States (opening in 1976), Saad Wholesale offers high-quality cuts of goat, lamb, poultry, veal, and fresh and frozen fish, and packages of Saad's subsidiary brand of Sharifa hot dogs and cold cuts. After browsing through the maze of cold cases and crystal-clear meat counters, customers can cash out with Aref Saad, the CEO and founder who often stands behind the cash register of his family-run establishment. For first pick of the finest cuts of meat, regulars recommend visiting early mornings, which isn't too hard, since Saad opens at 7am Monday through Saturday. Those looking for another option for fresh halal meat nearby should check out Berry & Sons Islamic Slaughter, located nearby at 2496 Orleans Street. At Berry & Sons, fresh cuts are whisked from the cooler to the lobby on mechanized meat hooks to preserve freshness, though we've found that it is best to call ahead to assure service. *2814 Orleans St., www.saadmeats.com, (313) 831-8126.*

» **Savvy Chic** - Savvy Chic's interior seems to be transformed into a stylish cottage in the French countryside through the creative expertise of owner, and College for Creative Studies alumna, Karen Brown. Brown achieved this effect by hand-painting the shop's original concrete with an aged-oak floor finish and coating exposed brick walls in a fresh dose of cream and crème de menthe stripes. Brown mixes her hand-painted space with a large selection of modern, Earth-friendly made-in-America housewares and one-of-a-kind antique decor. Stop in Thursday through Sunday to find vintage Victorian chairs, floral cloth napkins and aprons, an antique crafted-in-Detroit oven, gardening tools and golf gifts for dad, luscious bath and candle products, and a bit of imagination! *2712 Riopelle St., (313) 833-8769.*

Wigley's Meats and Produce - Wigley's is a long, narrow market with a meat and deli counter that stretches the entire length of the store. The market offers a small selection of fresh produce, dairy, and frozen desserts, but Wigley's mainly does meat, and does it well, as evidenced by its exceptional following of corned-beef fanatics, who have been enjoying the same top-secret Wigley family recipe since 1924. By offering a slightly sweeter take on the traditional Irish-American corned beef, Wigley's remains a big hit among locals who recognize the juicy flavors from their favorite coney island and deli establishments. This family-owned establishment employs Wigley relatives, who know their meat cuts and corned beef preparation, and the Detroit Free Press even named Tom Wigley one of Detroit's kings of corned beef. For those who are looking for a slightly more savory take on corned beef with a similar history, and who are willing to buy in bulk, try Grobbel's (2500 Orleans St.), a fellow Free Press–anointed king of corned beef, and a Detroit original since 1883. *3405 Russell St., (313) 833-3030.*

CULTURAL ATTRACTIONS

OMNICORPDETROIT - This quirky collaborative workspace was Detroit's first hackerspace. Defined by a do-it-yourself mentality and shared physical, financial, and informational resources between its members, OCD has transformed a once derelict, 7,300-square-foot building into a fully functional work and meeting space. Opening their doors every other Thursday on Open Hack Night for the general public, OCD is the place to go if you need access to power tools, space to work on a one-night project or advice from one of its many savvy members. Check out OCD's website to learn about other opportunities and regular event nights such as Moped Mondays. Admission is donation based. *1501 Division St., www.omnicorpdetroit.com.*

Red Bull House of Art - When approaching the House of Art, an unassuming, industrial entrance leads into the open floor plan of first-floor studios. There's a hyped-up, collaborative feeling throughout the workspaces, which are occupied by all kinds of visual artists. However, it's in the gallery space, in the lower level, where visitors can expect to be blown away. A dark corridor of stairs leads to a series of brick-walled tunnels, almost subway-like in appearance, glowing under ambient neon lights. The tunnels lead past a bar and some sitting areas, to what feels like another world: a vast, wide-open gallery. You'll feel as if you've been transported to New York's Meatpacking District, but this industrial-chic space exhibits only emerging, Michigan-based artists. Corporate logos are tastefully absent from Red Bull's House of Art, aside from a couple of fridges stocked with (free!) cans of the energy drink. *1551 Winder St. (In the E & B Brewery Lofts)*

» Salt and Cedar - Where Riopelle Street ends and Orleans Street transforms into Napoleon Street lies a little corner gallery and vintage letterpress studio called Salt and Cedar. Partners Megan O'Connell and Leon Johnson founded the company to supply the Detroit area with a letterpress publisher and to offer workshops to poets, writers, visual artists, and any looking to learn. Behind the bright green door of this Eastern Market space, visitors will find a table full of Salt and Cedar printing samples, from hand screen-printed hard covers to hand set poems. Look for their beautiful hand-printed posters and broadsides for shows at MoCAD and other venues. In the next room, visitors will find rows of vintage letter blocks, presses, and maple pew seating that invites guests to sit and gaze at the typeset prints decorating the walls. *2448 Riopelle St., www.saltandcedar.com, (207) 671-3462.*

» Signal-Return Press - Signal-Return is a modern, open space full of presses, antique letter blocks, working artists, and wordsmiths alike. The space reverberates with creative energy as artists work at long blonde wooden-block tabletops, surrounded by exposed brick walls and orange and white ceiling beams. Separating the retail and workshop areas are shelves stacked with chapbooks and art and design publications, as well as blank postcards, envelopes, and notebooks ready to be printed! A long string stretches along the length of the store, clothes-pinned with the latest screen prints and letter-pressed memorabilia for sale. The studio offers a variety of great classes (including letterpress printing, book binding, and linocut printing) and after taking two, students are eligible to use the shop's presses during open studio hours. *1345 Division St., www.signalreturnpress.org, (313) 567-8970.*

ENTERTAINMENT & RECREATION

The Detroit Flyhouse - Though not for the faint of heart, there's something spectacular about barrel rolls and flips performed 20-feet in the air. That's the Detroit Flyhouse, a destination yoga and acrobatics studio like no other. Set in a beautiful exposed-brick studio space in the rear of the FD Lofts building, silks and trapeze bars dangle from the ceiling 25 feet above. With patience, attentive encouragement, and bursts of excitement the instructors teach aerial yoga for singles and partners, aerial hoop dancing, and trapeze performance modeled after Cirque du Soleil. Those less inclined to a rigorous yet rewarding workout can catch the students and instructors when they perform around the city at both private and public events. Note: Locating the facility can be tricky—the entrance is found through the parking lot off of Erskine. Be sure to call ahead to get the entrance code to access the facility garden and studio entrance. *3434 Russell St., www.detroitflyhouse.com, (313) 674-6424.*

Trinosophes - Based in an 8,900-square-foot 1933 storefront, local musician and promoter Joel Peterson—who brought Detroit the now-legendary programming at the Bohemian National Home in the mid 2000s—has painstakingly rehabbed the space and quietly created one of the places in Detroit to hear independent music. The music-focused art space is centered around a formidable concert venue, but the facility is developing a cafe and a second home for People's Records (see separate entry), as well as a nascent People's-led Detroit Music Museum featuring music, ephemera, and memorabilia. While Peterson is finishing renovations, the space has a raw beauty with untreated walls and unfinished amenities—though the space is constantly evolving, much like the cutting-edge work it showcases. *1464 Gratiot Ave., (313) 737-6696.*

POINTS OF INTEREST

Brixel Murals - Conceived by artist Cedric Tai, these "brixel" murals (a mash up of brick and pixel) transform the uniform bricks on the sides of buildings into stunningly colorful geometric patterns. Although these murals have spread across the city, this is one of our favorites. *1492 Gratiot Ave.*

Eastern Market Cold Storage Mural - This colorful mural adorning the side of a warehouse features a bounty of fruit whimsically arranged to depict a heifer. The mural is the handiwork of architect Alexander Pollack, who painted the piece 1972 in an effort to enliven the market. At four stories tall, you can't miss this piece. *2531 Riopelle St.*

Eastern Market Welcome Mural - One of the popular large-scale commercial works painted in the market by artist Alexander Pollack in 1972, this mural depicts a forklift hauling what might be the world's largest watermelon and pulling cartloads of less absurdly scaled fresh produce. *2451 Napoleon St.*

Transmat Records - The headquarters for techno pioneer Derrick May since 1986. *1492 Gratiot Ave.*

CHAPTER 4
CORKTOWN

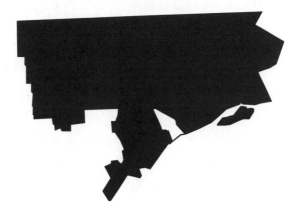

Near West
Side

New Center / North End

I-94

Burrell
Merrick
Putnam

Loraine

Warren

Hancock

Woodbridge

Core
City

Forest

Earl

Jefferies

Midtown

Lawton

Humboldt

17th

15th

Poplar

16th

Calumet

I-96

18th

Selden

Magnolia

Alexandrine

Mulberry

Selden

Hazel

Brainard

Martin Luther King Jr.

CORKTOWN

Sycamore

Ash

Ash

Elm

Grand River

Butternut

Briggs

Wabash

Vermont

Harrison

Butternut

Perry

Huron

Temple

North
Corktown

Cochrane

Perry

Spruce

Spruce

Pine

M-10

19th

18th

17th

16th

Vermont

I-75

Kaline

Cherry

Downtown

Michigan

Plum

Millenium
Village

Dalzelle

11th

Elizabeth

Marantette

Church

Southwest

15th

Vermont

Leverette

10th

Bagley

16th

Rosa Parks

Labrosse

Corktown

14th

Porter

Abbott

Trumbull

Howard

Hubbard
Richard

Lafayette

West Side
Industrial

Fort

Jefferson

Detroit River

| 0 | | 0.5 | | 1 |
Miles

Corktown is a historically working-class neighborhood and is characterized by its quaint, pastel-colored workers cottages and must-visit restaurants, bars and coffee houses. It is not only Detroit's oldest existing neighborhood, but also one of its most charming. For the purposes of this guide, Corktown is defined as being about 2.5 square miles, roughly bounded by Grand River Avenue to the north, M-10 (the Lodge Freeway) to the east, the Detroit River to the south, and a private railroad line and 16th Street on the west.

Comprised of French ribbon farms through the 1700s, Corktown began to develop as a neighborhood when Irish immigrants flocked to Detroit to escape the Irish potato famine of 1845 and settled in the eighth ward of the city, which included this neighborhood. Because immigrants to this area were primarily from the County Cork in Ireland, the neighborhood became known colloquially as Corktown. Developed as a working-class immigrant community, the tree-lined neighborhood rose quickly, as the small pastel, wood-frame workers cottages and multi-family row houses were constructed expeditiously: most were built by the 1860s. Though the tight-knit Irish immigrant population diffused over the years, as newcomers arrived from Germany, Malta, Mexico, and the American South, the historic association with Ireland has remained, including many subtle nods to the heritage in businesses around Corktown. The neighborhood also hosts the raucous annual St. Patrick's Day Parade.

Through the late 20th century, the neighborhood has been challenged by freeway construction, industrial development, the closure of Michigan Central Station, and, most recently, the move of the Detroit Tigers—and eventual demolition of the historic stadium, which had been a vital part of the neighborhood since 1912. However, despite these setbacks, Corktown has persevered, even flourished. Today, though home to only slightly more than 7,000 people, the neighborhood is frequently in the national spotlight for the unprecedented growth in small business and entrepreneurship, urban agriculture, grassroots development, and the arts.

Because of the path of I-75 (Chrysler Freeway), the area is commonly separated into two neighborhoods, Corktown and North Corktown. While they have a shared history, they have somewhat distinct personalities. The traditional Corktown neighborhood, which is south of I-75, is more historically intact and is where the Irish enclave began to establish itself. Today, it's a dense, active neighborhood that has seen substantial growth and development, especially around

Michigan Avenue. Characterized by its distinctive, charming streets, the neighborhood offers many walkable and bikeable amenities and is an enticing place to visit. North Corktown is composed of parts of the historic Core City and Briggs neighborhoods. Though the area went through a period of decline, recently, it has been reborn as a center for activism and urban farming, offering residents historic homes in close proximity to downtown, as well as open green space for gardens, greenhouses, and creative projects.

BARS & RESTAURANTS

» Astro Coffee - Serious coffee nerds, lovers of incredible homemade fresh sweets and sandwiches, and pretty much everyone else rejoiced when husband and wife team Daisuke Hughes and Jess Hicks opened this gem in 2011. A daily ritual for neighborhood folks and a destination for those from afar, Astro offers a near-endless rotation of high-quality and fair trade beans from across the world (looking for a Guatemalan roast with a thick mouth feel and notes of caramel apple? The chalkboard wall behind the baristas will give you tasting notes on your daily options). These are perfectly complimented by Jess' locally sourced, made-from-scratch, mouthwatering treats, though we caution that their polenta cakes, coconut Anzac cookies, and crème fraiche and egg sandwiches are proven to be dangerously addictive. Take a seat at the back counter, at a charming café table in the sunny front windows, or at the large communal table in the back and soak in some Corktown culture with your coffee. Like many successful fledgling Detroit businesses, this place is built on love, not snobbery, with baristas paying as much attention to your mood as to your (perfect) latte foam. *2124 Michigan Ave., www.astrodetroit.com, (313) 638-2989.*

» Brooklyn Street Local - This diner emphasizes locally sourced from-scratch meals for breakfast and lunch and is operated by two former Torontonians who decided to follow their dream of owning their own restaurant and moved to Detroit to make it happen. Located on Corktown's main drag, visitors traveling west on Michigan won't be able to miss the flowing, abstract mural by street artist Reyes that covers an entire side of the building. Inside, the establishment offers a warmer feel, a contemporary take on the classic diner aesthetic. Though Brooklyn Street serves all of the hearty home-cooked diner staples, with a fresh, local spin, it also offers a strong menu of vegetarian and vegan options—and even brings a touch of Canadian flavor to the menu with pea meal bacon and the best poutine this side of the Detroit River. *1266 Michigan Ave., www.brooklynstreetlocal.com, (313) 262-6547.*

Casey's Pub - Take the antique firefighter decorations to heart: Casey's Pub is Detroit's quintessential working-class bar. Bought by a retired fire captain in 1984, this Corktown joint still attracts a loyal crowd of neighborhood regulars and blue-collar heroes looking to douse a long day with a cold pint. There's no jukebox, but there are cheap pitchers and a house hamburger that gives some of Corktown's fancier eateries a run for their money. Expect to meet your local electrician, elevator mechanic, or the occasional off-duty Detroit police bomb squad technician. Be sure to take a spin through the men's room, where the soaring 14-foot brick walls and ceiling are covered with scrawled homages to the city's trade unions and firehouses. *1830 Michigan Ave., (313) 963-2440.*

Corktown Tavern - It was at ground zero when the Detroit Tigers decided to pack up and head downtown in 1999 (spitting distance from the ballpark is hardly an exaggeration). Today, it's a little rough around the edges, but the Corktown Tavern soldiers on with a mix of neighborhood regulars, hard-core Tigers devotees, rockers, bikers, and their kin. While at times you get a sense of a devil-may-care attitude from the bartenders and patrons alike (those plastic cups aren't for drinking water), there's plenty of vibrancy left in this Corktown dive. Take a walk up the creaky, narrow staircase in the back: Depending on the night, you might catch a DJ spinning classic punk records, your favorite new up-and-coming band, or the occasional full-fledged, packed-to-the gills dance party. Keep an eye out for the return of Dorkwave, Detroit's wildest party back at the turn of the millennium: Word is, they're coming back to the Tavern with a vengeance. *1716 Michigan Ave., www.corktowntavern.com, (313) 964-5103.*

Gaelic League and Irish-American Club of Detroit - Founded in December 1920 with the aim of preserving and promoting the "Irish race" in Detroit and beyond, the League remains a staple of the Corktown neighborhood with its historic dance hall and cozy tavern that look much the same as they did nearly a century ago. Known for its St. Patrick's Day festivities, the club documents parades gone by with a commemorative Master of Ceremonies plaque wall and scattered black and white photos. Though many of the social activities hosted at the League are reserved for members or the Irish-American

Club (just $20 annually), don't be intimidated by the "members only" sign on the door—anyone can enjoy a pint at the quaint bar inside. As an added incentive, lucky visitors can often catch live Irish folk tunes in the tavern. *2068 Michigan Ave., www.gaelicleagueofdetroit.org, (313) 964-8700.*

» Green Dot Stables - Recently purchased, retooled, and reopened by young entrepreneurs Jacques and Christine Driscoll, this jockey-themed bar and restaurant is hugely popular, and with good reason! Formerly frequented by cops, neighborhood folks, and in-the-know hipsters, Green Dot Stables is now frequented by just about everybody, and it's often difficult to get a seat, especially on Tigers game days. Fortunately, the simple, fun, tasty, and affordable menu of eclectic sliders, deliciously seasoned specialty fries, salads, sides, desserts, and full bar including Michigan craft beers and house cocktails, is well worth the wait. Mosey in through the swinging saloon doors and enjoy a drink at the bar by the cozy faux gas lamps while watching the ponies on TV, cuddle up in a booth under the cedar shake shingles, or bring a group and sit at one of the large round tables. If you head to the loo, be sure to check out the horse mural in the back. The à la carte menu boasts nothing above $3 (literally nothing—cocktails and beer included), so pick out a slider or three and be sure to get some fries. For the even more budget conscious, pop in for a bottle of domestic or Canadian beer for only $2. Although the menu is pretty meat-heavy, there is plenty to please the herbivores among us. The foosball table is a bona fide bonus. *2200 W. Lafayette Blvd., www.greendotstables.com, (313) 962-5588.*

Iridescence - Sitting atop the MotorCity Casino Hotel, 17 stories in the sky, Iridescence offers soaring views of the Detroit skyline from 40-foot-high windows that stretch 180 feet across in what is easily one of the most dramatic, if slightly ostentatious, dining rooms in the city. Hundreds of pendant lights in glass baubles float overhead while LED-lit panels subtly illuminate the walls and ceiling in a pearly glow of jewel-colored neon. And all of that is merely parlor dressing for the food. A multi-time recipient of the AAA four-diamond award and the Wine Spectator Award of Excellence, Iridescence truly does take fine dining to new heights. Drawing on French and Asian influences, Iridescence presents "deconstructed" American classics in a way that is nothing short of art. The 40-foot wine wall with an electronic pulley system that rotates its 300 or so on-hand labels will delight even the most casual oenophile. *2901 Grand River Ave., (313) 237-6732.*

» Le Petit Zinc - Quaint and charming, this casual French café offers reasonably priced crepes, sandwiches, salads, and espresso drinks, with lots of delicious options for vegetarians. Crepes are divided between sucre or sale—made either as a traditional French confection—such as jam, butter and granulated sugar or Nutella—or made with savory filling—like French sausage, ham and brie, goat cheese and greens, or ratatouille (all savory crepes are served with a small green salad). Simplicity and quality, not snootiness, are the touchstones. Diners refresh their water themselves family-style from repurposed red wine bottles. In warmer months, patrons can enjoy their meal on the restaurant's beautiful, verdant outdoor patio, complete with a water fountain and a stone bed. In unaccommodating weather, a bright interior and cozy zinc bar offer a cheery respite from cold, rain, or snow. *1055 Trumbull Ave., www.lepetitzincdetroit.com, (313) 963-2805.*

LJ's Lounge - Between the original mirrorball pillars, Budweiser "Great Kings of Africa" portraits and the massive fish tank perched behind the bar, LJ's Lounge is Detroit character with a capital "C." This Michigan Avenue dive attracts a cross-section of Corktown regulars, rock scene fashionistas, and awestruck tourists with its cheap beers and only-in-Detroit time-capsule comforts. It's been home to some of the city's most legendary (and mostly defunct) DJ nights, piloted from the bar's one-of-a-kind record library and DJ booth in the back. These days, don't miss Terry-oke, a freak-flag-flying Thursday night karaoke extravaganza. For extra localist-points, keep an eye out for Charlie, the blue-shirted spirit who's rumored to haunt the bathroom hallway at the back of the bar. *2114 Michigan Ave., (313) 962-0013.*

Maltese American Benevolent Society - In the heart of the Michigan Avenue Corridor lies the Maltese American Benevolent Society, where Maltese Americans—real, honorary, and self-declared—sip domestic beers or basic cocktails and swap news from Malta or downtown Detroit. The interior of the space will make even the unacquainted nostalgic for the home country: Pictures of Malta's sandy coastlines, architecture, star soccer players, and influential citizens decorate the club. For a couple of quarters, visitors can crank up the volume on a classic jukebox full of '90s hits and Motown classics. But the real fun here is to be had with the gracious and hospitable regulars, who are known to buy a drink for a fresh, friendly face. While food isn't normally served, on Sundays visitors can buy delicious a Maltese pastizzi pastry, full of ground beef, peas, and cheese. Although the club is membership-based, the public can join the fun on Thursday through Sunday each week. *1832 Michigan Ave., (313) 961-8393.*

McShane's Irish Pub and Whiskey Bar - The handiwork of Sean, Ryan, and Bobby McShane, this spot is a contemporary, upscale take on the classic sports-orientated shuttle bar format and a popular pre-game watering hole. Opened in 2012, this recently renovated sports bar offers a host of distractions from the game, including billiards tables, 17 TVs, a shotski (four shots affixed to a ski), jukebox, and an impressive draft list notably including local favorites by Arbor Brewing Company, Motor City Brewing Works, Bell's, and Dragonmead. If you'd like to fill up before being tempted by a rink-side wiener, you're in luck—the food is tasty. The menu is best described as upscale bar fare with an Irish slant, including most notably the veggie Philly supreme, Irish egg rolls, killer fish and chips (with thyme-seasoned fries), baked macaroni and cheese, and the Hammer of the Gods—a thick pile of ham, gouda, lettuce, and tomato on challah. *1460 Michigan Ave., www.mcshanespub.com, (313) 961-1960.*

» Mercury Burger & Bar - Mercury Burger & Bar delivers upgraded, home-style versions of American favorites: delicious burgers ground fresh daily, classic sandwiches, dogs, fries, homemade onion rings, tasty salads, and dreamy tater tots of your childhood, served in paper-lined baskets. They've got a full bar featuring Michigan craft beers and decadent hand-dipped milkshakes with addictive boozy "grown-up" versions available. The vibe at Mercury is casual and fun with a clean, subway-tile-and-chrome retro diner feel, a long bar, comfortable booths, and a handful of references to "Mercury," including a cool mercury-dime bar, and a larger-than-life Lincoln-Mercury photo. In the summer months, munch al fresco on the patio with a view of the iconic train station. *2163 Michigan Ave., www.mercuryburgerbar.com, (313) 964-5000.*

» Mudgie's Deli - In Detroit, meat is king—and Mudgie's is a top contender for the deli sandwich crown. This neighborhood eatery tweaks the well-worn lunch counter model with innovations such as its locally made Sy Ginsburg corned beef, adventurous daily soup specials and delectable apple potato salad. At lunch, it's packed but never overrun; its Sunday brunch is a hidden gem. The only frustrating thing about this restaurant is selecting from its 24+ sandwich menu, forcing carnivores and vegetarians alike into fits of indecision over which house specialty to devour. Plus, don't overlook the craft soda selections in the front cooler. *1300 Porter St., www. mudgiesdeli.com, (313) 961-2000.*

» Nancy Whiskey - If the bartenders like you—REALLY like you— they might pull out the tattered book with photos of Nancy riding a horse through the bar on St. Patrick's Days of yore. This beer-and-a-shot joint carries a liquor license dating to 1902, making it one of the oldest watering holes in the city. The veteran Corktown establishment has benefited from a massive, historically respectful facelift following a near-devastating 2009 fire but still makes good on the traditions that made it a Corktown legend: neighborhood vibe, live blues on the weekends, and enough Irish whiskey to kill... well, a horse. Be sure to let your bartender know if it's your first time in—he/she might have a special treat for you. *2644 Harrison St., www.nancywhiskeydetroit.com, (313) 962-4247.*

Nemo's - It's like Field of Dreams, but in reverse: One of Detroit's longest-standing and most-revered sports bars did booming business for decades, thanks to the crowds that flocked to Tiger Stadium a few blocks away. But once the Tigers moved downtown to Comerica Park, the crowds kept coming. This devotion makes Nemo's the city's ultimate sports bar to this day. During home games, the rear parking lots are packed with tailgaters, and the bar's fleet of buses (painted in Corktown green and white) shuttle hundreds of fans to the sporting events of the season. Inside, of course you'll find plenty of big-screen TVs, but the main decor of the tin-ceilinged bar consists of dozens of framed newspaper front pages chronicling the city's sports glory. With bartenders who could fill in for TV color commentators without breaking a sweat, and a hilariously no-frills food menu (burgers and chips, please), Nemo's is where the sporting crowd's true believers congregate. If you want to get a seat at the bar on Opening Day, get there early. *1384 Michigan Ave., www.nemosdetroit.com, (313) 965-3180.*

» PJ's Lager House - Continuously operated as a restaurant, bar, or speakeasy since 1914, the Lager House has forged a reputation as one of the best joints in the city to catch local and national indie, punk, and garage rock 'n' roll. Since purchasing it in 2007, owner and music guru PJ Ryder has breathed new life into the venue, which now hosts shows—and draws crowds—almost every night. In addition to bringing the jams, the bar boasts food a cut above normal bar fare, with solid options for vegetarians and meat eaters alike, aptly billing it as a "kitchen with Detroit attitude and a dash of New Orleans flavor." Think homemade burgers—both meat and veg—burritos the size of your head, real deal po' boys, and gumbo. On off-nights, and before shows, there is often ping pong in the Jerome P. Cavanagh Social Room or, of course, you can just hunker down with a Stroh's at the long, history laden bar. Don't miss our favorite pub quiz in town every other Tuesday, featuring intelligent and esoteric trivia thoughtfully pulled together by quizmaster John Pat Leary. *1254 Michigan Ave., www.pjslagerhouse.com, (313) 961-4668.*

» Slows Bar B Q - Often cited as a shining example of local business revival in Detroit, Slows' soul-satiating cuisine has won over the hearts of longtime Detroiters, new transplants, suburban old-timers, and New York Times critics alike. Established in 2005, Slows boasts a well-designed, contemporary interior built mainly of reclaimed wood in an urban-yet-homey atmosphere perfect for the comfort food it serves. In general, the brisket, ribs, and pulled pork are revered, and the must-try sandwiches include The Yardbird (pulled smoked Amish chicken, mustard sauce, bacon, mushrooms, and cheddar)—which was recently named one of the top three sandwiches in America by the Travel Channel—The Longhorn (beef brisket, onion marmalade, smoked gouda, with a spicy sauce), and The Reason (smoked pulled pork butt, coleslaw, and pickle strips). Vegetarians love the place, too, for The Genius—a faux chicken wonder. Round out your meal with one or two of the life-affirming sides: succulent waffle fries, the homemade mac and cheese, sweet-potato mash, green beans, cornbread, old-time applesauce and split pea and okra fritters—all of which are excellent receptacles for the many house-made sauces. Blame it on the huge selection of beers and bourbons, the mouth-watering entrees, or the overall affordable prices, but Slows gets packed at peak hours. Reservations are accepted for parties of six or more; otherwise it's recommended to come early—or wait it out at one of the many nearby bars in Corktown. *2138 Michigan Ave., www.slowsbarbq.com, (313) 962-9828.*

» **St. Cece's** - At St. Cece's, the patron saint is whiskey and worshipping at the altar is having a chair near the roaring fire on a wintry Detroit night. Replete with Celtic accents, stained-glass windows, pews, and wood elements, many of which were salvaged from abandoned churches in the city, the warm and inviting bar exudes an old-world, European charm, which is often augmented with live, traditional music. Bellying up to the bar, you'll find Michigan microbrews on tap, a comprehensive bar menu, and stiff drinks, including a house shot, which is dubbed the Sweet Baby Jesus—and with good reason. Out of the kitchen, St. Cece's serves up bar food with a high-end, yet unpretentious, twist—from pulled pork sliders, to their homemade ricotta ravioli, and signature angus hamburger. It's also a bartender's bar: look for your favorite barkeeps recounting bawdy tales on the weekend and join them in soaking up the Corktown spirit late into the wee hours of the night. *1426 Bagley Ave., www.saintceces.com, (313) 962-2121.*

Steak Hut Restaurant - Whether you're looking for a quick breakfast fix or a leisurely bacon and egg brunch, nowhere in Detroit serves the greasy staples with the same homey panache as the Steak Hut. If you're lucky, you might get a heaping side of worldly advice from Gus, the man at the grill. All this can be had on a meager budget that makes out-of-towners balk (get in before 11am, and you can treat yourself to the legendary $2 breakfast special). Don't miss Sunday mornings, when live acoustic country and folk musicians whip up a soundtrack that's well-matched to the Steak Hut's comfort foods. *551 W. Lafayette Blvd., (313) 961-0659.*

» **The Sugar House** - With an emphasis on pre-Prohibition refinement, the Sugar House is home to some of Detroit's most exceptional craft cocktails. In an elegant atmosphere replete with taxidermy, vintage photos, and dramatic brass chandeliers, vest-clad bartenders and servers tend to candlelit tables. Following the grand tradition of fine cocktails, all syrups and juices are freshly house-made, so you won't find any artificial flavors at this dram shop, only high-quality ingredients and a carefully vetted drink menu of the highest caliber. If the selections on the seasonal menu don't strike your fancy, there's always "dealer's choice"—select a favorite liquor or theme and let the bartenders expand your palette. Though there isn't a full menu, the bar offers a selective assortment of gourmet small plates and bar snacks. Visit on Saturday or Sunday afternoons for their "eye-opener menu," featuring Bloody Marys and bagels. If you're lucky (or check the schedule) you can catch Spanish guitar, DJs, or jazz music throughout the week. *2130 Michigan Ave., www.sugarhousedetroit.com, (313) 962-0123.*

SHOPPING & SERVICES

Bagley Vision - Owned by a man named George who occasionally refers to himself simply as "the old-timer," Bagley Vision is a curious optical emporium that the uninitiated often assume is closed—a misconception that might have something to do with the padlocked metal grate over the front door. However, if you are lucky enough to find your way in—the secret is calling ahead—you are in for a treat. While the "old-timer" stocks a sizable selection of standard optical fare in the normal mercantile displays, the real prize is his selection of "vintage frames"—a large cardboard box heaped with vintage and dead stock frames priced from $20. With lenses also around the $30 mark, the shop is astonishingly affordable and ideal for fans of a retro look. *2150 Bagley St., (313) 964-7994. (Do not call late—the old-timer lives in his store.)*

Brooks Lumber - The outgoing and dependable staff at Brooks is renowned for explaining projects and educating customers as they show them around the—almost—overwhelming inventory. Opened in 1900, the crowded shop retains the unassuming, packed atmosphere of old-timey hardware stores. Whether you're in the market for a flange, a stud, a key, or a sash lock, it's nearly impossible to leave without finding what you needed. Brooks also offers a full line of lumber, electrical, and plumbing supplies and specializes in historic home renovation necessities. The location is especially memorable for longtime residents, as former Tigers announcer Ernie Harwell was fond of saying, "They'll find that at Brooks tomorrow" after impressive home runs out of the old Tiger Stadium, which stood across the street. *2200 Trumbull St., (313) 962-6448.*

Detroit Athletic Company - Located in a charming old building steps away from the site of where Tiger Stadium once stood, this athletic-wear emporium has something for every Tigers, Pistons, Red Wings, or Lions fan. Though not a huge store, it packs in the merch and, in addition to a stellar selection of T-shirts, caps, and sweatshirts (including some classic vintage throwback styles), it has an impressive array of other goods emblazoned with your favorite team's logo. From simple T-shirts to lapel pins to Tigers-themed BBQ sets to photo-realistic woven Red Wings blankets, the Detroit Athletic Company is a one-stop shop to stock up on goods to show your team pride. *1744 Michigan Ave., www.detroitathletic.com, (313) 961-3550.*

Detroit Massage and Wellness - Located in the spacious upper suites of the St. Francis Cabrini Clinic—a compassionate holistic health care facility—lies Detroit Massage and Wellness. Founded in 2011, owner Hannah Lewis provides Detroiters with a tranquil, down-to-Earth massage experience that includes a meet and greet with a massage therapist, a customer intake survey, and a personal consultation—all of which takes place in addition to those 30, 60, or 90 minutes of nirvana on the massage table. Anticipate soothing nature sounds, tranquil lavender and mint wall colors, and a wide-range of services, including deep tissue, reflexology, aromatherapy, reiki, myofascial release, lymphatic, TMJ, Swedish, prenatal/postnatal, sinus/allergy, abdominal, hot stone, and chair massages. Call to schedule an appointment. *1234 Porter St., www.detroitmassageandwellness.com, (313) 355-0629.*

The Greening of Detroit - Formed in 1989 as a reforestation and beautification project for the city of Detroit, this environmental nonprofit has blossomed into much more than just trees. Throughout the years, Greening has expanded its efforts to include education, advocacy, and a Garden Resource Program that supports more than 1,300 community, family, and school gardens in the city. Before you start your home or neighborhood garden, be sure to check out the vast array of resources it offers, from affordable organically grown transplants to materials to raised beds. The nonprofit is also a mainstay at Eastern Market on Saturdays and the Wayne State University Farmer's Market on Wednesdays, helping to sell locally grown produce through Grown in Detroit. Go to its website for more information on the Garden Resource Program and to learn about upcoming events. *1418 Michigan Ave., www.greeningofdetroit.com, (313) 237-8733.*

» Hello Records - Small in size but stacked with wax, Hello Records is a great place to load up on music at fantastic prices. With beautiful hardwood floors and wall-to-wall record shelves, this unassuming store has a laid-back atmosphere made for browsing. Although they stock rock, soul, gospel, funk, jazz, disco, techno, hip hop, and folk LPs and 45s from all eras, this shop is especially popular among collectors looking for jazz, soul, and dance platters—particularly forgotten soul gems from Detroit's hundreds of local music labels. With Hello's low prices, customers can buy an album for a song, even on the deepest cuts. Knowledgeable owner Wade Kergan is without pretense, and his friendly staff is incredibly approachable and excited to introduce customers to new artists, albums, and genres. The store's popularity among both buyers and sellers leads to a constantly changing inventory. If you don't find what you're looking for, come back after lunch. *1459 Bagley St., www.hellorecordsdetroit.com, (313) 300-5654.*

» **John K. King Used & Rare Books** - If you're looking for an in-town escape, lose yourself in books at Michigan's largest used and rare bookstore, and one of Detroit's best and most beloved shopping experiences. This four-story former glove factory, once moved from its original moorings to make room for a highway six decades ago, is a bibliophile's sanctuary. With a collection of more than one million books, you can treasure hunt for hours through aisles upon aisles of floor-to-ceiling stacks. If you're not browsing for bargains, peculiarities, or happy accidents but have something particular in mind, just ask one of the incredibly helpful and knowledgeable staff members to point you in the right direction. Thankfully, the titles are well-organized. *901 W. Lafayette Blvd., www.rarebooklink.com, (313) 961-0622.*

National Dry Goods Co. - Since 1921, National Dry Goods has supplied Detroit with affordable, "durable, rugged, and comfortable"

clothing and shoes for school, work, and play. Women, men, and children can find everything from school uniforms to Dickie's work pants to Carhartt coats, gloves, and jumpsuits. It also offers custom screen-printing services. Other accessories—including umbrellas, colorful roll socks, wool berets, and ball caps—keep customers coming back to this one-stop apparel shop. *1200 Trumbull Ave., www.nationaldrygoods.com, (313) 961-3656.*

» Rachel's Place - Tucked away in a brownstone row house on a residential street just north of Michigan Avenue, Rachel's Place always seems like a wonderful secret, even though it's popular with in-the-know vintage lovers and is just steps away from all the Corktown action. Owner Rachel Leggs' fabulous style and eye are apparent in the selection and organization of this bountiful and well-curated store. Her friendly welcome will make you feel at home from the second you first set foot in the door. After only a couple of visits, when you walk in, she's likely to pull out spot-on finds that she's been holding behind the desk for you. If you like vintage clothes, it's nearly impossible to set foot inside without finding something to buy. *2124 Pine St., (313) 964-9008.*

Salvation Army - The Fort Street Salvation Army is a colossal thrift store with a choice selection of small housewares, linens, and tchotchkes for the discerning thrifter. The clothing selection is above average and extremely plentiful. In addition to these items, the store sells furniture, though this is not its strong suit. As a perk, this Salvo is cleaner than other area thrift stores and boasts restrooms and fitting rooms, which are fairly uncommon in similar outfits. *1200 W. Fort St., www.salvationarmyusa.org, (313) 309-3372.*

Xavier's 20th Century Furniture - Since 1985, Xavier's has brought the finest collection of modern, functional, and famous names in furniture design to Michigan Avenue. Here, owner James Slade keeps things fresh and lively from his burgundy brick building, which is accented with popping robin's egg blue trim and stunning window displays of his latest vintage furniture finds. Shoppers will not only admire modern pottery and glass, coffee tables, sofas, elegantly framed paintings, and rare Hudson's fur hats, but they will hear the history behind each piece and the story of each designer from Slade himself. Collectors will appreciate Slade's eye for Gilbert Rohde and Charles and Ray Eames pieces, as well as modern and contemporary furniture from the 1920s through the 1980s. Rare pieces, such as Art Deco Chase chrome candlesticks, appear as Slade discovers gems at antique malls and estate sales across the country. Xavier's cult following of customers snatches up these exciting items quickly, so be sure to visit often. Filmmakers and photographers are also welcome to inquire for prop rentals. *2546 Michigan Ave., www.x20th.com, (313) 964-1222.*

CULTURAL ATTRACTIONS

5e Gallery - With a brightly painted facade that reflects the explosion of talent among the young visual and musical artists who create here, the 5e Gallery educates youth and the public on the art and the elements of hip-hop. Founded in 2008, the alternative multidisciplinary arts space showcases and facilitates contemporary artwork while it engages its audience and community. The walls of the space are replete with colorful murals and street-art-style portraits. Drop in and you're likely to see students and artists editing video of music performances, creating mixes for dance groups, hosting hip-hop dance practices, or preparing for film screenings. Hip-hop fans should visit on Tuesday evenings for "The Foundation"—an event co-founded by local emcees Invincible and Miz Korona that seeks to celebrate and empower women in hip-hop. *2661 Michigan Ave., www.5egallery.org, (313) 355-2572.*

Imagination Station - Founded by a team of local creatives in 2010, the Imagination Station is a fledgling creative campus and public art space dedicated to exploring the intersection of technology, art, and community. Primarily housed in a vacant blighted 1880 home-turned art installation called "Righty," the Imagination Station is a raw, and lively space featuring a performance venue built out of a demolished adjoining house that was known as "Lefty," and a large open space. The Imagination Station offers an array of performances, talks, and artistic endeavors. Since opening, the station has played host to a variety of art installations, including a house-size camera obscura and—most recently—a free concrete "Urban Put Put" course made from found objects, including a vehicular obstacle. Although it is best to visit during one of its many public events, when volunteers may act as a docent, visitors can enjoy self-led tours to explore the station at any time. Outside of events, there are no regular hours. *2230 14th St., www.facethestation.com.*

Kunsthalle Detroit - Located inside an old bank building, Kunsthalle Detroit is the country's first museum dedicated to multimedia and light-based art. The non-collecting institution ("Kunsthalle" is German for "art hall") opened in summer 2011 with a knockout show featuring work by internationally acclaimed film and video artists like Bill Viola, Ange Lecci, and William Kentridge. Founded by former New York art consultant Tate Osten, Kunsthalle has an ambitious vision that includes becoming a leading force in Detroit's revitalization and the world's foremost museum of light-based arts. 5001 Grand River Ave., www.kunsthalle-detroit.org, *(313) 897-7000.*

North End Studios - Founded in the North End neighborhood in 2009, when founding member and CCS alumna Katherine Craig spearheaded a giant and now-iconic sky-blue mural on their original building on Grand Boulevard, this vibrant, young, creative artists collective has now set up shop in Corktown. Dedicated to working with the community and existing as a hub for artists to work, to exhibit, and to collaborate, North End Studios mounts high-quality exhibitions with adventurous and thoughtful new work, as well as progressive film screenings, community collaboration, residencies, music and performances, and, under its alter-moniker Sparklewood, raucous parties lasting into the early hours of the morning. *5101 Loraine St., www.northendstudiosdetroit.com.*

Ponyride - The latest project from model-turned-restaurateur-turned-philanthropist Phil Cooley, Ponyride transformed a declining 30,000-square-foot industrial office complex into a community-driven art space where tenants, composed of fledgling artistic enterprises, pay just 10 to 20 cents per square foot in exchange for sharing their craft and expertise with the surrounding community. The result is an inspiring, aesthetically beautiful space that, at least for the time being, is in a constant state of flux, as renovation continues in new areas of the labyrinthine building. As of the writing of this guide, some of our favorite enterprises housed in the facility include **Context Furniture,** a custom contemporary furniture manufacturer; **Detroit Denim Co.,** a boutique denim manufacturing company that responsibly and meticulously crafts jeans and other textiles by hand; a social enterprise called the **Empowerment Plan** that pays members of the homeless community to manufacture versatile outerwear; **En Garde!** Detroit, a full-service fencing studio; **RunJit,** a dance studio that parlays the art of Detroit's homegrown hip-hop dance style called jit; and **Stukenborg,** a virtuosic letterpress studio offering commercial printing and studio classes. Because the building itself does not hold regular public hours, be sure to contact the party you intend to visit prior to your trip. *1501 Vermont St., www.ponyride.org.*

ENTERTAINMENT & RECREATION

Abreact Performance Space - Theater in Detroit doesn't get more intimate than this. A comfortable Corktown loft becomes a singular performance space that seats about 40 and showcases work by big-name playwrights, as well as local talent. The productions range from challenging classics to over-the-top romps, but whatever the particulars, some things about the Abreact never change: the immediacy of experiencing live theater in someone's living room, the welcoming atmosphere, and the complimentary refreshments. (The Abreact doesn't charge admission, either, though donations are encouraged.) *1301 W. Lafayette Blvd., Apt. 113, www.theabreact.com, (313) 454-1542.*

Corktown Cinema - The reincarnation of the beloved Burton Theatre, Corktown Cinema builds upon the strong reputation set by local cinephiles David Allen, Jeff Else, Nathan Faustyn, and Matt Kelson in their first foray. Opened in 2011, this popular theater shows a thoughtfully curated selection of art house, indie, cult, foreign, and classic films. From their raw, simple space in a former brass foundry—which is still undergoing renovation—Corktown Cinema offers periodic indoor and outdoor screenings that approach critical films with a joie de vivre. Rumor has it that the theater will settle into new digs in the neighborhood in 2013 and resume a full schedule of screenings. Check their website for showtimes and the potential change of location. *2051 Rosa Parks Blvd., www.corktowncinema.com, (313) 473-9238.*

MotorCity Casino - Since opening in 1999, the MotorCity Casino has become renowned among area gamblers for its unique ambiance, attentive staff, dining options, and array of gaming machines. In a Las Vegas style reminiscent of a concept car, the exterior's wavy chrome and ostentatious neon light display complement the building's interior, which draws design and aesthetic inspiration from local automotive tradition, including fixtures modeled after automobile parts interspersed with architectural elements custom-made by West Coast automotive designer Chip Foose. The on-site casual dining options, including the Assembly Line Buffet and Pit Stop, offer unparalleled selection, and pay further homage to the area's automotive heritage. While even the most seasoned card shark will enjoy the wide assortment of table games, MotorCity Casino is better known for its gaming machines—especially its loose slots and video poker. The casino's 2,800 games include classic reel games, five-reel options, video poker, and video slots and come in denominations from $.01 to $50. *2901 Grand River Ave., www.motorcitycasino.com, (313) 237-7711.*

SITES

» Michigan Central Station - A hauntingly beautiful, captivating image of urban blight, Michigan Central Station has become an emblem of the city during the two decades since it closed. The building, set on the apron of Roosevelt Park, has been featured prominently in Hollywood and independent films, television, and music videos, and it has been enjoyed by countless clandestine visitors, the images of its interior and silhouette epitomizing the grandeur of a Detroit that was, but no longer is. The reality is more nuanced. Despite its massive, 500,000-square-foot, 18-story size and ambitious Beaux-Arts neoclassical flourishes—such as ionic columns and vaulted ceilings in marble rooms made to mimic Roman bath houses—MCS was never fully occupied after opening in 1913. But the station's elegance could not overcome logistical obstacles to its inhabitation. The building's disuse is realistically due to two separate blows: its inaccessibility to passengers when streetcars in Detroit were scuttled, and the post-war auto boom that coalesced

with new freeways to make driving more attractive than train travel. Regardless of the cause, the station changed hands and was gradually wound down before being closed in 1988, later purchased by local controversial bridge tycoon Manuel "Matty" Moroun. Since its closure, its future has been uncertain, with plans for both renovation and demolition being recommended. In 2012, lighting was added to illuminate the station at night, which is decidedly stunning. *2405 W. Vernor St.*

Tiger Stadium Field - For more than 100 years, the Tigers called "The Corner" home, from Bennett Park to Navin Field to Briggs Stadium and finally to Tiger Stadium. Evolving with each successive owner and expansion until its final game in September 1999, the site has seen many canonic moments in baseball—Ty Cobb stealing three bases on three consecutive pitches in 1911; the team's first World Series victory, in 1935; the end of Lou Gehrig's streak of 2,130 consecutive games, in 1939; Denny McLain's 31st win in the team's '68 championship season; Dave Bergman's dogged 13-pitch walk-off home run in '84; and Robert Fick's grand slam in 1999, as the last home run, RBI, and hit at Tiger Stadium. Since the hard-fought, heavily contested demolition in 2009, residents have bestowed the field with the name Ernie Harwell Memorial Park out of gratitude for the beloved longtime broadcaster's passion for Detroit and its ball club. Though technically not public, the storied field remains playable, tended by volunteer groundskeepers on an ad hoc basis. Residents are rumored to sometimes slip onto the field, beyond the unsecured fences, to enjoy America's favorite pastime on one of the sport's most hallowed diamonds.
Northwest corner of Michigan Ave. and Trumbull Ave.

Worker's Row House - Built in 1849, and one of the oldest surviving homes in Detroit, though now empty, this unassuming three-unit row house was occupied continuously for 150 years, originally by Irish immigrants, and then a steady succession of other hardworking Detroiters. In the early life of the building, density and rental rates were so high that as many as 12 people lived in each of the three 560-square-foot units at a given time. Though threatened by the development of a church parking lot, the Greater Corktown Development Corporation, which plans to develop the structure into a workers museum, rescued the historic building from the wrecking ball. In the meantime, Wayne State University is in the midst of a long-term archeological dig on the site, recovering everyday artifacts of 19th century Detroit life. *Located on 6th St. between Bagley St. and Labrosse St.*

POINTS OF INTEREST

Brother Nature Farm - This urban farm supplies a number of local restaurants with fresh produce, runs a community-supported agriculture (CSA) operation, and can be found at its stand every Saturday at Eastern Market. About once a week, the farm also sells prepared foods from an old Airstream trailer located next to its farmland. *2913 Rosa Parks Blvd.*

Catherine Ferguson Academy - A high school for pregnant teenagers and young mothers, the academy teaches life skills in addition to academics, and features a fully operational farm with horses, goats, rabbits, ducks, and chickens. *2750 Selden St.*

Corktown Mural - Jerome Ferretti painted this colorful mural in 2005 on Michigan Avenue, welcoming travelers exiting from Downtown into Corktown. *1236 Michigan Ave.*

Detroit Beautification Project - Fat Captain America Mural - As part of the Detroit Beautification Project, graffiti artist Sever painted this overweight Captain America, complete with a Big Gulp and a corndog. *4220 Vermont St.*

Hope Takes Root Garden - One of the older community gardens in the city, the plants here get a boost from the bees that the members keep on site. *2829 Wabash St.*

Joe's Auto Truck Welding Perforated Metal Installation - This abandoned auto repair shop received a striking makeover in 2012, when University of Michigan graduate students filled in its missing windows with undulating, geometric metal sheets. *2223 Perry St.*

Monumental Kitty - Artist Jerome Ferretti's brick sculpture of a huge cat head, paw, and tail was inspired both by the nearby former Tiger Stadium site, as well as the abundance of cats hanging around in North Corktown. *1717 Fisher Fwy.*

Spirit of Hope Farm - Operated by the adjacent Spirit of Hope Church, this farm aims to beautify the neighborhood, stock the church's food programs, and provide an educational opportunity for local children and adults alike. *1561 Myrtle St.*

CHAPTER 5
SOUTHWEST

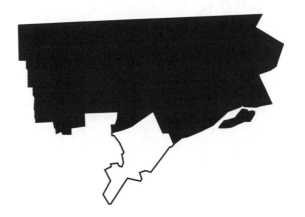

Near
West
Side

Midtown

Corktown

Warren

I-96

I-94

MLK

Briggs

Millenium
Village

Michigan

Grand Boulevard

Mexicantown

Hubbard
Richard

Michigan
Martin

Huhbard
Farms

Jefferson

SOUTHWEST

Livernois

Fort

Springwells

I-75

DelRay

Dearborn

Jefferson

Carbon
Works

Oakwood
Heights

River
Rouge

Melvindale

Boynton

Lincoln
Park

Outer

Ecorse

Detroit River

Outer

0   1   2
Miles

No visit to the city is complete without a trip to Southwest Detroit. This collection of historic neighborhoods is a regional destination for its Central and South American cuisine, vibrant commercial districts, and local cultural amenities. Foodies, history buffs, art and music lovers, bargain hunters, and architecture fans can spend a lifetime— or an afternoon—exploring Southwest Detroit and never soak everything in. As we define it, Southwest Detroit spans 13.3 square miles and is bounded by I-94 to the north, the Detroit River to the south, I-75 to the east and the city limits to the west.

Since becoming part of Detroit between 1857 and 1922, Southwest Detroit has remained one of the most ethnically, religiously, and racially diverse areas in the city. Drawn by the promise of Ford's $5 workday at the neighboring Rouge Plant, waves of German, Hungarian, Irish, Italian, Russian, Romanian, Czech, Armenian, Appalachian, and African-American workers flocked to Southwest Detroit through the postwar era. Today, this legacy of popularity among immigrants continues through the many South and Central Americans living in, and moving to, the area—Southwest is home to more than 60,000 residents and is growing. Many know parts of Southwest Detroit as Mexicantown, but alongside the many residents of Mexican heritage are smaller contingents of people of Argentinean, Bolivian, Chilean, Colombian, Cuban, Ecuadorian, Dominican, El Salvadorian, Guatemalan, Honduran, Nicaraguan, Panamanian, and Puerto Rican ancestry.

Southwest Detroit is home to a diverse group of neighborhoods, each with unique identities, development patterns, and evolutionary directions. Among others neighborhoods, Southwest Detroit is home to Boynton, Carbon Works, Claytown, Delray, Hubbard Farms, Hubbard Richard, Mexicantown, Michigan Martin, Oakwood Heights, and Springwells. Although each of these neighborhoods offers a distinct character, their shared historical popularity among immigrants has created many physical and aesthetic similarities. Because of the past—and in some neighborhoods, current—influx of immigrants and working-class residents, the area features blocks upon blocks of brick and wood frame homes in Foursquare, Craftsman, and Colonial Revival styles, most typically between 1,000 and 2,000 square feet and built between 1890 and 1930. The streets of Southwest Detroit are typically narrow, highly walkable, and flanked by beautifully aged trees. Along many residential blocks, visitors will find charming neighborhood bars or corner markets tucked away, far from major roads. Most of the Southwest neighborhoods straddle or abut the area's primary commercial artery, West Vernor Highway, which despite its name, is a stroll-worthy, narrow commercial corridor, with tree-lined shopping districts corralling unusually congenial traffic congestion, summer popsicle vendors on bikes pedaling in and out of side streets, and scores of independent businesses packed with locals.

Although nearly every neighborhood in Southwest has reasons to visit, a few areas rank among our favorites. Visitors looking to soak up some vintage character at a corner dive should follow their boozy divining rods to Springwells, Claytown, or Delray. Those looking to enjoy South and Central American cuisine should start their culinary adventure in Mexicantown or along the Vernor corridor but should explore further for more out-of-the-way locales. Visitors looking to stroll through a beautiful, tree-lined, historic neighborhood amidst the sweet smell of fresh tortillas and admire fine Romanesque, Colonial Revival, Beaux Arts, Cape Cod, Foursquare, Craftsman, and Italianate architecture should look no further than Hubbard Farms.

BARS & RESTAURANTS

Abick's Bar - Don't tell anyone, but Abick's might be the classiest secret in the neighborhood. Behind the unassuming facade of this bar at the intersection of two residential streets in Southwest Detroit lies a century-old family tradition. Maya Abick Soviak, the octogenarian owner and barkeep, has lived her entire life in the apartment upstairs and has a reputation for fine cocktails and better stories. Patrons are welcomed into a cozy, well-worn front room complete with a tin ceiling, beautiful brass cash register, and a bar-long wooden liquor cabinet featuring stained-glass windows. The bar offers a secluded, plush cigar lounge in the rear, which features two TVs, rental lockers, and a curated selection of cigars for sale. Bring a treat for Samson, the friendly and endearing bull mastiff and unofficial mascot. Pool table, darts, and limited menu. *3500 Gilbert St., (313) 894-9329.*

Angel's Place - Angel's is an excellent option for the peckish looking for lunchtime variety. This cheap, delectable Puerto Rican carryout joint on Michigan Avenue is easy to spot, with its bright red patriotico paint scheme, and tough to mistake for any other restaurant once inside. Dine-in service is possible at a few red-and-white clothed tables, but ambience skews toward the Spartan. Quick, cheap takeaways—like alcapurria (fried banana mash stuffed with chicken), pasteles (meat and potato stuffed fritters), and tostones (fried flat bananas)—are kept warm instead of made to order, so arriving earlier is better. Dinners of beef, chicken, and pork are served with traditional rice and beans. For beverages, customers may choose between Malta and Pepsi. *7824 Michigan Ave., (313) 846-7381.*

Armando's Mexican Restaurant - A favorite stop for many a hungry Detroiter, this charming Mexican restaurant offers large portions at small prices. Setting the scene with a tiled decor, a welcoming atmosphere, and traditional Mexican music, the kitchen whips up traditional fare, as well as Tex-Mex options, with standards like botanas, tacos, and enchiladas (with a special zesty sauce) serving as consistently stellar options. Every weekday, the spot hosts a flavorful all-you-can-eat lunch buffet, complete with homemade salsas and pitchers of margaritas. Open until 2am on weekdays and 4am on weekends, the place is an ideal postbar destination. For those lucky enough to skeeter in before last call, Armando's has a full bar, with extra solid margaritas and mojitos. *4242 W. Vernor Hwy., (313) 554-0666.*

» Café con Leche - A coffee-lover's oasis, Café con Leche, which is Spanish for "coffee with milk," features a menu of well-crafted renditions of the usual suspects, as well as Mexican specialties like champurrado (a warm, rich and mellow chocolate/masa concoction with plenty of texture) and shots of chocolate a la taza or yerba mate served in traditional gourds. Patrons relax in an open, comfortable setting decorated with local artwork and a canopy of burlap coffee sackcloth. Regularly hosting concerts, community meetings, and other events, Café con Leche has become a nucleus of the neighborhood. Also offering some Mexican products (Jarritos!), delicious baked goods, and homemade sandwiches, Café con Leche is a favorite place to hunker down and make use of the free Wi-Fi or chat with a friend over a bite. *4200 W. Vernor Hwy., (313) 554-1744.*

Cas Bar - A play on the name of the adjacent Casper Street, the understated curiosity-inviting vintage neon sign shining through the bar's hexagonal window is indicative of the tarnished treasure inside. While the galley-style bar, which almost entirely caters to grizzled neighborhood regulars, isn't polished by any means, it's an inviting and friendly verbal repository of Southwest Detroit lore. So, if you're feeling social, order a Stroh's, and prepare to talk shop. There's a pool table in the back. *7800 Michigan Ave., (313) 581-9777.*

Charlie's Bar - Detroit's response to the international shortage of Art Deco dive bars, Charlie's Bar draws from the best of 1930s style, 1970s entertainment, and 1980s drink prices. A small, friendly neighborhood bar on a lively strip of Springwells, Charlie's is a quiet space offering Centipede, a large projection screen, a pool table, darts, and a jukebox alongside the intricate Art Deco woodwork behind the bar. The impressive projector makes this a solid choice to watch the game, but the woodwork, darts, and pool table make this a great place to work on your elbow bends with friends. In contrast to most dives, cocktail drinkers will be impressed by the selection of liquors. *1503 Springwells St., (313) 849-3951.*

Chicago's Pizza - Whether you're craving a classic round or a deep, saucy, cheesy Chicago-style pizza pie, this family-owned carryout pizza joint has the pie for you. Not only does Chicago's Pizza serve up the classic sauce-on-top deep dish at a few dollars cheaper than Pizza Papalis (see separate entry), but delivery is also available. Wings and subs make great supplements to Chicago Pizza's iconic specialty, the Mexican Pizza, which piles Chorizo, ham, pepperoni, beans, onions, and peppers atop a classic round crust. Open late. *4650 W. Vernor Hwy., www.chicago-pizza-detroit.com, (313) 843-3777.*

Colombo's Coney - An adorable little old-school diner that's clean but not overly bright for those still recovering from late-night indulgences, Colombo's features shining red booth seating and plenty of counter stools for a good view of the grill top. Scrape together the last of your change to grab a deal your out-of-town friends will scoff at: a $2 breakfast special of eggs, toast, and hashbrowns (served 6am–11am) or splurge and pay an extra dollar to get some meat with that breakfast. *5414 W. Vernor Hwy., (313) 849-0995.*

Donovan's Pub - This pub wears the title "dive bar" with pride. Cheap, cold beers, the occasional musical act, and an off-the-beaten path vibe are sure to welcome you on any given night. The bar embraces a nonchalant joie de vivre—the Christmas lights, antique breweriana, and Detroit ephemera hanging on the walls are emblematic of the laid-back vibe and easygoing staff. From behind the old-timey bar, the affable staff digs into its deep inventory of greasy bar food, call liquors, and bottled beers to the sounds of classic rock, pop, and country. On the right nights, an array of acts—including local favorites such as Rodriguez and Tyvek—grace the stage, but one thing remains the same: no frills. If you're looking for a friendly barkeep and a place to drown your sorrows without having to worry about a

whopping bar tab, you've found your match. No drafts.
3003 W. Vernor Hwy., (313) 964-2267.

Donut Villa - With the vintage modernist signs and pungent doughnut aroma drawing customers in from throughout the neighborhood, it's no wonder that it's usually hard to find a seat at the counter. Open since the Eisenhower administration, Donut Villa is a thrifty sweet tooth's paradise: The cheerful staff makes all of the more than 30 varieties of 65-cent doughnuts—including the ever-popular pumpkin doughnuts—and coffee all day, ensuring you're always getting fresh treats. Don't leave without ordering a handful of nickelnuts—the renowned 5-cent doughnut holes. Gambling fans will be relieved to know you can purchase lottery tickets at the counter. *5875 W. Vernor Hwy., (313) 849-4752.*

» Duly's Place Coney Island - Not a place for claustrophobics, Duly's is at most a 12-foot-wide shotgun style diner with a handful of tightly packed tables reminiscent of a Depression-era lunch counter—with Depression-era prices. Open 24 hours, the coney is dotted with memorabilia, newspaper clippings, photographs, and regulars who look like they've been there since the place opened in 1921, giving it a certain indescribable charm. While the faithful who ascribe to the Duly's dogma will attest to the fact that the counter serves up the best coney in the city, this is an argument for the ages—one that can be settled only with a first-person sample. Those who aren't coney fans can sample the breakfast, which is served all day and night, or the tasty homemade soups. Just look for the logo that's the well-dressed hot dog equivalent of Mr. Peanut. *5458 W. Vernor Hwy., (313) 554-3076.*

» El Barzon - Although you might think serving both Italian and Mexican food is a novelty act, it's anything but. Tucked into a quiet Southwest Detroit neighborhood, El Barzon owner and head chef Norberto Garita offers cheap tickets to Puebla and Rome with his exquisite, split menu. The restaurant's bistro decor, exposed brick walls, white tablecloths, wooden chairs, and marble-top bar imbue an atmosphere of casual elegance. The menu reflects the decor. Through both his Mexican heritage and Italian culinary training, Garita demonstrates a faith in the power of fine, fresh ingredients, which lends dishes on both the Italian and Mexican sides of the menu an unparalleled zest and intensity. Although revered for the delightfully rich, citrusy homemade mole sauce and the incredible and celebrated homemade pastas, guests can explore the diverse menu with confidence—nary an option misses the mark. The Involtino di Vetello (veal stuffed with prosciutto), Vongole Ecozze all Arrabiata (mussels and clams in a tomato broth), and Barbacoa de Chivo al Horno (poblano goat barbecue) are all peerless and make excellent options on a third visit, after a thorough sampling of the mole and pasta. Each of these choices will leave guests snitching from the doggy bag on the way home. If you leave room after your delicious, affordable meal, try the lemon ripieno sorbet. *3710 Junction St., www.elbarzonrestaurant. com, (313) 894-2070.*

El Club Lounge & Mexicantown Fiesta Center - You might believe you're in a divey Mexican cantina when standing in the spacious, charmingly overgrown grassy patio of this unique Southwest Detroit classic. Seated under a labyrinth of gazebos and party tents, guests are surrounded by pots of artificial flowers and live plants, picnic tables, and curious decorations as mariachi songs waft from inside the old building. Originally a Lithuanian social club, the interior features a skylight with original plaster molding. The friendly owner and hostess, Dolores Sanchez, will be glad to give you an ad-libbed history of the bar as she pours you a brewski or shot of bottom-shelf tequila. These days, the sometimes-sleepy bar is brought to life with occasional live punk and rock shows and the regular outdoor Happy Hour DJ night through the summer. The bar is usually open Wednesdays, Thursdays, and Fridays and for special events, but patrons should call ahead. The large adjoining hall is also available for event and show rentals. *4114 W. Vernor Hwy., (313) 841-0400.*

El Papa de los Pollitos - Take a lesson from the cheerful chicken sheriff mural on the front facade: Get in line. There are few things as tasty—and perhaps as popular—as juicy, succulent, tender, perfectly grilled chicken basted in house-made sauce served with hot rice and beans. El Papa de los Pollitos—"father of the chickens"—might be a small, timeworn restaurant with a handful of tables and walls that haven't been on the business end of a paintbrush since Ronald Reagan left office, but it often barely keeps up with demand, no matter how tightly the expert staff pack the 12-square-foot outdoor grill. Along with its famous barbecued chicken—made outdoors year-round—tasty dishes, such as tacos, taquitos, and other Mexican treats, comprise an ever-changing menu based on what the restaurant has in stock. Call ahead or cross your fingers—the chicken is in high demand. Expect to leave sated for only a few simoleons. *4047 W. Vernor Hwy., (313) 729-0259.*

El Rancho Restaurant - Serving up authentic Mexican fare inspired by flavors of their hometown San Louis Potosi, owners Lucia and Alfonso Avila have built upon their stellar reputation since opening in 1983. Charming murals of Mexican towns adorn the sunny-yellow walls and traditional weavings and cowboy hats rest above the comfortable, cushioned brown booths. In addition to the extremely affordable lunch specials—entree, soup, chips and two varieties of delicious salsa for $5—El Rancho offers a comprehensive, tasty, dinner menu, including delicious flautas (deep fried tortillas rolled in beef or chicken), camarones al a veracruzana (shrimp in tomatillo sauce), and menudo (tripe soup). The breakfast options shouldn't be overlooked either, particularly the chilaquiles (scrambled eggs with corn tortillas, cheese, and vegetables). A full-service bar also offers a wide selection of tequila and Mexican beer. Complete your meal with El Rancho's famous flaming ice cream dessert (think baked Acapulco). *5900 W. Vernor Hwy., www.elranchomexrest.net, (313) 843-2151.*

El Rincon Taraxco - Affectionately called ol' Rincy by some locals, this hole-in-the-wall eatery serves some of the city's best Mexican seafood, or "mariscos," as the aqua-inspired letters on the facade indicate. Forget chips and salsa, this is a fish joint, so look for an incredible tuna and mayonnaise spread to greet you at your table. With a focus on palate, not aesthetics, house specialties include Chilaquiles de Camaron (shrimp in a fried tortilla drizzled with salsa and cheese), Caldo de Siete Mares (a flavorful seven-seafood soup), and Ceviche (cold fish "cooked" with lime juice as the acidic catalyst on a toasted tortilla). Though everything is in Spanish at this authentically Mexican restaurant, don't be shy about asking your server for some translation assistance—the staff is happy to guide you. Seafood selections are best washed down with a fresh-squeezed lime margarita from the full bar. *1414 Junction St., (313) 843-6595.*

El Zocalo - You haven't been to Mexicantown if you haven't navigated through El Zocalo's labyrinthine kitchen to get to its cushy dining room. Housed in an ornate 1920s bank building, the cheerful interior of this popular eatery is clad in bright colors, colorful reproduction Aztec and Mayan artifacts, and vibrant South and Central American paintings. The comprehensive menu is stacked with Mexican comfort food, and tasty takes on traditional Mexican and South American favorites, including menudo (tripe soup), chiles rellanos (stuffed fried peppers), and nopalitos (cactus pads), as well as more pervasive options like tacos, burritos, and enchiladas. With such options, the place would be a medal contender in any Mexicantown tacolympics. El Zocalo wins for its cheap beer, carafes of margaritas, excellent sangria, lovely patio, and stellar service. And don't miss its queso flameado, the best in town. Patio seating available. *3400 Bagley Ave., (313) 841-3700.*

Evie's Tamales & Family Restaurant - Evie's is a Mexican restaurant famous for its satisfying tamales, but also drawing crowds for cheap and generous breakfasts and lunches. Breakfast here hits the main points—an emphasis on eggs and meat with large quantities at good prices, but flavors are tart and spicier; grits or potatoes are swapped for rice and beans; tortillas pinch-hit for toast. The trappings are basically low-key: Earth tones, nods to Detroit icons like the Boblo boat, and Mexican trinkets, but the menu—full of Mexicantown standards—makes Evie's a real draw. Dine-in tamales are served with homemade salsa and run only 70 cents a pop, while terrines of rich and hearty pozole (pork and hominy soup) or menudo (hominy and tripe) will slake any appetite. Word of caution: Restrooms at Evie's barely outsize airplane johns. *3454 Bagley Ave., (313) 843-5056.*

Family Treat - Family Treat's motto, "Serving Southwest Detroit's best foot-long coney for more than 54 years," is a perfect description of this retro neighborhood diner. With the original vintage decor and seemingly original prices—including 90-cent ice cream cones—this neighborhood spot serves as much charm as it does delicious foot-long coney dogs. While the entire menu is popular, the foot-long dogs, fried mushrooms, fishwiches, and all 12 flavors of milkshakes are renowned. Stop by on Tuesday for taco night or Thursday for foot-long night. Closed November through January. *2010 Springwells St., (313) 841-3522.*

General George S. Patton P.L.A.V. Post 11 - The Patton post for the Polish League of American Veterans in Detroit is a bar with a simple rental hall open to anyone. The bar is a tiny, relaxing den with room for a handful of navy monogrammed "Patton Post Bar" stools and seating at small tables, making it a welcome place to sit, chat, and listen. Two portraits of the decorated World War II general watch over the place, and there is a wood-carved Polish Eagle and a U.S. crest as emblems. The jukebox leans heavily on old favorites, with Bruce Springsteen's 1984 anthem "Born In The U.S.A." being one of the newest releases. The entrance is on the south of the building, up a short flight, and next to a flagpole flying Old Glory. Closes at midnight. *4930 Central Ave., (313) 842-9178.*

» Giovanni's Ristorante - Arguably the best Old World Italian food in the city, Giovanni's is a hidden jewel. Part of a stalwart Italian enclave that has survived the encroachment of surrounding industry, the restaurant opened in 1967 and still oozes pride and tradition. Though the decor in the three dining rooms is reserved, the gentle accent lighting, black tablecloths, and light-hued walls are complemented by classy touches, such as photographs of Tony Bennett and Frank Sinatra dining at the establishment—which are as good an endorsement as any. The cuisine is exceptional, evidenced in the preparation and subtlety of what is served. Of the many varied options, standouts are the homemade pastas (all made from scratch on-site), the alfredo gnocchi, ricotta cannelloni, braciole (beef tenderloin rolled with prosciutto, braised in a tomato sauce), and richly flavorful tiramisu. Foodies looking to brush up on their Italiano will be pleased to know that Berlitz-style "learn Italian" dialogues are broadcast in the restrooms. As a suggestion, those traveling from the east should make it a point to travel across the Oakwood Avenue Bridge, a small engineering splendor from another time. *330 Oakwood Blvd., www.giovannisristorante.com, (313) 841-0122.*

Gonella's Italian Foods - Gonella's subs are better. On a quiet block in Oakwood Heights lies this charming corner Italian grocery and deli that has kept Detroiters well fed for more than 70 years. This neighborhood corner market puts its Italian pride on display inside and out, from murals of the Tuscan countryside painted above the refrigerators to the green, white, and yellow storefront awning. The highlight of the place is at the large deli counter, where Gonella's serves renowned, layered Italian subs built with fine, fresh-cut deli meats and fresh-baked hard and soft rolls. Although customers can order from the menu, veterans go custom, selecting from the wide variety of meats—including ham, turkey, bologna, salami, capicola, prosciutto, and pancetta—and delicious assortments of cheeses, vegetables, and dressings. One word describes what you're about to enjoy: delizioso. Aside from the beloved deli counter and a selection of prepared pasta and salads, Gonella's sells cannolis that are hand filled by a local Italian grandmother, alongside a fine selection of olives, olive oils, homemade sausages, pillowy Italian breads, balsamic vinegars, wines and a variety of other Italian kitchen staples. *295 Oakwood Blvd., (313) 841-3500.*

Ham Palace / A&L Restaurant - Though "palace" might be overselling it a bit, A&L is a haven for grabbing a cheap, tasty, quick, and filling breakfast or early lunch. This diner on the edge of Delray decked in patriotic tri-color paint fits the bill for a convenient stop-in—customers can choose from thick-cut off-the-bone ham, breakfast specials with amply portioned sides, and grilled sandwiches. The setup at A&L consists of worn vinyl stools for counter patrons, cozy booths, and a smattering of porcine set pieces from piggy banks, to cookie jars, to just plain decorative pigs. Patriotism and piety accompany succulent ham here—icons of the Madonna, the Messiah, and Mother Teresa preside over all service, which is friendly and conversational. *9405 W. Fort St., (313) 841-1309.*

» **Hygrade Deli** - The sparkly blue, red, and gold vinyl seats, vintage fixtures, old-school wood paneling, and Art Deco-esque facade, make a marvelous stage for the real stars of this show: the corned beef and pastrami. Since opening in 1955, owner Stuart Litt's deli has built a legion of adoring fans that love tender texture, glistening presentation, exceptional flavor, and outstanding, perfectly brackish, corned beef. Although beautifully shaved in house, the corned beef and pastrami are made up the street at United Meat and Deli, keeping the meat juicy, and aromatic. Lunch customers can't miss with the renowned mile-high reuben, egg salad sandwich, hot pastrami, corned beef on rye, and split pea soup. If you're an early bird, try the corned beef hash—it's so divine, you'll find yourself contemplating abandoning silverware and eating like a caveman. After you fall in love with Hygrade, you won't be alone—the affable staff serves 400 pounds of corned beef a week. *3640 Michigan Ave., (313) 894-6620.*

Johnny's Ham King - Set underneath the Ambassador Bridge is a strong embassy for dive counter food. Though the neighborhood has seen better days and decoration inside is pretty sparse, both the hungry and hungover will find much to like here. Johnny's titular meat is well worth its bargain prices—house-cured, thick-cut slabs of saline ham carved fresh are available in sandwiches, omelets, or as part of massive egg breakfasts with homemade hash browns ringing in around $4. Aside from breakfast, a full coney menu is available, with a few options for the cholesterol-averse. Service is attentive and professional, so any bleary-eyed wanderer in need of coffee fill-ups will wait minimally for refueling. Closes at 3pm. *2601 W. Fort St., (313) 961-2202.*

La Terraza - Though it's off the beaten path and has minimal signage, La Terraza has built a well-deserved reputation as a destination for tasty Mexican seafood. Patrons who make their way to the one-story brick building will find a pleasant but understated interior with dark hardwood tables and booths that afford guests a direct view of the action in the kitchen. Though traditional Mexican food is available, the house specialty is seafood. Offerings include a variety of fish and seafood soups, with highlights being a pre-Columbian pozole, unique fish and shrimp tostadas such as a Marlin tostada served in smoky Mazatlan sauce and garnished with avocado slices, and an incredible fish cocktail. La Terraza doesn't serve alcohol, but Jarritos, Mexican Coke, and delectable homemade agua fresca are a solid substitute. *1633 Lawndale St., (313) 843-1433.*

Las Brisas - Home to mariachi bands, Las Brisas mixes a weekend dance club scene with a large authentic Mexican menu. From corn tortillas to homemade sauces, Las Brisas' menu delivers. In the evening, Mariachi singers will visit each table and serenade customers—and even take requests—making this restaurant a great place to embarrass a birthday guy or gal. After 10pm on weekends, the focus shifts toward DJs and dancing. Customers flood the new stainless steel bar, framed by exposed brick archways and glowing mood lights. This turn-of-the-century industrial interior meets a Mexican theme with mural scenes of the oceanside, dramatic sconce lighting, and spicy salsa music. *8445 W. Vernor Hwy., www. lasbrisasindetroit.com, (313) 842-8252.*

Los Altos Restaurant - Just a bit off-the-beaten-path, Los Altos is the favorite Mexicantown spot for many Detroiters and is definitely worth the minimal extra effort. Start your meal with complimentary chips served with four or more delectable house-made salsas and other dips, and then order one of Los Altos' plentiful, affordable entrees. If you only go once, a must-have is the taco al pastor—pork marinated to perfection and topped with cilantro and onions—though everything from burritos to botanas (and even the beans and rice) are outstanding. Wash it all down with a bottled Coca-Cola or horchata. Though its food is tops, the cozy dining room is part of the draw, with comfy booths aplenty and warm, charming lighting. *7056 W. Vernor Hwy., (313) 841-3109.*

Los Corrales - While most of Mexicantown's eateries are clustered together, Los Corrales is somewhat of an island north of Junction, but it's well worth the detour. Cheap, abundant food with a range of choice is the specialty here, including a selection of seafood dishes, such as fried whole tilapia, shrimp and cactus, or ceviche tostadas. Traditional Mexican tacos with the usual meats—chicken, tongue, brisket, pig stomach (crispy, salty, succulent) or tripe (perfectly cooked)—are especially delicious. All food ordered-in is served with fresh chips and a delectable variety of homemade salsas. The dining room has a terra cotta color scheme, red brick archways, and an ad hoc tiki cantina with a light assortment of call liquors to satiate thirsty guests. Though dubbed a "billar," the games are on hiatus, making food the main event. *2244 Junction St., (313) 849-3196.*

» Los Galanes - One of the real highlights of the heart of the Mexicantown strip, this Southwest Detroit-family-owned restaurant has been a favorite since the early 1990s. The sprawling restaurant is great for large groups (check out the upstairs) or for an intimate meal for two in the colorfully painted and tiled dining room. The menu is vast and extensive—enjoy everything from traditional goat stew to a full menu of fresh seafood or some solid vegetarian options. The covered light-strung patio is a highlight of the summer and can't be beat for ambience and people-watching. Enjoy a margarita or several or a bevy of Mexican beers while a mariachi band serenades you. Visit the second floor on a weekend night to find Los Galanes transformed into one of the neighborhood's favorite dance spots. *3362 Bagley Ave., www.losgalanesdetroit.com, (313) 554-4444.*

Mexican Village Restaurant - For a cheesy, delicious, take on south-of-the-border comfort food in a fiesta atmosphere, pull into the secured lot. The ambiance is wonderfully kitsch, with vivid paintings of dramatic desert scenes, ponchos and sombreros on the wall, and colorful flowers and candles at every table. Open since

1958, owner Connie Azofeifa and her crack staff offer a dizzying array of delicious, rich, options on the comprehensive menu, most notably including the El Tejano Burritos (deep-fried burrito with the works), and Enchiladas Rancheras (enchiladas with ranchera sauce). Veterans start off with a Botanita Appetizer (a kitchen sink nachos and what the menu calls "A Special Treat!!!"), which might be a white tablecloth's nightmare but a dream for the rest of us. Try an incredible homemade Sopapilla (fried pastry) if you've managed to save room. The ambrosial margaritas are available by the glass and the liter. *2600 Bagley St., www.mexicanvillagefood.com, (313) 237-0333.*

Mike's Famous Ham Place - To the chagrin of kosher diners everywhere, Mike's Famous Ham Place is so confident in the taste of their inexpensive, savory and delectable sliced ham, that it sees little reason to offer much else. Actually, since 1974, this legendary, charming old school diner has been dishing out one thing and one thing only: killer ham. Outside of the occasional pie or daily special, the menu includes only five items: a heaping plate of sliced ham; ham and eggs; bean soup (with ham); pea soup (loaded with ham); and the

tastiest, largest ham sandwich known to man (garnished with ham). Portions are outrageously large, so be ready for a doggy bag. *3700 Michigan Ave., (313) 894-6922.*

» **Motz's Hamburgers** - Don't let the lack of a crowd fool you. Motz's distinctive large, juicy sliders have been among the best in the city since it opened in 1929. While the early White Tower architecture— replete with vintage dining counter and retro diner-facing grill— would be reason enough to visit, its renown is burger-based. Motz uses Eastern Market–fresh, never-frozen, beef grilled on a bed of onions to create its big, rich, and tender sliders. Motz is not quite the carnivore stronghold it once was: Vegetarian visitors will enjoy the veggie burger sliders. *7216 W. Fort St., www.motzhamburgers.com, (313) 843-9186.*

Neveria La Michoacana - La Michoacana's hand-painted signs and welcoming purple and teal chairs will carry visitors back to their own favorite childhood ice cream parlor—and make them wish that the Superman sundaes of their younger years had tasted as good as La Michoacana's frozen pineapple popsicle. Known for its homemade fruit popsicles and the giant $4 La Michoacana Sundae—featuring four scoops of classic ice cream flavors layered with desirable toppings—this shop has a huge selection of cold treats. Try an agua fresca (a fruit-juice-like drink that is sometimes made with cream), horchata, frozen chocolate-covered bananas, or delicious fresh strawberries drizzled in homemade sweet cream. Most menu items are listed in Spanish and English, accompanied by hand-painted illustrations, but the welcoming staff is happy to answer questions or offer you a sample to try before you buy. *4336 W. Vernor Hwy., (313) 658-3217.*

Pollo Chapin - Pollo Chapin and its Guatemalan pride add a different dimension to the Mexican-restaurant-heavy Southwest neighborhood palate. The scent of perfectly seasoned fried chicken wafts from the restaurant, located in a renovated bright yellow house full of orange chairs, smiling patrons, and incredibly friendly servers. Though the house fried chicken is divine (available barbecue or spicy), the delectable sides with authentic Guatemalan flair are a highlight, including the Curtido beet and cabbage salad, the macaroni and cheese with jalapeno, and chocolate flan. While you wait for your order, take a peek at the colorful wooden display cases full of Guatemalan imported jewelry, woven bags, and trinkets for sale. *2054 Junction St., (313) 554-9087.*

» Pupusaría y Restaurante Salvedoreño - This small, cinderblock, hidden gem is set far back from the street in an unlikely neighborhood, and it's easy to miss. With eight booths and four tables for four, it's tiny, but festive with South and Central American, African, and Asian flags for decor. Pupusas are a traditional El Salvadoran empanada-like dish made of corn flour and filled with such delightful combinations as cheese/beans/loroco flowers, pork/beans/cheese, jalapenos/cheese, and chicken/squash/cheese. In addition to the pupusas, the tamales, pasteles, and the fried plantains with crema and frijoles are to die for. Be sure to make heavy use of the delicious salsa and curtido accompanying your order. There's no booze, but there is a bountiful selection of non-alcoholic drinks, including a tasty horchata. To top it off, this joint is astonishingly cheap—you'll be belt-looseningly full for well under $10, including drinks and sides. *3149 Livernois Ave., (313) 899-4020.*

R&R Saloon - Primarily billed as a bear and leather gay bar, this night spot welcomes everyone with its motto: "Be who you are at the R&R." Serving drinks to Detroit since 1977, the R&R offers daily drink specials, a seasonal patio, DJs, a pool table, video games, karaoke, and one of the best monthly dance party in town—Macho City. Prepare yourself for cutoffs, pint jars of draft beer, and amazingly danceable disco tunes that last into the early-morning hours (till 5am on the weekends). If you work up an appetite dancing, they have a full kitchen cooking up barfood staples—and if you find yourself partying tlil dawn, you can even catch breakfast here starting at 2am. Voted "Best Leather Daddy Bar" by Metro Times readers. *7330 Michigan Ave., www.rnrsaloon.com, (313) 849-2751.*

Red's Park-In Bar - Long a haven for Southwest Detroit's Appalachian community, this husband-and-wife-owned country-western dive endures in a changing neighborhood thanks to hospitable service, cheap drinks, and one of the best jukeboxes in Detroit. Red's, occupying the first floor of a red brick two-story, is darkly lit with a black ceiling, wood-paneled walls, and racing car hoods for decoration. A low-slung lampshade hangs above the pool table and illuminates nearby signs prohibiting gambling on pool. The jukebox has popular choices like Hank Williams, Ernest Tubb, bluegrass classics, and even pop crooners like Nat King Cole. Original owners Chuck and Sue still live upstairs, and their dachshund is usually around as a lookout. Red's opens around 10am and closes by 8pm or so. *4442 Central St., (313) 841-1858.*

Señor López Mexican Restaurant - The chiles rellenos alone are worth the trip. These culinary masterpieces are lightly battered and fried poblano peppers hand-stuffed with cheese and topped with unmatched ranchero sauce. The chiles rellenos, however, are not your only path to Mexican nirvana: the Cochinita Pibil (marinated pork), Chiles En Nogada (stewed poblano peppers over rice), and delicate yet straightforward tacos loaded with fresh-cut cilantro and onions and your choice of meat are all outstanding. Open since 2002, Señor López is quickly building a strong following, so getting one of the handful of tables can be difficult on some days. Carryout isn't a bad option, however, as the quiet, if not divey, atmosphere is rather unremarkable, and Dingeman Park is a few blocks up. *7146 Michigan Ave., www.senorlopezmexicanrestaurant.com, (313) 551-0685.*

» Southwest Detroit Taco Trucks & Grills - Southwest Detroit is home to a wide array of tasty taco trucks and outdoor grills slinging Mexican street food. In general, at either trucks or grills (which sometimes include indoor seating) food is cheap, quick, and made from a variety of meats with other ingredients are fresh, and a beverage selection that is limited to Coke products and water, with the occasional Jarritos. Food and service are the focus, while the typical parking lot ambiance takes a backseat. April to October is the surest time to catch the widest selection, but several joints are open year-round. Hours vary by eatery, but none open later than 11am or close before 7pm, and most are open much later. You'll find most of the taco trucks and grills between Junction Street and Lawndale Street, on or around Vernor Highway, Dix Street, or Springwells Street. All locations are cash only, and vegetarian options exist but aren't the strength of most vendors. These are a few of our favorite spots:

- **El Primo:** A smaller selection of meat than others, but lightning-fast, generously portioned tacos for $1.25. Very popular. *Dix St. at Central Ave.*

- **El Taco Veloz:** The early bird's taco truck. Open at 8am, seven days a week, until as late as 11pm weekends. Excellent grilled onion or jalapeño, anyone? *6170 Toledo St.*

- **El Taquito:** Featuring shrimp quesadillas, and affordable as they come. The al pastor tacos are outstanding. Seven days a week. *6060 W. Vernor Hwy.*

- **La Mexicana Supermercado:** An outdoor grill connected to a grocery store. Serves delectable tacos, including pollo, carne asada, and lengua. Open until the cows come home, year-round. *7934 W. Vernor Hwy.*

- **Loncheria el Parian:** $1 tacos and a huge variety. The Springwells location has an authentic al pastor rotating spit. The charming Dix cart is reminiscent of a carnival wagon. Both offer delicious tortas. Open until 11pm on Friday and Saturday. Burgers and hot dogs available. *Two trucks: Dix St. at W. Vernor Hwy. and Springwells St. at I-75.*

- **Pollo los Gallos:** Outdoor grill famed for roast chicken. $1.25 tacos, and meals of much, much more. Open seven days, 10am to 9pm. *7170 Dix St.*

- **Tacos el Toro:** Hearty portions cooked spot-on, a full selection of meats, carrot and radish sides, and a choice of red and green salsas. Closed Tuesday. Two trucks: *2142 Springwells St. and Michigan Ave. at Central Ave. or McGraw St. at Addison St.*

- **Taqueria El Rey:** See separate entry.

Tamaleria Nuevo Leon - For more than 30 years, Tamaleria Nuevo Leon has served authentic, savory and sweet tamales by the half-dozen from its picturesque locale. Two friendly women work behind the counter of this family-owned spot, preparing masa to the perfect consistency and cutting meat for fresh tamales. For about $5 customers can feast on six tamales and a tasty side of salsa. Parking is available on the side street, Ste. Anne Street, making this little restaurant perfect for carryout. Just down the street from the infamous Michigan Central Station, you'll see the restaurant's charming terra cotta roof tiles and whitewashed facade nestled next to the curious blue "dome home." Veggie-friendly tamales available. *2669 W. Vernor Hwy., (313) 962-8066.*

Taqueria El Naciemento - In the thick of the vibrant West Vernor strip lies El Naciemento, named for its owner's hometown in Jalisco, Mexico. Decidedly more authentic than some of its brethren down the street, this taqueria and full bar, which is popular with locals, might lay claim to the most extensive selection of taco, burrito, and torta fillings this side of Texas. Though all the bases are covered handily, if you're looking to move beyond the tenets of American-Mexican fare, this is your place. Expand your palate with expertly executed classics like fried pork carnitas, seafood, goat, steak, tongue, and chorizo, or push your boundaries with stomach, brain, or head. To complement the tasty edibles, the interior of El Nacimiento has a thoughtful, cozy Mexican villa feel that transforms into a neighborhood hangout when locals arrive, which is usually later in the evening. Don't miss out on the yummy homemade juice. Open until midnight during the week and 4am on Friday and Saturday. *7400 W. Vernor Hwy., www.elnacimientorestaurant.com, (313) 554-1790.*

Taqueria El Rey - Beyond the unpolished facade and aromatic siren song of grilled chicken, the unassuming Taqueria El Rey offers some of the city's finest Mexican food. While the prosaic atmosphere might remind you of an orthodontist's office or dive bar, the food might remind you of the Mexican food served behind St. Peter. Although the supporting cast is outstanding, the belle of ball on this menu is the grilled chicken. Cooked right outside at the adjoining walk-up taco stand, the excellent dry rub, smoky flavor, and perfectly cooked, tender texture of these slabs of heaven will leave you ordering seconds. Not a bird nerd? Look no further than the outstanding tostadas de camaron, hamburguesa de camaron, burrito estilo california, or torta de lomo adobado. If you need to take the edge off, try one of the renowned margaritas originales from the full bar. *4730 W. Vernor Hwy., www.taqueria-elrey.com, (313) 357-3094.*

Taqueria Lupita's - In a neighborhood flush with tasty Mexican options, and on a street that's one of the epicenters of the action, it can be hard for a taqueria to distinguish itself, but if you're willing to pass on the margarita, Lupita's does it with a bevy of inordinately inexpensive real-deal authentic Mexican street food. Highlights at this divey self-proclaimed "house of the original Mexican taco" include hearty pozole soup and chorizo, carnitas, and especially al pastor tacos, which are legendary in these parts. Don't be afraid to get adventurous here, that lengua taco won't eat itself. *3443 Bagley St., (313) 843-1105.*

Taqueria Mi Pueblo - Affectionately dubbed the "Mexican Applebees"—more for its decor than the quality of the food—Mi Pueblo stands out among the many Southwest Detroit Mexican eateries as a spacious, cheery, and inviting restaurant, with broad appeal for various palates on a budget. It has all the Mexican staples in its many-page colorful, laminated menu—try the chorizo tacos, carnitas, and tamales—and that includes the really Mexican staples like menudo, beef head, and tongue tacos. The complimentary chips and salsa are plentiful and delicious, and there are plenty of vegetarian options. Flavors are bright and products are fresh, and did we mention that it's really, really cheap? *7278 Dix St., (313) 841-3315.*

Taqueria Nuestra Familia - Aside from the brightly lit cashier's counter glowing from the back-lit images of delicious pork street tacos, fresh-pressed corn tortillas, and green-sauced enchiladas, patrons will admire Taqueria Nuestra Familia's rainbow of hand-painted tables and chairs depicting the tropical landscape scenes of Mexico. The colorful atmosphere matches the demeanor of the friendly wait staff, as well as the delicious taste of the house-made salsa. Enjoy the $2.95 taco lunch special or go for an evening out and sip on $4 margaritas or a glass of Pacifico at the full bar. *7620 W. Vernor Hwy., www.nuestrafamiliarestaurant.com, (313) 842-5668.*

» Telway Hamburgers - Owned by octogenarian Earl Owens since 1944, the Telway is a "hamburger system" that offers sliders by the bag and the self-proclaimed "best coffee in Detroit" (a statement that's hard to dispute). The burgers are steamed on a bed of onions, giving the meat an incredibly tender, juicy, consistency that melts on your tongue and melds with the flavor of the wonder buns and gooey cheese. The onion rings and fries are made fresh and have an outstanding texture. Telway serves 3,000 hamburgers a day out of its beautifully vintage White Tower building from the 1940s. Eat your burgers at the counter or sit on your car in the parking lot. You'll never go back to White Castle. *6820 Michigan Ave., (313) 843-2146.*

Tommy T's Pub - Tommy T's Pub is a unique neighborhood dive bar in a residential area that emphasizes comfort and selection. The simple yellow awning outside belies a modern, sand-colored interior, which is clean, cool, and massive. In addition to a counter that stretches more than 50 feet, Tommy T's offers six pool tables for customers, who are usually locals, meaning that soccer is extremely popular viewing, Mariachi is often heard on the jukebox, and the Spanish is the lingua franca, though the staff is bilingual. The drink menu includes bottles of Pacifico and Modelo with Mexican Coke for teetotalers. *3511 Clippert Ave., (313) 897-5967.*

Vicki's Barbecue & Shrimp - You can't miss Vicki's if you're in the neighborhood—"where there's smoke, there's barbecue." Established in 1960, this carryout joint serves a focused menu of tender smoked ribs in either regular or hot sauce, oven-pit chicken, and fried shrimp. The restaurant is unmistakable for its distinctive sharp V out front and the tufts of deep, rich oven smoke continuously piping out of the building's roof. Step inside and you'll see the brick smoke oven with a steep black metal hood behind the kitchen glass from the vantage of a small red brick colored lobby. Pro tip: The "sandwich" (which is actually just ribs with bread on the side) and fries with sauce on top are especially delicious. *3845 W. Warren Ave., (313) 894-9906.*

Vince's Italian Restaurant & Pizzeria - There's a reason they've been using the same recipes for more than 50 years: Vince's is classic Italian food at its best. In a homey dining room that feels like a visit to your Italian grandparents' basement, bedecked with murals of Italian cities, this Springwells favorite is family-owned by four generations of the same family, and it shows. Founded by Italian immigrants Vincenzo and Maria Perfili in 1960, what began as a small pizza parlor serving up pies for workers at Southwest Detroit's Cadillac Fleetwood Plant grew into a beloved family restaurant. In addition to its popular old-school pizzas, Vince's serves house-made pastas and sauces and wonderful ravioli and manicotti. All the dishes are made to order, so it's not a good option if you're in a rush. Be sure to stay for dessert—the tiramisu is the best in town and the cannoli is sublime. *1341 Springwells St., www.vincesdetroit.com, (313) 842-4857.*

Xochimilco - One of the more popular eateries in Mexicantown, Xochimilco (that's pronounced "zo-she-mill-co," in case you were wondering)—which is "small" for the area with seating for only 240—is best known for its intimate homey decor with dark rooms, antique chandeliers, and large velvet oil paintings hanging on the walls. With a menu leaning toward the Tex-Mex side of the spectrum, house specialties include botanas (Mexican small plates), cheesy nachos, boozy margaritas, and homemade chips and salsa. For night owls, both the kitchen and bar are open until 2am daily. *3409 Bagley St., (313) 843-0179.*

SHOPPING & SERVICES

Algo Especial Super Mercado - This small but charming mom-and-pop market supplies all the staples of an authentic Mexican meal. Pick up cactus or sweet pepper from the exclusive selection of fresh produce, order a fresh cut of beef from the meat counter, and browse through aisles of spices, corn flours, dessert mixes, and tortilla presses. Try the carryout tamales if you're in a pinch for lunch, or just choose a snack from the wide selection of Mexican candies, sodas, and juices. While you shop, swap stories with the community members congregated in the Latin CD and DVD section, or ask the charming elderly man behind the counter about the latest in neighborhood gossip. *2628 Bagley St., (313) 963-9013.*

California Wine Grape Co. - A little corner of Italy lies tucked away on West Fort Street, where the facade of California Wine Grape Company displays a sunny mural of rolling hills and tangled grapevines. This bright shop is a Mecca for wine drinkers and winemakers alike. Inside the massive 10,000-square-foot showroom and warehouse, visitors will find rows upon rows of grapes (including 16 reds and 13 whites), juices, de-stemers, oak casks, demi-johns, custom glassware, presses, pumps, and starter kits. Shop owner and Abruzzo, Italy, native Giuseppe Pracilio brings a great deal of sophistication to the craft, and often serves as an oracle of oenophilia to the scores of rookie and veteran home winemakers who come for advice. Pracilio makes his own legendary wines, which are highly sought after and available by the half gallon. The shop becomes a hive of activity each year when California Wine Grapes sells more than 20 truckloads of grapes over the six week harvest season in early autumn. *7250 W. Fort St., www.californiawinegrapeco.com, (313) 841-0590.*

Chilango's Bakery - This little panadería y pastelería—or bakery and pastry shop—carries a huge selection of authentic Mexican baked goods, including breads, pastries, and sweets. Self-serve style, use parchment paper and plastic tongs to make your selections from the long glass display case. Feel free to ask the friendly staff for explanations about each item, since the labels are listed in only Spanish. With huge portions and reasonable prices, the shop can be an economical alternative to some of the larger, better known bakeries in the neighborhood. *5427 W. Vernor Hwy., (313) 554-0133.*

Detroit Farm and Garden - With gardens and farms popping up all over the city, the need for quality supplies and gardening resources has bloomed. Opened by owner Jeff Klein in the former Detroit Police Department Third Precinct building, Detroit Farm and Garden supplies growers with everything needed for verdant greens from compost and soil to growing media and tools to organic fertilizers, feed, seeds, and hay. The shop is also a hub for resource sharing and education, with information and regular classes that help the food-growing community keep its gardens as local, sustainable, healthy, and tasty as possible. If you're going big, there is plenty of space for loading bulk purchases in the entrance in the back off of 21st Street. *1759 20th St., www.detroitfarmandgarden.com, (313) 655-2344.*

Diana's Bakery - This friendly bakery offers traditional bountiful Mexican desserts and fresh sandwich breads. While shopping, you can peek at treats being made on the large metal tables that are dusted in flour or covered with fresh dough. The selection changes daily, so pastries are not labeled. But just ask Diana—the bakery's namesake and the owner's 8-year-old daughter—who knows the ins and outs of the pastries, cookies, and breads. After school, she sits behind the cashier's counter with her coloring book and pauses from her work only to offer her recommendations on her father's specialties. From brightly frosted yellow and pink cookies to cheese-filled shortbread pies, Diana's Bakery offers a variety of tasty goodies each day of the week. *1401 Lawndale St., (313) 842-0987.*

E&L Supermercado - Founded in 1948 and family-owned for three generations, E&L is a beautiful, bountiful full-service grocery store. Owned by the Fienman family, their legacy in the food industry is apparent by the vast selection of fresh, quality meats, fresh baked goods, Mexican specialties, and produce available. In addition to its in-house bakery, fresh tortillas and chips come straight from Hacienda Foods next door, while the meat counter offers competitive prices for choice cuts. If you're looking for a more immediate snack or dinner, the store has a fresh foods counter where shoppers can pick up delicious, authentic tacos for a buck a pop. Despite its size and scope, E&L Supermercado maintains a homey feel with its outstanding service and inviting atmosphere. *6000 W. Vernor Hwy., (313) 552-2140.*

Hacienda Mexican Foods - Supplying the public with wholesale Mexican goods and locally produced taco shells, tortillas, corn chips and tostadas since 1994, Hacienda Mexican Foods offers wholesale prices and wholesome service. From bulk spices, fresh avocados, and frozen chorizo to Mexican sodas and candy, owner Lydia Gutierrez takes pride in the outstanding quality of her goods, which are sold across the country, and available to the public in bulk quantities at the West Vernor location. The beautiful storefront was recently renovated and includes two beautiful murals by Chilean artist Dasic Fernandez, including the well-known "Mano de Obra Campesina" (2010), which emphasizes the importance of corn cultivation in Latin American culture. Although offering limited options, hungry Detroiters can also get straight-from-the-factory tortillas at La Michocana Tortilla Factory *(2600 Bagley Ave., (313) 554-4450) 6022 W. Vernor Hwy., (313) 895-8823.*

Hector's Men's Wear - For more than 75 years, the shining black Art Deco facade has drawn customers into this old-timey classic menswear store. Though the original owner is no longer around, the new owners are a charming couple that takes pride in their business in their Southwest Detroit community. In addition to a selection of affordable classic menswear and accessories for boys and adults, such as caps, button-up shirts, suit coats, belts, dress shoes, and watches, the store sells work clothes and everyday wear from suppliers like Dickies, Guerilla Cut, and Reebok. *5449 W. Vernor Hwy., (313) 554-2044.*

Honey Bee La Colmena - The most common retort to the misguided assertion that "Detroit has no quality grocery stores," Honey Bee has been constantly expanding since 1956 and is a beautifully managed Mexican-oriented full-service grocer. With a killer selection of fresh, inexpensive produce, every kind of hot sauce imaginable, lots of locally made tortillas, organic and vegetarian options, and completely incredible house-made guacamole and salsas (available for sampling at the entrance), this shop is a destination and a real treat. In addition to groceries, it carries a solid selection of Michigan and Mexican beers and Mexican sundries (like loteria cards, soaps, and candies), and it has a wonderful hot food counter at the back of the store featuring delectable burritos and tacos. If you're looking to round out your fiesta, check out the large and festive selection of piñatas for sale displayed around the store. *2443 Bagley St., www.honeybeemkt.com, (313) 237-0295.*

La Gloria Bakery - After being greeted by the aroma of baked treats and the cheerful staff, visitors should equip themselves with tongs and plastic trays and begin their self-guided cafeteria-style confection safari. This small, bright, and unassuming space is packed with cases upon cases of freshly baked pastries, cakes, tamales, breads, and tortillas set out on wooden racks. Take your time. In a room seemingly bursting with flans, turnovers, cannolis, conchas, galletas, pan de polvo, and tres leches, La Gloria rookies often miss some of the best delicacies. Although the racks are typically lacking in details or descriptions of the goods for sale, all of the options are delicious. The pan dulce, empanadas, and churros are held in especially high regard by regulars. Visitors can easily buy enough desserts to rot a tooth with pocket change, so stock up. *3345 Bagley St., (313) 842-5722.*

Life Style Soccer - Soccer heads rejoice! With the recent surge in interest in soccer south of 8 Mile Road, Life Style Soccer has quickly become a popular outfitter for the city's players and fans of all ages. The small, straightforward, unassuming shop stocks an impressive variety of cleats, shin guards, balls, jerseys, and other soccer paraphernalia for aspiring players. The store carries both youth and adult sizes, although it has a larger selection for younger patrons. For the city's armchair midfielders, Life Style Soccer carries a bevy of jerseys and posters for supporters of most major European and South and Central American clubs. The friendly and knowledgeable bilingual staff are always willing to make recommendations. *4848 W. Vernor Hwy., (313) 841-8412.*

Luna's Bakery II - Quietly tucked into a checkerboard-tiled storefront with decorative wrought iron window gating is this treat of a bakery. Specializing in uncommonly cheap, quick, handy confections such as Mexican sugar cookies, tarts, seasonal fruit pastries (don't miss pumpkin in the fall!), traditional favorites like concha or bolillo (sweet and savory breads, respectively), Luna's lets customers serve themselves from behind a horseshoe of display cases on simple lunch trays. Fresh cakes, brownies, savory breads and tamales are also available, but call ahead for tres leches or other less common delectables. And for the inquisitive, there's curiously not a Luna's Bakery I. *5680 W. Vernor Hwy., (313) 554-1510.*

Lupita Laundromat - Equal parts neon light museum, community hangout, and bargain-priced laundromat, Lupita Laundromat is the Detroit launderer's paradise. The rainbows of neon lights adorning every wall illuminate the large and diverse collection of exotic plants on display throughout the building. With more than 100 washers and dryers, Lupita always has available machines, and it also offers same-day and two-day drop-off services for on-the-go launderers. The taco truck across the street makes for a great spin-cycle snack. *3938 W. Vernor Hwy., (313) 843-2133.*

Markowycz's European Homestyle Sausage - Markowycz's is a destination traditional meat vendor in southwest Detroit. A distinct site marked by vintage cerulean plastic letters, a metal awning, and a red-and-green neon window signs, Markowycz's has been subject to many a carnivore's pilgrimage since it opened in 1954, and it retains its original charming look. Renowned by some as the best in Michigan, all sausages and lunch meats are processed and smoked on site and sold alongside imported Polish groceries such as canned sprats, pickled vegetables, crackers, and other savory items to complement sausage. Though not for sale, the mounted sport fish and massive steer horns on the walls are an interesting view while you wait for your order. Closed Monday and Tuesday. *8616 Michigan Ave., (313) 846-6870.*

» Mexicantown Bakery - This inviting, convivial bakery in the heart of Mexicantown is popular among locals for good reason: It provides customers a range of fluffy pastries and sweet treats for any sweet tooth, from Mexican cookies and pastries like conchas, to traditional favorites like cannoli and cake, indulgent renditions of classics like tres leches cake, pan de muerto, or budin de pan, and its own distinctly popular chocolate "mice" (vegetarian friendly). The beautiful, loft-like interior features exposed brick, hardwood floors, and bright displays of piñatas above the wall of pastry displays. Conveniently, also available is a beautiful, albeit curated selection of Latin American groceries and beverages in the back of the store. *4300 W. Vernor Hwy., www.mexicantown.com/bakery, (313) 554-0001.*

Ornela's Bakery - Distinguishing itself with murals inside and out that depict individuals who would make Sir Mix-A-Lot proud, the brightly lit interior of this authentic Mexican panaderia features three walls of glass-encased treats. Ornela's displays are filled floor to ceiling with a wide-selection of cookies, flans, and sweetbreads baked fresh twice daily, as well as a selection of ice cream, slushies, coffee, and fresh fruit. Be sure to ask for a sample of one of the house specialties, the delicious caramel sauce, which simmers for five hours each Saturday before being packaged and sold for the week. At 5pm the staff begins baking an evening batch of fresh treats, making this the bakery to visit for fresh goodies after work or dinner. Customers looking to complete their grocery spree should also stop by La Carreta next door, which sells produce and dairy, as well as a wide selection of spices, obscure candies, and dry goods. *6915 Michigan Ave., (313) 554-9722.*

Peoples Brothers Bakery - This charming bakery has been a neighborhood staple since 1976. From behind the mismatched stools and counter, the delightful house pastry chefs in flour-dusted white aprons pour fresh-brewed coffee and help customers select from the incredible selection of Southern-style baked goods. The mammoth pastry display case are stuffed with delicious sweet and savory treats, including outstanding custard donuts, sweet potato pie, Danishes, cream puffs, lemon tarts, hand-iced cakes, and dinner rolls. Owner James Peoples' double-crust sweet potato pie, especially, is to die for—the rich flavor and creamy consistency are almost unparalleled.

Sit down or carryout. Irregular hours. *2765 S. Fort St., (313) 383-9090.*

Prince Valley Gigante Supermercado - In addition to offering customers perhaps the most regal name and logo combination in the city, Prince Valley Gigante Supermercado offers customers a seven-days-a-week full-service grocery. The huge store features a solid selection of dry and canned goods where customers would be remiss to miss the salsa and hot sauce selection. However, the highlights of the store are its bakery department with fresh empanadas and Mexican breads, fabulous deli, and frozen meat selection—which includes harder-to-find items like frog legs, and its incredibly cheap produce. Because Prince Valley welcomes shoppers until 10pm, it's also the perfect place to run for a late-night snack, to grab a 30-rack, or to cure your post-dinner sweet tooth with the wide selection of Mexican soda and candy. *5931 Michigan Ave., www.gpvsupermarket.com, (313) 898-9717.*

Rodriguez Vaquerita - With a name derived from the Spanish word vaquero, which means cowboy, Rodriguez Vaquerita specializes in western apparel. The understated storefront on West Vernor Highway is packed floor-to-ceiling with a wide-variety of items, including racks of embossed leather cowboy and biker boots, timeless cowboy hats, fringed leather vests, silver belt buckles, denim clothes, and—perhaps best of all—pearl-snap cowboy shirts. Though the store heavily focuses on clothing and apparel of the cowboy variety, they also (curiously) sell children's communion clothes and shoes as well soccer gear. Yee haw! *5698 W. Vernor Hwy., (313) 849-0746.*

Sam's Barber Shop - With an understated but charming retro facade marked by only a simple black letter sign and neon in the shape of a pair of scissors, you might miss Sam's if you didn't look carefully. However, it would be a mistake to miss this small gem. Inside, amid decorative barber poles and lighting, Sam snips up quality $10 men's cuts in his four old-school red and gray barber chairs. Before you pay at the antique cash register, inquire about hot straight razor shaves. *7109 Michigan Ave., (313) 841-2323.*

Sheila's Bakery - As a temple to the grain corner of the food pyramid, this pantheon of pastry is worth the pilgrimage. Located on a lively strip of Springwells Street, this large, modern Mexican bakery offers a diverse selection of sweet and savory treats in its nineteen bakery cases, as well as fresh-brewed coffee. Sheila's offers a wide-variety of traditional and delicious Mexican treats including arroz con leche, conchas, and buneulos, as well as equally delicious, albeit unorthodox, offerings such as the "Ding Dongs Mexicana." However, the house specialty of this Southwest gem is its cake—specifically the to-die-for tres leches cakes, which are baked fresh frequently and always on hand. Cake customization is complementary. Carryout only. *2142 Springwells St., (313) 841-8480.*

Southwest Detroit Outdoor Mercado - A Southwest Detroit destination for down-and-dirty flea market action, vendors gather at this unmarked gravel lot on West Vernor Highway to sell everything from antique tools to knock-off purses. Everybody and their uncle shows up to shop between 7am and 7pm Friday through Sunday, but Saturday usually draws in the most customers—and the tastiest food trucks! Keep an eye out for savory delights from taco trucks and Middle Eastern food carts parked among the secondhand furniture vendors during the lunchtime rush. *6408 W. Vernor Hwy.*

Xochi's Gift Shop - The word "xochi" means "flower" in Nahuatl, and there couldn't be a more perfect name for this blossoming depot of Mexican imports located in the heart of Mexicantown. Owned by the Rosas family since 1985, Xochi's stocks its space with a wide assortment of gifts and souvenirs from the floor to the ceiling. Get outfitted with multicolored sombreros, traditional ponchos, authentic Wrangler embroidered shirts, silver jewelry, and leather boots. Then deck out your home with classic margarita glasses, pottery, tapestries, canvas paintings of Frida Kahlo, Our Lady of Guadalupe, Pancho Villa, and more. Heading to a fiesta? Bring a bouquet of the large, vibrant paper flowers (made by Xochi's) and a piñata (Xochi's makes those, too!). *3437 Bagley St., www.xochis.net, (313) 841-6410.*

CULTURAL ATTRACTIONS

555 Non-Profit Gallery and Studio - Housed in a former police precinct, 555 Gallery has turned a complex of former squad rooms, detective's offices, and holding cells into a raw, dynamic, and distinct art space. Bare concrete ceilings are mirrored by polished concrete floors and lit naturally by floor-to-ceiling windows with flowing, rust-colored arches created by 555's founding members outside. Offices are used as studios or workshop space and the holding cells have been repurposed as workrooms. Founded in 2002, and all volunteer- and artist-run, in addition to mounting exhibitions, 555 regularly holds concerts and events, offers affordable artist studio space for rent, and hosts residency and arts education programs. On permanent display is a massive stencil by the street artist Banksy, which was removed from the Packard Plant and is now legally owned by the gallery. *2801 W. Vernor Hwy., www.555arts.org, (888) 495- 2787.*

Tuskegee Airmen National Museum - Inside Historic Fort Wayne, the Tuskegee Airmen National Museum is dedicated to commemorating the history of the African-American men who flew and trained as combat pilots during World War II. The legacy of the airmen, among whom former-Mayor Coleman Young is counted, is recounted through exhibits including authentic combat artifacts, films, and documents. The museum scored a coup in 2010, when it purchased an authentic 1943 T-6 aircraft used in training the Tuskegee airmen, though this is housed at City Airport and not on-site at the Fort Wayne location. Prospective visitors should plan on inquiring ahead—hours to view exhibitions are by appointment, and admission is not included with entrance to Fort Wayne. *6325 W. Jefferson Ave., www.tuskegeeairmennationalmuseum.org, (313) 843-8849.*

Whitdel Arts/ Ladybug Studios - Vacant until it was beautifully renovated in 2007, the historic Whitdel building offers affordable apartments for artists and houses two arts organizations in the garden level, Ladybug Studios and Whitdel Arts (formerly Ladybug Gallery). Ladybug Studios is a cooperatively run clay studio and gallery space offering workshops and exhibition opportunities for local artists and community members. Whitdel Arts is a gallery that is a division of the Contemporary Art Institute of Detroit and presents a wide range of exhibitions in its spacious, contemporary 1,800-square-foot space showcasing work by established and emerging artists. In addition to gallery shows, Whitdel Arts hosts community arts workshops. *1250 Hubbard St., Ladybug Studios: www.ladybugstudios.wordpress.com, Whitdel Arts: www.whitdelarts.com.*

ENTERTAINMENT & RECREATION

Clark Park - A lush, lively, 29.8-acre recreational, athletic, and cultural jewel set amidst old homes, a vibrant commercial corridor, and dense neighborhoods, Clark Park has been a vital center for Southwest Detroit for generations. Since its donation to the city by real estate and fisheries magnate John P. Clark in 1888 and more recent adoption by the nonprofit Clark Park Coalition in 1991, the park has built a reputation for both its fine physical amenities and its exciting programming. While most of the park's physical assets are located in the southern end of the park—south of Christiancy Street—the northern end of the park is a scenic wooded area built for strolling and picnics, with dense stands of trees that become beautiful with changing seasons. Among other amenities, the southern end of the park is home to a regulation-size outdoor ice rink, baseball and softball diamonds, playscapes, football and soccer fields, tennis courts, a clubhouse, basketball courts, a scenic wooded area, a number of public art installations, and an amphitheatre. The amphitheatre and ice rink, especially, play host to numerous festivals, performances, matches, one-time events, and tournaments, such as the annual Cinco de Mayo festival, Police Department/Fire Department hockey charity match, and Winter Carnival. Among the many activities at the park, these stand out:

- **Ice Rink:** The regulation-size outdoor sheet, complete with stands, scoreboard, and dashing boards, offers free skating and skate rental and has been known to host outdoor Red Wings practices.

- **Public Art:** Between the storied Clark Park Sculpture Project and more recent art additions, such as ornamental brickwork by Lisa and Mary Luevanos and the mosaic installation "Bridge the Divide" (2012) by Gary Kulak and Vito Valdez, the park's northern portion makes for a scenic walk.

Bordered by W. Vernor Hwy., Clark St., Scotten St. and Lafayette Blvd., www.clarkparkdetroit.com, (313) 841-8534.

Latino Mission Society - Forty-five years ago, bowling was a major part of Detroit life and culture. So much so, in fact, that in addition to the 47 bowling alleys that once graced the city's neighborhoods, dozens upon dozens of Detroit civic, institutional, and religious buildings added private bowling alleys—from churches to the mayoral residence. Though most of these lanes and alleys have been lost to time, one of those that remain can be found in the basement of what was formerly the Bethlehem Lutheran School and is now the Latino Mission Society. Predating the Depression, the fully operational and nonmechanized four-lane alley is a curious marvel. Constructed almost entirely of wood, cloth, and leather, the alley requires "pin boys" to hustle and return balls on the rickety track while they reset the pins with the surprisingly efficient hand-operated contraption. In addition to the alley, which is private but available and economically priced for party rental, the secular organization offers performances, music classes, and nutrition courses for the community. Call for bowling rental. *1450 McKinstry St., www.latinomission.org, (313) 841-2377.*

Matrix Theatre Company - A beloved Southwest Detroit institution, Matrix Theatre was founded in 1991 and is a community-based socially engaged theater company and venue offering and fostering creative original and heritage theater and opportunities for youth and adult community participation. In addition to live theatre, Matrix creates and performs with impressive larger-than-life puppets on-site, throughout the city, and through schools and after-school outreach programs. Watching a play in the intimate theater is an experience not to be missed—check the website for upcoming performances. *2730 Bagley Ave., www.matrixtheatre.org, (313) 967-0999.*

Senate Theatre / Detroit Theater Organ Society - Best known for its historical one-of-a-kind instrument, the Senate Theatre boasts an original 1928 Wurlitzer console and organ of 2,300 pipes, specially commissioned by the Fisher brothers for their eponymous theater and relocated to its current home by the (now) Detroit Theater Organ Society in 1964. The massive, ornate console is still decked in its original Mayan-themed makeup with resplendent gold paint, but the organ's voice is what brings members and visitors. Only Wurlitzer parts are used to keep the instrument's rich, mellow sounds bellowing through the theater. For analog aficionados, the organ and its set of 34 instrument voicings are entirely air-driven, powered offstage by a 25-horsepower motor. A gilded age theater, the Senate opened in 1926, and features an enormous vertical marquee and a recently remodeled lobby with comforts of lush gold, burgundy trim and antique furniture, as well as a 19th century wood melodeon. The theater was originally used by DTOS as a venue for club organists to play and gather, but is now an all-purpose venue featuring monthly and semi-monthly film screenings, live music, and event rental, including weddings, with a capacity of 800. *6424 Michigan Ave., www.dtos.org, (313) 894-0850.*

SITES

Ambassador Bridge - One of the most notable landmarks in Detroit, the Ambassador Bridge is a graceful suspension bridge and a gleaming, towering testament to the beauty of Art Deco and Art Moderne design and the innovation of the Modern Age. It was the longest suspension bridge in the world when it was built in 1929, and the lights on the bridge's cables can be seen at night from miles around, glimmering and reflecting on the Detroit River. The busiest border crossing in North America, the bridge carries 25% of all trade volume between the United States and Canada and is privately owned by controversial billionaire Manuel "Matty" Moroun through the Detroit International Bridge Company. As is standard with most international crossings, it's equipped with duty-free shops and a duty-free gas station (also owned by Moroun). *2744 W. Fort St., www.ambassadorbridge.com, (313) 963-1410.*

Bagley Pedestrian Bridge - In 2010, 40 years after being severed by the chasm of the I-75 and I-96 freeways, Mexicantown was re-connected by the Bagley Pedestrian Bridge. With a lofty mission of re-establishing communal unity, the bridge succeeds with a design that

invites interaction. An impressive 417 feet across, the most distinct feature of the contemporary asymmetrical crossing—which is the only cable-stayed footbridge in Michigan—is the 155-foot tall angular pylon that towers over the bridge it supports. With a price tag of $5 million, the bridge is dotted throughout with decorative lighting, seating, and landscaping, which, combined with the fact that it allows visitors to sit atop 10 lanes of traffic—and affords an incredible view of the Ambassador Bridge—makes it an unforgettable destination for carryout from the many nearby restaurants. Of course, for those that aren't hungry, it can simply be a place to meditate on neighborhoods, development, and what being the "Motor City" has meant for Detroit. *The bridge starts at Bagley and the I-75 service drive on the West side, and Bagley and 21st on the East Side.*

Dome Home - Built in 1998 by Leo Gillis, cousin of Jack White (nee Gillis), the bright blue 4,000-square-foot residential mini-complex is based on the geodesic domes developed by Buckminster Fuller in 1948. The only geodesic domes in Detroit, the complex's reinforced concrete structure was constructed from a kit and cost $110,000 to build, including materials and labor. The structure is privately owned, so please restrict visits to the sidewalk. *Located at the intersection of W. Vernor Hwy. and Johnson St.*

Historic Fort Wayne - Situated on 96 acres along the Detroit River, Fort Wayne was originally built to repel a British invasion from Canada that never materialized. These days, the only battles you're likely to find are between competing bargain-hunters both eyeing the same tschotske at the fort's biannual flea market or simulated ones put on by Civil War re-enactors. The main, star-shaped fort building and stunning limestone barracks were constructed between 1843 and 1851, but additional construction continued until 1931, resulting in a number of smaller structures, including additional barracks, officers' quarters, stables, shops, etc. Not all have been well-preserved, and many are off-limits to visitors, but history enthusiasts will have a ball wandering around the vast premises and exploring the buildings that are accessible. It's also a great spot for a picnic, a bike ride, or any number of events that regularly take place there, including the flea market and battle re-enactments, as well as races, veterans' events, historic commemorations, and holiday celebrations. *6325 W. Jefferson Ave., www.historicfortwaynecoalition.com, (313) 628-0796.*

Hubbard Farms - Bounded by West Vernor Highway to the north, Clark Street to the west, West Lafayette to the south and West Grand Boulevard to the east, the Hubbard Farms historic district is a two-century old enclave named for developer Bela Hubbard, one of the founders of what would grow to become the Detroit Institute of Arts. Historically, the land that now comprises the scenic neighborhood was a Pottawatamie village and was dotted by elaborate burial mounds, which were later joined by French ribbon farms (narrow plots designed to maximize fresh water access). However, both the remnants of the gravesites and the farms were cleared to make way for the city's increasingly explosive growth at the end of the 19th century. Largely developed between 1880 and 1920, the neighborhood attracted upper-class residents employed as managers in industry and manufacturing. Housing styles in the neighborhood—which has been well-maintained, especially in recent decades—include a range of attractive Victorian, Romanesque Revival, Beaux Arts, Italianate, and Colonial Revival residences. Though the neighborhood is more reserved in its grandeur than Boston-Edison or Palmer Woods (see separate entries) it makes for a scenic two- or four-wheeled historic home tour.

J.W. Westcott Co. - At the foot of 24th Street on the Detroit River sits the most unique post office in Detroit—and maybe the United States—a mobile marine mail delivery service that claims to be the only mail service in the world that delivers while vessels are under way. "Mail in the pail," as it's called, was first provided by John W. Westcott in 1874 from his rowboats to passing steamships, and the service expanded over the decades to come. In 1948, Westcott's company was assigned its own ZIP code—48222 (the only floating ZIP code in the United States)—and today the 24/7 operation averages about 30 deliveries in a solar day. A contract post office, walk-up customers can visit the land-based office to send mail to all destinations, floating or not, and purchase nautical charts, books of nautical history, and trade publications. Business is seasonal—J.W. Westcott operates from April to mid-December. Visitors should try to watch a delivery from the most optimal location, the adjacent Riverside Park, which provides fence-free seating on the waterfront. *12 24th St., www.jwwestcott.com, (313) 496-0555.*

Lawndale Market - With its walls, racks, and ceilings plastered with more than 10,000 Polaroid pictures of customers, Lawndale Market is more folk museum than liquor store. Between 1995 and 2008 (when

Polaroid ended film production), owner Amad Samaan decorated his store with his celluloid garlands and wallpaper by photographing local children who did well in school and other customers who piqued his interest. This otherwise modest party store has an impressive selection of South and Central American beers. Hours vary wildly, so visitors should call ahead. *1136 Lawndale St., (313) 841-2531.*

Ste. Anne de Detroit - Considering its heritage as the second-oldest continuously operating Roman Catholic parish in the United States, it's appropriate that a church named for the grandmother of Jesus has provided sanctuary to Detroiters as long as the city has existed. Construction of the first church began just two days after the city's founder, Antoine de la Mothe Cadillac, arrived in 1701, though the parish was forced to rebuild eight times over three centuries because of urban renewal and fires, including a scuttling by the Fort Pontchartrain settlers themselves during the first Fox War. The current edifice was completed in 1887, and boasts elegant Victorian Gothic features, including some uncommon for American churches— soaring flying buttresses, spired wood pews, and an ornate carved wood elevated pulpit. The church also has a shrine of the patroness saint (worshipped at special Novena services) and still retains the wood altar from the church constructed in 1818 in its chapel, where the renowned local 19th century priest Gabriel Richard is interred. There are also two majestic organs—one 26-rank organ above the entrance to the sanctuary, and another in the chapel. Detroit's history can be traced from the church's comprehensive historical records, which trace the city's evolution from a French colony to U.S. metropolis. Spanish mass offered. *1000 St. Anne St., (313) 496-1701 www.ste-anne.org*

Woodmere Cemetery - Founded in 1867, Woodmere is one of Detroit's oldest cemeteries and the resting place of many of its most influential businessmen, especially those who made their fortunes before the auto industry—in tobacco, lumber, steel, newspapers, shipping, and even soda. Established as a rural oasis in the sleepy township of Springwells, today, Woodmere is part of bustling neighborhood in Southwest Detroit. It's huge—more than 200 acres—so it helps to bring wheels, two or four, when you visit. *9400 W. Fort St., www.woodmerecemeteryresearch.com, (313) 841-0188.*

Notable burials include:

- David Dunbar Buick (1854 - 1929): Founder of Buick Car Company, inventor of a method for enameling bathtubs still in use today. *Section Allendale, Lot 631.*

- John Judson Bagley (1832-1881): Tobacco magnate, governor of Michigan, and one of Woodmere's founders. *Section D, Lot 149.*

- James Vernor, Sr. (1843-1927): Inventor of Vernor's Ginger Ale and longtime member of Detroit's Common Council. *Section D, Lot 146.*

- Ford Hunger March victims Joseph York, Joseph Bussell, Kalman Leny and Joseph DeBascio: Killed March 7, 1932, during a labor demonstration. *Section Ferndale, Lot 18.*

- Hamilton Carhartt (1857-1937): Founder of the Carhartt line of work clothes. *Section North Lake.*

- David Whitney (1830-1900): Lumber baron whose former home is now The Whitney restaurant. *Section F.*

- James E. Scripps (1835-1906): Founder of the Detroit Evening News (today's Detroit News). *Section A5.*

Zug Island - Across a shipping canal from the hardscrabble Del Ray neighborhood lies Zug Island, a heavily industrialized dystopian iron island that belches smoke and fire like a post-apocalyptic volcanic monster. Originally a small peninsula in the Detroit River, the island was owned by furniture magnate Samuel Zug who fancied it for the site of his dream home, until it was found to be too swampy, vermin-infested, and inhospitable. In 1888, Zug permitted a canal to be cut through his property to allow ships easier access to the Rouge River, transforming the peninsula into an island. Zug sold the island in 1891, and it quickly became a compact industrial center, with the first of its three blast furnaces being constructed in 1902. Today, the island is owned and operated by United States Steel and is formally called the Great Lakes Works, but we'll stick with Zug Island. It's connected to the mainland by only two bridges, but don't even think about turning onto one of them to try to enter the island. Few have seen the interior of this industrial works because of its intense high security level, and you'll be turned away. That's OK, though: You can marvel from the mainland at the strangely beautiful, jaw-dropping site with blast furnaces lighting up the sky and producing an entrancing glow that can be seen for miles. Though technically, the private island is located

in River Rouge, it is best observed from Southwest Detroit. Trivia bonus: Zug Island was supposed to be the final destination of the ill-fated Great Lakes freighter the Edmund Fitzgerald that sank off of Whitefish Point in Lake Superior in 1975.
W. Jefferson Ave. and Zug Island Dr.

POINTS OF INTEREST

Cadillac Urban Gardens - In a former parking lot for GM executives, this urban garden features raised beds built from repurposed shipping carts. *McKinstry St. and Merritt St.*

Cloud Bridge - This cheerful transformation of a grimy overpass into a blue sky dotted with clouds was the work of local artists Davin Brainard and Dion Fischer. *665 W. Grand Blvd.*

Del Ray Crib in The Hood - A folk art oddity in the heart of one of the city's grittiest, most industrial neighborhoods, this private home is surrounded by a makeshift plywood fence and guarded by hand-painted ceramic lions. *8475 Dearborn St.*

Diversity Is Our Strength - In 1995, 18-year-old Arturo Cruz designed this huge mural on the side of the popular Mexican restaurant Los Galanes. The celebration of the diversity of people that make up the region was executed by a multicultural, multigenerational group of more than seventy people.
3362 Bagley Ave.

Ford Hunger March Site - On March 7, 1932, thousands gathered to march toward the Dearborn office of Henry Ford to demand better employment opportunities and the right to organize. The loud, but peaceful, protesters were met with violent resistance from the Dearborn Police and Ford Security, who sprayed machine gun fire into the crowd, killing five and injuring more than 60.
W. Fort St. and Miller St.

Gabriel Richard Grave at Saint Anne's Church - The French-born Catholic priest served as a nonvoting delegate of the Michigan Territory from 1823 to 1825. Father Richard opened the first printing press in the city, was a cofounder of the Catholepistemiad of Michigania, which would later become the University of Michigan, and gave the city its motto (Speramus meliora; resurget cineribus; in English: "We hope for better things; it will arise from the ashes") shortly after a fire leveled the city in 1805. *1000 Ste. Anne St.*

Hotel Yorba - Made famous by the White Stripes song and video of the same name, this once economical hotel is now permanent housing. *4020 Lafayette Blvd.*

Jack White Home - The White Stripes frontman spent his early years in this Southwest home, later turning it into a recording studio. *1203 Ferdinand St.*

Jimmy Hoffa Home - This is the childhood home of the infamous Teamsters president whose death remains a mystery to this day. *4742 Toledo St.*

Malice Green Memorial - The mural here, painted by artist Bennie Israel, commemorates the site where Malice Green was brutally beaten to death by Detroit police during a traffic stop. *3418 W. Warren Ave.*

Old Boblo Docks - This oversize blue mural is all that remains of what was once the docking place for the steamers Columbia and Ste. Claire, which took happy families to Boblo Island, an amusement park located on an island in the middle of the Detroit River. *4436 W. Jefferson Ave.*

Romanowski Park - An example of grassroots volunteerism and dedication, this park, once little more than a weedy lot, now contains athletic fields, a 100-plus fruit tree orchard, and a handful of community gardens. *4401 Lonyo St.*

Target Mural - This 1975 mural by renowned Cass Corridor artist Robert Sestok was commissioned by James F. Duffy Jr., an avid patron of the Detroit art scene and the owner of the warehouse on which it's painted. The work connects itself to the city's industrial roots with a kinetic circle resembling a whirring sawblade or a cross section of a working pipe. *5840 W. Jefferson Ave.*

Salt Mines - About 1,200 feet below the city, this enormous mine, host to 100 miles of underground roads, has been intermittently in operation since 1910. It's currently producing rock salt used to de-ice roads. *12841 Sanders St.*

St. Francis D'Assisi Parish - Completed in 1903, the two five-story towers of the historically Polish Catholic Church flank the ornate three-story Corinthian-columned entryway. *4500 Wesson Ave.*

CHAPTER 6
NEW CENTER/NORTH END

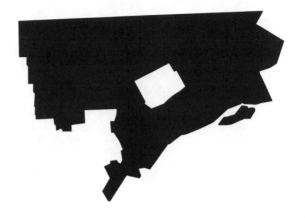

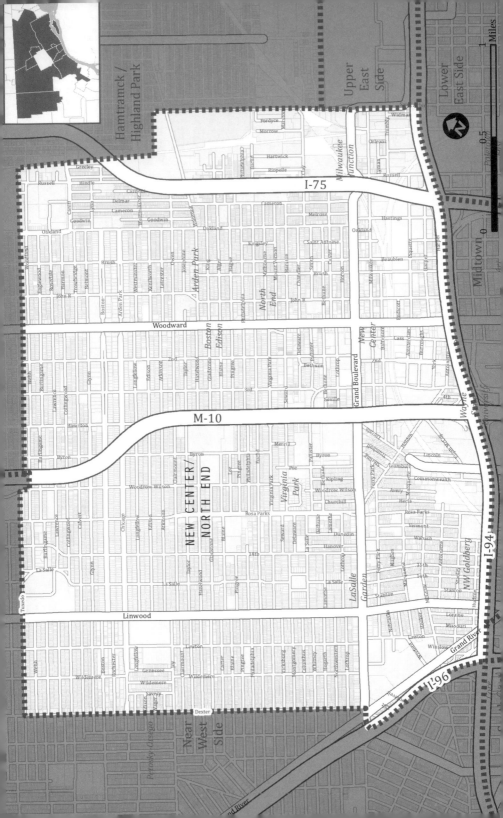

From renowned neighborhood shops and local eateries to authentic dive bars and live entertainment, the New Center/North End area of Detroit is the perfect destination to view stunning architecture, soak in the region's history, and admire diverse, character-rich local art. Collectively, the commercial and residential neighborhoods in this area are filled with big city history, culture, and flavors that draw people from throughout the region.

New Center/North End, as we define it, covers more than seven square miles and is bounded by I-94, Hamtramck, Highland Park, Dexter Avenue, and Tuxedo Street. This area is home to a constellation of neighborhoods, including Arden Park, Boston-Edison, LaSalle Gardens, Milwaukee Junction, New Center, North End, Northwest Goldberg, and Virginia Park. Most neighborhoods within this area date to the earliest days of the city's automotive renaissance, having been annexed between 1827 and 1915, and originally built primarily between 1900 and 1929. The area is steeped in automotive history and is home to Henry Ford's first plant, the former Fisher Body factory, a neighborhood for automotive magnates, the General Motors headquarters from its golden years, and large swaths of automotive workers' housing.

Today, New Center/North End is home to 33,000 people. It includes the city's most diverse collection of historic architecture and an array of neighborhoods that have evolved in different ways because of the ongoing diminution of the local automotive industry. Although defined here together as New Center/North End, the neighborhoods that collectively comprise the area have distinct histories and disparate trajectories. Despite these differences, the neighborhood can be divided into three areas—southern, central, and northern and western—that are unified by similar histories and physical characteristics.

For shoppers and hungry or thirsty visitors alike, the New Center district—the southernmost part of the area covered in this chapter—is among the city's most significant commercial corridors and offers one of city's most diverse collections of restaurants, bars, and independent shops set in some of the most breathtaking commercial architecture in the city, making it a destination for enjoying local art and culture, shopping, and flavors.

Abutting Chicago Boulevard, the central area of this chapter, including neighborhoods like Boston-Edison, Arden Park, and the slightly more modest Virginia Park, are home to lush boulevards lined with palatial

World War II-era mansions, which were once home to many of the earliest auto barons, making them popular with those looking to experience a scenic, stately, historic urban neighborhood.

The northern and western areas of the neighborhoods covered in this chapter have experienced considerable population loss and are consequently home to many vacant homes and lots. These areas have recently begun to become home to some new younger creative residents who, alongside their older neighbors, have begun to work to revitalize some of these areas with gardens, art installations, galleries, and artistic live-work spaces. For those looking to experience some of the city's most diverse venues for folk and independent art, the North End, Milwaukee Junction, and Northwest Goldberg neighborhoods offer a fascinating environment to see creative work and grassroots community projects.

BARS & RESTAURANTS

Apex Bar - If these walls could talk! In the boom years of Detroit's automotive area, the Apex Bar was a mainstay of the northern extension of the Hastings Street entertainment district that, along with the adjacent Paradise Valley neighborhood, had a vibrancy that rivaled Harlem and Chicago's south side. The bar is best known as the place where a little-known Mississippi bluesman named John Lee Hooker first cut his teeth before he was catapulted into the pantheon of blues history. Over the next 50 years, the neighborhood surrounding Apex fell prey to an all-too familiar story in Detroit: freeway construction, "urban renewal," flight, blight, and decay. The bar still holds on today, thanks to the pluck of its civic-minded matriarch, Marvelous Persell. She's serving cheap drinks to a crowd

of down-on-their-luck neighborhood regulars that are the mainstays of most neighborhood bars in the city, but with a self-bestowed honor that emphasizes the determination that keeps the doors open: she makes sure the bar lives up to its modern-day reputation as "the cleanest bar in Detroit." Be sure to skip Sundays, when Ms. Persell closes the doors for a little R&R. *7649 Oakland St., (313) 873-1190.*

» City Wings - Owner Grant Lancaster's sleek, inviting, and modern space is a wing lover's paradise. The clean lines, bright colors, and industrial loft aesthetic of the large dining room offer a cheerful atmosphere, while the re-arrangeable nature of the small tables accentuates the social nature of wings. Visitors can see the open kitchen and watch as the cooks turn massive pieces of fresh Amish chicken into one of 16 flavors of chicken wings. Although every type of wing is outstanding, the hickory smoked BBQ, and Parmesan and garlic flavors are exceptional. City Wings' non-wing menu is also delicious. Standouts include the fried okra, baked beans, and turkey chili. Vegetarian options are limited, but the veggie plate—any combination of three sides—is available and tasty. *2896 W. Grand Blvd., www.citywingsinc.com, (313) 871-2489.*

Cuisine - Enjoy elegant, contemporary French-American cuisine by candlelight in this little gem tucked away in a charming historic home on a tree-lined street behind the Fisher Theatre. The cozy house was a speakeasy in the 1920s and has been a series of restaurants since the 1950s. It's not for the budget conscious, but it's worth every penny of the splurge. Cuisine offers a seasonal menu of innovative, fresh food with a French influence from chef and owner Paul Grosz, who studied under chefs in France, had a stint at Le Cordon Bleu, and was a chef at the Whitney in Midtown before opening Cuisine. The beef tenderloin and scallops are especially sublime, and the truffle mac and cheese is outstanding. The menu doesn't cater to vegetarians, but there's usually at least one veggie-friendly entree, such as an asparagus risotto. Ask the friendly servers for advice on wine pairings for your meal. *670 Lothrop Rd., (313) 872-5110.*

Firewater II Bar and Grill - Part bistro and part dance club, by day, this popular neighborhood joint is a New Center destination for mid-priced business lunch and low-key dinner and drinks. The raised round tables—and large open bar—offer a welcoming atmosphere for tuna melts, grilled salmon salads, ribs, and other mealtime staples. By night, the bar and grill transforms into a place "where class is a requirement, not a request," often requiring a $5 cover charge and a dress code: no boots or sneakers. On the central wooden dance floor, a cult following of eager Chicago steppers and other dancers ignites the bar with clapping heels in front of the DJ stage, which also plays host to live music on weekends. For those dancers who are a little green, lessons are offered on Tuesday afternoons. *6521 John R St., (313) 872-0812.*

Mr. Mike's - Serving cold drinks and hot steaks to the New Center community since 1936, Mr. Mike's is a dim, old-timey steakhouse and bar that oozes character. The vintage leather upholstery, intricate woodwork, and stained glass all contribute to the vintage bistro ambiance. It is a destination for a three-martini lunch, a romantic date—or a raucous night of karaoke. Mr. Mike's transforms each day from a quiet lunch spot to a professional-grade R&B karaoke bar. Although Mr. Mike's is known for its outstanding strip steaks, the other options on the relatively concise menu—such as the turkey club, the onion soup au gratin, and the liver and onions—are all delicious. Mr. Mike's has a strict dress code prohibiting jogging suits, hoodies, white T-shirts, and baseball caps. *6064 Woodward Ave., www.mrmikeskaraoke.com, (313) 871-6722.*

New Center Eatery - Despite a diverse menu loaded with delicious Southern staples—such as turkey sausage, grits, chicken fajitas, fried green tomatoes, gumbo, and baby back ribs—the belle of the ball on this Dixie menu is the chicken and waffles. Whether you're visiting this charming yet unassuming breakfast-and-lunch spot for hangover treatment, a social breakfast, or a business lunch, get the chicken and waffles and be prepared for a yin and yang combination of sweet and savory featuring lightly breaded chicken, fluffy waffles, juicy strawberries, buttery butter, and warm syrup. This New Center classic can be busy during weekday lunches, so many regulars get carryout and head over to the nearby New Center Park. *3100 W. Grand Blvd., www.newcentereatery.com, (313) 875-0088.*

» Northern Lights Lounge - Decked out with mid-century swank, the Northern Lights Lounge is one of the classiest establishments in New Center. The bar is elegantly decorated with a retro lounge decor: dark wood trim, velvet upholstery, elevated vinyl booths, and candlelit tables. Though shuffleboard is on the bill every night, there is frequently live entertainment, which varies from rock concerts—including a residency by Detroit legend and Funk Brother Dennis Coffey every Tuesday night—to burlesque shows or DJ nights. There are drink specials most nights, and food is served until midnight. The menu offerings are more dive bar than four-star, but with half off on Thursday nights, you can't complain. *660 W. Baltimore St., (313) 873-1379.*

Parks Old Style Bar-B-Q - Get ready for meltingly tender and mouthwateringly flavorful ribs served in Fred Flintstone–size portions. From within the sleepy building and its modest interior, owner and barbe-guru Constance Parks has been barbecuing some of the city's finest ribs and chicken since 1964. Although the slightly unkempt building and interior waiting area appear unchanged since opening, it is a very clean space, with a cheerful atmosphere and friendly staff. While the simple menu lists only two meats—ribs and chicken—customers can order them in a variety of preparations, including slabs, rib sandwiches, wing dings, half chickens, and rib tips. The barbecue chicken is, naturally, tender and perfectly cooked and seasoned, but the rib portions of the menu are the highlight. The ribs are outstanding, drawing a perfect balance between being well-done and juicy, sweet, and spicy. Perhaps most importantly, the ribs are smothered in the house vinegar-based barbecue sauce. Don't forget to ask for extra napkins. *7444 Beaubien St., www.parksoldstylebar-b-q.com, (313) 873-7444.*

Stella International Cafe - Set just off the breathtaking lobby of the Fisher Building with cafe seating under the ornate concourse, Stella is a small, European-style coffee shop in the most elegant of settings. In addition to brewing Illy coffee, from Trieste, Italy, the cafe offers six locally roasted varieties, including our favorite, the Cyclers Choice Breakfast Blend, a perfect cup of Joe for two-wheeled commuters on the go. To augment its caffeinated offerings, Stella offers bagels from exceptional New York Bagel in Ferndale, as well as a wide variety of fresh pastries, breakfast delights, house-made sandwiches, and hot grilled paninis. Visitors headed downtown can find Stella's satellite location in the Guardian Building. *3011 W. Grand Blvd., www.stellacafe.com, (313) 664-0400.*

Turkey Grill - Home to Detroit's turkey burger for more than 15 years, the Turkey Grill offers healthy and tasty alternatives to typical carryout at comparable prices. Order at the counter, and in about 10 minutes the turkey-Tom goodness will arrive hot off the grill for you to enjoy to-go or at one of the spacious booths. From the classic turkey burger to breakfast specials with turkey sausage to Cajun-fried turkey wings, the Turkey Grill offers a tasty variety of Southern-style dishes for less than $10. Be sure to drop in Fridays for the Louisiana-style gumbo special. Fried sides and a few salads are vegetarian-friendly, but the main dishes offer turkey, turkey, or turkey! *8290 Woodward Ave., www.turkeygrilldetroit.com, (313) 872-4624.*

Woodward Cocktail Bar - Said to be the oldest operating gay bar in America still in its original location, the Woodward has been a nexus for the LGBTQ community to socialize, relax, drink, and dance since 1951. The address of the bar belies its rear entrance—patrons buzz to get in and are served in a den of exposed brick with a low ceiling and rose-tinted lighting. The dance floor is a raised wooden stage and features a colored light rig, with DJs spinning seven nights a week starting at 10pm. The Woodward is largely a destination bar for members of Detroit's African-American gay community, but there's no litmus test for prospective regulars. Standard pub grub and smoking patio available. Monday is drag nights Monday. *6426 Woodward Ave., (313) 872-0166.*

Z's Villa - Roll up your sleeves and get ready for bonfires, horseshoes, and volleyball over beers and pizza. Set in a deceivingly quaint home, this lively bar and restaurant specializes in what can only be described as "party food"—pizza, ribs, wing dings, potato skin boats, clam strips, and nachos. In addition to its yummy food, Z's has a well-stocked bar and a commendable beer list. While popular for lunch and dinner year-round, this spot is especially popular in the summer, when the horseshoe pits and volleyball court come alive. The free shuttle makes this a great option for catching some vittles before downtown sporting events. *42 Piquette St., www.zsvilladet.com, (313) 874-2680.*

SHOPPING & SERVICES

» African Bead Museum - Equal parts gallery, bead shop, and museum, it's hard to miss the mirage-like light shimmering from the thousands of fragments of mirrors adorning the exterior of the building and the colorful painting and sculptures in the adjacent lots. Its external ornamentation is only a preamble to an even richer interior: Visitors may stop in to shop from a selection of thousands of fascinating and beautiful authentic folk beads from throughout Africa, take part in African dance classes, or check out the museum's collection of African artifacts, which includes sculptures, textiles, and pottery from the last several hundred years. Founded in 1985 by celebrated local artist Olayami Dabls, the museum moved to this

17,500-square-foot location in 1998. Stop in any weekday or on Saturdays, and if you're lucky, you'll be able to enjoy a thoughtful conversation with Dabls himself about beads, art, African artifacts, and Detroit. *6559 Grand River Ave., www.mbad.org, (313) 898-3007.*

Big Book Store - "Little" brother to Corktown's four-story warehouse, John K. King Used & Rare Books (see separate entry), the still massive Big Book Store also carries a variety of used books, but specializes in comics and magazines. The large open room houses floor-to-ceiling shelves of paperbacks and boxes of periodicals in every genre. If you find the maze of books at John K. King a little too extensive, and you're searching for a variety of affordable reads, the Big Book Store is the perfect, more manageable, place to browse. Don't be dissuaded by the long list of no-nos posted at the entry to the store—the staff is friendly, and if you ask to see the Big Book Store's collection of vintage adult titles, they'll be happy to help you. *5911 Cass Ave., www.rarebooklink.com, (313) 831-8511.*

Detroit Gallery of Contemporary Crafts - Appropriately located on the first floor of the magnificent Art Deco Fisher Building, Detroit Gallery of Contemporary Crafts showcases traditional craftspeople and artists from across the nation. This store features handmade ceramics, jewelry, handbags, knits, tapestries, furniture, home decor, and even hand-dyed and handcrafted women's clothing and hats. The gallery has been the perfect place to find a meaningful gift or a unique personal piece for your home or wardrobe for more than 30 years. *3011 W. Grand Blvd., Ste. 104, (313) 873-7888.*

Detroit Hardware Company - Run by generations of the Webster family since 1924, Detroit Hardware Company has been a frequent destination for generations of the city's shade-tree handy folk. In addition to offering expert advice on projects—and especially historic rehabilitation projects—the knowledgeable and warm staff offer a variety of services, from watch battery replacement to custom glasswork. More than a hardware store, the shop sells a wide array of items across its two floors, including beautiful cast iron pans, hunting licenses, and an assortment of home goods. *6432 Woodward Ave., www.detroithardwareco.com, (313) 875-0838.*

Dittrich Furs - Harkening back to Detroit's days as a fur-trading post for Ojibwe trappers and French merchants, Dittrich keeps the tradition of fine furs alive. As one of the oldest family-owned retail business in Detroit, Dittrich was founded in 1893 and is one of the leading fur retailers in the United States. The store offers a selection of more than 1,000 furs, as well as garment design and manufacturing services, garment repair and restyling, and state of the art cleaning and storage. Known for wonderful service, Dittrich employees greet every visitor as if they had walked into the family's own living room. If for any reason you can't find what you are looking for at Dittrich, try Silver Fox Furs (3031 W. Grand Blvd., (313) 872-4260), which specializes in custom and one-of-a-kind fur apparel and accessories. *7373 Third St., www.dittrichfurs.com, (313) 873-8300.*

London Luggage - Since opening in 1948, London Luggage has been outfitting area travelers and businesspeople with its extensive inventory of suitcases, briefcases, purses, satchels, writing instruments, and handbags. Enthusiastic owner Ward Dietrich and his staff have a passion for baggage, and love explaining products to customers, while helping them navigate the huge 6,500-square-foot showroom and warehouse. Though the window display showcases the iconic luggage brands, such as the reliable Briggs and Riley, classic Samsonite, and sturdy Swiss Army, a wealth of caches populate the contemporary sales floor. Dooney and Burke handbags, sturdy laptop cases, and fine briefcases are just a few items available in addition to first-rate luggage brands. In the sparkling glass showcases, admire the Mont Blanc fountain pens, Cross pens, and fine watches. *5955 Woodward Ave., www.londonluggage.com, (313) 831-7200.*

Ms. Lottie's Ice Cream and Candy Factory - Nestled in the corner of John R and Kenilworth and named after the owner's grandmother, Ms. Lottie's brown factory facade opens into a magical, multicolored toy chest full of collector's tin lunchboxes, classic 10-cent candies, frozen Good Humor treats, and chilled Huggies juice barrels. Don't let the wild weeds at the adjacent corner dissuade you from visiting Ms. Lottie's, because the Ice Cream and Candy Factory and the neighboring Transformations Barbershop are part of a project to re-envision the neighborhood as a family-friendly retail block. Sit with locals and listen as they share their vision for the neighborhood as you nibble candy on Lottie's freshly painted brown bench: a repurposed church pew that rests along the sidewalk. *9405 John R St. (313) 415-5566.*

» Pure Detroit - What began as a small T-shirt company and shop in the David Whitney Building in 1998 has grown into a thriving Detroit business and a beloved local brand. Though the company also maintains storefronts in two prominent Downtown architectural icons—the Guardian Building and the Renaissance Center (see separate entry)—its flagship store is located in the palatial Fisher Building. Accessible just off of the architectural gem's Lothrop Road entrance, the bi-level store offers the largest selection of Pure Detroit's signature Detroit tees, totes, sweatshirts, magnets, undies, pet leashes, and belts and purses made from old seat belts—as well as Detroit gifts such as mouth-watering Sanders treats, delicious McClure's pickles, and Faygo pop. Pure Detroit has become a destination for visitors and locals alike looking to stock up on some Detroit swag. *3011 W. Grand Blvd., Ste. 101, www.puredetroit.com, (313) 873-7873.*

Recycle Here! - If you've got a dash of trash to stash, steer your rear to Recycle Here! Home to numerous murals, cheerful staff, interactive art installations, and a free rummage trailer—the "junk hole"—Recycle Here! is Detroit's response to the recycling blues. The center offers residents a chance to recycle their paper, cardboard, plastic, glass, plastic bags, Styrofoam, and broken electronics while visiting with their neighbors and having a good time. Recycle Here! is a multi-stream facility, so recyclers must sort their recyclables into appropriate bins. Visitors should also plan on checking out the two sister operations: the Greensafe Store—which offers environmentally friendly disposable foodservice supplies, including sugarcane compostable bowls and cornstarch utensils—and the Lincoln Street Art Park, a self-described outdoor "Ghetto Louvre" which features art made from found and recycled materials, and an array of exciting, unorthodox, and curious outdoor events, as well as live shows. *1331 Holden St., www.recyclehere.net, (313) 871-4000.*

Value World - A thrifter's thrift store, the shop is an insider's location that offers a healthy selection of men's and women's clothing at excellent prices. Though it's a little rough around the edges, it frequently affords steadfast visitors big scores, such as vintage designer apparel, furs, jewelry, and an impressive selection of flannel shirts. Though clothing, and especially women's clothing, is the focus of the store, there is a small area dedicated to housewares, toys, and electronics off to the side. As resale market prices continue to rise, it's nice to know a thrift store like this still exists. Part of a regional thrift store chain, other Value World (sometimes Value Village) locations can be found throughout the metro area, including a location in nearby Hamtramck. Be sure to look online for the elusive 50% off coupon before visiting. *8300 Woodward Ave., www.valueworld.net, (734) 728-4610.*

Vera Jane - Founded by the team behind Pure Detroit, Vera Jane has been offering handbags, superfine undergarments, re-fashioned vintage jewelry, and clothing to shoppers in New Center since 2003. Situated in the Fisher Building, the store's poured concrete floor and exposed ceiling recession contrast the opulent brass and marble lobby outside—but Vera Jane's blend of contemporary style with retro touches, such as a vintage hair salon chair and a smattering of commemorative Art Deco tomes (for sale), bring a warmth and welcoming feel to the space. The store is small—think boutiquette or cozier—but its selection is a unique mix of goods from modern designers, including seatbelt handbags by Harvey, Cosa Bella lingerie, coats and hoodies by Alternative Apparel, and specially commissioned jewelry pieces. *3011 W. Grand Blvd., (313) 872-VERA.*

CULTURAL ATTRACTIONS

» Model T Automotive Heritage Complex - Perhaps the nation's most significant automotive heritage site, the Model T Automotive Heritage Complex at the Ford Piquette Avenue Plant is an impressive museum in a storied 1904 structure. The building, a New England mill-style plant, was the first structure built by the Ford Motor Company and the birthplace of the Model T, the "Tin Lizzy." The beautiful three-story red brick building, with its original wooden columns and maple floors, and patches of original paint, untouched since 1910, affords visitors the opportunity to walk in history. The museum, spread across the second and third floors of the building, showcases a number of authentic vintage Piquette-era Fords, including several models of the Model T and earlier Model S. In addition to the many antique Fords and period artifacts on display, the museum offers a constellation of innovative interpretive displays that explain the assembly process with original Model Ts and display panels that underscore the historic importance of these iconic cars and the people and building that created them. A museum gift shop sells a range of Model T memorabilia, clothing, and Ford-related items. In addition to regular programming and exhibits, the museum acts as a de facto Model T enthusiast's meeting place, and frequently, collectors are on hand to offer rides in one of the legendary cars. The complex is open from April to October, Wednesday to Sunday. Check out the original wooden elevator. *461 Piquette St., www.tplex.org, (313) 872-8759.*

» Motown Historical Museum - A Mecca for music lovers from all over the world, the Motown Historical Museum is housed in Hitsville U.S.A., the birthplace of Motown Records, one of the most influential and significant music labels in U.S. history. Between 1961 and 1971, Motown had 110 top 10 hits—more than any other label during the period—and introduced the world to critically acclaimed and best-selling artists such as The Four Tops, Michael Jackson, The Jackson 5, Marvin Gaye, The Isley Brothers, Gladys Knight & The Pips, Martha Reeves and The Vandellas, Smokey Robinson and The Miracles, The Supremes, The Temptations, Mary Wells, and Stevie Wonder. In 1959, Berry Gordy, the founder of Motown, purchased a house and lived upstairs after converting an attached photography studio into a well-engineered recording studio, "Studio A," where nearly all of Motown's hits were recorded for a decade. In 1985, Esther Gordy Edwards, Berry Gordy's sister, began rehabilitating the space to its Motown-era condition and acquiring artifacts. Today, the space has been beautifully restored and features thousands of historic photos, stage outfits, records, posters, gold records, original sheet music, and artifacts, including Michael Jackson's black fedora and studded glove. The museum offers regularly scheduled one-hour tours that take visitors through the large interpretative display area, the original echo chamber, the uniform wardrobe room, Berry Gordy's second-floor flat, the perfectly preserved control room, and the fabled "Studio A." A highlight of the tour experience is the brief Motown dance

lesson, held in "Studio A." The professional docents are friendly and outgoing and have seemingly unparalleled knowledge of the label's history and culture. Stars such as Reeves or Wonder occasionally drop in to greet fans, particularly on weekends. Don't forget to "Shop Around" at the well-stocked gift shop. *2648 W. Grand Blvd., www.motownmuseum.com, (313) 875-2264.*

Russell Industrial Center - The brainchild of Greek immigrant entrepreneur and controversial figure Dennis Kefallinos, the Russell Industrial Center is a massive arts incubator space housed in a sprawling, 2.2-million-square-foot former chassis manufacturing complex originally designed by Albert Kahn in 1915. Since being reimagined as an inexpensive home base for artists and craftspeople in 2003—so far, 650,000 square feet of the complex have been renovated and leased—the facility has become the headquarters, workshop, studio, or office of 300 creative small businesses, from architects to glassblowers, candle makers to artistic welders. Compartmentalized into hundreds of smaller, private units, the best time to explore the facility is during one of its seasonal open houses, when the majority of the tenants open their doors to the public and share their work and space. Some of our favorite tenants with public hours are **Cave Gallery,** a contemporary art gallery that showcases emerging and established artists; **Detroit Industrial Projects**, a raw, for-lease industrial gallery space that plays host to a wide-ranging cast of exhibits; the **Detroit Center for Contemporary Photography**, a nonprofit gallery space dedicated to lens-based work; and **Michigan Hot Glass Workshop,** a mammoth 4,000-square-foot glassblowing facility and gallery that offers classes for all skill levels. In addition to the studio space in the building, the complex is also the host of the weekly Russell Bazaar on the ground floor, which features 150 vendors in a flea market atmosphere, with sellers slinging folk art, shea butter, sunglasses, jewelry, food, and everything in between. The facility also hosts the annual People's Art Festival, a DIY craft and music fair, on its grounds. Don't miss the unmistakable mechanical lion mural, which greets passing motorists on the I-75 expressway. Though the doors are often unlocked, because the building itself does not hold regular public hours, unless you are attending a pre-scheduled event, be sure to make contact with the party you intend to visit prior to your trip. *1600 Clay St., www.ricdetroit.org, (313) 872-4000.*

Submerge Records - Submerge Records is a Detroit techno distributor that has offered an archive exhibit and retail outlet in New Center since 2003. In accordance with the culture and legacy of the music, the facility is discreet: its building bares no signs signaling that it's there, and it doesn't hold regular open hours. However, the minimal planning required to arrange a visit to Submerge and its store somewhere in Detroit is well worth it. The archive, Exhibit 3000, is situated in a mellow, sleek lobby framed with glass display cases that highlight the technological, social, artistic, and apocryphal aspects of Detroit techno. Artifacts on display include the sequencer used by Kevin Saunderson to make the track "Big Fun," a 1920s-era lathe used to press numerous unique and landmark Detroit releases, gold and platinum record awards from the UK, and original album artwork. The archive, though small, is greatly enhanced by tours of the exhibit that give context, anecdotes, and personal perspective to the role Submerge played in the music, as well as the larger techno scene itself. The store, set bunker-style in the basement, features thousands of signatures from the visitors who've come from all over the world. The store sells Underground Resistance clothing and relevant 12-inch and 7-inch records. Tours and visits must be arranged by e-mail *(support@submerge.com)* in advance, except during the annual DEMF open house. *3000 E. Grand Blvd., www.submerge.com.*

Tangent Gallery & Hastings Street Ballroom - This gallery and performance venue built in a former paper plant has been offering performers the chance to rent unique and adaptive space for more than a decade. The gallery is whitewashed with an elevated stage at the front and has a full sound system, while the ballroom is curtained in black with a full stage at its front—with a full liquor license available at either for events. Notable performers at the space have included John Sinclair, Kevin Saunderson, and Thornetta Davis. Check the website for upcoming shows, concerts, and happenings, or for more information about hosting your own. *715 E. Milwaukee St., www.tangentgallery.com, (313) 873-2955.*

ENTERTAINMENT & RECREATION

Fisher Theatre - One of Detroit's oldest theater venues, the Fisher is Detroit's home for touring Broadway productions. Located in the lavish Fisher Building (see separate entry), the Fisher Theatre originally featured an ornate Aztec-themed interior replete with live macaws, a goldfish pond, and banana trees. After a several-decade stint as primarily a movie and vaudeville house, it was completely remodeled in 1961 and transformed into a simple, yet still elegant, midcentury modern design with marble, walnut and Indian rosewood paneling, and crystal and bronze details. It also has superior acoustics and 2,100 seats, all with good sightlines. Broadway greats from Mary Martin to Bernadette Peters and Lynn Redgrave have graced the Fisher's stage, and it has hosted the world premieres of Hello Dolly and Fiddler on the Roof, among others. Check the website to see the schedule for upcoming shows and to buy tickets. *3011 W. Grand Blvd., www.broadwayindetroit.com, (313) 872-1000.*

Jam Handy Building - A two-time Olympic bronze medalist in aquatic sports (1904 and 1924), Henry Jamison "Jam" Handy was also a successful commercial filmmaker who dominated the field of short-format film production through the late-1960s. His production company produced countless instructional videos and advertisements for major clients such as Lucky Strike and Chevrolet. While hundreds of Jam Handy films can be found on YouTube, the essential view is Detroit: City on the Move, a film produced in 1966. Though the production company has long-since vanished and the building is somewhat rundown, renovations are ongoing and the facility is selectively open to the public. What was once the company's main film studio, complete with 40-foot ceilings, exposed-brick walls, cat walks, and large loading bays, is now used intermittently for live-theater productions and is the home of Detroit Soup (see listing in events). The front rooms play host to the Jamison Social Club, which holds its own dinners and social gatherings. *2900 E. Grand Blvd., Jamison Social Club: www.eepurl.com/i5BX9, Detroit Soup: www.detroitsoup.com.*

New Center Park - A tranquil, well-manicured pocket park and outdoor venue in a scenic, urban setting, New Center Park is surrounded by some of Detroit's most majestic architecture. Though it's open daily as an escape from the office blues, under the night sky, with the surrounding buildings illuminated, the popular park offers a rich summer calendar (June-September) of free programming. Classic crowd-pleasing movies are screened outdoor movie theater style on Wednesday evenings; live jazz and blues acts take the stage on Thursdays; and local bands take it up a notch on Saturdays. With a luscious, rolling hill well-positioned for optimal viewing of the stage and screen, grab one of the provided red folding chairs or bring a blanket and hunker down on the lawn. As part of the attraction, in the attached contemporary conservatory cafe that opens to the park, visitors can grab sandwiches, burgers, and booze to augment the show-going experience. *2990 W. Grand Blvd., www.newcenterpark.com, (313) 784-9475.*

The Schvitz Health Club - Perhaps the most-discussed but least-experienced gem of old Detroit, the Schvitz was built in the 1930s as a classic Russian bathhouse and was a notorious Purple Gang hangout back when that was a terrifying phrase. It's an unmarked building in a seriously rough-and-tumble part of Detroit's North End. If you pass muster with the doorman, you'll enter a weathered main lobby, replete with a cursing parrot. Strip down at the lockers, take a quick shower, and then proceed downstairs into the steam room, which is basically a high school shower room with tiered wooden benches and a steam oven the size of a Volkswagen. Grab a seat on the bench next to one of the Schvitz's diehard regulars (think middle-aged to elderly, suburban, Jewish, wealthy, and fearlessly nude) and prepare for 30 minutes in the most extreme sauna of your life. Noobs sweat it out on the bottom benches, while the lifers gravitate toward the top, where temperatures are rumored to hit 180 degrees, chatting about their boats and mistresses. The air is thick with the aroma of the plaitza, soaped massages the men give to one another with homemade oak leaf brooms (did we mention everyone is naked?). After sweating it out for as long as you can handle, you exit the steam room and take a dip in the ice-cold pool, don a bathrobe and buy yourself a steak dinner in the lounge, washing it down with the bottle of liquor you brought with you. We must stress, this is the oldest of old-boys clubs in Detroit and tradition reigns supreme, so approach it gingerly. The regulars are an intensely tight-knit group, so unless you've lucked out and found a veteran to vouch for you, expect a serious once-over. Ladies are out of luck, unless you muster the chutzpah to go on Saturdays, when the joint hosts a notoriously liberal "Couples Night" (get your mind in the gutter, and you've pretty much got the right idea what that means). We'd recommend sticking to one of the boys' nights and buying your girlfriend an evening at a more "traditional" spa. Men-only on Wednesday and Thursday evenings and Sunday mornings, Couples Night Saturdays. $20 to enter. *8295 Oakland Ave., (313) 871-9707.*

SITES

» Boston-Edison - Once one of Detroit's most prestigious addresses, Boston-Edison is home to some of the city's most stately and breathtaking turn-of-the-century residential architecture. Comprised of 900 residences on 36 blocks, the neighborhood is bounded by Boston Boulevard to the north, Woodward Avenue to the east, Edison Avenue to the south, and Linwood Street to the west. Developer Edward Voigt, who began acquiring land for the neighborhood in 1884, established building restrictions and a stately boulevard and street pattern to assure and encourage the construction of the city's most palatial homes by its most elite citizens, the first of whom arrived in 1905. Largely constructed by 1925, the archetype of American individuality is evident in the eclecticism of classical design present in the neighborhood, with masterful examples of English Revival, Roman Revival, Greek Revival, French Provincial, Colonial Revival, Italian Renaissance, Prairie, and Vernacular. All of the homes in the neighborhood are impressively large, built of brick, stone, or stucco, and set back at least 30 feet from the front lot line, creating a stately appearance augmented by elaborate exterior details, extensive landscaping, slate or tile roofs, and leaded-glass windows. Though the neighborhood has transitioned from a residential capital of world commerce to a middle-class enclave, because of the dedication of committed residents, much of the original character and quality of the neighborhood is preserved to this day, and self-guided tours, whether by foot or on two or four wheels, still capture the magic of a time when Detroit was the world's foremost industrial power and the captains of industry lived in this neighborhood. Visitors to the area should be sure to also explore Arden Park, a 92-home historic district across Woodward, just east of Boston-Edison, on East Boston and Arden Park streets, between Woodward Avenue and Oakland Street. With a similar history and similar stature of residents, the neighborhood was developed at the same time as Boston-Edison, but was begun later. While nearly every house in the neighborhood is a sight to behold, notable highlights include:

- Berry Gordy Jr. Mansion: Founder of Motown Records.
  918 W. Boston Blvd.
- Five (of the seven) Fisher Brother Mansions, of automotive fame:
  - Charles T. Fisher Mansion. *670 W. Boston Blvd.*
  - Alfred J. Fisher Mansion. *1556 W. Chicago Blvd.*

- Edward F. Fisher Mansion. *892 W. Boston Blvd.*

- Frederick J. Fisher House. *54 Arden Park Blvd.* (Located in Arden Park)

- William A. Fisher Mansion. *111 Edison Ave.*

- Henry Ford Mansion: Ford's residence from 1907 to 1915, until the construction of the Fairlane Estate in Dearborn. *140 Edison Ave.*

- J.L. Hudson Mansion: Founder of Hudson's Department Store, now Macy's. *121 E. Boston Blvd.* (Located in Arden Park)

- Joe Louis Home: The modest home of the American icon and Heavyweight Champion of the World. *1683 Edison Ave.*

- John Dodge Mansion: Along with brother Horace, founder of the Dodge brand of automobiles, now a part of Chrysler, *75-91 E. Boston Blvd.* (Located in Arden Park)

- Sebastian S. Kresge Mansion: Founder of S.S. Kresge stores, now Kmart. *70 W. Boston Blvd.*

- Walter Briggs Mansion: Auto baron and owner of Detroit Tigers. *700 W. Boston Blvd.*

- Walter P. Reuther: Early UAW labor leader. *2292 Longfellow St.*

Cadillac Place - Listed as a National Historic Landmark, the building now known as Cadillac Place was designed by Albert Kahn in 1919 to be the world headquarters for General Motors—the largest company in the U.S. for more than 70 years. When it was completed in 1923, it was the second largest office building in the world. Kahn designed the Neo-Classical building made of limestone, granite, marble, and steel, with four parallel 15-story wings to allow sunlight and ventilation to each of the hundreds of offices housed in the building. The exterior of the building features a crown of exquisite two-story Corinthian columns and a colonnade of ionic columns around the base, which hint at the ornate interior, the most noteworthy feature of which is the lobby arcade with its vaulted ceilings made of Italian marble. Although since converted into a cafeteria, the lower level once housed two swimming pools for use by executives. The building is connected to its neighbor across Grand Boulevard—The Fisher Building—by an underground pedestrian tunnel. After General Motors moved its headquarters to the Renaissance Center in 2001, the building underwent one of the largest historic renovation projects in United

States history and was renamed Cadillac Place, in tribute to Detroit's founder. It now houses offices for many major state officials, including several Michigan Supreme Court Justices, and the former executive suite now serves as the Detroit office for Michigan's governor and attorney general. If Cadillac Place looks familiar, you may recognize it from the Michael Moore film Roger & Me, in which it was featured prominently, and the Jack White-curated album Sympathetic Sounds of Detroit. *3044 West Grand Blvd.*

Cathedral of the Most Blessed Sacrament - The elegant Gothic Revival seat of Detroit's archbishop, this cruciform cathedral boasts striking architecture and magnificent sculptures, and stained glass to match. Though built between 1913 and 1915, the church's elaborate ornaments were finished more gradually, with many installed after Pope Pius XI's 1938 designation of the facility as a cathedral. Beneath the cathedral's massive rose window, the main archway is lined with intricate relief carvings and flanked by a pair of traditional pinnacled Gothic bell towers soaring 135 feet in the air. Most Blessed Sacrament's symmetrical facade features sweeping architectural traceries, buttress facings, and most notably, beautiful statuary by legendary sculpture Corrado Parducci. In addition to the fine ornamentation, the design's clean lines showcase the fine natural grain of the Ohio sandstone and Indiana limestone of the interior and exterior. Inside, the sanctuary is brightly lit by the church's 22 stained-glass windows and dominated by the formal presbytery. The church is best visited in the afternoon, when the setting sun makes the stained glass glow, flooding the nave with colored light. *9844 Woodward Ave., www.archdioceseofdetroit.org, (313) 865-6300.*

Clairmont and 12th: 1967 Riots Site - The northwestern corner of Clairmont Street and Rosa Parks Boulevard, now home to Gordon Park, played an integral role in the city's history as the point of origin for the 1967 Riots. Today this modest park is home to benches, chess tables, and a large purple metal polyhedric sculpture, Jack Ward's Trinity, but offers no explanation of the significance of the site. In the early morning hours of July 23, 1967, Detroit Police officers raided an after-hours party at a blind pig celebrating the return of two Vietnam veterans. Crowd anger over the raid escalated into widespread clashes, resulting in five days of looting, police brutality, and mob violence that saw 43 people killed, 467 injured, 7,231 arrested, and 2,509 buildings burned or looted. Nearly 13,000 U.S. Army and National Guard troops were deployed to quell the rioting, while prominent citizens like Detroit Tiger Willie Horton and congressman John Conyers made direct appeals to crowds to stop the violence. Ultimately, nearly a quarter of the city was physically affected by the violence and destruction, but its impact as an evocative symbol of contemporary racial discrimination and conflict was felt around the country and still resonates in the city today. While surveying the aftermath, then-Mayor Jerome Cavanagh said, "Today we stand amidst the ashes of our hopes." Although most frequently described as riots, today, some now refer to the grim event as a rebellion, uprising, or civil disturbance to reflect a more nuanced view of the circumstances and context leading up to the violence. Many commentators now agree with the findings of President Lyndon B. Johnson's Kerner Commission: that racial tensions over police brutality, economic discrimination, and dissatisfaction with housing and educational options were the catalysts for the violence. The events of the summer of 1967 have been cited as both political protest highlighting grievances in Detroit's black community and as an accelerant to the city's pre-existing population and economic decline. Today, the quiet Gordon Park offers visitors a poignant place to sit and reflect on the ongoing social inequity and racial tension that continue to divide our region. *Clairmont St. and Rosa Parks Blvd.*

Fisher Body 21 - At one time, the Milwaukee Junction district was a major hub of Detroit industry, and Fisher Body Plant 21 was its epicenter. Built in 1919 by Detroit architect Albert Kahn—as famous for his many ornate commercial and residential structures as for his industrial designs. Kahn's work revolutionized factory design with walls of windows to let in light and used reinforced concrete to withstand the vibrations and weight of heavy machinery. Founded in 1908, Detroit's Fisher Body Company set the industry standard in auto bodies and made bodies for Cadillac, Ford, Studebaker, and Hudson, among others. As the company expanded rapidly, it grew to more than 40 plants in the Midwest, including this six-story factory, located just down the street from Henry Ford's original workshop. After 75 years of operation, the plant was finally abandoned in 1994. Now the domain of scrappers, explorers, and artists, graffiti lines the interior and exterior, and eerie stalactites cling to the ceiling over the winding abandoned track that once moved bodies through the assembly line. *700 Piquette St.*

» Fisher Building - Dubbed Detroit's largest art object, the 441-foot cascading Art Deco tower of the Fisher Building has been dropping jaws since its completion in 1928. Originally intended to be a complex of three buildings—a 60-story behemoth flanked by two 30-story skyscrapers—only the first of the lesser towers was completed before the onset of the Great Depression, and the grand plans were simplified. The wealthy Fisher brothers of Fisher Body fame viewed the project as a gift to the city of Detroit and gave virtuoso architect Albert Kahn free reign to build "the most beautiful building in the world" to be their company headquarters and, along with the General Motors Headquarters (now Cadillac Place), to establish New Center as a center for shopping and entertainment. Beyond the artful exterior, the highlight of the masterpiece is the opulent interior exemplified by the stunning and ornate three-story lobby, which features forty varieties of marble and hand-painted barrel-vaulted ceilings which were described upon the building's unveiling as "a mass of gorgeous color, shimmering like the plumage of exotic birds." In addition to being a world-class architectural attraction, the Fisher Building is a world of shops, theater, and art. See the separate entries for the building's other rich offerings, including the Fisher Theater and the building's many shops. *3011 W. Grand Blvd.*

The Lee Plaza - A seemingly out-of-place 15-story skyscraper in an otherwise low-density neighborhood, the Lee Plaza went from being a towering symbol of Detroit's wealth to a sad symbol of the city's decline. Built by real-estate magnate Ralph T. Lee in anticipation of future growth into the area, the Lee Plaza opened in 1929 as a "residential hotel," complete with luxuriously furnished rooms, concierge service, room and maid service, a shopping center, and an upscale grocery. The architectural flourishes and sculptures by Corrado Parducci were extravagant but fitting for its high-class tenants. Unfortunately, due initially to the Great Depression, the city's development and growth never caught up with the hotel, which stood as a lone sentinel on West Grand Boulevard. Since closing in 1997, the building has been ravaged by scrappers, including the notable thefts of its copper roof and 50 terra cotta lion heads from its facade. Now a windowless relic, the ghostly ruin is a popular site for photographers and stands as a reminder of the city's architectural legacy. *2240 W. Grand Blvd.*

Pallister Street - Beginning in 1978, General Motors began a development called New Center Commons, just north of what was then the location of its world headquarters in New Center. Designed to simultaneously attract General Motors employees to the neighborhood, while revitalizing beleaguered residential areas, the complex project entailed rehabilitations, new construction, traffic rerouting, and street closures. The most beautiful phase of the development project remains the brick-paved, pedestrian-only block of Pallister, between Second Avenue and Third Street. With a park-like setting created by the trees and antique-style lamps that line the brick street, a stroll down Pallister more closely resembles a period film set of old Detroit than the active residential street that it is. Though it's small and difficult to find because of road closures, the photogenic turn-of-the-century homes and picturesque brick street are worth the trip. *Pallister St. from Second Ave. to Third St.*

Sacred Heart Major Seminary - This awe-inspiring, sprawling red brick complex was completed in 1926 in the English Tudor Gothic style, and is a Catholic seminary affiliated with the Archdiocese of Detroit, offering both vocational divinity programs and an Institute for Ministry, geared toward laity. The entire structure was constructed at one time—rather than in sections—prompting claims that the resulting stability would ensure the structure would stand 300 years. It is bedecked with Tudor flourishes throughout, such as small paned windows and steeply gabled roofs, however, the focal point of the exterior is the imposing square bell tower topped by four intricately detailed spires. In recent decades, one of the most distinct attractions at Sacred Heart has been the shrine on the southwest corner of Linwood and Chicago featuring a statue of a black Jesus, painted such during the '67 riots, perhaps as a rejoinder to the violence. Regardless of its inspiration, Sacred Heart has subsequently maintained the statue and its challenge to prevailing racial assumptions. The interior of Sacred Heart offers an artisanal wooden reredos (a decorative altarpiece) of the apostles and is home to the largest collection of Pewabic tile in the world, with gorgeous inlays in both chapels and the school facility. *2701 Chicago Blvd., www.shms.edu, (313) 883-8500.*

United Sound Systems - Though less renowned than its big brother up the street, Hitsville U.S.A., this humble recording studio has had nearly as great an impact, serving as the production house for some of the most influential recordings in music history. Opened by Jimmy Siracuse in 1933, the facility was Detroit's first major recording studio. With Siracuse's son Joe in the engineer's booth, United Sound Systems recorded cuts for stars living in Detroit at the time, such as Miles Davis, Charlie Parker, and John Lee Hooker, who recorded his seminal song Boogie Chillen' in Studio A. In 1958, a young Berry Gordy bought studio time at United Sound Systems to produce "Come to Me" by Marv Johnson. After recording the record, Gordy was inspired to open his own studio nearby, which would become Motown Records, and mimicked many of the facility's design features. After Don Davis purchased United Sound Systems in 1971, the studio's musical palette expanded. Though soul masters like Aretha Franklin and Marvin Gaye continued to record at the facility, acts such as Isaac Hayes, Funkadelic, the Rolling Stones, the MC5, and Underground Resistance, grew the breadth of the studio's output. Though it has been boarded up for nearly a decade, the historic sign from the Don Davis era is still in place and stands as a beacon reminding passersby of the building's legacy and contribution to music history. *5840 Second Ave.*

POINTS OF INTEREST

Aretha Franklin Home - The Queen of Soul lived in this amazing home in historic Boston-Edison, surrounded by a canopy of trees. *649 E. Boston Blvd.*

Best Deals Market - Now operating as a liquor store, this building's history as a former Purple Gang headquarters can still be seen in the metal letters affixed to the facade, which spell out the name of the gang's number-making chief, "Charlie the Pencilman." *Oakland Ave. and Clay St.*

Bloomtown Detroit - Architect Ellen Donnelly's project of planting these six monochromatic gardens was intended to reference the houses that once stood in their place. *8010 Oakland St.*

Buffalo Bill Train Crash Site - On July 20, 1900, the train carrying the Buffalo Bill Wild West Show infamously crashed here, killing one and injuring nine. *E. Grand Blvd. and Russell St.*

Bust of MLK - This gorgeous three-foot-tall aluminum bust acts as the centerpiece of a small pocket park at the intersection of Rosa Parks and West Grand Boulevard. *7334 Rosa Parks Blvd.*

Charles Brady King Auto - Three months before Henry Ford built his first automobile, Charles Brady King built a gas-powered automobile on this, the former site of Lauer's Machine Shop. Ford, on his bicycle, was reported to have been following King's horseless carriage as it became the first of its kind on the streets of Detroit. *618 Antoine St.*

Collingwood Manor Massacre Site - Now a parking lot, on September 6, 1931, three Chicago mobsters were gunned down in the Collingwood Manor Apartments, which once stood on this site. The shooting led to a trial that would send important members of the notorious Purple Gang to prison, ultimately leading to the downfall of the powerful crime syndicate. *1740 Collingwood Ave.*

D-Town Records - This reserved, historic three-story home was the home base of Mike Hank's soul imprint D-Town Records, which pressed a bevy of now legendary singles between 1963 and 1966. Essential listen: "Detroit, Michigan" by Ronnie Love. *3040 E. Grand Blvd.*

Food Field Garden - This urban farm, located on the former site of Peck Elementary, is committed to growing all of its produce organically and can be found at many of the farmer's markets around the city. *1600 Lawrence St.*

Fourth Street - This single block is the last remnant of what was once a thoroughfare of homes demolished for M-10 and I-94. Today, this shared history and small area has fostered a vibrant tight-knit community. *Fourth St. and Holden St.*

Golden World Records - Before being bought out by Motown in 1966, like its sister label, Ric Tic, in 1968, Ed Wingate ran his soul and R&B label, alongside Joanne Bratton, from his home on the western edge of Boston-Edison. *2307 Edison St.*

Lots O' Greens Farm - These formerly vacant lots are now home to this well-kept raised-bed community garden. *749 Taylor St.*

Metropolitan United Methodist Church - Completed in 1926, this elaborate English Gothic church was constructed with ochre grant from Massachusetts, and features a traditional cruciform and, especially off of Chandler Street, beautiful traditional detailing. The interior boasts large murals depicting the history of Protestantism and Methodism, as well as Michigan's second largest organ. *8000 Woodward Ave.*

Motown Records Original Site - Before moving into the iconic location on West Grand Boulevard, this was where Berry Gordy officially started Tamla Records, a forerunner to Motown Records in 1959. *1719 Gladstone St.*

Oakland Sugar House - Now a vacant lot, the bar that once occupied this site was the home base for the infamous Purple Gang, organized criminals who ruled much of the city's illegal alcohol trade during Prohibition. *8606 Oakland St.*

Olympia Stadium Site - Designed by C. Howard Crane, the Detroit Olympia, also known as The Old Red Barn, was the home arena for the Detroit Red Wings from 1927 to 1979. It also hosted a number of other athletic events, as well as concerts, including by The Beatles and Elvis Presley. The building was demolished in 1987. *5920 Grand River Ave.*

Reinvented Detroit Flag Mural - This clever muralist's reinterpretation of the City of Detroit flag includes Old English Ds, urban gardens, a Cadillac, and greater racial diversity, incorporated into the traditional design. *918 Custer St.*

Rosa Parks Home - Although she was born in Alabama and earned her civil rights reputation through her actions on that famous bus in Montgomery, Parks moved to Detroit in 1957 and lived in this modest apartment from 1961 until her death in 2005. *3201 Virginia Park St.*

Silverbolt - Molded from automobile bumpers, this John Kearney horse sculpture stands proudly in front of the Children's Museum, which currently is not open to the public. *6134 Second Ave.*

Smokey Robinson Home - The Motown favorite grew up in this house just a few doors down from Diana Ross and just around the corner from Aretha Franklin. *581 Belmont St.*

The Illuminated Mural - It's hard to miss this massive nine-story mural, designed by Katie Craig, which looks like a beautiful melting rainbow. The installation uses paint splatters to convey a sense of movement and action. *2937 E. Grand Blvd.*

Ty Cobb Home - The all-time Detroit Tigers great—famous as much for his surly demeanor as he is for his astounding skill on the baseball diamond—lived in this relatively modest home. *800 Atkinson St.*

Walter P. Reuther Home - The famed UAW president lived in this well-kept home on the city's west side until his death in a plane crash in 1970. *3240 W. Philadelphia St.*

Westbound Records - This modest residence was once home to the funk and soul label most famous for records from Funkadelic. *5603 Sixteenth St.*

CHAPTER 7
LOWER EAST SIDE

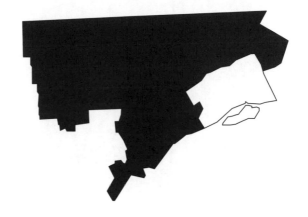

Grosse Pointe Park

Jefferson
Chalmers

MorningSide

*Chandler
Park*

Ravendale

I-94

Upper East Side

*Conner
Creek*

*Marina
District*

LOWER EAST SIDE

*Joseph
Berry
Subdivision*

*Indian
Village*

*East
Village*

*Gold
Coast*

*West
Village*

Van Dyke

*Island
View*

Grand Boulevard

Detroit River

*Belle
Isle*

Gratiot

Mack

Jefferson

McDougall-Hunt

Warren

*Poletown
East*

*Elmwood
Park*

Riverfront Warehouse District

*Forest
Park*

Eastern
Market

*Lafayette
Park*

I-75

I-375

*New Center /
North End*

*Art
Center*

*Medical
Center*

Midtown

*Brush
Park*

Downtown

Running along the north shore of the Detroit River, the lower east side is among the most photographed districts in the city and is popular among locals and visitors for its delicious eateries, scenic vistas, historic neighborhoods, memorable cultural amenities, emerging shopping and entertainment districts, and its incredible island park, Belle Isle. The lower east side, as we define it, is bounded by the Detroit River, I-75, Eastern Market, I-94, and Alter Road.

As one of the city's oldest areas, the lower east side is steeped in local history. This portion of the city was once home to most of the city's ribbon farms—long, narrow farms that typically measured 250 feet by one to three miles, to maximize river access. Beginning in 1707, Detroit's founder, Antoine de La Mothe Cadillac, granted 34 farmers much of the land in what is now the lower east side of the city. Many of these early families are remembered in the city's street names, such as Witherell, Livernois, Riopelle, St. Aubin, Chene, Beaubien, Moran, and De Quindre. As the city developed, the area blossomed as a stately residential corridor along Jefferson Avenue, with industrial land along the river and Beaufait Street, and block upon block of modest single-family homes. In the early 20th Century, the western end of the area became known as Black Bottom—named for the rich soil—and grew to be a renowned, vibrant African-American neighborhood in the prewar era of housing discrimination. In the postwar era, much of this history and vibrancy was lost in the wake of urban renewal projects, such as freeway development, factory and public housing construction, and widespread demolition.

Annexed into a growing Detroit between 1832 and 1917 and primarily built out between 1880 and 1954, the lower east side is distinctive both for its role in the city's history and for its diverse physical design. This 19-square-mile area is home to 70,276 people and encompasses a host of neighborhoods, including Chandler Park, Conner Creek, East Village, Elmwood Park, Forest Park, Gold Coast, Indian Village, Island View, Jefferson Chalmers, Joseph Barry Subdivision, Lafayette Park, Marina District, McDougall-Hunt, Poletown East, Ravendale, Rivertown Warehouse District, and West Village. Although each neighborhood is distinct, with a unique history and architecture, they collectively showcase the diversity of forms in architecture and urban design during the city's peak development years, including grand apartment complexes, scores of Cape Cod, Craftsman, Foursquare, and Tudor homes, stately mansions, and prewar commercial thoroughfares along once-grand streetcar lines.

No visit to the city is too short for visit to the lower east side. The area is a destination for its fine architecture, emerging entertainment district, and recreational and cultural assets. Although many areas in this chapter make for a fine visit, five stand out. For those looking to admire historic architecture, the picturesque group of neighborhoods collectively called The Villages—Berry Subdivision, East Village, Gold Coast, Indian Village, Island View, and West Village, but especially Indian Village—offer some of the city's finest architecture, with hundreds of opulent mansions set back from lush lawns and stunning tree-lined streets, alongside the fledgling retail district in West Village. Visitors looking to experience modern architecture should head for Lafayette Park's impressive array of Ludwig Mies van der Rohe-designed townhomes, shops, and apartment towers set in a verdant park-like campus. Followers of art shouldn't miss the controversial and essential outdoor multi-block Heidelberg Project and the storied, historic Pewabic Pottery. For thirsty visitors, the Rivertown Warehouse District offers a bevy of independent bars and eateries, most of which showcase the beautiful aesthetic potential of adaptively reusing warehouses. For all visitors, the city's island playground, Belle Isle, offers some of the city's finest cultural experiences, athletics facilities, public art, and recreation space.

BARS & RESTAURANTS

» **Andrews on the Corner** - Opened in 1918 by Gus Andrews—and still owned by his grandson Tom—this charming old-school sports bar and grill maintains much of its original character, complete with its beautiful woodwork, retro detailing, and tin ceiling. Prepare your taste buds for a dance with all-fresh Eastern Market meat and a menu a cut above regular bar food—including the ever-popular club and au jus sandwiches. In addition to its extensive food options, Andrews has more than 25 beers on draft and an impressive liquor selection. Although the plethora of TVs and a free shuttle to the stadia make this an excellent sports bar, Andrews also offers "Drinking With Doggies" night on Tuesdays—a chance to bring your pooch along for some hooch—and live music on Thursdays and Saturdays. *201 Joseph Campau St., www.andrewsonthecorner.com, (313) 259-8325.*

Atwater Brewery Tap Room - This might be Detroit's hardest-to-find-bar: hidden in the Rivertown Warehouse District, you have to weave between towers of kegs, pallets of bottles, and zipping forklifts to discover the modest bar nestled inside the burgeoning brewery. Atwater started with a brewpub more than 15 years ago but ditched the restaurant a few years back to focus on what it's best at: making delicious microbrews. More of a warehouse with a few taps than a full-fledged bar, drinking a cold pint to the clatter of production and the yeasty smell of a new batch being boiled is one of the most intimate drinking experiences around. The bartenders are passionate about their brews, and they tend to let the drinks speak for themselves. And it works: With the brewery preparing to ramp up production and distribution by as much as 40%, we can expect only that this brewery-with-a-bar to get more crowded, and more prized in the coming years. *237 Joseph Campau St., www.atwaterbeer.com, (313) 877-9205.*

Bai Mai Thai - Offering customers a refined, contemporary, and warm interior highlighted by beautiful wood accents and a babbling stone fountain, this fine dining restaurant in Lafayette Park offers an extensive menu of traditional Thai cuisine and a full bar. The restaurant treats patrons to generous daily drink specials complemented by familiar dishes like edamame, matsaman, pad prik, pha-naeng, and, of course, pad Thai—all delivered with an enthusiastic, welcoming smile. For dessert, try the green tea ice cream. *1541 E. Lafayette St., www.baimaithai.com, (313) 567-2484.*

Bayview Yacht Club - A nearly century-old institution devoted to freshwater sailing in Michigan, the Bayview Yacht Club occupies five acres along Detroit's riverfront, with a marina of more than 100 slips that accommodate yachts as large as 70 feet. Since 1925, the club has run the renowned Port Huron to Mackinac Race, a competitive midsummer regatta that attracts hundreds of majestic sailboats, and is noted as one of the longest freshwater races in the world. In addition, the club holds a private, local racing series, and offers sailing lessons for those still gaining their sea legs. Inside the clubhouse, members and their guests can dine in understated elegance at the riverfront restaurant, which serves classic American cuisine, while the bar offers a condensed menu to pair with its touted cocktails. *100 Clairpointe St., www.byc.com, (313) 822-1853.*

The Clique - Though it's attached to a drive-up motel, don't miss out. This old-school greasy spoon serves up some of the best diner-style breakfast in town (and serves it until 3pm). Turning out all the staples with working-class panache: The hash browns are buttery; the grits are mild and perfectly textured; the cinnamon rolls are split and cooked on the flattop; the French toast is fluffy; and the bacon is perfectly thin. The joint draws an eclectic, colorful mix of patrons and has been popular with celebrities visiting Detroit, such as Stevie Wonder and Aretha Franklin, who have autographed placemats and napkins, which adorn the walls. As an added perk, the restaurant is strategically located near the Riverwalk, so you can scenically walk off your indulgences. *1326 E. Jefferson Ave., (313) 259-0922.*

» Ivanhoe Cafe / Polish Yacht Club - Run by Polish pub keeper Patti Galen, this cheerful, old-school Polish restaurant and neighborhood watering hole has been delighting east siders for generations. Open since 1909, the century-old Ivanhoe Cafe is in its original brick building, replete with a tin ceiling, hand-carved bar, walls decked with antique photos and newspaper clippings, and fresh flowers, candles, and vintage lamps on tables in the cozy dining rooms. In addition to the full bar, the restaurant offers a delectable Polish menu, including stuffed cabbage, kielbasa, homemade coleslaw, pan-fried perch, pierogi, and hearty potato pancakes, along with variety of classic bar fare sandwiches, including the renowned Polish Reuben—kielbasa, sauerkraut, and cheese. The landlocked cafe plays host to the Polish Yacht Club, a good-natured social club and charitable organization with a tongue-in-cheek alias. Founded in 1961, the club's landlubber "commodore" and members often sport sailor's attire and love sharing stories and good cheer with guests. *5249 Joseph Campau St., www.ivanhoecafe-pyc.com, (313) 925-5335*

Kita Pita - This sandwich spot on the east side is a welcome addition to the neighborhood. Family-run and named for the owner's mother, Nikita, this lunchtime eatery offers customers tasty, generously portioned favorites at good prices. The building is tough to miss from the outside—a bright red color scheme with mustard yellow script pivots into a hand-painted mural of a sandwich wrap whose sultriness belies the family friendliness within. Inside the candy-heart pink lobby, customers voice their favorite pitas on a specially designated graffiti wall. And wraps aren't all there are: $5 chicken and waffles, cheap duos of corned beef sliders, fried PB&J and sides of French fries slathered in Cajun seasoning round out the good bargains. Customers can order any soft drink they want, as long as they want Faygo. *10307 Mack Ave., (313) 822-1780.*

Louisiana Creole Gumbo - Sister to the downtown location at the Rosa Parks Transit Center, this original carryout location of Louisiana Creole Gumbo welcomes visitors with a large, toothy brass gator that stretches across the storefront's bay window. The gator remains the signature mascot for this delicious establishment, which has a variety of gumbos and classic jambalaya that include seafood, sausage, and crab. Visitors can dress up any order with bacon, cheese, and other tasty toppings for less than a dollar more. Vegetarian options include red beans and rice, award-winning cornbread, and famous candied yams. Gumbo-lovers, note that Creole gumbo is less spicy than the Cajun style, but packs a ton of flavor! A friend once claimed that if the gumbo was this good in Louisiana, she never would've moved here. *2053 Gratiot Ave., www.detroitgumbo.com, (313) 446-9639.*

Marshall's Bar - Just north of the Fox Creek neighborhood lies this blue-collar watering hole that celebrates the area and its customers. Owned by Ted Kapuscinski, a starting pitcher for the Tigers' farm system in the 1940s and 1950s, Marshall's is a low-key watering hole with cheap drinks, zero fuss, and enough personal touches to give it plenty of character. So, tip back an Old Milwaukee, grab a grey faux-leather stool, and abseil into incandescence. Marshall's is partisan to showing Detroit sports but runs old movies with the sound off when there's none on. *14716 E. Jefferson Ave., (313) 821-0610.*

Mr. Lovely Williams & Sons Ice Cream - Despite what you might think—based on the relative lack of signage and the dreary façade—Mr. Lovely's is indeed open. Windows, signage, eye contact, and air-conditioning are all amenities you'll forget you're missing as you sink your incisors into Mr. Lovely's handmade ice cream. As visitors walk into the shop—a room about the size of a large restroom stall, where every bit of wall is covered with candy wrappers and handwritten ice cream menus—they're greeted by a jovial, mysterious, and radio-worthy baritone voice: "Welcome to Mr. Lovely's!" While this friendly phantom proprietor serves some of the best ice cream on the east side, Mr. Lovely is best known for his fruit flavors. Those looking for something less cone-based can enjoy one of the seemingly infinite types of candies. *10700 Mack Ave.*

My Dad's Bar - Someone raised the kids right. The brother and sister team that runs My Dad's Bar—Frank and Lola Gegovic—have given the joint a level of character uncommon for low-key watering holes. With a skillfully thrifted decor that surreally emulates the best of 1950s basement bars, the upscale dive is appropriately named. Seat yourself at the multicolored bar stools, refashioned hardwood card tables, or on the outdoor patio to soak in the class of carefully chosen, stylishly retro decor, such as decommissioned typewriters, a shapely mannequin lamp, vintage bar accessories, and framed photos of the fathers amongst us. Cheap wells, domestics, and local imports are among the offerings, along with board games and, yes, TV. Don't forget to bring some quarters for the well-curated jukebox. *14911 Kercheval St., (313) 831 3237.*

Rattlesnake Club - This elegant riverfront restaurant is a popular destination among the city's movers and shakers, thanks to sweeping views of the river and the city's skyline, a lavish yet chic interior, and renowned upscale American cuisine. The au courant dining room features beautiful table settings and a fine collection of two- and three-dimensional art. Executive Chef Chris Franz's seasonal menus feature certified prime Angus beef and offers an emphasis on organic and sustainable ingredients. The "upscale dude food" menu includes an irreproachable apple-cider-cured duck breast, better dunkel braised beef short ribs, and sizzling, tender porterhouses that could feed a small family. The staff and managers are warm and professional, with the knowledge to suggest wine pairings and experience to make informed recommendations. The wine list is thorough and interesting, with fine offerings from Traverse City to Bordeaux. *300 River Place Dr., www.rattlesnakeclub.com, (313) 567-4400.*

Raven Lounge - Open since the 1950s, this unassuming east side club is the oldest continuously operating rhythm and blues bar in Michigan. According to legend, if Motown stars of the day weren't playing the stage, they were sitting in the audience. While much of the surrounding neighborhood has rejoined the earth, the near-legendary venue is still rocking strong and remains a destination. Look for a packed house of welcoming regulars and first-timers every Thursday, Friday, and Saturday with $5 soul, funk, and rhythm and blues shows. Though music is the highlight at the Raven, the bar offers a sizeable selection of beers and call liquors, and the kitchen rounds out the experience with a full menu of soul favorites. If you come to the Raven once, you'll come twice. And, as the owner of the club, Tommy Stephens, will let you know, if you return to the Raven, "you're family." *5145 Chene St., www.theravenloungeandrestaurant.com, (313) 924-7133.*

Royal Barbecue Pizza - Look for the building that's an amalgamation of Spanish Revival and strip mall Chi-Chi's, and you will have found this unexpected gem of a barbecue, pizza, chicken, burger, and deli joint. With a late-night drive through and delivery, and comfortable, modern booth seating for dine-in customers, the eatery offers a wide-variety of heavy-duty greasy spoon takes on American classics, one of the house specialties being a BLT made with a pound (!) of bacon. Yep. King me. *5844 Mt. Elliott St., www.royalbar-b-q.com, (313) 923-2222.*

Sindbads - Named for one of the greatest (mythical) sailors to ever wander the high seas, Sindbads has been a staple on the Detroit waterfront since 1948. With a retro, nautical ambiance, the classic eatery offers floor-to-ceiling windows that afford guests beautiful, sweeping views of the Detroit River. In the spacious, scenic dining room, patrons can choose from a wide selection of classic sandwiches and "treasures from the land and sea." House specialties include thick Angus steaks, a "man-size" chicken sandwich called the Land Lubber, and, of course, selections from the comprehensive seafood offerings—of which we suggest The Mariner, a triple threat of fresh white fish, scallops, and frog legs. While Sindbads is a decidedly Surf & Turf establishment, it happily accommodates vegetarian guests off-menu. The restaurant also features a large wooden bar, which is usually packed with regulars discussing pressing issues. While most guests come by land, if you're looking for a more scenic route, Sindbads has a private marina with 86 boat slips—and offers economical overnight rates. *100 St. Clair St., www.sindbadsdetroit.com, (313) 822-7817.*

Southern Fires - Located on the first floor of a former warehouse, Southern Fires has become a classic upscale soul food destination on the east side. The menu is a modified prix fixe—all entrees, such as succulent marinated chicken, fish, or ribs, are served with two sides (the dulcet sweet potatoes are delicious) and buttery, moist cornbread. Dine-in in the sprawling, warm, open dining room at tables with tall wooden benches or grab your meal to go. Check out the panoramic street scene mural reminiscent of the iconic painting Sugar Shack in the back of the dining room. *575 Bellevue St., www.southernfiresrestaurant.com, (313) 393-4930.*

Steve's Soul Food and The Key Club - In a beautifully restored industrial brick building, near the Detroit River, you'll find Steve's Soul Food and The Key Club. Steve's buffet stretches the length of the building and offers all the standard soul food fare from catfish to mac and cheese and all varieties of pie. Guests can take carryout, or they can dine-in on the main floor with airy lofted ceilings and tall booths or open tables surrounding large flat-screen televisions. Venture up to the third floor of the Key Club for a great view of the Detroit River and downtown—there's no cover charge if you stop by during the day. At night, The Key Club often hosts special events from concert after-parties to birthday celebrations. Check the bulletin board for upcoming Key Club events, or call. *1440 Franklin St., (313) 393-0018.*

» Sunday Dinner Company - A culinary and aesthetic jewel, Sunday Dinner Company has been winning epicurean hearts since opening in 2010. Set in a beautifully restored 1886 post office, the charming dining room features exposed brick walls, original artwork, and strings of Christmas tree lights crisscrossing the ceiling, giving the space a homey, contemporary ambiance. Amid this warm, delightful atmosphere, chef Eric Giles prepares sublime soul food at this gourmet buffet-style eatery. With this reinvention of cafeteria-style dining, staff escort and serve guests from the constellation of delectable options. In addition to seasonal dishes, guests can expect exquisite takes on soul and Southern staples, including fried chicken, catfish, sweet potatoes, dirty rice with shrimp, black-eyed peas, collard greens, dumplings, and mac and cheese. The fried chicken, like the other proteins, is made-to-order and unparalleled: The buttermilk breading and fresh chicken is at once crispy and juicy, tender and crunchy. This stunning food is served with a mission. As a socially conscious, community-orientated business, Sunday Dinner Company actively hires at-risk youth and adults in need of a second chance. *6470 E. Jefferson Ave., (313) 877-9255.*

Tashmoo Biergarten - Named for a beloved Great Lakes steamship whose captain owned the house that once occupied the site, Tashmoo—which, conveniently, is also a Native American word for "meeting place"—is a charming and lively DIY outdoor biergarten in historic West Village. The anchor of a nascent small-business revival at the intersection of Agnes and Van Dyke, Detroiters of all stripes gather at long, communal tables amongst festively lit trees and bask in the late fall (and sometimes spring) sun. In addition to a rotating tap of tasty Michigan brews from bubbly lagers to rich stouts, guests can also sample an array of artisanal food-cart fare, including locally made sausage and pierogi. Though beer is the order of the day, Tashmoo is family-friendly, and offers classic board games and Corn Hole, the popular Midwestern game of bean bag toss. The biergarten operates seasonally, so be sure to know before you go. Per their motto, meet up and drink bier! *1416 Van Dyke St., www.tashmoodetroit.com, (616) 862-8834.*

They Say - So, what exactly are they saying? Good things. If the curious name doesn't attract your attention to this jazz club and restaurant, the exposed brick, wood trim, and Art Deco bar will. Nestled in a spacious and handsome historic former warehouse building in the resurgent Rivertown Warehouse District, They Say brings live jazz and blues talent to its first-floor lounge five nights a week—and occasionally on afternoons, as well. Out of its impressively small open kitchen, the joint turns out a solid but compact menu of standards, many of which involve a Cajun twist. Of its offerings, favorites are the Buffalo wings, thick-crust pizza, and steak, which are backed up by a cornucopia of other options. Though it is sometimes overtaken by a club atmosphere—and cover—during less inclement months, the scenic outdoor patio on the second floor offers unmatched views of the Renaissance Center and a soothing breeze off the nearby river. Check the restaurant's Facebook page for upcoming events. *267 Joseph Campau St., (313) 446-4682.*

Trolleys - Historically a sleepy neighborhood sports bar, Trolleys is undergoing a gradual transition toward becoming a Filipino restaurant. This transformation makes for a fascinating aesthetic and cultural juxtaposition and makes the place a destination for delicious Filipino fare. Aside from the usual sports bar options, Trolleys offers lumpia—a type of beef eggrolls, adobo—chicken cooked in vinegar, fried rice—and tom kha soup, alongside a host of other Filipino offerings. Besides the varied decor and Filipino food, the joint is also home to an Internet jukebox, a pool table, and cheap, stiff drinks. By far the best place to have pancit noodles and a Budweiser while watching the game. *17315 Mack Ave., (313) 886-1060.*

Walt's Spirits & So Much More - The lower east side claims a classy, amicable speakeasy in Walt's, a beautiful neighborhood watering hole that is simultaneously upscale and affordable. Though ownership has changed hands over the years, Walt's retains its original crescent-shaped nickel bar, the original black cherry wood bar cabinet that stretches 20 yards, and original antique woodwork. A friendly mixture of neighborhood regulars and local businessmen make up the clientele at Walt's, who are drawn by the personable cocktailians, the mellow atmosphere, and a competitive selection of call liquors. A smallish bar menu is available, and Walt's regularly hosts live music or game day events without cover charge. *6452 E. Jefferson Ave., (313) 259-4470.*

Ye Olde Tap Room - With more than 280 draft and bottled beers from six continents, including many hard-to-find Belgian and German varieties, this storied tavern is a bona fide brewski-lover's fantasy.

Once a gambling hall and a house of ill-repute, the place became a blind pig in 1922 during Prohibition and has been in continuous operation as a bar ever since. Inside, the dark, cozy beer hall has wood tables and a fireplace that hint at its past and make it a popular east side destination. For the hungry set, tasty, well-paired cheese and sausage are available, as are complimentary peanuts that will help keep you thirsty. For entertainment, the bar frequently hosts live music and offers darts to keep patrons active and help them work off some of their caloric intake. Don't miss the annual Repeal Day party, which always packs the house. *14915 Charlevoix St., (313) 824-1030.*

SHOPPING & SERVICES

Franklin Furniture - Equal parts office furniture store and alternate view of Detroit businesses past, Franklin Furniture is crammed with inventory. Owner Jim Snyder procures furniture from defunct Detroit-area businesses—often with old documents still in the filing cabinets! You can wander through the dimly lit furniture-lined hallways to find vintage pieces or hang out in the front of the shop to browse through smaller office supplies. The warehouse doesn't have a distinct sign, but visitors can enter through what looks like a back door facing Franklin Street in the winter months and an open garage door in the summertime. Once inside, you'll be overwhelmed by the seemingly endless supply of often vintage office chairs, desks, conference tables, filing cabinets, and just about every other office accoutrement you can imagine. *2128 Franklin St., (313) 393-2500.*

Gardella Furniture - Decorating Detroit area homes from the same gorgeous brick building since 1939, Gardella Furniture fills three floors—20,000 square feet—with the latest in classic, modern, and contemporary furniture. The exposed brick walls are decorated with unique decor for the home and office, and reproduction antiques, including a linen travel map of Detroit from the 1700s. A rounded glass-block corner window sheds light on the large selection of bedroom furniture and couches, fabric swatches, dining tables, chairs, kids furniture—even drapery, light fixtures, and rugs. The large selection may seem overwhelming, but interior designers are on-hand to offer consultations. Closed Thursdays and Sundays. *2306 Gratiot Ave., www.gardellafurniture.com, (313) 567-7470.*

Harbortown Market - A destination for discerning east siders for more than 20 years, this midsize, full-service grocer is renowned for its fresh produce, impressive deli, quality meats, fresh flowers, fresh cheeses, high-end beer and wine selection, and an array of local and organic foods. Thanks to an extensive renovation in 2010, the shop is a bright, modern, and lively space that allows visitors to easily navigate the considerable selection. Owner Tom George stocks a constellation of gourmet items such as almond milk, imported cheeses, and organic Amish chicken, and his store is known for a relatively remarkable vegetarian selection. The gourmet store is popular with local gourmands: It is the city's largest seller of Häagen-Dazs ice cream. *3472 E. Jefferson Ave., (313) 259-9400.*

Korash Florists - This family-operated florist, known for its good service and fresh, high-quality flowers bears the name of its original owner, who long-provided the east side with thoughtful, elegant, and promptly made flower arrangements and bouquets, a tradition that continues today. After buzzing to enter, visitors enter a cool sanctuary of lush green baskets and symbolic arrangements, flanked by charming glass-paneled, pastel green wooden coolers with black metal handles filled with prepared bouquets. Call ahead. Delivery available. *7200 Gratiot Ave., www.korashflorist.com, (313) 923-9100.*

On The Rise Bakery - This arm of the Capuchin Soup Kitchen is much more than a bakery. On the Rise is part of the ROPE (Reaching Our Potential Everyday) program established in 2006 to develop life skills for former prisoners and addicts and to prevent recidivism or relapse by providing them a stable environment in which to work and regular income while they reintegrate into society. On the Rise serves a wide selection of yummy, homemade sweets and baked goods, including cakes, breads, cookies, rolls, and other treats, with a special flair for fruit pies. Located in a historic brick building, the retail counter for the social enterprise is warm and welcoming and exudes the positivity inherent in the organization's work. *6110 McClellan St., www.cskdetroit.org/bakery, (313) 922-8510.*

People's Restaurant Equipment Company - Occupying a four-room warehouse with a freshly painted brick facade and sign inviting shoppers to "the party place," People's is packed with every supply imaginable for kitchens and restaurants. Think everything from five-gallon barrel barbecues to drink muddlers and strainers, giant margarita glasses, party picks, chef uniforms, basic glassware, beer pitchers, knives, a rainbow of tablecloths and matching napkins, and even commercial stainless steel tables, deep fryers, and barstools. Even though the store caters to restaurants and commercial clients,

it stocks a wide variety of goods useful for home kitchens, and individuals are welcome to stop in to shop. *2209 Gratiot Ave., www.peoplesrestaurantequipco.com, (313) 567-1944.*

» **Pewabic Pottery** - Founded in 1903 by ceramic artist Mary Chase Perry Stratton and her partner, Horace James Caulkins, as part of the Arts and Crafts movement, Pewabic Pottery is a renowned National Historic Landmark. Known for its distinctive iridescent glazes, hundreds of Detroit's most prestigious buildings and homes contain Pewabic tiles, and installations of them can be found across the country from the Shedd Aquarium in Chicago to the Nebraska State Capitol. Stratton was an important figure in the arts scene in Detroit in the early 20th century, serving as a trustee of what is now the Detroit Institute of Arts and founding the University of Michigan ceramics department. Now run by a nonprofit, Pewabic maintains an active fabrication studio creating commissioned large-scale installations as well as its traditional tiles, dishes, ornaments, and gifts. Shop for these smaller wares, as well as work by talented local ceramic artists, in its wonderful on-site shop, or check out its wide array of fantastic class and workshop offerings for a chance to hone

your pottery skills in a historic, intimate setting. When you visit, be sure to take a self-guided tour of the production facility to see ceramic artists at work creating pieces in much the same way that Stratton did more than 100 years ago. *10125 E. Jefferson Ave., www.pewabic.org, (313) 626-2000.*

» Wheelhouse Detroit - Scenically located on the Detroit RiverWalk, the Wheelhouse is a small, but exceedingly well-curated, contemporary bike shop that serves as the home base for RiverWalk bicycle traffic. Enter through the raised glass garage door to find a well-stocked selection of essential accessories and new bicycles, with a range of options available for both beginners and two-wheeled veterans. If you don't see something that's quite the right fit, the staff is known to happily, and speedily, assist in special ordering any part. To keep you moving, the shop also offers an exceptional repair service, boasting some of the city's most experienced and amicable bike mechanics. However, despite these offerings, the Wheelhouse is most loved for its bike rental and tour services. Make your selection from the 11 bike rental options—from road bike to cruiser, BMX, or tandem—and cruise the streets of Detroit right—on two wheels! On weekends and some weekdays, the Wheelhouse runs a variety of bike tours, including architecture, public art, automotive heritage, and local dining. Open seasonally. Check the website for hours and tour offerings. *1340 E. Atwater St., www.wheelhousedetroit.com, (313) 656-2453.*

CULTURAL ATTRACTIONS

» Anna Scripps Whitcomb Conservatory - This historic conservatory was designed by Albert Kahn in 1904 (modeled after Thomas Jefferson's Monticello) and features an 85-foot central dome. Sitting on a scenic 13-acre parcel of Belle Isle featuring a formal perennial garden, a rose garden, and a serene lily pond, the conservatory itself is packed with beautiful native and exotic plants of all kinds, including large palms, a cactus room, a fernery, the largest municipal collection of orchids in the country (including rare orchids saved from Britain during World War II and transported to Detroit). It is a long Detroit tradition to visit the conservatory on Christmas and Easter to see the special seasonal displays. Of special note is the annual fund-raiser plant sale held the Saturday of Memorial Day weekend, specializing in unusual plants and heirloom tomatoes. Free admission. *876 Picnic Way, www.belleisleconservancy.org, (313) 852-4064.*

» Belle Isle Aquarium - Designed by Albert Kahn, the 10,000-square-foot Belle Isle Aquarium opened in 1904. The grand entrance opens into a large gallery with tank-lined walls and an incredible arched ceiling covered in shimmering green glass tile to mimic the feeling of being underwater. Though the facility was closed to the public in 2005, it was maintained by volunteers and reopened by the Friends of Belle Isle on the aquarium's 108th birthday in 2012. While volunteers are still working to restore and repopulate 60 of the aquarium's tanks, more than a dozen have been reactivated and are teeming with aquatic life, including turtles, eels, and a wide variety of salt and freshwater fish. Because the aquarium is run completely by volunteers, it is currently open only regularly on Saturdays. Admission is free, but donations are welcome. *3833 Insulruhe Ave., www.belleisleconservancy.org.*

Belle Isle Nature Zoo - Opened in 2005 to replace the larger Safariland, the Belle Isle Nature Zoo is a lively interpretive center dedicated to showcasing Michigan's native flora and fauna. The updated facility is always abuzz with the sounds of enthusiastic children enjoying the zoo's many educational programs and installations, including the native deer enclosure, lecture auditorium, turtle exhibit, indoor beehive, reptile and amphibian areas, spider display, and crafts area. The friendly and knowledgeable staff brings these offerings to life, particularly for the youngest Detroiters. The zoo complex is also home to a protected six-acre forested wetland, an impressive trail network, and a large bird watching and observation area. The well-maintained bathrooms are open 362 days a year, making it a popular place to discover nature when nature calls for many island visitors. *176 Lakeside Dr., www.detroitzoo.org, (313) 852-4056, Ext. 3023.*

Boggs Center - Since 1995, the James and Grace Lee Boggs Center to Nurture Community Leadership has operated as a nonprofit organization in the Boggs' home, located just north of Belle Isle. In this green, grassy neighborhood full of old-growth oaks and colorful houses blossoms new ideas and networks for transformative leadership. Named for the couple, which settled in Detroit in the 1940s and dedicated their lives to organizing in labor unions and the civil rights movement, the Boggs Center organizes conferences and international publications, such as Reimagining Work and The Next American Revolution. Visitors may discuss community building in their own neighborhoods with Grace Lee Boggs, who at 97 years old continues to evolve her philosophy for visionary organizing in the 21st century. By appointment only, visitors are encouraged to call ahead to schedule a visit for what will likely be a transformative experience. *3061 Field St., www.boggscenter.org, (313) 923-0797.*

Dossin Great Lakes Museum - A must-see for any historian, maritime enthusiast, or imaginative child, the Dossin Great Lakes Museum is located on the south side of Belle Isle and is home to several notable exhibits, including the first speedboat to reach 100 miles per hour (Miss Pepsi), the opulent smoking lounge from the steamship City of Detroit III, and intriguing rotating exhibits pertaining to the Great Lakes. Most exciting for the young or young-at-heart is the pilot house of the William Clay Ford, mounted atop the museum and facing the river—allowing any visitor to "captain" a Great Lakes freighter. One of the best features of the museum—and one that can be enjoyed from the comfort of your own home—is the Dossin Great Lakes Museum Detroit River Watch webcam, which you can remotely maneuver to spy on passing freighters, boats, and rowers. Be sure to check out the cannons on the way in—they were captured from the British during the Battle of Lake Erie in the War of 1812. Hours vary seasonally, but winter brings spectacular views of an ice-filled river. *100 Strand Dr., www.detroithistorical.org, (313) 852-4051.*

» The Heidelberg Project - A labor of love and an act of resistance, the Heidelberg Project is Detroit's best-known outdoor art installation, and one of its most controversial. When Tyree Guyton and his grandfather Sam Mackey started painting polka dots on abandoned houses and attaching stuffed animals to trees in 1986, it was a defiant gesture meant, in part, to draw attention to their crumbling east side neighborhood. In the years since, Heidelberg has continued to grow, transforming two full blocks into a constantly evolving, imaginative wonderland of found objects that is as angry and challenging as it is colorful and inspiring. While elements of the project were demolished by order of two separate mayoral administrations, today, the Heidelberg is an internationally acclaimed destination (visited by more than 275,000 people a year), a 501(c)3 nonprofit, and an art education center. A must-see. *3600 Heidelberg St., www.heidelberg.org, (313) 974-6894.*

ISKCON Temple of Detroit at the Fisher Mansion - Built in the 1927, the Fisher Mansion was a monument to auto-body magnate Lawrence Fisher. The 22,000-square-foot Spanish Mission-style estate boasts a music room with Japanese ceilings, a dining room with pillars from a 15th century German castle, a covered boat slip that once held Fisher's 104-foot yacht, and, according to rumor, hidden Prohibition-era wine cellars. That era's gilded grandeur has vanished. But with every death comes a new beginning, as Bhaktivedanta Swami Prabhupada—founder of the Hare Krishna movement—might say. The mansion was donated to the Krishnas in 1975 by Alfred Brush Ford (great-grandson of Henry Ford) and Elisabeth Reuther (daughter of union leader Walter P. Reuther) and now serves as a temple and cultural center, which are headquartered in the former ballroom. Outdoors, the four acres of landscaped grounds are still beautifully maintained and are home to altars of sacred icons, three fountains, a waterfall, and peacocks that grace the facility with their presence. The center offers free prasadam feasts after public worship and lecture on Sunday evenings. Visitors are asked to remove their shoes. *383 Lenox St., www.detroitiskcon.org, (313) 824-6000.*

ENTERTAINMENT & RECREATION

»**Belle Isle** - Discover some of the city's most popular cultural amenities, cycling routes, scenic natural landscapes, public art, outdoor athletic venues, historic architecture, and picnic spots on Belle Isle. The city's second largest park, and the nation's largest public island park, Belle Isle spans 982 acres and includes the region's most diverse collection of programmed amenities, many of which have been delighting Detroiters for generations.

The park, which measures five miles around, is home to a host of natural features, including four lakes—Takoma, Muskoday, Blue Herron Lagoon, and Okonoka—and a dense woodland, making it a popular destination for ducks and migrating birds—including warblers, geese, and birds of prey, and the birders that love them. Belle Isle is in the nation's busiest inland waterway, making for picturesque views of Detroit, Windsor, and the frequent Canadian-side freighter traffic. On windy days, lucky visitors will pick up the sweet smell of corn from the nearby Canadian Club distillery.

Deemed Île aux Cochons—"Hog Island"—by the 18th century French settlers who used livestock to eliminate the rattlesnake infestation and to keep their hogs from mainland coyotes, the island first entered private hands in 1769, when George McDougall traded Ottawa and Ojibwa residents eight barrels of rum, three rolls of tobacco, six pounds of vermilion, and a wampum belt for the island. Belle Isle changed hands twice before being renamed in honor of Governor Lewis Cass' daughter Isabelle "Belle" Cass, or French statesman Charles Louis Auguste Fouquet, duc de Belle-Isle—depending on whom you ask. In 1879, the City of Detroit purchased the island for $200,000, with plans on creating one of the nation's premier parks. Toward this end, the city enlisted renowned landscape architect, Frederick Law Olmsted—who designed New York City's Central Park—to design the park in 1883. Since the Olmsted plan, the park has been the beneficiary of numerous incidental projects, which, together, create a vibrant patchwork of art, woodlands, and recreational destinations. Although the island is home to a constellation of sites and recreational and cultural opportunities, including a band shell, model yacht basin, giant floral clock, coast guard station, and numerous picnic shelters, a number of attractions stand out. *Entry to the park is via the MacArthur Bridge on E. Jefferson Avenue at E. Grand Boulevard. www.belleisleconservancy.org.*

- **Anna Scripps Whitcomb Conservatory -** See separate entry in this chapter.

- **Athletic Field & Field House** - Built in 1898, the Field House was designed as a bicycle rental facility by local architect Edward A. Schilling and anchors the 36-acre Athletic Field. The Athletic Field includes nine baseball diamonds, 10 lighted tennis courts, a running track, the World Cup Soccer Field, handball courts, racquetball courts, and basketball courts. Loiter Way and Vista Drive.

- **Beach & Water Slide** - Open from the second week of June through Labor Day, the public beach is a well-maintained, half-mile artificial beach, fronting a large, buoyed swimming area. The adjacent water slide offers two curvilinear slides—a three-turn, two-story slide, and a seven-turn three-story slide. The beach is home to Jazz On the Beach during summer Sunday evenings, June through August. Riverbank Road at Oakway Trail.

- **Belle Isle Aquarium** - See separate entry in this chapter.

- **Belle Isle Casino** - Named not for gambling, but for its intended resemblance to an Italian villa, this elegant 1908 design features a yellow-brick facade, four corner towers, a two-story arcaded veranda, and a terra cotta tile roof. Originally used as a park management and visitor dining facility, today the casino is used for public and private events and is available for year-round rental. Casino Avenue and The Strand, (313) 628-2081.

- **Belle Isle Nature Zoo** - See separate entry in this chapter.

- **The Belle Isle Practice Center** - See separate entry in this chapter.

- **Borreal Wetlands Forest** - The island's 200-acre woodlands are one of the last remaining remnants of the region's original old growth forests, which once covered Southeast Michigan. Visitors will find diverse species including bur oak, pin oak, hawthorn, silver maple, shagbark hickory, and pumpkin ash. The island's woodlands are home to miles of trails and paths for walking, running, birding, and mountain biking. East side of the island, along Woodside Drive, Central Avenue, and Oakway Road.

- **Detroit Boat Club** - Built in 1902, this large Spanish Colonial Revival-style structure was the first concrete structure in the United States and was once the opulent center of boating and rowing on the Great Lakes before falling into disrepair. Today, the storied Detroit Boat Club Crew calls the facility home and sponsors competitive and recreational rowing classes and competitions at the club. 6 Riverbank Dr., www. detroitboatclubcrew.com, (313) 642-0555.

- **Detroit Yacht Club** - See separate entry in this chapter.
- **Dossin Great Lakes Museum** - See separate entry in this chapter.
- **Fishing Piers and Bulkheads** - Although fishing is permitted on all of the shores, canals and lakes—except for the protected Blue Heron Lagoon—anglers are most commonly found on the island's two piers and two bulkheads. While the Detroit River is home to game fish like walleye and sturgeon, the piers are best for panfish, including yellow perch, white bass, bluegill, rock bass, and smallmouth bass. Located along Riverbank Road and The Strand.
- **Flynn Pavilion** - Designed by Eliel Saarinen and opened in 1949, this beautiful, modernist structure on the bank of Lake Takoma allows visitors to rent charming two-seater swan-shaped paddleboats and explore the inland waterways. The recently renovated structure is available for private rentals during the offseason. Loiter Way and Picnic Way, (313) 628-2069.
- **Giant Slide** - Take a ride in a potato sack down this blazing fast, four-story metal slide. The supervised facility is lighted and open during only the summer. Central Avenue and Inselruhe Avenue.
- **Hipster Beach** - Though it is unsanctioned and, according to authorities, unsafe, the sandy inlet unofficially known as Hipster Beach is the semiprivate outdoor bathing oasis of choice for bohemians of all types and anyone in the know. To get there, drive or bike to the east end of Belle Isle. When The Strand turns north, park in the dirt lot on the right side of the road, by the swings. Follow the path around the William Livingstone Memorial Light, and continue across the cement footbridge. Follow the path until you spot the mythical place on a narrow canal: Hipster Beach. The whole hike is just more than a mile. Please be cautioned that the area is not a sanctioned beach. There is no lifeguard on duty, and bathers are subject to potential police reprimand.
- **Ice Tree** - What began as the "Ice Fountain," a Washington Boulevard tradition in 1910s, the Ice Tree is a 30-foot-tall ice

sculpture created by the City of Detroit and built from ice-covered Christmas trees. Riverbank Road at Inselruhe Avenue.

- **James Scott Memorial Fountain** - A monument to millionaire gambler and Detroit playboy prankster James Scott, the Scott Fountain and associated bronze sculpture were built amid great controversy, as many residents were hesitant to accept Scott's funds to memorialize such a rascal. Designed by architect Cass Gilbert, who designed the U.S. Supreme Court Building, this lavish, white marble fountain was completed in 1925 and is adorned with lions, dolphins, and even the head of Neptune, Greek god of the sea. Casino Avenue and The Strand.

- **Kids Kingdom Playscape** - This expansive, half-acre playground features brightly colored play equipment for children 12 and younger, including swings, tunnels, slides, climbing surfaces, climbable animal sculptures, and a large space capsule-themed merry-go-round. Central Avenue and Inselruhe Avenue.

- **MacArthur Bridge** - Among the nation's first cantilevered arch bridges, the General Douglas MacArthur Bridge was built in 1923, after its predecessor burned following a construction accident. The bridge's 19 spans run 2,356 feet. Shortly after being named for MacArthur in 1942, the Belle Isle side of the bridge played host to the beginning of a three-day race riot when a now-disproven rumor suggested a white man had thrown an African-American woman and her baby from the bridge in 1943. The riot, which stemmed from a simmering controversy surrounding the construction of the Sojourner Truth Homes and housing discrimination facing African-American war material workers, caused 600 injuries, 34 deaths, and more than 1,200 arrests. For its aesthetics and history, the bridge is a national historic landmark. E. Grand Boulevard and E. Jefferson Avenue.

- **Nancy Brown Peace Carillon** - Unveiled in 1940, this bell tower was built with public donations from 60,000 loyal readers of Detroit News columnist Annie Louise Brown, who used the nom de plume Nancy Brown. At the behest of the tower's pen-namesake, the 85-foot Neo-Gothic bell tower is dedicated to world peace. The automated, computer-controlled 49-bell carillon chimes every half hour. Muse Road and Picnic Way.

- **Statuary** - In addition to the opulent James Scott Memorial Fountain (see above), Belle Isle is home to beautiful statuary spread across the island. Most impressive among these, perhaps, is the Levi L. Barbour Memorial Fountain, a breathtaking black granite and bronze 1936 installation by famed sculpture Marshall Fredericks. The fountain, Fredrick's first public work, centers on a wheeling bronze gazelle surrounded by black granite depictions of a grouse, a hawk, an otter, and a rabbit. Other notable works on the island include Allen Newman's bronze Spanish-American War Monument (1932), Samuel Cashwan's bronze James J. Brady Memorial (1927), Herman Martzen's bronze Johann Friedrich von Schiller Sculpture (1907), Raefello Romanelli's bronze Bust of Dante Alighieri (1927), and Richard Bennett's stainless steel Gazelle (1991).

- **William Livingstone Memorial Light** - The nation's only marble lighthouse, this 1929 Art Deco structure memorializes Great Lakes shipping safety advocate William Livingstone. Designed by Albert Kahn, the fluted 80-foot tall white Georgia marble structure features a brilliant, bronze 11,500-candlepower lantern that can be seen for up to 15 miles. Located on the far east end of the park, off of Lakeside Drive.

The Belle Isle Practice Center - Putter have a little patina? Open March through Thanksgiving, the Belle Isle Practice Center is perhaps Michigan's finest golf practice center and a destination for Detroiters and college and high school teams from throughout the region and state looking to improve their game. Located on a scenic portion of the east end of Belle Isle, the practice center offers a 30-bay full-length driving range—including grass tees—three putting greens, four chipping greens, three sand traps, a full acre grass fairway, and a short, albeit challenging, five-hole course. The grounds and facilities are beautifully maintained, and the professional staff is friendly, knowledgeable, and happy to share pointers. The clubhouse offers complimentary club rental, and offers a variety of new and used equipment at reasonable prices. See you on the links! *175 Lakeside Dr., www.thebelleislepracticecenter.com, (313) 821-5218.*

Chandler Park Golf Course - Located in the northern half of Detroit's verdant Chandler Park, the Chandler Park Golf Course has been delighting generations of golfers since opening in 1929. The subtle slopes and gentle terrain on this Williams, Gill & Associates-designed course make it easy on the dogs and on the scorecard. This merciful, par-71 course measures 5,832 yards from the blue tees and features wide sweeping tree-lined fairways and forgiving greens, making it popular among those new to the game—and those who play like it. Aggressive golfers should be wary of the sand and grass traps flanking many of the fairways, which favor those with a solid irons game. The greens and fairways are watered, so the course stays green into the summer. The course was truncated when I-94 was built, so the front nine is shorter than the back. If you're playing only nine and want more of a challenge, play the back nine. The course is home to a putting and chipping area for pregame warm-ups, as well as a beautiful, full-service pro shop. *12801 Chandler Park Dr., www.chandlerparkgolfcourse.com, (313) 331-7755.*

Chene Park Amphitheater - Perched at the water's edge, with a stunning view of downtown Detroit and Canada, Chene Park offers a capacity of 6,100, in the form of both lawn and outdoor theater seating. With its enormous, defining, white tent structure that resembles a ship's sails, the amphitheater hosts an annual summer concert series featuring an exciting music menu of jazz, R&B, hip hop, and soul. Though sometimes the outdoor acoustics are known to be a little imbalanced, it has established itself as a scenic gem of the summer entertainment season, and a popular date spot for an evening of music, food, and drinks while watching the sunset on the river. *2600 Atwater St., www.cheneparkdetroit.com, (313) 393-7128.*

City Sports Center - Open year-round since the first puck dropped in 1993, City Sports Center's frozen sheets are a destination for those looking to lace up for figure skating, hockey, or broomball. With two NHL-regulation size rinks, 500-person capacity stands, a weight room, locker rooms, glass-walled meeting space for hockey widows, and a kiss and cry for successful skaters, the beautiful and utilitarian facility has become home base for hockey clubs, from Wayne State University and many area high schools. The expert, family-orientated staff leads figure skating lessons, hockey clinics, supervised pick-up hockey, and league games for boys, girls, teens, and adults. Visitors can set their watch to the Zamboni service, which keeps the rink's renowned "fast ice." The center offers daily open skates and welcomes private event reservations. Occasionally, the Detroit Red Wings are known to practice at the facility, and fans are allowed to drop off memorabilia for autographs, provided they don't bother the players. No skate rental. *3401 E. Lafayette St., (313) 549-4214.*

» Dequindre Cut - A former Grand Trunk Railroad line converted into an east side recreation path in 2009, the Dequindre Cut runs a happy 1.35 miles from Gratiot (near Eastern Market) to Woodbridge

Street, connecting with the Riverwalk (to the east and west) from there. The handsomely landscaped, 20-foot-wide path has designated space for pedestrians and cyclists, and is home to some of Detroit's most accessible and vibrant street art (much of which existed before development and was wisely left in place). Located 25 feet below grade, the Dequindre Cut manages to feel at once enclosed and airy, public, and intimate. It's great on its own for a leisurely stroll or as a handy connector on a longer excursion. *Between Gratiot Avenue and Woodbridge Street, parallel to St. Aubin. Entrance ramps at Gratiot Avenue, Lafayette Street, and Woodbridge Street, www.detroitriverfront.org/dequindre.*

Detroit City Futbol League - A spirited co-ed recreational futbol league, the Detroit City Futbol League has united Detroit's neighborhoods through the "beautiful game" since 2010. Composed of teams assembled from Detroit's historic neighborhoods, the adult league debuted with 11 clubs but now boasts 30. The teams compete each season for pride, bragging rights, and the illustrious Copa Detroit title, which is granted to the winner of the end-of-season tournament of the same name. The competitive but sporting games are lively and thrilling to watch, especially when some of the more colorful teams are playing, such as Cass Corridor and their "Suck it" flag, boombox, and PBR-swigging, or "upper crust" Indian Village and their postgame martinis. Games are free and open to the public and are played Saturdays throughout the summer. Games are played at the World Cup Soccer Field on Belle Isle and at Historic Fort Wayne. Check out the website for schedules and standings: *www.detroitcityfutbol.com.*

Detroit Yacht Club - Founded in 1868, the nearly 100,000-square-foot DYC is the largest yacht club in the United States and one of the grandest, most storied, clubs in Detroit. Located on a private island adjacent to Belle Isle, the current facility, which was designed by architect George D. Mason, was designed in the Mediterranean style and completed in 1922. The historic clubhouse and grounds feature a 380-slip marina, two swimming pools, athletic courts, casual and formal dining rooms, ballrooms, and exercise facilities. The club offers a packed schedule of family-friendly activities, including sailing lessons and races, summer camp, and special events, the highlight of which is the annual Venetian Night. Since 1921, the club has been a title sponsor of the annual hydroplane races, a tradition it began with the encouragement of legendary racer and club member Commodore

Gar Wood. Though only members and guests are allowed into the club on most days, select rooms are available for public event rental. Discounted memberships are available for young people. *1 Riverbank Dr., www.dyc.com, (313) 824-1200.*

East Side Parks - Don't tell anyone, but tucked along the Detroit River on the city's east side lies one of the area's greatest secrets: a string of 12 quiet, scenic, and pastoral parks with unparalleled views of the river. The 12 massive parks—Henderson, Owen, Alfred Brush Ford, Mariner, Chene, Peter Maheras-Bronson Gentry, Mt. Elliott, Orleans Atwater, Riverfront-Lakewood, Gabriel Richard, Stockton, and Memorial Annex—total more than 210 acres. Although a few of them offer lovely amenities—such as the five baseball diamonds at Peter Maheras-Bronson Gentry, the amphitheater at Chene, or the playground equipment at Stockton, these east side parks are largely unprogrammed and intentionally left as lush, green space. While the parks' general simplicity allows visitors to enjoy the serenity of nature, many visitors make use of the river access and open expanses to go fishing, fly kites, take romantic picnics, bird watch, launch model rockets, play lawn games, and watch the passing freighters go by. Although all of the parks are worth a visit, three offer truly unique features: Stockton is next to the Manoogian Mansion, Peter Maheras-Bronson Gentry includes a large island, and Mariner is home to an operating lighthouse. While a secret to many residents, area geese are no stranger to these parks and often leave behind tokens of their appreciation, so plan on wearing shoes. *The parks are along or south E. Jefferson Avenue, between E. Grand Boulevard, and Alter Road.*

Family Aquatic Center at Chandler Park - Based in the southern half of beautiful Chandler Park, the Family Aquatic Center is a destination for those looking for un-watered-down aquatic fun. The updated, 22,000-square-foot facility accommodates up to 2,023 patrons and offers a range of activities, including two massive water slides that allow 15 mile-per-hour tube or body sliding, a 570,000-gallon wave pool with nine-foot crests, and a toddler area with more than 100 spray fountains and other water rides. If you forget your trunks or need a snack, visit the well-stocked Tiki Hut, which offers swim gear and other accessories or the concession canteen that serves up summer grub. Visitors must be 48 inches tall to ride the slide. Open Memorial Day through Labor Day. Call ahead for prices and relevant weather information, or to inquire about event rental. *12660 Chandler Park Dr., (313) 822-7665.*

The Goatyard / Boatyard / Detroit Sail Club - With about 25 boat slips, The Goatyard—or Boatyard—is not the biggest marina in town, but it certainly has the most character. The yard occupies the property of an old brick factory and is situated on a musty canal near Detroit Edison's Conner Creek Power Plant, with the city's only private tugboat bar and a weathered dock that floats barely two inches above the water next to a sunken schooner. It's home to the city's most unique sailboats, including the first fiberglass-hull, "unsinkable" Crescent sloop, which was designed in Detroit by engineer Dick Hill in 1953. The yard is littered with a host of industrial relics, including a derelict brick-making machine, several trucks, a pair of school buses (one of which serves as an office), rusty bikes, abandoned motorcycles, and of course, tons of boats. Goatyard members are known to the rest of the Metro Detroit sailing community as the Pirates of Lake St. Clair. If you want to become a pirate, or just want to have a good time sailing with the laid-back manager Stephen Hume and his partner Susan McDonald in the Detroit Sail Club, reserve your slips early in winter because they're hard to come by. *10 St. Jean St.*

John's Carpet House - Every Sunday in the summer between 2pm and sundown, music fans in the know can catch live (amplified) music from some of Detroit's finest blues musicians in the fields of the near east side. The event started as a regular jam session in the garage of John Estes, who insulated the walls with carpet to muffle the sound, inspiring the nickname of the ad hoc venue. Though Estes passed away long ago and his house and garage no longer occupy the site, the honored tradition of a free public Sunday jam session continues today. Visitors are welcome to bring their own brown-bagged food (or beverages) but can also enjoy tasty fried chicken and other down-home vittles from the food trucks and stands that set up shop near the action. If you feel like dancing, you're in luck—just make sure you bring your best moves because the regulars put on a show. Though there's no admission fee, guests are encouraged to "put a ducket in the bucket" to give the musicians a little something for their time and to make sure the grass gets mowed and the Porta-Johns get emptied. *St. Aubin Street at Frederick Street.*

The Players Club - With an exterior designed in the Florentine Renaissance style, and an interior that is somewhere between Art Deco and Medieval castle, the 90-year-old Players Club is a pint-size architectural treat maintained by caretakers who have remained faithful to the club's historic legacy and the traditional Shakespearean method as an all-male amateur theatrical organization. Amid breathtaking narrative Art Deco murals and stunning classical architectural flourishes, guests sit at private tables as they enjoy three one-act theatrical productions called "frolics." *3321 E. Jefferson Ave., www.playersdetroit.org, (313) 259-3385.*

William G. Milliken State Park and Harbor - Serving as a link to Chene Park, the Dequindre Cut, and Rivard Plaza, this oasis is the only Michigan state park to be located in an urban area. On the Detroit River, just east of downtown, the 31-acre park has restored wetlands, which mimic the original botanical shore life and attract migratory birds. This restful, beautifully designed park provides welcome facilities for fishing, picnicking, walking, bicycling, and boating, as well as a 52-slip harbor marked by a lighthouse at the entrance. *1900 Atwater St., (313) 396-0217.*

SITES

Detroit's Last Lustron Home - Designed by Carl Strandlund in 1947, Lustron homes were all-steel modernist prefabricated homes clad in porcelain-enameled steel that rose to prominence during the postwar housing shortage. Stemming from the same impetus and ideology as Buckminster Fuller's Dymaxion House, the comparatively traditional Lustron homes featured built-in furniture, integrated appliances, and enameled steel walls, ceilings, drawers, doors, and floors. Strandlund marketed the homes as offering a "new and richer experience for the entire family," where "Mother has far more hours." The company went bankrupt in 1950, after building only 2,500 homes nationwide. Only a fraction of these remain unaltered. The last unaltered Lustron home in the city, 654 Ashland St., is an unparalleled example of a two-bedroom Model 02 Westchester Lustron home complete with the original maize yellow enamel. An architectural gem of the Jefferson Chalmers community, the home features massive red street numbers, making it easy to find. This home is serial #00708. Because the home is privately owned and occupied, please be respectful and only check it out from the street. *654 Ashland St.*

Ossian H. Sweet House - In 1925, Ossian Sweet—a prominent African-American physician—purchased a one-and-one-half story brick bungalow in an all-white neighborhood. When word spread around the neighborhood, segregationist white neighbors took arms, and Sweet, fearful for his life, invited a number of family and friends to spend the night. On the night of September 9, 1925, an angry mob of 500 neighbors encircled the house and pelted the home with stones, while shouting death threats and slurs. A single shot rang out from the house, killing one member of the mob. Police immediately arrested the family and charged them with murder. At the behest of the NAACP, legendary attorney Clarence Darrow—fresh off the renowned Scopes Monkey Trial—served as defense counsel before presiding Judge Frank Murphy. Despite facing an all-white jury, Darrow successfully argued self-defense and, after an impassioned seven-hour closing statement, the Sweets were acquitted. The landmark case played a pivotal role in the subsequent overturn of racial redlining laws and was the inspiration for author Kevin Boyle's award-winning book Arc of Justice. The home is an occupied private residence, so visitors should be respectful of the owner's privacy. *2905 Garland St.*

» **Elmwood Cemetery** - With acres of sculptural grave markers and ornate mausoleums, rolling hills, defiant spires, stone angels, towering old trees, benches designed by Robert Moses for the 1932 World's Fair, and centuries of Detroit history at every turn, Elmwood is the oldest nondenominational cemetery in Michigan, and it's a sight to behold. A park-like urban oasis established in 1846, Elmwood is the final resting place of numerous notable figures in the city's long history, including 29 former mayors of Detroit, as well as state and U.S. senators and representatives, Michigan governors, a postmaster general, presidential cabinet members, and soldiers and officers of every American war since the Revolution, including 205 Civil War veterans. Its 86 acres were sumptuously landscaped by influential American landscape architect Frederick Law Olmstead, making it one of Detroit's most remarkably scenic and serene outdoor spaces, representative of Detroit's natural topography prior to development. Even the tranquil creek in the valley has a story to tell: In 1763, British soldiers attempting to ambush Chief Pontiac's camp were surprised to find the Indians expecting them. Legend has it that the creek ran red from the carnage and was known thereafter as Bloody Run. This resplendent, contemplative setting is ideal for a leisurely stroll, bike ride, or historical exploration. Expect to see many graves bearing names that are familiar now as Detroit streets. Notable burials include:

- **Lewis Cass (1782–1866)**: Michigan territorial governor, ambassador to France, secretary of war under President Andrew Jackson, secretary of state under President James Buchanan, and Democratic nominee for president in 1848. *Section A, Lot 25.*

- **William Woodbridge (1780–1861):** Secretary of the Michigan Territory and, after statehood, Michigan's second governor and U.S. senator from Michigan. Namesake of the Woodbridge neighborhood. *Section A, Lot 13.*

- **Coleman A. Young (1918–1997):** World War II Tuskegee Airman and Detroit's first black mayor; served five terms. Equally revered and reviled, the powerful, polarizing Young presided over a period of social and economic change in the city. *Hazel Dell.*

- **Bernhard Stroh (1822–1882)**: German immigrant founded Stroh Brewery Company, maker of Stroh's beer. *Section Q.*

- **Zachariah Chandler (1813–1879):** Mayor of Detroit, four-term U.S. senator, secretary of the interior under President Ulysses S. Grant and was nearly a candidate for president. *Section B, Lot 49.*

- **Fred "Sonic" Smith (1949–1994):** Guitarist for MC5, husband of singer Patti Smith. *Section V.*

- **Hiram Walker (1816–1899):** Distiller, founder of the Hiram Walker & Sons Distillery Company in Windsor, Ontario, makers of Canadian Club whiskey. *Section A2.*

In the cemetery's southeast corner is Beth El, a small lot purchased from Elmwood in 1850 that's the oldest Jewish graveyard in the state. Across the eastern fence is Detroit's oldest extant cemetery, Mt. Elliott Cemetery, founded for the city's Catholics in 1841. Families of blended religious heritage would sometimes buy plots along the fence line and bury their Protestants on one side, Catholics on the other. *1200 Elmwood Ave., www.elmwoodhistoriccemetery.org, (313) 567-3454.*

Harbor Island Canal Area - Yes, there's island housing in Detroit. Along Alter Street, south of Jefferson Avenue, are some of the most unique backyards in the city—lush backyards with hoists, finger docks, greenery, and watercraft jutting into Fox Creek and the many narrow man-made canals and small bridges that form the neighborhood, making the area popular with adventurous Jet Skiers and kayakers seeking one of the city's most unique aquatic navigation opportunities. While only small watercraft can explore the creek and canals, landlubbers and seafarers alike can explore the extended Creekside area. Mariner Park, an island formed by Fox Creek, two canals, and the mouth of the Detroit River, is a kempt, treed, and lush green park that features river's edge fishing spots (with dedicated rod-holders) and Windmill Point Lighthouse. Across the river, visitors can spy Peche Isle, a partier's haven, and can watch the heavy traffic of sail and motor boats, freighters, and kayaks during the day. Close to the west, also an island, but one that is reachable by land, is Riverfront-Lakewood Park, an unmaintained park that is delightfully rambunctious with nature, bringing pheasants, cattails, and thick, tall grass. Who needs Venice?

Fox Creek: *Along Alter Road, south of E. Jefferson Avenue.*

Harbor Island: *Lakewood Street south, right on Harbor Island Drive.*

Klenk Street: *Alter Road south, right on Klenk Street.*

Mariner and Riverfront-Lakewood Parks: *Alter Road south continues to Riverside Drive west.*

» Indian Village - One of Detroit's most exquisite historic neighborhoods, Indian Village contains 352 stately homes and mansions—some as large as 12,000 square feet—designed by some of the city's most esteemed architects. Bounded by Mack Avenue to the north, Seminole Street to the east, Jefferson Avenue to the south, and Burns Street to the west. The land was originally occupied by the Rivard and St. Aubin ribbon farms (narrow farms running perpendicularly out from the river) but became a state fairground and then horseracing track before being purchased by developer James Owen in the 1880s. Owen playfully dubbed the development Indian Village after the streets, Iroquois and Seminole, which were named for popular local thoroughbred racehorses—not directly after Native American tribes, as one might infer. Between 1895 and 1929, the area, which was then a relatively remote, rural oasis, became a bedroom community for Detroit's captains of industry. Set back from the street, with carriage houses larger than many middle-class homes, the impressive homesteads were designed by such names as Louis Kamper, C. Howard Crane, Albert Kahn, George D. Mason, and Smith, Hinchman & Grylls. Outfitted with intricate ornamentation and flourishes, leaded and stained glass, sculpture, and other exterior details, prominent architectural styles in the neighborhood include Georgian, Federal, Colonial Revival, Arts and Crafts, Romanesque, and Tudor Revival. Because of the dedication of committed residents, much of the original character of the charming tree-lined neighborhood is preserved to this day, and self-guided tours, whether by foot or on two or four wheels are essential for fans of historic homes and architecture. A tradition since 1958, the best time to see Indian Village is during its home and garden tour the first Saturday of June. Though smaller, there are also lovely homes in adjoining historic **West Village** to the west, on Van Dyke Street and Parker Street, between Kercheval Street and Jefferson Avenue. While nearly every structure in the regal neighborhood is magnificent, notable highlights include:

- **Arthur and Clara Buhl House:** Gothic Tudor Mansion. *1116 Iroquois St.*

- **James Hamilton House:** Tudor Revival Home. *8325 E. Jefferson Ave.*

- **Bingley Fales House:** A Neo-Georgian. At 15,000 square feet, it is the largest home in Indian Village. *1771 Seminole St.*

- **Louis Kamper House:** Neo-Renaissance Home of the renowned architect. *2150 Iroquois St.*

- **Henry Leland House:** Tudor Revival home of the founder of Lincoln and Cadillac Motors. *1052 Seminole St.*

- **Edsel and Eleanor Ford Honeymoon House:** Home of Henry Ford's son from 1917 to 1921, and birthplace of Henry Ford II. *2171 Iroquois St.*

- **Mary S. Smith House:** A palatial Neo-Renaissance mansion. *8445 E. Jefferson Ave.*

- **Frederick K. Stearns House:** An impressive Tudor Revival. *8109 E. Jefferson Ave.*

- **Detroit Waldorf School:** Designed by Albert Kahn, originally the Liggett School, now a private school in the Steiner tradition. *2555 Burns St.*

- **Jefferson Avenue Presbyterian Church:** Stately Gothic Revival church designed by Wirt Rowland in 1926. *8625 E. Jefferson Ave.*

Joseph Berry Subdivision - Largely built between 1898 and 1929, Berry Sub, as it's known locally, is part of the Villages neighborhoods, and its 90 homes—heavy on Tudors and Colonials—are tucked away east of Indian Village, on four streets, between Jefferson Avenue and the Detroit River. The neighborhood boasts a dynamic, diverse mix of residents, including Kid Rock and the mayor (who resides in the Manoogian Mansion, the official mayoral residence at the east end of Dwight Drive) and some of the city's most recognized leaders in local politics and business. Of special architectural note are the seven homes on Dwight Drive along the Detroit River, which include the Manoogian, as well as lumberman Joseph Weber's Colony. The colony was comprised of the westernmost five homes, all built in 1920, as the family's private compound. Although all the homes are owned independently today, the pipes that heated all five from a central heating plant still run through their basements. Berry Sub residents enjoy the quiet, country-like setting on the river, and relish in a rich variety of wildlife, including pheasants, red foxes, opossum, raccoons, rabbits, waterfowl, and even the occasional turtle or bird of prey. *E. Jefferson Ave. at Fiske Rd.*

» **Lafayette Park** - Completed between 1958 and 1965, Lafayette Park is a seminal work by renowned architect Ludwig Mies Van Der Rohe and a masterpiece of the International Style. Spanning 78 verdant acres, the beautiful campus is home to 186 one- and two-story townhomes, four high-rise apartment buildings, a covered pedestrian shopping mall, and a school, making the complex the largest collection of Mies van der Rohe structures in the world. The townhomes, especially, are distinctive for their clean lines, simple aesthetic, minimal presence, structural order, perfect proportions, and tinted glass-and-aluminum-clad exterior, all of which embody the intrinsic design elements characteristic of Mies van der Rohe. The development includes thoughtful details, such as parking lots that are recessed below the sightline of the nearby dwellings, pathways to school that aren't interrupted by streets, and a spare but breathtaking 19-acre park that offers inspiring views of the surrounding masterpiece of modernity. *The complex is located North of Lafayette Ave., between Rivard St. and Orleans St.*

Liberty Motor Car Company Headquarters - Detroit is the only metropolitan area in the world with two full-size replicas of Philadelphia's iconic Independence Hall. Though Henry Ford commissioned such a structure for Greenfield Village in 1929, he was not the first auto baron to do so. In 1919, now defunct Liberty Motor Car Company was a fledgling automobile brand looking to expand. With founder Percy Owens—a man with East Coast ties—at the helm, the company selected this site for its new factory and stately Liberty Hall-copping headquarters. Though the company sold 21,000 cars in

1921, because of supplier competition with the big four (Ford, GM, Packard, and Hudson) the company went defunct by 1923—leaving this curious replication as its legacy. Though the building was used by Thyssen-Krupp until 2007, it is now vacant. *Located on a private, guarded drive at 2909 Connor St.*

Packard Motor Car Company - You have to see it to believe it—even then you might not trust your eyes. At 3.5 million square feet of abandoned steel and concrete extending over 40 acres of property, the Packard Plant is either an urban explorer's dream or a city planner's nightmare. Both have fretted over the fate of the Detroit's largest symbol of bygone prosperity. Completed in 1911 and designed by Albert Kahn, the state-of-the-art plant assembled luxury vehicles until Packard Motor Company merged with Studebaker and halted production in 1958. There have been several demolition attempts, but because of the intimidating cost and scale of the endeavor, none has come to fruition. Artists, some internationally renowned, have used the plant as their canvas, most notably Banksy's "I Remember When All This Was Trees"—now at the 555 Gallery (see separate entry)— and Scott Hocking's "Garden of the Gods." Because of the uneven state of structural soundness, exploring the complex can be dangerous. *1540 E. Grand Blvd.*

St. Albertus Church - Though it closed and was desanctified in 1990, St. Albertus has been painstakingly maintained and remains one of the city's most historic and most visually striking religious monuments. Completed in 1885, it was the first church in the city to be constructed with steam heating and electric lighting, and it is the oldest standing Polish church building in the city. Though stately, the red brick exterior with its central oxidized copper steeple belies the stunning and opulent interior in which the sweeping turquoise vaulted ceiling hovers 40 feet above the sanctuary. Illuminated by the rainbow of hues that emanate from the numerous narrative stained-glass windows, the nave—with capacity for 2,500 parishioners— terminates at the stunning altar, which features intricate reliefs, sculptures, and painted details. While the parish is no longer active, the church is actively maintained by the Polish American Historic Site Association, which loosely operates the facility as a Polish heritage site and a center for Polish history and culture. In addition to special Roman Catholic masses held twice monthly, the association offers tours and hosts events, including the annual St. Albertus Fest, which features local rock bands and homemade pierogi and acts as a grand

opportunity to explore the architectural riches inside.
4231 St. Aubin St., www.stalbertusdetroit.org, (313) 831-9727.

Sweetest Heart of Mary - Completed in 1893, this magnificent Gothic Revival church was once the nation's largest Polish Catholic church and among the area's most beautiful. Begun by a splinter congregation from the older St. Albertus Church, Sweetest Heart of Mary grew to be a largely Polish parish, peaking at 4,000 families. The red brick cruciform structure features a gabled roof, an elegant entranceway with oak bas-relief doors in arched doorways, twin buttressed 217 foot spires, and three bells named for Saints Mary, Joseph, and Barbara. The structure's most stunning architectural feature, however, may be the original, monumental stained glass windows lining the sanctuary. Depicting several saints, Jesus, and Mary with vivid colors, the windows won numerous awards at Chicago's famed Columbian Exposition World's Fair. The nave is perhaps more elegant than the facade. The exquisite sanctuary features groined vaulting clad in gold tapestry, marble pillars with intricate Corinthian capitals, religious murals, and an intricate red oak Vatican II altar. Visitors should attend mass, schedule a tour, or visit the annual pierogi festival to admire the interior. *4440 Russell St., www.sweetestheart.org, (313) 831-6659.*

Water Works Park & Hurlbut Memorial Gate - Once one of the city's most popular attractions, when the 110-acre site was selected for the city's principal water pumping station in the 1870s—as it remains today—it was also designed to serve as a park. Though it featured a lagoon, tennis courts, a baseball diamond, an 8-foot-tall mechanical floral clock, playground equipment, and 12 pear trees said to have been planted by the city's French settlers, the highlight of the park was the opulent 185-foot-tall minaret-style stand-pipe tower that not only maintained water pressure but doubled as a breathtaking observation deck for tourists. Though the tower, which was demolished in 1945, and other amenities have been lost to time, the ornate Hurlbut Memorial Gate remains. More an opulent monument to Beaux Arts architecture than a gateway, the intricate stone gate was restored in 2007, stands 50 feet high and 132 feet wide, and has a dual stairway leading to a terrace 12 feet above the ground. Though entrance is no longer permitted, visitors to the Brede-Mueller masterpiece, which fronts the street, can also spy the classical, historic High Lift Building pumping station, which is still in operation today, behind the wrought iron fence in the distance. Please note that the horse troughs on the gate are no longer operational, so please seek water for your steed elsewhere. *Located at the intersection of Cadillac Blvd. and Jefferson Ave.*

POINTS OF INTEREST

Cow Head - Built in 1959, this curious piece of commercial statuary—a gigantic bull head—sits atop a shuttered neighborhood dairy. You may have caught a glimpse of it in the movie 8 Mile. *13099 Mack Ave.*

Birdie Records - This abandoned storefront, just across the street from the blistering glow of "The Gold Mine," was once home to the 1980s label that produced a mix of soul, funk, and disco from artists such as Ronnie Hudson, Salvatore, and The Exportations. *6352 Gratiot Ave.*

Charles Trowbridge House - Sitting quietly on the southern side of busy East Jefferson Avenue, this Victorian home is the oldest building in the city, built as a private residence in 1826. The building is now home to a handful of small businesses. *1380 E. Jefferson Ave.*

Christ Church of Detroit - The oldest Protestant church in Michigan, this Episcopalian English Gothic Revival church was completed in 1863. The stunning light-stone church features ornate stained-glass windows and a five-story bell tower topped by an ornamental spire. *960 E. Jefferson Ave.*

Design on the Prairie House - Built in 2009 by a team of Cranbrook Academy of Art architects, this home is a model of contemporary architecture set in a largely vacant area, creating a stark, beautiful juxtaposition. *2126 Pierce St.*

Earthworks Urban Farm - Founded in 1997 as a small garden, this now sizable farm grows fresh produce that goes directly into the meals served at the attached Capuchin Soup Kitchen and serves as a learning and advocacy center to help all people get access to fresh food. *1264 Meldrum St.*

Farnsworth Neighborhood - This small, dynamic, collaborative, tight-knit, neighborhood is home to the Farnsworth Community Garden, Rising Pheasant Farms, and several other family farms and pocket gardens, as well as a couple of community arts organizations and endeavors such as The Yes Farm and the Ocelot Print Collective. *Farnsworth St. and Moran St.*

Father Bernard "Solanus" Casey Grave - Father Casey, the first U.S.-born man, officially named "venerable" by the Vatican (the second step along the Catholic path to sainthood), is buried here in Saint Bonaventure Monastery. Miraculous cures have been attributed to Father Casey and account for the pilgrimages some people make to this resting place. *1740 Mt. Elliott St.*

Father Gabriel Richard Sculpture - This bold granite sculpture depicting one of Detroit's most important historical figures was commissioned by the Works Progress Administration in the late 1930s and executed by sculptor Leonard Jungwirth.
7478 E. Jefferson Ave.

Faygo Factory - A favorite since 1907, Detroit's popular Faygo soda pop has been manufactured and headquartered here since 1935.
3579 Gratiot Ave.

Feedom Freedom Garden - This community garden beautifies its neighborhood and acts as a platform for the social justice mission of its founders, Myrtle Thompson Curtis and Wayne Curtis.
876 Manistique St.

Gospel Hands Car Wash - This abandoned church/car wash is perhaps proof enough that the business idea you had a few years ago wasn't as original as you thought. *8700 Mack Ave.*

Indian Village Centennial Garden - Maintained by the Indian Village Men's and Women's Garden Clubs, this beautifully landscaped ornamental garden features wrought-iron gates and a gazebo and manicured lawns. *2568 Seminole St.*

Indian Village Tennis Club - Established in 1912, this members-only tennis club's three clay courts fit neatly in this neighborhood of stately homes. With a $5 guest pass, visitors can swing racquets with higher-income brackets. *1502 Parker Ave.*

Manoogian Mansion - Located in the historic Berry Subdivision, this 1928 Mediterranean Revival Style mansion serves as the official residence of the city's mayor. *9240 Dwight Dr.*

Martha Reeves Home - This two-story building was home to the young singer as she was moving up the ranks at Motown Records. *2409 Townsend St.*

Michael Jackson Death and Obama Inauguration Commemorative Murals - These two larger-than-life murals depict a smiling, radiant President Barack Obama post-2008 inauguration, and a Smooth Criminal-era Michael Jackson.
Fischer St. and Gratiot Ave.

Moses W. Field House - Now sandwiched in an early 20th century city block, this 1860s brick and stone home is one of only two known remaining farm houses in the city, built when the area around it was countryside. *2541 Field St.*

Sippie Wallace Grave - Buried in Trinity Cemetery, Sippie Wallace was one of the great blues singers of her time—with a career stretching across much of the 20th century and featuring collaborations with Louis Armstrong, B.B. King, Johnny Dodds, and Clarence Williams. *5210 Mt. Elliott St.*

Small Ville Learning Farm - What started as an idea to engage at-risk youth and clean up a blighted block, has turned into a full-time urban farm that emphasizes organic growing methods and using gardening as an opportunity to strengthen community bonds. *6068 Barrett Ave.*

Sonny Bono Home - The non-Cher half of Sonny and Cher spent his first year of life in this cozy east side home. *5380 Holcomb St.*

Summer in the City Jefferson East Mural - Painted by the group in 2005, this lively installation is a meta-mural, featuring a colorful collage of other favorite Summer in the City murals, including ionic columns and contrasting geometric shapes, alongside the Woodbridge giraffe. *14367 E. Jefferson Ave.*

University Club - This Collegiate Gothic-style building, finished in 1931, was built as a gathering place for college graduates and included squash courts, a two-story great hall, and apartments for both permanent members and visiting guests. It's currently unoccupied. *1411 E. Jefferson Ave.*

Yondotega - A brick wall keeps prying eyes out of this exclusive and incredibly secretive club, which has offered its 150 members fine food and the company of other "true gentlemen" since 1891. They've been located at this location since 1959, after the first headquarters was demolished to make room for the Chrysler Freeway.
1450 E. Jefferson Ave.

Ze Mound - When the nearby marina was dredged, this enormous, grassy hill was the inadvertent byproduct. Today, it serves as a spectacular place to have a picnic or watch the International Freedom Festival fireworks display, and plays host to an annual Bastille Day celebration. *1687 Atwater St.*

CHAPTER 8
UPPER EAST SIDE

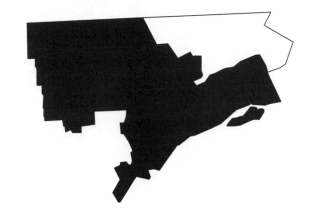

As the second-largest chapter in this book by area and population, the upper east side as defined by this guide covers nearly a quarter of the city and, consequently, offers visitors perhaps the most diverse range of experiences. The area, roughly bounded by I-94, Hamtramck, Highland Park, Woodward, 8 Mile, and the city limits, encompasses a host of neighborhoods steeped in history that often showcase resident pride and energy. These neighborhoods—including Conant Gardens, East English Village, Gratiot Woods, Greenbriar, Grixdale, Krainz Woods, LaSalle College Park, Mohican Regent, MorningSide, Nortown, Pulaski, Regent Park, Von Steuben, and Yorkshire Woods— typically feature wide, tree-lined streets with homes ranging from starter bungalows and red-brick Tudors to stately historic homes. The upper east side is among the newest areas in the city, having been annexed into Detroit between 1915 and 1926 and constructed beginning in the late 1920s through the post-war period.

As in most areas of the city, population decline and abandonment have taken a toll on many parts of the upper east side, though the impacts may be more apparent here than elsewhere. Many of the area's once prim and charming neighborhoods have developed a patina of decline punctuated by vacant homes and vacant land. In many neighborhoods, blocks have lost half or more of their homes. These challenges have at once sparked an unparalleled evolution in the traditional urban fabric and showcased the resolve of dedicated residents. In many neighborhoods beset by encroaching vacancy, residents have responded with a host of gardens, community spaces, beautiful murals, and community-led redevelopment projects. These remarkable efforts make the upper east side a destination for visitors looking to admire the city's burgeoning population of urban farms and gardens.

The city's east side is home to a majority of the city's industrial land. This proximity to industrial work has made it popular with generations of industrial workers and, as a result, this area has been home to many waves of new immigrants from other countries, other states, and other parts of the city, including large numbers of Germans, Flemish, Romanians, Italians, Poles, Czechs, African-Americans, and, more recently, Chaldean and Hmong residents. Although the area is now predominantly African-American, many former residents have left their mark in the form of active ethnic businesses that continue to operate alongside the many African-American-owned businesses.

Like the neighborhood's ongoing residential evolution, many of the upper east side's commercial corridors have a few missing teeth. These thoroughfares, namely East Warren, East McNichols, Gratiot, Mack, John R., Woodward, and Harper, offer a range of destinations, including an array of antique stores, outstanding Detroit-style barbecue, and other legendary Detroit dining institutions—including a Belgian mussel bar, a German beer hall, and the city's most famous Detroit-style pizza joint. Because these destinations lack consistent density, however, the upper east side is best explored by car.

Like any major city, Detroit has some neighborhoods that are best visited during the day or in groups. Although many neighborhoods within this chapter are safe and vibrant, some areas may be unsafe late at night, and we recommend exercising a bit of caution and practicing the same safety rules you would when visiting parts of any urban center. Many of these businesses offer secure parking.

BARS & RESTAURANTS

8 Mile Pancake House - Since this island pancake joint offers an expansive menu of lunch favorites and breakfast options, including a selection of more than 25 kinds of omelets, 8 Mile does much more than just pancakes well. That said, the namesake dish at this diner are fluffy, Frisbee-size delights, available with a variety of mix-ins, such as pecans, fruit, or chocolate chips, and are priced affordably to accommodate any carbo-loader. Visitors dine at the counter on well-used faux leather stools, or at similarly well-loved booths, in a warmly colored and mellow-lit dining room. Closed by 4pm. Wi-Fi available. *12930 E. 8 Mile Rd., (313) 839-7030.*

Asian Corned Beef Deli - As a self-proclaimed "Asian-Jewish" restaurant, Asian Corned Beef is a New York-style dive deli serving a unique take on deli fare, including its home-cured pastrami and corned beef, home-roasted turkey, and hand-brined pickles. While the deli offers a host of delicious—and more typical—deli options, it is most renowned for its delectable corned beef and pastrami egg rolls, and kimchi-laden Asian wraps. Offering only a single table, visitors should plan on carryout. Vegetarians might look elsewhere. *2847 E. 7 Mile, (313) 893-1650.*

Blue Pointe Restaurant - A laidback, refined classic since 1982, Blue Pointe Restaurant is an upscale east side destination for fine Italian and fresh seafood. The beautiful interior features elegant woodwork, fine nautical art, a host of taxidermy mounts, and a friendly, unpretentious atmosphere. The polite staff is knowledgeable and approachable, capable and willing to make scotch recommendations or discuss the merits of different cuts of meat. Although the menu is dominated by delicious Italian and seafood fare straight from the boot or the sloop—including veal scallopini, shrimp llene, fresh oysters, escargot, and fresh perch—don't overlook delectable takes on American staples, such as the crab cakes and New York strip steaks. If all steaks were this good, more cows would be cannibals. Live music on the weekends. *17131 E. Warren Ave., www.thebluepointerestaurant.com, (313) 882-3653.*

Bogart'z Cafe - This neighborhood bar and grille, dedicated to the man who believed "a hot dog at the game beats roast beef at the Ritz," stays true to form: Bogart'z offers an upscale take on bar fare in an ideal game-watching environment. Especially popular with neighboring Grosse Pointers, Bogart'z is a large, charming space dominated by Humphrey Bogart-related decor, a number of TVs, church-pew booths, and an impressive array of contemporary woodwork. Although known for its mouth-watering Buffalo burger, Bogart'z is no one-hit wonder. The less well-known Cajun burger, salmon tacos, and crab cake sliders all put on Oscar-worthy performances and are rightly revered by regulars. The carefully curated beer list and solid liquor choices offer ample reasons to raise a glass. *17441 Mack Ave., www.bogartzcafe.com, (313) 885-3995.*

Bread Basket Deli - Don't judge this book by its cover. Behind a sleepy facade, utilitarian waiting area, and bulletproof glass, the Bread Basket Deli offers a bevy of traditional delicatessen staples, including pastrami, peppered beef, corned beef, turkey pastrami, and potato knishes, alongside dishes with a distinctly Detroit flavor, such as pastrami sliders and Detroit-style sweet potato pie, which incorporates bacon as a key ingredient. The food is of unparalleled freshness. Many of the ingredients, including the corned beef, pickles, and bread and rolls, are locally made and delivered daily. Don't be deceived by the affordable prices—portion control is a foreign concept to this meat palace. The small waiting area is carryout only. Along with the west side location, located at 15603 Grand River Ave., this location is one of two Detroit locations in this small, regional chain. *17740 Woodward Ave., www.breadbasketdelis.com, (313) 865-3354.*

» Buddy's Rendezvous Pizzeria - Opening in 1936 as a neighborhood bar, Buddy's began serving its now-famous, deep-dish square pizza in 1946. It's the originator of what has come to be known as Detroit-style pizza—a deep-dish square pie with Sicilian roots featuring a deliciously greasy, chewy, and crispy crust with the sauce on the top and toppings under the cheese to prevent scorching. True to its Detroit roots, the square-shaped pizza is the result of being baked, not in a pizza pan, but an automotive parts tray. Buddy's is now a small Metro Detroit chain, but this is the original (and, in our opinion, best) location. It's got an unpretentious 1950s vibe and charming decor including a pizza-themed homage to Diego Rivera's Detroit Industry fresco cycle in the entryway. While it serves a full menu of burgers, sandwiches, soups, salads, and more that are reportedly delicious, we've never been able to resist just ordering one of its many award-winning pies. Enjoy your pizza with a pitcher or boomba of beer and be sure to step out back for a game of bocce ball after dinner. *17125 Conant St., www.buddyspizza.com, (313) 892-9001.*

» Cadieux Cafe - A destination bar on the east side for delectable Belgian cuisine and heady Trappist ales, Cadieux has been serving lovers of Flanders and Wallonia for more than 50 years. The comfy, mellow dining room is decorated by portraits of famous Belgians and is the perfect place to enjoy steamed mussels, Belgian pommes frites with mayonnaise, its notable Belgian beer soup, or Sunday rabbit dinner. In addition to live sets from local bands, the cafe features the only feather bowling in the United States, a game similar to bocce but with flattened wooden balls rolled down earthen lanes toward a feather at the other end, open to the public all nights except Tuesday or Thursday, when League experts go to work. *4300 Cadieux Rd., www.cadieuxcafe.com, (313) 882-8560.*

Capers - A destination steakhouse for the carnivore on a budget, Capers puts menu first and dispenses with unnecessary fussiness. Hidden behind an unassuming facade on Gratiot's northeast stretch, the mellow, wood-paneled dining room is usually packed to the gills with chummy, convivial regulars. Serving priced-by-the ounce steaks, Capers may offer the best cuts of meat for the value in the city. Patrons looking to prioritize their drinks over their eats can perch on the wooden stools at the bar while they sip on the gargantuan, bargain-priced 32-ounce beers. Customers may park in the private lot for free and are buzzed in. Although the beef comes a la carte, combo meals and hearty portions of sides are available at an affordable price. Dress code is casual and reservations are impossible—calling ahead is recommended. *14726 Gratiot Ave., (313) 527-2100.*

Cleopatra Mediterranean Grill - Since hanging the shingle in 2012, owner Sam Tobia's quaint neighborhood Middle Eastern spot has been pleasing east side palates with some of the city's finest, fit-for-a-pharaoh Mediterranean fare. The low-key restaurant is pleasantly clad in Egyptian mementos and ancient-Egypt-themed artwork. This unassuming ambience contributes to the restaurant's accessible atmosphere. The offerings are highly navigable for ghallaba greenhorns—the menu has vivid descriptions of every dish, and while all the dishes are flavorful, the spices are not overwhelming. The menu is large and varied, featuring outstanding takes on saji, shawarma, crushed lentil soup, koshary and mujadara. Cleopatra emphasizes quality over quantity, and while the portions are ample,

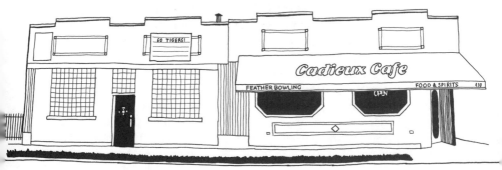

they are not particularly shareable. After your bicuspids discover the heavenly shawarma, however, you won't want to share. Great vegetarian options. *19027 Mack Ave., www.cleopatragrill.com, (313) 640-9000.*

Dairy World Food and Treats - Although it offers a menu that is as eclectic as it is delectable—including authentic pierogis, abbas, chimichangas, lasagna, tacos, four types of grape leaves, and burraks—Dairy World Food and Treats' true specialty is its ice cream and soft serve treats. Given the incredible variety of ice cream and soft serve flavors available—including root beer and praline—the range of cone options, and the number of possible toppings—such as chocolate cake and baklava—there are 129,600 possible ways to order a cone. This is, of course, in addition to the ice cream cakes, malts, milk shakes, smoothies, floats, flurries, and sundaes available. Carryout only. *19010 Woodward Ave., (313) 731-8570.*

» The Dakota Inn Rathskeller - Celebrating Detroit's rich German heritage since 1933, this charming, authentic, historic rathskeller, replete with dirndl-clad servers, dishes up delicious, hearty German food and beers (more than 20!). The original owner, Karl Kurz, worked at the Highland Park Ford Plant and toiled away during nights and weekends to transform a dilapidated Chinese laundry into this traditional German-style rathskeller in the architectural style of his native Wiekersheim, Germany. The original establishment consisted of a tiny three-stool bar, but over three generations, his family has greatly expanded on the original building and tradition. Currently run by the grandson of Kurz, the cozy, dark-wood-paneled interior is decorated with German beer steins, trophy animal mounts from family hunting trips, and hand-painted German scenes. Many nights feature live bands, and most conclude in a rousing sing-along to the traditional Schnitzelbank drinking song depicted in a lively mural in the dining room. Once a year, Dakota Inn pitches its yellow-and-white-striped tent for an authentic German beer garden, complete with German bands and polka contests, and September and October bring Oktoberfest, an especially celebratory time featuring oompah bands, chicken hats, joyous sing-alongs, and, of course, plenty of beer. Vegetarians will enjoy the vegetarisch plate. The Dakota Inn also has a downstairs banquet room available for private parties for up to 50 people, and it offers off-site German catering. Open for only lunch Wednesday-Friday and dinner Thursday-Saturday. Check the website for frequent special events. *17324 John R. St., www.dakota-inn.com, (313) 867-9722.*

Dish - There is an awfully large amount of high-quality food coming out of the tiny kitchen at Dish, a lunch-and-dinner takeout counter on the east side. With a menu shaped by a professional chef and described by customers as "gourmet," Dish offers an array of new American cuisine, including thoughtfully prepared sandwiches, salads, soups, quesadillas, pasta dishes, and a rotating selection of specials (potato-encrusted salmon is a popular option), with an emphasis on locally sourced ingredients. Wait times are minimal, and patrons concerned with their environmental footprint will appreciate Dish serving its food in biodegradable containers. *18441 Mack Ave., www.dishdetroit.biz, (313) 886-2444.*

» Dutch Girl Donuts - A magnet for Detroiters for more than 50 years, Dutch Girl is Detroit's place for doughnuts. This independent corner shop is a beloved local favorite, featuring quaint vintage blue and white awnings and signage with illustrated emblems of its namesake lass. Inside are a few spots for customers to indulge in delectable, handmade fried dough delights in flavors like blueberry, raisin, and chocolate cake, as well as traditional favorites like glazed or jelly. Open 24/6 (closed Sundays), cash only. *19000 Woodward Ave., (313) 368-3020.*

Dyer's Bar and Grill - Dyer's is one of the few places standing in its neighborhood, which makes it easy to spot and tough to pass by—which customers shouldn't. Dyer's is a true community bar—owned by the landlord of the upstairs apartments, whose tenants find themselves enjoying this dark, subdued dive with a horseshoe bar, beaded lamps, vinyl bar stools, cheap beer, and a 7-for-$1 jukebox that plays honest-to-goodness classic 45s—like Elvis, Petula Clark, Bob Seger, and Marvin Gaye. Dyer's is a speakeasy-style buzz-in joint with only well liquors and no actual "grill" food. *12241 Gratiot Ave., (313) 521-6767.*

East Bar - In a town where you can't swing an empty Stroh's without hitting a neighborhood dive bar, few stand out. The East Bar stands out. With boatloads of sailing bric-a-brac, a knotty pine interior, over-the-bar aquarium and exposed beams, this charming spot has an unassuming atmosphere reminiscent of bars in Northern Michigan. Despite the fire-sale prices on its impressive beer list, this friendly dive is more than a gymnasium for practicing Milwaukee curls. The pool table, occasional live music, dog-friendly policy, dartboard, and jovial staff make this spot a destination for a laid-back good time. Owner Clyde's small kitchen also offers a limited but delicious menu of bar fare. *15045 Mack Ave., (313) 885-6630.*

Georgia Cafe - The heir to the classic east side joint Geneva's, both in location and spirit, Georgia's has duly taken on the mission of serving east siders stick-to-the-ribs food at a price anyone can afford. This shotgun-style sliders-and-more counter is a cozy, charming place to get a quick breakfast or lunch. The restaurant features a plain white laminate interior, and customers eat sitting on short, comfy, chrome stools with the scent of grilled onions wafting over from the grill. Grab a bag of hot, fresh sliders (five for $4.50) with minimal wait. *17179 Harper Ave., (313) 882-8262.*

Golden Gate Cafe - Golden Gate Cafe's welcoming, colorful exterior is a contrast to the surrounding neighborhood, which is largely vacant. Part healing center, part vegetarian cafe, and part bohemian meeting place, Golden Gate is a surprising oasis of friendly conversation, delicious food and a warm atmosphere. Dine inside at the counter or at a warm booth nearby or eat in the serene sculpture garden outside replete with wandering chickens and a fountain. They also offer non-traditional chiropractic services combining natural chiropractic practice with cranial sacral work, shiatsu, applied kinesiology, and nutritional counseling. *18700 Woodward Ave., www.innatedetroit.com, (313) 366-2247.*

Hashbrown Cafe - Less than a mile down the road from the Conant Gardens Historic District lies this mom-and-pop business, a brunch and soul food cafe famous for fried catfish, salmon croquettes, and hand-cut hash browns. From morning to night, the menu selections are cooked to order, so visitors often take one of the purple, red, or yellow seats at the diner counter and watch the cooks chopping up fresh ingredients through the window to the kitchen. In typical diner fashion, the cafe features spacious booths lined along the front window, where families can dine and watch the Conant Street traffic. *19458 Conant St., (313) 366-0433.*

Krakus Restaurant and Bar - Though this restaurant is located just outside of Hamtramck, the little brick building maintains all of the Polish flare found there. Krakus is a family-run place with homey '70s decor, authentic homemade food, a full bar featuring Polish beers and vodka, and plenty of polka music. Some locals even prefer the food at Krakus to the Hamtramck heavy hitters Polish Village Cafe and Polonia (see separate entries). The portions are large and a great value—the Ukrainian borscht, dill pickle soup, homemade pierogi, and potato pancakes are divine—at this low-key spot for regulars and neighborhood folks who want to pop in for delicious carryout. On Saturday nights, Krakus is the place to party, with a live polka band playing until 2am with secure parking. *12900 Joseph Campau St., (313) 368-4848.*

» La Dolce Vita - The sweet life renews itself at this Italian restaurant hugging the edge of Palmer Park. Temporarily exit contemporary America in favor of lambent old-world elegance and understated class. La Dolce Vita serves traditional and modern Italian/continental fare, including a popular lasagna béchamel, decadent escargot, homemade gnocchi, and flavorful seafood, all with an emphasis on freshness and distinct flavor profiles. Among the desserts is a world-renowned tiramisu (OK, perhaps just city-renowned, but you could have fooled us). The entrance is off Parkhurst, through the restaurant's utopian garden patio, which is available for al fresco dining and occasional live music in the summer. Despite its popularity, the restaurant retains an allure of seclusion, making it suitable for a romantic meal or a peaceful brunch. *17546 Woodward Ave., www.ldvrestaurant.net, (313) 865-0331.*

Louie's Ham and Corned Beef - An east side favorite for more than 40 years, Louie's Ham and Corned Beef is a charming yet unassuming gem with a healthy dose of both hominess and pluck. The restaurant is simple and straightforward with formica booths, porcine-related art, and a vintage open kitchen. In a city known for its high corned beef standards, Louie's stands out for its tender, fresh, and flavorful corned beef. Although the entire menu—including the all-day breakfast items—will not disappoint, the renowned stacked ham sandwich and Louie's Combo—stacked pastrami and corned beef on grilled rye—are the belles of the ball. *16661 Harper Ave., (313) 881-4250.*

Marcus Hamburgers Restaurant - Opened in 1929, this unassuming dive diner is best known for its acclaimed Marcus burger—a harmonica-shaped burger served in a hot dog bun with onions. With the ever-present gang of bantering regulars at the distinctive horseshoe counter providing free entertainment, visitors can enjoy Marcus burgers or one of the many slobber-worthy Polish options, such the handmade pierogi or chicken dumpling soup. With recipes honed over several generations, Macedonian-immigrant owners Mike and Louie Lozanovski never disappoint. A great place for a sighting of Detroit's finest. *6349 E. McNichols Rd., (313) 891-6170.*

» Milt's Gourmet Barbecue - Founded by Milt Goodson in 1989, Milt's has been bringing delicious, drool-worthy barbecue ribs and chicken to the city's east side for a generation. Don't be fooled by the sleepy facade and spare dining area—the food is unbelievably outstanding. Milt's specializes in authentic Detroit-style barbecue, a rich, juicy, fatty, sauce-laden take on the more common St. Louis or Texas styles. In addition to the renowned chicken and ribs, Milt's offers delectable catfish and turkey, toothsome mac and cheese, and nectarous turtle cake. Hire a veggie-sitter and make this one a carnivore's night out: Of the 32 main dishes on the menu, none are vegetarian-friendly.
19143 Kelly Rd., (313) 521-5959.

Nunn's Barbeque - Barbecue is a hot topic in Detroit, and while people are passionate about their opinions, this is definitely the kind of city where there is room for more than one kind of 'cue. Nunn's is carryout-only and offers barbecue in the Southern soul food tradition: meaty fall-off-the-bone ribs cooked in a massive smoker and slathered in Nunn's own seasoning blend and spicy-sweet sauce, hand-battered jumbo shrimp, garlicky greens, decadent yams, pig feet, and homemade banana pudding and peach cobbler. There's nothing fancy about this sparkling-clean BBQ joint, but it takes its food seriously, and serious barbecue fans need to do their lives a favor and check this place out—it's "the meat that can't be beat!"
19196 Conant St., (313) 893-7210.

Other Side Lounge - Whether you're in the mood for a fishbowl-size Long Island iced tea or a glass of wine, this LGBTQ lounge in a contemporary setting offers more than a full bar bathed in pink light and crisp sound system. The modern zen décor, complete with bamboo green walls, stone tiles, and a fenced-in outdoor oasis smoking patio area, creates a relaxed atmosphere for gathering with friends. Secure parking is available, as is free Wi-Fi access.
4933 E. 7 Mile Rd., www.othersidelounge.com, (313) 305-7793.

The Sandwich Shop - Since opening in 2012, these maestros of meat have been winning—and perhaps clogging—the hearts of east siders with their brilliant and delicious sandwiches. While the exterior of the recently rehabbed space is adorned with murals of anthropomorphized sandwiches merrily chasing one another, the interior is far more plain and unassuming, dominated by a handful of tables and a large wall of bulletproof glass. Thankfully, this glass is not sandwich proof. Although The Sandwich Shop has a fairly diverse menu—including jumbo shrimp, catfish, stuffed potatoes, and fried okra—the focus is on its 12 equally delicious signature sandwiches and burgers. Among these, the Texan—a half-pound of ground beef stuffed with corned beef and Swiss cheese—and the Renaissance—a half-pound of corned beef with Swiss, coleslaw, and Russian dressing—are the most exceptional. In every case, the meat is fresh, well-seasoned, and cooked perfectly. Vegetarians should wait in the car. *19153 Van Dyke Ave., (313) 826-1437.*

The Stone House Bar - Billed as "Michigan's oldest continuously operating bar," the Stone House has been voted Michigan's best biker bar for three years running and has the history to back it up: The Purple Gang ran a brothel out of this 1860s farmhouse during Prohibition, complete with a tunnel dug under Woodward Avenue (then a dirt road) to smuggle in the hooch. It was a carnie haven during the life of the recently shuttered State Fairgrounds. These days, you can expect a mix of bikers, neighborhood eccentrics, and Detroit lifers. Its defining feature is the two-story front porch, where you can grab a bird's-eye view of the surrounding environs on a lazy summer afternoon. In addition, there's a horseshoe pit outside, but don't step up to the plate unless you're bringing your A-game: The regulars are pros. The bar hosts fowling (a combination of football and bowling) on Wednesdays and holds live rock and blues shows most Saturday nights. *19803 Ralston St., (313) 891-3333.*

Two Way Inn - Although called Two Way Inn, its name stems from the fact that it has two ways out—when your old lady comes looking for you through the front door, you can dash out the back. If these walls could talk, you could expect a lot of winking wisdom from the venerable Two Way Inn. Originally opened in 1876, it's Detroit's oldest existing bar, and it looks the part, with an interior of ancient wooden floors, antique kegs, and long-abandoned farm tools decorating the walls. These days, the bar draws a steady crowd of Hamtramck boosters, who make the short trek every first Friday for a neighborhood hootenanny. Be careful with that bell above the bar though—give it a ring, and you might find yourself buying a round for the bar. *17897 Mt. Elliott St., (313) 891-4925.*

Vergote's - This affordably priced "you buy, we fry" joint on the east side is the oldest of its kind in Detroit—around since 1939 and still family-owned and operated. A large selection of fresh fish—filleted or whole—is available, as well as an assortment of chicken cuts, visible in dozens of feet of display cases, as well as frozen selections, breading, seasoning, and sauces. "You buy, we fry" is just what it sounds like—fresh or frozen is available for in-house frying, grilling, Cajun prep, or uncooked. There is also a carryout menu of dinner specials available and house-made soups—gumbo, etouffee, and chowder. *16523 Harper Ave., (313) 882-9030.*

SHOPPING & SERVICES

Allemon's Landscape Center - In the garden and landscaping business for 80 years, Allemon's has been an east side green thumb's destination for three generations. With a well-organized, but packed, shop that spills out of the traditional red brick commercial building, through the large open-air sheds, and onto the sidewalk, the store stocks seeds, flowers, shrubs, trees, fountains, mulch, pavers, fencing, lighting, and every other outdoor necessity you can or can't think of. Thanks to their years in the business, the seasoned staff is full of bona fide experts on the subject of landscaping on hand to answer all manner of relevant queries. *17727 Mack Ave., www.allemons.com, (313) 882-9085.*

All Star Books - Packed with finds, All Star Books is a book and comic fan's paradise, with literally hundreds of thousands of titles. Both a new and used bookstore, the shop specializes in pulp fiction, 1930s and '40s collectibles (think vintage action figures, radios, and other paraphernalia), mainstream and offbeat graphic novels, and comics. In addition to shelves and boxes stuffed with used comics, the shop stocks almost 500 active comic book serials. In addition to the family-friendly fare, All Star carries a curated selection of adult titles. A word of warning: Though it's worth the digging, alphabetization is a bit of a lost art for All Star's collection of used comics. *16725 Mack Ave., (313) 881-7599.*

Another Time Antiques - With the sounds of Vivaldi pouring onto the sidewalk past the intricate shop window displays, it's hard to resist stopping in. Located in the heart of Antique Row, this charming neighborhood antique shop is home to a diverse selection of elegant and winsome antiques, and possibly the city's finest antique lamp repair operation. Specializing in smaller early 20th century goods—and especially period lamps and clocks—this small shop has affordable rates on its typically high-end offerings. *16239 Mack Ave., (313) 886-0830.*

Archer Record Pressing - One of the last 10 record-pressing plants in the world, this third-generation family business has been working hard for Detroit music since 1965. Because record production equipment hasn't been manufactured since the mid-1980s, Archer family members employ specialized repair skills and knowledge of the finicky equipment to keep the plant's five presses running. From Motown artists to rock 'n' roll to hip-hop to techno and other electronic music, Archer has helped create the music that has put Detroit on the map. With record pressing plants closing as owners retire without anyone left to take the torch, we're so glad that business is up at Archer, due in large part to the major Detroit techno artists who rely on vinyl, such as Kevin Saunderson, Juan Atkins, Derrick May, and Theo Parrish releasing internationally acclaimed records pressed locally. Archer is a favorite among local groups large and small who want to put out LPs the old-fashioned way.
7401 E. Davison St., www.archerrecordpressing.com, (313) 365-9545.

Arts & Scraps - Arts & Scraps is a crafter's paradise! This nonprofit recycles 28 tons of reusable industrial material a year, sorting it into hundreds of affordable, useful, creative, and learning materials, like cans, frames, sewing notions, cardboard, papers of all sorts, fabrics, tickets, canisters, yarn, you name it. Be sure to check out the craft kits it assembles from donated materials ($2 each, with discounts for multiples). Arts & Scraps gives back to the community to help people think, create, and learn through its many programs, in all providing recycled scraps for minimal cost to 3,300 organizations and classrooms annually, reaching 275,000 people of all ages and abilities each year, and it can even bring programs and materials to those who can't get to the facility with the ScrapMobile bus. Arts & Scraps is open only Tuesdays, Thursdays, and Saturdays for shopping, but check the website for information on workshops, birthday party hosting, field trips, volunteer opportunities, and more.
16135 Harper Ave., www.artsandscraps.org, (313) 640-4411.

Better Made Potato Chip Factory & Store - Distinguished by the bonnet-clad Miss Better Made who graces every bag, Better Made potato chips have been a Detroit institution since 1930. Located on a once-busy stretch of Gratiot Avenue, the factory, which sources Michigan potatoes for eight in-season months, processes 60 million pounds of potatoes every year through an automated system of lifts, conveyors, washers, peelers, slicers, fryers, and packaging machines. While it no longer offers factory tours, the factory store is the only place to buy the classic thin, crispy chips fresh, straight off the line. In addition to all of the standard varieties—and they do have all the standard varieties—the factory store sells dozens of harder to find snack foods, such as chocolate covered potato chips, potato sticks, a variety of popcorns, and the famously elusive Rainbow Chips—made from potatoes with a higher sugar content, which gives them color marks and a slightly sweet taste. *10148 Gratiot Ave., www.bmchips.com, (313) 925-4774.*

Bike Tech - Whether you're looking to hit the beach, the trails, the ramps, or the streets, or just looking to ride off your February thighs, the knowledgeable and friendly mechanics at Bike Tech can help you whip your whip into shape or find you the perfect new ride. Owner Brian Pikielek's large shop carries an almost-unparalleled selection of restored vintage bicycles alongside their impressive selection of new bicycles—namely, Raleigh, Diamondback, and Fuji models—and diverse parts selection. Though the shop is unique for its knowledge of classic road bikes, the knowledgeable staff works on everything from penny-farthings to pursuit bikes. Ideal for the cost-conscious cyclist. *18401 E. Warren Ave., www.biketech.us, (313) 884-2453.*

Bishr Poultry and Food Center - While this Yemini market offers standard dry goods, canned items, dairy products, and frozen foods, it also offers freshly slaughtered Amish chicken. Stroll past the store-length buffet counter to scan the aromatic selection of prepared halal poultry in every style imaginable, including rotisserie, fried, broasted, and grilled. Any poultry dish may be coupled with Yemini side dishes, ranging from vegetables and hummus to basmati rice. The real excitement of this store hides in the back room, where clear

vinyl curtain strips give way to the halal butchering area. Animal lovers, beware! Thrill-seekers and poultry purists may observe the butchering process, and shoppers may even pick out their desired white-feathered Amish chicken from the cage. Soft-stomached customers can get their kicks at the front of the store, where bulk spices may be purchased by the pound. Customers can scoop desired amounts of fresh saffron, cinnamon, and other spices into clear plastic bags from the self-serve Plexiglas wall unit. *12300 Conant St., (313) 892-1020.*

Eastside Locksmiths - While still maintaining the mom-and-pop lock shop appeal, Eastside Locksmiths has serviced the east side since the 1930s. Every size and kind of key hangs from hooks on pegboard walls, while antique key-cutting machines and tools remain on display behind the cashier's counter. Opened in the 1930s as a bike shop, the store got into the lock business first by selling bike locks and offering locksmith services during slower winter months. In the 1970s, the globalized economy flooded the bike market with cheaper options sold at department stores and other chain locations, so the store switched to sell only locks. Now, the store continues to innovate to meet the neighborhood needs by offering lock services and lawn mower and snow blower repair. *15138 E. Warren Ave., www.eastsidelocksmithsllc.wordpress.com, (313) 881-0280.*

Energy 4 Life Health Food Store - Energy 4 Life is a veritable apothecary of alternative remedies and supplements. Customers walking in the store will enjoy a bouquet of herbs, loose teas, nettles, and seeds emanating from the oversize glass jars along the sidewall and available by the ounce. Aside from teas and supplements, the store also sells cleanses and hygiene products, and services such as infrared saunas and herbal body wraps. The setting for Energy 4 Life is far from boilerplate new age, instead a simple black tin ceiling, white walls, worn furniture, and durable wood cabinetry, underscoring the emphasis of the devotion dedicated to craft, rather than image. *16135 Mack Ave., www.energy4lifehealth.com, (313) 640-5790.*

Joe Randazzo's - Since 1953, Randazzo and his family have been selling locally grown fruits and vegetables at extremely competitive prices at its original location on Outer Drive and later at subsequent satellites in the suburbs. In addition to standard produce options, Randazzo's is loaded with trays upon trays of exotic fresh fruits and vegetables from around the world, including hard-to-find Indian bitter melons, young Thai coconuts, a multitude of spicy peppers, and plenty of other fresh goodies. As one of the largest produce retailers in the state, Randazzo's has become a go-to wholesale option in addition to retail. Shopping can get congested on evenings or weekends, so customers are advised to take advantage of the 6am opening time. *5240 E. Outer Drive, www.joerandazzos.com, (313) 892-0093.*

The Lobster Pot - A neighborhood seafood market that's been peddling the bounty of the lake (and sea) to the east side for more than 50 years, the Lobster Pot sells an assortment of fresh and frozen seafood unparalleled in the neighborhood in quality and variety. Located in a charming, two-story brick building dotted with large arched-windows, retro neon-signs, and murals of shorelines and lively lobsters, the store is the retail front end of Michigan Food Sales, a large regional wholesale seafood business that supplies nearby stores, restaurants, and country clubs. Because of the large-volume wholesale business conducted in the back of the house, the seafood available at the Lobster Pot is maximally fresh, and large catches like swordfish and tuna are filleted in house. Look for seasonal specials like stuffed flounder, and don't be shy about special requests. *16901 Harper Ave., (313) 882-7400.*

Mike's Antiques - On his piece of the east side, Mike might be considered the neighborhood "pops." He gives advice to the younger visitors, offers them deals on bikes and secondhand household items, and discusses his ideas about politics and the world today. Customers won't find a specialized selection of antiques, but Mike's Antiques carries more and more secondhand items that people in the neighborhood are looking for. Come for the conversation, for the advice on antiquing (and life), and for the chance to dig around through stacks of books, lamps, paintings, furniture pieces, and a few racks of vintage clothing. *11109 Morang Dr., (313) 881-9500.*

Park Antiques - The largest shop along Antique Row, this large, friendly, and eclectic neighborhood antique shop is known for its relatively modest prices and impressive selection of picture frames, bookends, and equestrian-themed gewgaws. Given the eclectic array of products from the mid-19th through mid-20th centuries, it is hard to leave empty-handed. Visitors are free to wander the narrow trails between saturated shelves of curiosities and vintage goods among the store's four large rooms. *16311 Mack Ave., (313) 884-7652.*

Sunnyside Bakery & Deli - An institution and one of Detroit's oldest neighborhood bakeries, Sunnyside has lived on while much of the neighborhood that surrounds it has faded. Recognizable for the campy murals depicting anthropomorphic coffee and doughnuts, the bakery, which specializes more in mid-century style baked goods than whole-grain items, still produces fresh bread, buns, doughnuts, and other sweets in-house, which it wholesales throughout the Metro Detroit area. Though some assortment of baked goods is available throughout the day, the best selection—much of it hot—is found in the morning. *5422 E. McNichols Rd., (313) 366-3277.*

CULTURAL ATTRACTIONS

Parade Company Tours - Take a peek backstage and see the Parade Company studio at work. The Parade Company—the beloved nonprofit that hosts the nationally televised America's Thanksgiving Parade, the Target Fireworks, and the Turkey Trot fun run—allows visitors to see behind the scenes as the staff prepares for the next Thanksgiving parade and to explore its extensive 110,000-square-foot warehouse. The exceedingly friendly and knowledgeable tour guides introduce visitors to the artists who develop costumes and floats and show visitors 60 beautiful floats, more than 3,000 costumes, and the world's largest collection of papier-mâché heads. While a guaranteed hit among younger visitors, adults will enjoy seeing floats up close and seeing how they're built. *9500 Mt. Elliott St., www.theparade.org, (313) 923-7400.*

ENTERTAINMENT & RECREATION

Balduck Park - Balduck Park is actually two separate well-maintained parks on either side of Chandler Park Drive on the city's far east side. One is a campus with an open field with baseball diamonds (including backstops), and soccer or peewee football areas, outdoor basketball courts, a small fieldhouse, and Balduck's most-loved feature, which sees use typically only a few weeks a year: a sledding hill—perfect for youths or irrepressible grownups on plastic discs to carom down with abandon on snowy days. Across Chandler Park Drive is a much smaller field surrounded by a small urban forest that is great for barbecuing and summer gatherings. In recent years, Friends of the Alger Theatre has offered free feature movies on the hill every summer, including live music, cartoons, and refreshments. *Chandler Park Dr. between Radnor St. and Canyon St., www.algertheater.org, (313) 343-9087.*

Bel Air 10 Theater - In a town with only two first-run movie theaters, the 10-screen Bel Air is a relative mammoth. Tucked off 8 Mile Road in the Bel Air Center Plaza shopping center, the theater boasts many contemporary updates, including digital projection, Dolby Digital 7.1 Surround Sound, and 3D projection capability. In addition to a healthy selection of first-run titles, which favors action and horror films, the theater also offers live projections of Detroit Lions football games. Pricing is generally a bargain: Matinees are $5, regular adult pricing is $7, and sports broadcasts are free with a concession purchase. *10100 E. 8 Mile Rd., www.belair10theater.com, (313) 438-3494.*

Detroit Rugby Football Club - Detroit Rugby has a legacy in Detroit that is more than 40 years old and more than 1,500 players proud. A men's team originally dubbed the Cobras (for its players who engineered the Ford sports car) began playing competitive national rugby on the fields of Belle Isle in 1968 and moved its practice and home field to northeast Detroit in 1979. DRFC has three teams, including a Division II men's team, a Division I women's team that won national championships in 2003 and 2004, and an over-35 Detroit Old Guys Select (D.O.G.S.) that plays under modified rules. The verdantly gritty Farwell Field hosts three pitches, which are cleared of tall grass for clean, proper play. Spectating at spring and fall matches is welcome, though seating is BYO. Alcohol prohibited. *Farwell Field: 4400 E. 8 Mile Rd., www.detroitrugby.org.*

Dorais Velodrome - The Dorais Velodrome, initialized during the '67 riots and completed (perhaps apocryphally) the day Neil Armstrong set foot on the moon, is a certain anomaly for the Motor City. This 250-meter ovular concrete bicycle racing track with 45-degree banks and a green median featuring sunflower plants has endured a generation of neglect and abuse to persist in its present state. The track has been tagged with spray paint and is scarred with cracks and patches up to 4 inches in height, so road riding is somewhat dicey, but attentive riders will find the track navigable. The track is set in a well-maintained Dorais Park at the foot of Derby Hill but sees little casual use. Several times a year, the velodrome comes alive for Thunderdrome, a Woodstock-on-wheels-style bike, moped, and motorcycle race—see more in the events listings.
Mound Rd. and E. Outer Drive, www.thunderdrome.com.

Fowling Warehouse - What the heck is fowling you ask? Popular with tailgaters and juggalos (ICP has been know to celebrate Juggalo Day here), but tons of fun for everyone, fowling is a football and bowling hybrid where teams are positioned across from one another with the objective of knocking down the other team's 10 pins with a football. The Fowling Warehouse is located in a massive old toy factory—with a vividly painted facade covered in large images of toys—a space it shares with the Chocolate Cake Design Collective and a Cranbrook graduate art gallery and workspace. There is usually open play during weekdays, but Mondays and Fridays are league days. Admission is $5-10, which gets you unlimited fowling until close on the first-come, first-served lanes. The warehouse tends to get pretty hot in the summer and chilly in the winter months, so dress appropriately and feel free to stop at the party store on the way for BYO libations. In case you were wondering, fowling rhymes with bowling. Check the website for special events, including rock-and-fowl. *17501 Van Dyke St., www.whatsfowling.com.*

Harpos Concert Theatre - This independent cinema-cum-rock-hall, which books its own shows, is known in the area as the optimal venue to see thrash, metal, hardcore, speed, industrial, and modern crossover acts. Built during an era when economic depression was waiting for world war to spark the country into action, Harpos has endured over the years to become a destination metal hall. Originally the Harper Theatre, this movie house built in the Art Moderne style mutated into a discotheque in the 1970s, giving it its (seldom-deployed) light-up dance floor. The end of the decade saw Harpos reinvented as a rock venue, featuring bands like Bachman-Turner Overdrive and Blue Öyster Cult, even introducing U2 to the Motor City concert scene. Eventually, Harpos transitioned to a venue fully devoted to metal and hardcore, attracting major acts such as Motörhead, Anthrax, The Misfits, Slayer, and GWAR to perform from its prominent 10-foot stage deep into the cavernous remnants of an ornate ballroom. Action is fueled by affordable alcohol. *14238 Harper Ave., www.harposconcerttheatre.com, (313) 824-1700.*

Renaissance Bowling Center - With an exterior decorated in bright red triangular stalactites and a neon-fringed sign, this community bowling area is impossible to overlook. Inside Renaissance are 50 new lanes outfitted with modern score computers and screens with evening games asking only $2.50 per person, in addition to daily bowling specials, as well as an updated bar and a kitchen for rollers to refuel. Renaissance prides itself on being the only bowling alley in Michigan owned by a black woman and emphasizes providing a venue for local residents to meet and socialize. Group deals, event rental, and opportunities for fund-raisers are all available. Closed Monday. Call for daytime hours. *19600 Woodward Ave., (313) 368-5123.*

SITES

Georgia Street Community Collective - GSCC is a campus of vegetable gardens, fruit orchards, animal pens, a small park, library and computer lab, and community center. At the collective, food and resources are shared among residents, including myriad vegetables, fruits, duck and chicken eggs, and goat's milk. The campus encompasses numerous lots on a quiet east side intersection, used and supported by the neighborhood. GSCC is the result of the efforts of local resident Mark "Cub" Covington, who began reclaiming the area in 2007 by clearing vacant lots of trash, and then planting gardens to create litter-resistant space. Cub hosts an array of public events, including a street fair, movie nights, Easter egg hunts, and holiday dinners. GSCC attracted international interest when London's Observer wrote about it in 2010—which led British trance label Anjunabeats to pay for landscaping work and park resources. GSCC is a destination for those looking to visit one of the city's most renowned urban farms and visitors looking to make a difference: GSCC is constantly seeking partners and donations of any kind—tools, school supplies, dry goods, financial support, and volunteer teachers to further their admirable mission. Although Cub welcomes visitors to admire and explore the garden at any time, it is best to visit during one of his public events. *8902 Vinton St., www.georgiastreetcc.com, (313) 452-0684.*

Power House Productions - Acclaimed local artists and husband-and-wife-team Mitch Cope and Gina Reichart founded a collaboration called Design 99 in 2007 out of a Hamtramck storefront to explore contemporary art and architectural practice. Since 2008, the pair has focused their work in their neighborhood, beginning with the Power House—an abandoned home they bought for a widely reported song, and used to investigate off-grid power and public art with neighborhood participation. The Power House is run on solar and wind power, and Cope and Reichert hope to turn the system into a replicable model. Since the house's launch and vast media exposure, the project has grown quickly and expanded into a constellation of other homes and sites in the neighborhood as they've taken on new projects, helped others buy homes, and worked with their neighbors and dozens of local and international artists (including a residency program sponsored by Juxtapoz Magazine). Now a nonprofit called Power House Productions, it utilizes the space and neighborhood as a laboratory for methods, explorations, off-grid energy solutions, public art initiatives, and as a center for fostering community and collaboration. The recent Ride It Sculpture Park, a new collaborative skate park off of the Davison Freeway and Conant Street, is a great example of how the pair's endeavors continue to evolve. The Power House is located at 12650 Moran St. at Lawley Ave.; and other projects are located in the immediate neighborhood. *The Ride It Sculpture Park is located at E. Davison St. and Klinger St.*

Ulysses S. Grant Home - Following his service in the Mexican-American War—long before he was a dominant Union leader in the Civil War or elected president of the United States, Ulysses S. Grant was assigned to a post in Detroit and lived in this home. Though this Greek Revival house was originally located on Fort Street, just outside of Fort Wayne, it was bought by the Michigan Mutual Liability Company in the 1950s and moved to the State Fairgrounds to preserve its historical legacy. Naturally, it was during his time in Detroit that then-Lieutenant Grant developed the "taste for good times" that would eventually lead to him being decommissioned in 1854—until his career was redeemed by a desperate Lincoln. *Though the home is not currently open to the public, it is visible from State Fair St., just east of the foot of Ralston St.*

POINTS OF INTEREST

Blessed Hands Hair and Nail Salon Sign - This salon has finally figured out a way to merge the Detroit skyline with Egyptian pyramids, disembodied hands, and an incredibly muscular pharaoh who is emerging from the Detroit River. *19111 Helen Ave.*

C.C.C. Club - It was here in 2006 that rapper Proof, mentor to Eminem and member of the hip-hop group D12, was tragically shot and killed during a fight over a game of pool. *15304 E. 8 Mile Rd.*

Coleman A. Young International Airport - Though it no longer offers commercial flights, Coleman A. Young International Airport (formerly City Airport), FAA code DET, was the city's main airport until 1947. Today, it fields primarily private planes. *11499 Conner St.*

Eastside Check Cashing Mural - The angelic visage of former mayor Coleman A. Young looks down over the social and political history of Detroit in this intricate mural. *13240 E. McNichols St.*

Faygo Ghost Sign - This absolutely gorgeous old mural coats the side of a building in vibrant colors, advertising Detroit's favorite Faygo soda. *8745 Mt. Elliott St.*

GM Poletown Plant - Once home to the active Poletown community—and its 4,200 residents—the neighborhood was contentiously erased through eminent domain to make way for this plant in 1981. The protests, some of which turned violent, resulted in Supreme Court rulings that restricted municipal takings. *Harper Ave. and Mt. Elliott St.*

John DeLorean Home - This cozy home on the northeast side of the city was where the man famous for designing the car immortalized in the Back to the Future films spent most of his childhood. *17199 Marx St.*

Laid in Detroit - Playing off the phrase "Made in Detroit," this small plot on the east side of the city is host to a fabulous duck farm and acts as a great resource for anyone looking for help raising poultry of all kinds. *4121 Neff Ave.*

Malcolm X Home - Born in Omaha, Nebraska, and spending much of his life on the road, Malcolm X spent some important time living here with Nation of Islam member Robert Davenport and his wife, Dorothy. *18827 Keystone St.*

Marshall Mathers Home - Hip-hop superstar Marshall Mathers (better known by the moniker Eminem) lived in this house as a teenager in the late 1980s and early 1990s. The home was featured on the cover of his 2000 album "The Marshall Mathers LP." *19946 Dresden Ave.*

Midland Steel Strike - In 1936, 1,200 day-shift steelworkers sat down and halted production for eight days at this location, performing the first sit-down strike in the city's history. *6660 Mt. Elliott St.*

Mondrian Building - This vacant store has been wonderfully wrapped in a mural that recalls the iconic paintings of artist Piet Mondrian. *14606 Harper Ave.*

The African Amalgamation of Ubiquity Mural - On an especially beat-up intersection, this mural, depicting important figures in African and African-American history, stakes its claim to fame with one of the greatest titles in mural history. *9980 Gratiot Ave.*

Theatre Bizarre - From 2000 to 2009, this was the site of an elaborate, unlicensed Halloween spectacle highlighted by enormous hand-built sets. Shut down by the city in 2010, the artists have moved the party to the Masonic Temple (see event listing), but the sets remain behind. *967 W. State Fair Rd.*

Tom Selleck Home - This east side home was where the young actor gained his appreciation for the Detroit Tigers and, presumably, beautiful mustaches. *10530 Lakepointe St.*

Tuba Records - Run by Marvin Jacobs, the label based here in the 1960s released records by Dee Edwards, Johnny Lytle, Derek Martin, and many others. *2952 W. Davison St.*

CHAPTER 9
NEAR WEST SIDE

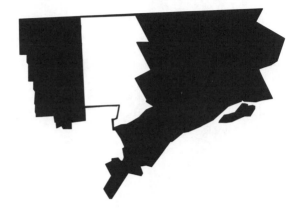

Spanning more than 30 miles, nearly 200,000 people, several vibrant neighborhoods, and one of the most diverse commercial corridors in the city, the near west side is a destination for historic sites, breathtaking architecture, and some of the city's finest comfort food. The area bounded by Greenfield Road, 8 Mile Road, Highland Park, and I-94—the area we call the near west side—is geographically the largest chapter in Belle Isle to 8 Mile, covering more people and a greater area than any other.

More than perhaps any other chapter in this book, the near west side is defined by its neighborhoods. This largely residential area is home to a constellation of communities, including the Avenue of Fashion, Aviation Subdivision, Bagley, Barton-McFarland, Fiskhorn, Green Acres, Oakman Boulevard, Palmer Park, Palmer Woods, Petosky-Otsego, Russell Woods, Sherwood Forest, and University District. Annexed into the city between 1875 and 1926, most homes in the area were built between 1920 and 1959, although many were built earlier. The neighborhoods in this chapter showcase the varying physical forms of the city's developmental history, from small brick Tudor, Cape Cod, and foursquare homes, to stately Mediterranean mansions, and large brownstone apartment buildings. Many blocks include beautiful, tree-lined streets with large porches hugging the sidewalk, creating a dense urban landscape that is especially picturesque with the fall colors.

Like many of the geographically broad chapters in this book, some areas have fared quite well in the intervening generations since their construction, while others have faced immense social, economic, and physical challenges as their residents became part of the Detroit Diaspora. For those looking to admire intact, vibrant, historic urban neighborhoods, Green Acres, Palmer Woods, Sherwood Forest, and the University District are among the city's finest, most historic residential neighborhoods and exemplify the potential impact of resident commitment and dedication. Other areas, such as Petosky-Otsego, have experienced more loss and are home to many vacant homes and vacant lots. In the face of these challenges, however, many near west side residents have beautified their communities with murals, gardens, and public art, making these neighborhoods an engaging destination for different reasons.

Although the chapter includes a number of commercial corridors, including Livernois Avenue, Fenkell Street, Grand River Avenue, McNichols Road, Oakman Boulevard, and 8 Mile Road, the most intact commercial center is the Avenue of Fashion, a resurgent shopping and services corridor along Livernois Avenue, between McNichols Road and 8 Mile Road, although mostly concentrated north of 7 Mile Road. While the corridor earned its name as a regional hub of apparel and accessory showrooms, retailers and wholesalers, the area has grown more diverse today, with the addition of galleries, salons, restaurants, and professional services.

Because of the scope of this chapter and the variety of neighborhoods, destinations featured here vary widely and are often geographically dispersed. Although many neighborhoods within this multifarious chapter are safe and vibrant, some areas may be unsafe late at night, and we recommend exercising a bit of caution and practicing the same safety rules you would when visiting similar areas of any urban center.

BARS & RESTAURANTS

1917 American Bistro - Tucked behind its charming retro sign and floor-to-ceiling cafe windows—and appropriately located on the Avenue of Fashion—this understated, contemporary restaurant was opened in 2010 by Donald Studvent, an automotive-worker-turned-gourmet-chef. Though the upscale atmosphere and food were recognized by Gourmet Magazine with its "Top Tables Award," the restaurant caters to all palates and budgets, with high-quality crowd pleasers like $6 build-your-own burgers, catfish, steaks, well-priced juice bar smoothies, and decadent desserts. Enjoy a drink at the small, cozy bar or stay for a meal on the rooftop garden, where open mic performances take place on Wednesday nights. *19416 Livernois Ave., www.1917americanbistro.com, (313) 863-1917.*

Akbar's Restaurant - Akbar's wears its basic food premises on its sleeve: Food should be homemade, fresh, affordable, and pork-free. This independent diner proudly advertises its support for the Detroit-born belief system of the Nation of Islam, whose most visible adherent is former Detroiter Malcolm X. Akbar's has a casual dining room of bright red wooden booths, low-key incandescent lighting, and artwork and portraiture commemorating the history and development of the civil rights movement. By no means, however, is creed a barrier to the agnostically hungry—Akbar's maintains a base of regulars with friendly service, quality ingredients, and excellent value. A breakfast special including eggs, beef sausage, potatoes, toast, and grits checks in at under $4. Open early and seven days a week. *12943 Fenkell St., (313) 491-9398.*

Brooksey's - While it hasn't always been Brooksey's, there has been a bar at 7625 W. Warren since 1925. Ownership has changed, but the antique dark wood bar and back bar remain, adding a touch of old-timey class to a modern social spot. Inside is a deep, cavernous place with a well-loved dance floor flanked by two poles available for use as long as patrons keep clothed with amber-tinted lights around a brass-colored ceiling rail turned on when action mellows. Brooksey's brings a variety of visitors and is known among locals as a familiar spot. The outside wall bears a mural of the bar's namesake—the owner's departed father. Brooksey's maintains a community interest—open mic nights, open pool nights, and event rental are offered. *7652 W. Warren Ave., (313) 898-8099.*

Caribbean Citchen - Famous in northwest Detroit for its tender curry goat, jerk chicken, oxtails, and alliteration, Caribbean Citchen serves excellent food in the Jamaican tradition. In addition to its tasty entrees, be sure to try some of the succulent sides. Be forewarned that you'll have plenty extra for lunch tomorrow! Carryout orders comprise a majority of its business, along with catering to any occasion, but should you find yourself in the mood for the Jamaican-themed ambiance, the Citchen offers a small dining area with courteous service. Friday features escovitch snapper or kingfish, but the place sells out fast enough to warrant calling ahead. *10500 W. McNichols Rd., (313) 345-3746.*

Connie & Barbara Soul Food - The retro White Tower facade, well-loved paneling, vintage mismatched chairs and tables, and shining metal grill top smothered with hash browns and pancakes intimate the fact that Connie and Barbara haven't strayed from their winning formula for generations. Although a little rough around the edges, this otherwise charming neighborhood breakfast spot is packed with regulars and longtime fans of the restaurant's delicious collision of soul food and breakfast, such as catfish and grits, and salmon croquettes and pancakes. From the house hot sauce to a secret Kool-Aid recipe, most everything here is homemade, and the servers have a knack for remembering every visitor's name. Bring a few quarters to feed the R&B-packed jukebox. Breakfast and lunch only. *13101 W. McNichols Rd., (313) 862-5240.*

Da Kitchen II - In its bright orange and red brick building, Da Kitchen II serves up delicious Southern home cooking for everything from brunch to dinner in a spacious dining room. The butter yellow walls and bright green booths look lived-in, but they sure are comfortable, and the ample seating appeases people waiting for their freshly chopped and cooked Western omelets, salmon croquettes, and soul food dinners. Da Kitchen also serves up a wide variety of catchy slogans. When serving to-go orders, cashiers emerge from the Plexiglas-encased kitchen to personally tell customers: "See you tomorrow!" and signs state, "It's GOOD food, not FAST food." But the painted abbreviated slogan on the building may be best of all: "Cum 2 da kitchen & c what UR missin!" *15250 W. 7 Mile Rd., (313) 341-3100.*

El-Lynn's Soul Kitchen - Inside a faded, classic White Tower building, El-Lynn's has been serving cheap, satisfying soul food at its whitewashed shotgun-style counter for more than 40 years. In that time, not a single instance of unnecessary modernization has taken place—the stools are chrome with split black covers, the coolers are the original steel, and the pink-and-white metal paneling provides the same homey atmosphere it did during the Ford administration. El-Lynn's is great for its food, of course—well-portioned, homemade, and highly sought after, but for those who are spending more than a quick lunch hour, it will be apparent that friendly, honest conversation is an unexpected perk and an obvious draw for El-Lynn's many regulars. Kool-Aid is the only beverage (save for water). Closes early. *15201 Livernois Ave., (313) 862-9687.*

Elmer's Hamburgers - With an exterior that is the definition of classic White Tower architecture, Elmer's has been serving up its unique take on sliders for more than 50 years. Though the immediate neighborhood surrounding the burger palace has seen better days, faithfuls still line up for the joint's sliders, which are well done yet extra juicy, with a massive, balanced flavor, and laid out over a bed of sautéed onions and pickles. Don't let the Plexiglas separating patrons from the cashier temper your curiosity, at $1.25 each, Elmer's trademark burgers—which are larger than normal sliders—are worth the trip. Open 24 hours. *8515 W. Chicago St., (313) 933-7766.*

Gregg's Pizza & Bar-B-Que - These distinctive hand-tossed pizzas and barbecued chicken have been the talk of the neighborhood for more than a generation. Gregg's specializes in perfectly cooked thin crust pizza loaded with toppings—which includes the de rigueur options and more fresh and obscure options, like shrimp and Italian-style broccoli—which make for a healthier pie with flavors evocative of summertime. Although the diverse menu runs the gamut of the popular options, the chicken parmesan pizza, steak and cheese pizza, and supplí Italian rice balls stand out. The unassuming, Spartan interior is all business, with a small waiting area, from which customers can witness their carryout pies being spun in the air and wings dumped in the fryer. With meals that can feed a family for less than the cost of a parking ticket, this place offers an affordable option for hungry Detroiters. *17160 Livernois Ave., (313) 341-2400.*

Lou's Deli - Corned beef connoisseurs will meet their match at Lou's Deli, a carryout sandwich shop that boasts more than 10 "good-for-the-beli" creations centered around that salty-sweet deli meat. Beefheads might find it hard to look at corned beef again after tackling the intimidating Big Louie—a full pound of juicy corned beef nestled on an onion roll for $14.24. For customers who aren't looking to break the bank or bust any buttons on their pants, Lou's Deli also serves up more than 20 sandwiches and subs with heart-healthy deli meats, salads, and fried sides. Expect four-inch tall sandwiches no matter the meat, so plan on sitting and enjoying these hot specials. *8220 W. McNichols Rd., www.lousdeli.net, (313) 861-1321.*

Motor City Soul Food - Behind the simple yellow awning lies this carryout restaurant, a favorite of the Travel Channel's Bizarre Foods America. Motor City Soul Food serves up a genuine soul food buffet, featuring classic candied yams and ham hocks, perch, and meatloaf sandwiches. Hot, fresh, and ready to go, each dish is refreshed quickly as lines of loyal customers push politely through the buffet line and point through the plate glass at each item ready for their carryout boxes. *12700 W. 7 Mile Rd., (313) 863-7685.*

Panini Grill & Juice Bar - Hungry Detroiters rejoice! From her modest counter inside the Coinless Laundromat, Lynda Laurencin has elevated the lowly Panini into gourmet fare. Easily the city's best (and only?) laundromat restaurant, the Panini Grill uses all fresh ingredients and innovative flavors to produce some of the city's finest sandwiches and smoothies. Although the delicious, gobbler-laden Jive Turkey is the best-seller, the shop is unique for the wide variety of carnivore-approved vegetarian offerings, such as the Corny Beef—an incredible TVP corned beef Panini—and the Ribless—an outstanding faux-beef riblet Panini. Although delivery is available, the nearby launderers make for good people watching. *1281 Oakman Blvd., www.paninigrilljuicebar.com, (313) 334-4001.*

Rono's Family Dining - Though the exterior may look a little institutional, don't be fooled: Rono's is the place for really, really good

Caribbean Cuisine. Opened more than 30 years ago by Mama Rono, the restaurant, which emphasizes flavor over decor, has become a destination for island specialties, such as oxtail, meat patties, curry goat and turkey, ackee and saltfish, and—of course—jerk chicken, authentically smoked on a wood-chip-burning grill. Any dish is best chased with a bottle of the exceptional house-made ginger beer and followed up with a desert, like the vegan-friendly Jamaican Coconut Drops: diced coconut drizzled in brown sugar and ginger and hardened into a perfect, crunchy clump! *14001 W. McNichols Rd., (313) 862-1295.*

Stanley's Other Place - Though passersby might not be able to tell from the plain brick facade of Stanley's Other Place, stepping into this family-owned Chinese restaurant is like stepping back into a 1950s Hollywood Chinese theater. Some might wonder where Stanley's original place is, but after enjoying an evening in this vintage glamour setting, most won't care. The black lacquered tables, shining red cushioned booths, wood cut-out archways, 1950s foil wallpaper and high ceilings create the perfect atmosphere for a special night out that is easy on the pocketbook. The main dining room can accommodate a group of 20 or more—all at one round table—and the gravy-doused entrees are large enough for two to share. For a lighter meal, and a smaller bill, try the fried rice and one of Stanley's signature Mai Tais. *2411 W. 8 Mile Rd., (313) 893-9696.*

Teresa's Place - Once visitors pass through the first entryway full of signage asking customers to "keep it classy" and to abide by the two-drink minimum, Teresa's Place transforms into a dimly lit, but surprisingly sleek neighborhood hangout that lies somewhere between dive bar and upscale lounge. The interior features exposed brick walls, a flaming copper fireplace, tall, intimate booth seating, and a full bar serviced by a white-collared bartender who jokes with the regulars perched along the leather cushioned stools. Patrons are mature, polite older folks who are far from shy, so come ready to swap stories over strong drinks! Aside from good conversation, customers can enjoy tasty bar food specials like wings and burgers, while dining in or taking out. *14000 W. McNichols Rd., (313) 862-2831.*

Tom's Tavern - Affectionately dubbed the "Slanty Shanty," this legendary west side watering hole is a dive's dive as unique as they come and a favorite among nearby University of Detroit Mercy students and devoted regulars (rumored to have included the Purple Gang) since 1928. Housed in a cozy, charmingly ramshackle one-story bungalow with a sloping bare cement floor with bar stools specially tailored to fit along the incline, belly up to the bar for a bottled beer and some good conversation, take a turn on the upright piano, or feed the jukebox full of classic rock, soul, and jazz favorites. Tom's hosts an infamous annual Babe Ruth Birthday Party, which is not to be missed by any fan of the Great Bambino (or anyone else, for that matter). If you think Tom's looks closed, look again and give the door a knock; this joint is speakeasy-style. A car parked in front is a good sign that they're probably open. That said, hours vary, so it's wise to call ahead. And bundle up in the winter—it's cold inside. *10093 W. 7 Mile Rd., (313) 862-9768.*

Uptown BBQ - Follow the bright blue arrow dotted with light bulbs to Uptown BBQ, a carryout haven for fans of Detroit's own surf and turf: the rib and shrimp dinner. The most notable feature of this simple, unassuming building might be the wonderful aromatic siren's song of fresh barbecue that hangs in the air inside and out. The welcoming staff—perhaps the city's friendliest service behind bulletproof glass—are famous for making some of the city's most tantalizing ribs, with delicate seasoning, tender texture, and smoky flavor. Thanks to its renowned barbecue sauce—with a perfect balance of sweet, salty, and smoky flavor—most of the entrees are solid, including the catfish, turkey wings, perch, chickens, pork chops, and beef ribs. On the long list of sides, the collard greens, candied yams, and mac and cheese are the tastiest triumvirate. *15700 Livernois Ave., www.uptownbbq. zoomshare.com, (313) 861-7590.*

SHOPPING & SERVICES

Bosco Fish Market - Bad day fishing? Head to Bosco. Open since 1951, this longtime seafood market offers a host of fresh fish and shellfish that are delivered daily. Their impressive inventory includes common offerings like perch, catfish, orange roughy, cod, tilapia, salmon, red snapper, lake trout, shrimp, crab, and oysters, alongside less-seen options like whiting, blue gill, smelt, and croaker. For the more successful anglers, Bosco also offers fish cleaning for your daily haul. Aside from fresh seafood, Bosco also offers a you-buy-we-fry service and a limited menu of yummy carryout options like hush puppies, onion rings, and chicken nuggets. The vintage signage, friendly service, and convenient location make it a pleasure to visit. *16227 Livernois Ave., www.boscofishandseafood.com, (313) 863-8675.*

Detroit Police Auctions - Looking for the perfect gift for that special someone? Nothing says love quite like medical scales, exotic animal care equipment, or gently used Sawzalls. Held the first Saturday of every month, the live Detroit Police Seized Goods Auctions at The Auction Block offer Detroiters an opportunity for an unusual cultural experience and a chance to score bargains with stories. Although the items vary widely and depend on the season's enforcement priorities among Detroit's finest, savvy shoppers can score antique cameras, power tools, DVDs, watches, knives, sports cards, coin collections, video equipment, and furniture at prices that are a steal—both figuratively and perhaps literally. Detailed auction lists—featuring pictures—are posted online several days ahead of each auction. All bids start at $5. *12660 Greenfield Rd., www.theauctionblock.com, (313) 659-3376.*

Detroit Store Fixture Company - A Mecca for those looking to hang their shingle since 1898, the Detroit Store Fixture Company offers a cornucopia of cornucopias, baskets, mannequins, display cases, slatwall panels, bins, racks, shelving, signage, and other store fixtures and supplies. The store's simple yet well-merchandised interior demonstrates the company's expertise in store displays and design. The store's vast inventory is spread across two showrooms and includes both new and used fixtures, assuring customers of finding just the right left-hand mannequin at a price within their budget. For those looking for custom fixtures, try Basrah Store Fixtures (7451 W. 8 Mile Rd.), a neighboring store specializing in contemporary and custom fixtures. *7545 W. 8 Mile Rd., www.detroitstorefixture.com, (313) 341-3255.*

Eric's I've Been Framed - If the pun or wall-length Obama mural are any indication, this frame shop is anything but typical. The warm, gold and purple walls are decorated with immaculate examples of Eric's custom framing work, racks of music and art posters, and local artwork. In addition to offering a vast selection of more than 3,000 frames and custom mats to choose from, employees are eager to design a showcase for any unique heirloom or collector's item, and have a picture frame, shadow box, or custom Plexiglas case for any item on any budget. The store also carries a variety of other gifts and decor, including reprints of vintage advertisements, memorabilia, and a large selection of fine art photography postcards. If you're looking for a more low-key, bread-and-butter mat and frame service, check out Jo's Gallery down the street, at 19376 Livernois Ave.—another great frame shop with many local art pieces for sale. Closed Sunday and Monday. *16527 Livernois Ave., www.ericsivebeenframed.com, (313) 861-9263.*

Kingpin Airbrushing Academy - Home to Kingpin Kustomz, Liquidman Bodyart, and Cori "Tha Guru King" Tattoo, this studio is most famed for its virtuosic airbrushing, for which it caters to customers across the nation, from Beyonce to Drake. Buzz at the door, and resident artist Felle will usher you into his showroom, which is dominated by a hyper-realistic airbrushed ocean scene that stretches from floor to ceiling. In the showroom, they offer a wide-selection of pre-painted masterworks, from tromp l'oeil motorcycle helmets to decked out kicks, Kingpin artists will customize anything, from T-shirts to SUVs to concert backdrops. Don't be afraid to inquire about Celebies—dolls realistically custom painted to resemble celebrities, complete with embedded MP3 speech and song. *20094 Livernois Ave., (313) 415-6308.*

Lewis Trade Center - For 15 years, the Lewis Trade Center has been the perfect place to score treasures you didn't know you needed. With narrow winding "aisles" beset on all sides by 12-foot piles of finds—from lawn ornaments to VHS tapes to mod vases to lawn mowers—this classic, massive, neighborhood junk shop will keep the curious interested and the interested curious. Don't be afraid to ask for assistance. The proud staff will help you navigate the oft disorderly array—or will help remove obstacles from your path. *4500 Oakman Blvd., (313) 834-2023.*

Lucki's Gourmet Cheesecakes - The brainchild of 22-year-old Lucki Word, Lucki's Gourmet Cheesecakes specializes in exceptionally soft,

delicate cheesecakes, in more than 50 flavors. Covering all the bases, the establishment deliciously slings all the standards, like strawberry and Oreo, but also takes daring forays into new territory, with potentially less-enticing varieties, such as junk food and salmon and sausage. In addition to her cheesecakes, Lucki whips up homemade cobblers, ice cream, and cakes of the cheeseless persuasion, including a number of sugar-free varieties. To tempt your sweet tooth and help you make a selection, the staff offers up plentiful free samples of Lucki's tasty treats. If you're feeling as creative as the staff, you can even design your own dessert and order custom cakes.
7111 W. McNichols Rd., www.luckischeesecakes.com, (313) 272-3190.

Mike's Fresh Market - As a neighborhood institution since opening in 2007, Mike's Fresh Market is a grocer's grocer. Between greeting customers with his toothy smile, owner Mike Koza runs the largest grocery store in the city, replete with a bakery, deli, flower stand, large produce section, and meat and seafood counter. While reminiscent of some chain grocers, Mike's Fresh Market is distinct for its significant Asian, Middle Eastern, and organic food offerings, and for the cheerful decor and staff. Locavores will be pleased to see a wide variety of Michigan-grown produce, as well the city's best selection of local foodstuffs, such as McClure's Pickles, Velvet Peanut Butter, and La Jalisciense Tortillas. *19195 Livernois Ave., www.mikesfreshmarket.com, (313) 345-4711.*

Murray Lighting and Electrical - Part lighting fixture showroom and part hardware supermarket, beyond the retro walls of this large cement warehouse lies every product remotely related to the field of electrical work and lighting installation. From ballasts to breaker boxes, chandeliers to chimes, meter cans to motor starters, and streetlights to security cameras, Murray has got you covered. Since it opened in 1963, commercial builders and DIY weekend warriors alike have taken advantage of its uncommon expertise and vast selection. If you're feeling particular, inquire about custom fixtures.
10227 W. 8 Mile Rd., www.murraylighting.com, (313) 341-0416.

New World Antique Gallery - Perched on a quiet block of Grand River Avenue, New World Antique Gallery has been serving northwest Detroit for more than 20 years. Despite the elegant name, the shop is more of a no-nonsense rummage sale—you are more likely to find an old lawn Santa or bucket of vintage doorknobs than ancient pottery. Although the fascinating and sometimes bizarre products are loosely organized into large piles with categories such as "metal" and "outdoors," the friendly owner will expertly guide you. Plan on spending a while here—the gallery is built for browsing. Haggle-friendly. *12101 Grand River Ave., (313) 834-7008.*

Professional Racquet Services - Since 1984, Professional Racquet Services has kept Detroit's squash, tennis, badminton, and racquetball players serving in style. Here you'll find every piece of equipment you'll need, from racquets to Rec Specs. Step back 30 years in time into the neighboring discount showroom to browse through dead stock tennis attire: a rainbow of tennis skirts, Wilson polos, and multicolored windbreakers. Looking for a place to play? Just ask the friendly and quirky owner, who hand-strings racquets behind the sales counter—he knows every court within city limits. *19444 Livernois Ave., www.prsracquets.com, (313) 863-1880.*

Shrine of the Black Madonna Cultural Center and Bookstore - Founded in 1970 as a nonprofit educational and cultural institution, the shrine is equal parts museum, art gallery, bookstore, and gift shop. The cultural center is affiliated with the Shrine of the Black Madonna Church, which was founded in Detroit by civil rights activist the Reverend Albert B. Cleage Jr. in 1953. Visit to browse through the largest African-American owned bookstore in the nation, chat with the helpful staff about the variety of African art pieces, or purchase African clothing and handcrafted jewelry. Visitors can walk through the museum and gallery on their own, but they should call ahead to schedule a guided tour. *13535 Livernois Ave., www.shrinebookstore.com, (313) 491-0777.*

Simply Casual - Since 1997, Simply Casual has been a destination on the historic Avenue of Fashion. Despite its name, shopping here is far from a casual experience and keeps its customers well-dressed in a range of urban to dressy to business-casual styles. Shop for everything from basic, everyday clothing to high-end designer goods in its clean, contemporary setting featuring a former dry cleaners' conveyor that allows a two-level display of up to 1,800 garments, or sit in the red velvet chairs and play a game of chess while you wait for a friend in the fitting room. Designer selections range from Betsey Johnson to Seven for All Mankind to Sean Jean, but generous sale prices and attentive salespeople make it easy for anyone to find the perfect outfit. *19400 Livernois Ave., www.simplycasual.org, (313) 864-7979.*

Terry's Enchanted Garden - From a glance at the bright tropical plants and tall vases perched in the window, this floral and gift shop might seem slightly out of place on the garment-themed Avenue of Fashion. However, in addition to being a full-service florist, this women-owned business has a shop-within-a-shop! Inside of Terry's you'll find Tara's Unique Boutique offering thoughtful gifts and women's clothing and accessories for any occasion. In business since 1980 and well-known in the Detroit corporate world for delivering unique fresh flower arrangements, plants, and gift baskets, the main floor of Terry's Enchanted Garden is divided between a selection of potted plants and home and garden accessories and a range of gallery quality jewelry, sculpture pieces, and greeting cards. Stroll to the back of the shop to find the Unique Boutique's selection of flowing skirts, colorful jeans and blouses, formal dresses, and women's accessories. *19338 Livernois Ave.,*
www.terrysenchantedgarden.com, (313) 342-3758.

Tradewinds Liquor & Wine Shop - Tradewinds Liquor and Wine Shop is the go-to destination for thirsty Detroiters with a discerning palate. Whether you're in the market for a fine elixir or a potable present, you won't be disappointed by this classy shop, its friendly, knowledgeable staff, or the reasonable prices. Tradewinds has an unparalleled-in-Detroit local and international beer and wine selection—organized by origin—alongside its impressive liquor and liqueur selection, which features harder to find inebriants like absinthe, Cachaça, Pimm's, Rumple Minze, and Chartreuse. As tough as it may be, no road sodas/cruise-voisier, please! *17521 Livernois Ave., (313) 342-0700.*

CULTURAL ATTRACTIONS

Ant T Bettie OK Puppets Museum - If Sesame Street comes with a take-away point—besides the "letter of the day"—it's that children love to learn from puppets. Although she wasn't inspired by Elmo but by her own interest in arts and crafts, retired Detroit Public Schools teacher Ms. Bettie created her own papier-mâché puppets as teaching aids. Throughout her career, Ms. Bettie brought elementary school lessons to life using her depictions of Native American leaders, larger-than-life models of ants, and hand puppets. Today, she decorates her home as a gallery and museum with collections of local artists and her own paintings. Portraits of Bettie's mother and influential civil rights leaders, Matisse-esque still-life paintings, and miniature dolls and puppets hang on display in her living and dining rooms. However, Ms. Bettie keeps her prized puppet collection in her basement, perched atop the felt black curtains of her homemade puppet theater. Ms. Bettie still dreams of owning a gallery space in Northwest, but for now she requests that visitors please call ahead to schedule a visit to her home art collection. *(313) 861-7426.*

Curtis Museum at the House of Beauty Hair Mall - Although featuring information on a range of figures that punctuate contemporary black history—including Nelson Mandela, Ed Bradley, Dr. Martin Luther King Jr., and General Colin Powell—this small, albeit fascinating, storefront museum and local curiosity lives to celebrate the life and work of longtime Detroiter Dr. Austin Wingate Curtis Jr., chief lab assistant to famed peanut researcher George Washington Carver. Located inside of the affiliated House of Beauty Hair Mall since its founding in 2000, the eccentric space winds through a series of brightly lit rooms that document different aspects of Curtis's life. The museum has an impressive array of scattered artifacts, ephemera, and art that chronicle the life of its namesake, including handmade figures in the doctor's likeness, photos of Curtis with Carver, and correspondence between the two men. Museum co-founder Mary Jones, who leads many of the tours, has a passion for sharing her knowledge and enthusiasm for the legacy of Dr. Curtis and this interesting chapter in black history. Visitors should call ahead to make an appointment, as hours vary from those posted. *14022 W. McNichols Rd., (313) 341-1512.*

Detroit Repertory Theatre / Millan Theatre Company - Off the beaten path, just outside of Highland Park, lies this cultural gem. The Detroit Repertory Theatre produces four major productions and approximately 180 performances each year with a strong focus on interracial casting and community involvement. Backed by expansive sets, intricate costumes, and stimulating performances, the Detroit Repertory Theatre is a must for theatre lovers and novices alike. The small, charming space features a full bar and 184 seats, creating an intimate theatrical environment and atmosphere. *13103 Woodrow Wilson St., www.detroitreptheatre.com, (313) 868-1347.*

Plantation House - A retired line worker, 83-year-old Jother Woods, grew up in a sharecropping family in rural Horseshoe Lake, Louisiana. As a young man, he moved to Detroit to seek his fortune, but he never relinquished his lifelong fantasy of one day owning one of the palatial

Southern plantation homes he admired as a boy. Over the past three decades, Woods realized his dream and hand-built his own country estate—at 1:30 scale. Built slowly, evolving and growing piece by piece, the folk-art masterwork is now 52 feet long and six feet wide. Tinkering in the basement of his lower flat, Woods painstakingly constructed the artwork with tens of thousands of discarded found objects. All to scale, a highway roars past a private drive, which winds through well-manicured gardens, over a lake, past the 16-room gated mansion and private pool, before giving way to a farm, silos, and horse barn. Filled with surprises at every turn, every minute detail, every flower, tree, road, vehicle, and structure is made from someone else's trash, beautifully reimagined here as another man's tranquil dream world. Though the project is too big for Woods to keep in one piece, he displays it, in sections, throughout his home and proudly grants tours of the grounds of his plantation to visitors lucky enough to see it. Mr. Woods requests that visitors make arrangements to see the work through the G.R. N'Namdi Gallery in Midtown. *(313) 831-8700.*

ENTERTAINMENT & RECREATION

» **Baker's Keyboard Lounge** - What started in 1933 as a small sandwich shop in the middle of farmland has turned into one of the most iconic and revered jazz venues in the country. The world's oldest continuously running jazz club, Baker's intimate stage has been graced by the likes of John Coltrane, Sarah Vaughan, Nat "King" Cole, Dave Brubeck, Cab Calloway, Miles Davis, and Ella Fitzgerald. Its intimate Art Deco interior features a distinctive curved, piano-shaped bar painted with a keyboard motif and tilted mirrors installed so the audience can watch the pianist's hands playing the gorgeous Steinway piano, which was handpicked by Art Tatum in the 1950s. Steaming crisp fried chicken, creamy mac and cheese, and the city's best collard

greens come rolling out of the kitchen to the dim and cozy dining room that is centered around the stage. Enjoy a stiff drink, snuggle up in a booth, and experience one of the greatest cultural assets Detroit has to offer. *20510 Livernois Ave., www.theofficialbakerskeyboardlounge.com, (313) 345-6300.*

Detroit Golf Club - Tucked between historic Palmer Woods, the University of Detroit, and the stately University District homes on Fairway Drive is this prestigious, private club. Established in 1899, the club is home to two verdant 18-hole courses—the par-72 North Course and the par-68 South Course—designed by famed course designer Donald Ross. Measured from the black tees, the North Course spans 6,837 yards and is a formidable challenge for players of any golf handicap. The tall trees, narrow fairways, and plentiful sand traps force golfers to play with the entire bag. The South Course, in contrast, is a short 5,967 yards, and favors those with local knowledge. Defined by its tight landing areas, steep ridges, and poor sightlines, this course—and especially the sixth hole—is built for golfers with long irons. Hang out on the green or at the 19th hole long enough and you're sure to spot famous Detroit movers and shakers or sports stars, such as the mayor of Detroit (who always has a complimentary membership), Tigers pitching ace Justin Verlander, manager Jim Leyland, or retired NFL halfback Jerome Bettis. The impressive Albert Kahn-designed clubhouse was added to the club in 1916. The club is available for weddings and other elegant functions. *17911 Hamilton Rd., www.detroitgolfclub.org, (313) 345-4400.*

Doll's Go Kart Track - With the elephant-size speaker pumping bumping disco jams, Doll's is hard to miss, which is a good thing for go kart fans, because the next closest facility is almost a half hour drive away and would most assuredly offer less attitude. Especially on weekends, Doll's pulls in a steady rotation of aspiring racers, and boasts five laps around the tire-lined oval track for a mere $3. Though they don't offer the latest in video entertainment, video game fans will be relieved to know that Doll's does offer a small arcade, so bring quarters. Doll's is open seven days a week. Come on now, go, kart! *4455 Oakman Blvd., (248) 508-3747.*

Palmer Park - Located along Woodward between McNichols Road and 7 Mile Road, Palmer Park is a verdant, beautiful, green city gem. The sprawling park, designed by Frederick Law Olmsted and Charles Eliot at the turn of the 19th century, spans 296 acres of lush lawns, woodlands, recreational amenities, and a lake. The park's many trees make it beautiful year-round, punctuated with beautiful gardens, changing fall colors, and serene snowfall. The park is home to more than 13 miles of hiking and biking trails, the Detroit Mounted Police station, a scenic lake, 16 tennis courts, an 18-hole golf course, a historic log cabin, and numerous picnic pavilions and playscapes. The log cabin was built in 1885 for the park's namesake, Senator Thomas W. Palmer and his wife, Mary, and remains as a charming reminder of the city's history and earliest architecture. The park's par-71, 18-hole golf course stretches 6,007 yards and is remarkable for its flat elevation and generous landing areas, making it forgiving for golfers of all ages and abilities. In recent years, a local community group called the People for Palmer Park has begun implementing physical improvements to the park, such as a new 800-tree apple orchard, and hosting fun community events such as bike rides, fund-raisers, free yoga classes, and tennis leagues. *910 Merrill Plaisance St., www.peopleforpalmerpark.org, (313) 757-2751.*

University of Detroit Mercy Titans Men's Basketball at Calihan Hall - Though more of a potential March Madness Cinderella than a perennial powerhouse, that doesn't stop the UDM Titans from putting on a great show at home. Since the arena known as Calihan was opened in 1952, the squad has won more than 70% of its home games and held the current best home winning streak of 39 games from 2001–2002. Notable team alumni include Dave DeBusschere, Bad Boy John Long, and iconic former coach and broadcaster Dick Vitale, for whom the court was named in 2011. Calihan Hall is a great intimate venue for college basketball. The gymnasium holds 8,300, and the steep, tight seating arrangement ensures good sightlines and an energetic crowd. *4001 W. McNichols Rd., www.detroittitans.com, (313) 973-1305.*

SITES

The Birwood Wall - Detroit's Berlin Wall, the Birwood Wall, is a relic and symbol of the city's historic and ongoing racial strife and segregation. At the time of the wall's construction in 1940, the neighborhood to the West, Blackstone Park, was predominantly African-American and consequently a victim of federal mortgage redlining. To circumvent federal restrictions, the developer of the nascent all-white middle-class neighborhood to the east, Eight Mile Wyoming, constructed this six-foot-tall concrete slab wall, that spans more than a half mile, to enable potential purchasers to get mortgages and to protect housing values. Today, the wall has been reimagined as an artistic canvas popular among area muralists and graffiti artists. *The Birwood Wall is located between Mendota Street and Birwood Street, running south from 8 Mile Rd.*

The Blue Bird Inn - Though it appears insignificant from the outside and has been shuttered for nearly 20 years, the Blue Bird Inn was opened in the 1930s in a small enclave on the city's west side and has a prominent place in the annals of jazz history. A popular club throughout the modern era—attracting acts such as Charlie Parker, John Coltrane, and Yusef Lateef—it is most notable for being the venue that is said to have saved the career of a young Miles Davis. As a promising horn player in New York, by the early 1950s, Davis had developed an uncontrollable heroin habit that threatened his future as a musician. He came to Detroit in 1953—where the drugs were said to be weaker than those on the East Coast—to kick his habit and was recruited as a resident player at the Blue Bird. According to legend, Davis beat his addiction there and returned to New York five months later to continue his ascent into stardom. Because of the club's contribution to jazz music, there are at least two pieces that identify the humble landmark: Thad Jones' 5021 and Tommy Flannigan's Beyond the Bluebird. *5021 Tireman St.*

Dorothy S. Turkel House - Though he was born in 1867, Chicago native Frank Lloyd Wright is known as arguably the most important and innovative architect of the 20th century. While Wright—who is famous for his prefabricated concrete designs, flat roofs, use of natural light, and integration with nature—designed 30 buildings in Michigan, the Turkel House is the only structure the pioneering architect designed in Detroit. Dorothy S. Turkel commissioned the home in 1955 after she read Wright's book The Natural House. The L-shaped, 4,300-square-foot home, which cost $525,000 in today's dollars, is designed in the architect's Usonian Automatic style, which entailed precast reinforced concrete blocks designed to expedite and streamline construction. Though the home is intriguing from the street, with its immaculately manicured gardens, 400 windows, two-story all-glass living room, and a second-story terrace with a bank of custom doors, it is most breathtaking from the inside, as it has recently been lovingly restored and features original built-in hardwood furniture and hundreds of intricate interior pre-cast concrete details. The home is privately owned and occupied, so please be respectful and only admire it from afar. *2760 W. 7 Mile Rd.*

The Grande Ballroom - Though it's been shuttered for more than 40 years and functioned as a music venue for only six, the Grande Ballroom has firmly secured its status as a pantheon of Detroit rock 'n' roll history. Built in 1928, the music palace was designed by Charles N. Agree, and was used as a dance hall venue through its early life. This changed when local schoolteacher Russ Gibb took over the building in 1966. With house bands the Stooges and the MC5—whose breakout live album Kick Out the Jams was recorded at the venue in 1968—playing weekly, the ballroom became a revolving door for future Hall of Fame talent. Among hundreds of others, the Velvet Underground, Led Zeppelin, Pink Floyd, Chuck Berry, Howlin' Wolf, John Lee Hooker, Cream, John Coltrane, the Who, and Sun Ra graced the stage. Though the building is long abandoned and has fallen into extreme disrepair, the walls still ooze history. If you listen carefully, you can still hear Rob Tyner urging us to "Kick out the Jams." *8952 Grand River Ave.*

» Palmer Woods - One of the premier historic neighborhoods in Detroit, Palmer Woods' 188 acres were originally part of a donation by Thomas Palmer, Detroit land developer, Michigan senator, and ambassador to Spain. The neighborhood was designed by renowned landscape architect and William Le Baron Jenney disciple Ossian Cole Simonds, who implemented the area's trapezoidal property lines to force architects to create distinctive designs, as each parcel had a one-of-a-kind shape. The area is known for its beautiful, winding elm-lined streets, flowing lawns, and recessed large brick and stone houses in a variety of classical architectural styles. The neighborhood's 298 homes showcase a range of designs, featuring examples of the Colonial Revival, Tudor Revival, Arts and Crafts, Neo-Georgian, Mediterranean, and Modern architectural styles. Although some homes were built later, the neighborhood was largely built between 1917 and 1929, by renowned architects such as Albert Kahn, C. Howard Crane, Maginnis & Walsh, and Richard H. Marr, with later additions by Minoru Yamasaki and Frank Lloyd Wright. The neighborhood offers a scenic and charming destination for a bike ride or walk. Though Palmer Woods offers the grandest homes in northern Detroit, those looking to admire historic homes nearby are encouraged to explore Sherwood Forest to the west and University District, Green Acres, and Palmer Park to the south. Palmer Woods is bounded by Strathcona Dr. to the North, Woodward Ave. to the East, W. Seven Mile Rd. to the South, and Strathcona Dr. to the West. Although nearly all of the homes in Palmer Woods are architectural treasures, highlights include:

- Bishop Gallagher Residence: Detroit's largest home, at 40,000 square feet. *1880 Wellesley Dr.*
- Two (of the seven) Fisher Brother mansions, of automotive fame:
  - Alfred Fisher Mansion: 1*771 Balmoral Dr.*
  - William Fisher Mansion: The city's second largest home, at 35,000 square feet. *1791 Wellesley Dr.*
- Dorothy S. Turkel House: A Frank Lloyd Wright design. See separate entry. *2760 W. 7 Mile Rd.*
- Brooks Barron Home: An understated home by Minoru Yamasaki. *19631 Argyle Crescent.*

Marygrove College and University of Detroit Mercy Campus Architecture - Two historic urban educational institutions, Marygrove College and the University of Detroit Mercy are an oasis of architectural integrity and pastoral beauty in a sea of neighborhoods and busy boulevards. Originally established in 1905 as a Catholic women's college in Monroe, Michigan, **Marygrove College** moved its campus to the once rural and heavily forested area of Six Mile and Wyoming in 1927. Oscar D. Bohlen was selected as the architect to design the Liberal Arts building and the adjoining Madame Cadillac hall, which to this day remain the focal points of the campus. Designed in the Tudor Gothic style, the Bedford stone buildings bring a classic collegiate appearance to the grounds. The campus is flanked by a gorgeous Indiana Oolitic limestone gate that sets the campus' aesthetic tone for visitors. Due east of the school lies the **University of Detroit Mercy**, which has roots dating back to 1877. A private Catholic university in the Jesuit and Mercy traditions, the school is the largest Roman Catholic university in Michigan. Though less consistently architecturally splendid than its sister to the West, UDM's sprawling, lush campus has many highlights. The campus is anchored by the World War I Memorial Tower, which is a functioning clock tower that was built in 1926 and still regulates the school day. The campus is also dotted by an impressive array of early 20th century Spanish Baroque architecture, demonstrated in the School of Architecture Building, Chemistry Building, and Lansing-Reilly Hall. Though both campuses are guarded and private, they are accommodating to respectful visitors and photographers—and maybe picnickers. *Marygrove College is located at 8425 McNichols Rd., UDM is located at 4001 W. McNichols Rd.*

Woodlawn Cemetery - Established in 1895, Woodlawn was once a place where barons of industry were laid to rest in temple-like mausoleums far away from the city. It has since been surrounded by the city and has become the cemetery of choice for Motown greats (Stevie Wonder and Diana Ross, long may they live, have both reserved Woodlawn plots). Wooded with giant pine and oak trees, Woodlawn is best explored on foot or by bicycle, and it's exceptionally pretty in the fall. Its collection of family mausoleums is one of the largest in the country and gives the cemetery the character of a small, silent city. *19975 Woodward Ave., www.woodlawncemeterydetroit.com, (313) 368-0010.*

Notable burials:

- Rosa Parks (1913–2005): Activist and "first lady" of civil rights, buried in the Rosa Parks Freedom Chapel.
- J.L. Hudson (1846–1912): Founder of Hudson's department store. *Section 10.*
- John (1864–1920) and Horace (1868–1920) Dodge: Founders of Dodge Bros. Motor Company. Their Sphinx-guarded mausoleum is one of Woodlawn's most famous. *Section 10, Lot 5.*
- Edsel B. Ford (1893–1943): Son of Henry Ford and president of Ford Motor Company from 1919 until his death. *Section 10.*
- Hazen S. Pingree (1840–1901): Mayor of Detroit, governor of Michigan, and "idol of the people."
- Alex Manoogian (1901–1996): Armenian-American entrepreneur, founder of the Masco Corporation, and donor of the Manoogian Mansion, now Detroit's mayoral residence.
- James Couzens (1872–1936): Vice president and general manager of Ford Motor Company, U.S. senator, and mayor of Detroit.
- David Ruffin (1941–1991): Lead singer of the Temptations. *Section 3, Lot 243.*
- Levi Stubbs (1936–2008): Lead singer of the Four Tops. *Section 3, Lot 325 (directly behind the office).*
- James Jamerson (1939–1983): Bassist for Motown studio band the Funk Brothers. *Section 37, Lot 265.*
- Michael Jackson (1958–2009): Not actually buried at Woodlawn, but you can visit a memorial to him, where gifts that were left at the Motown Museum after his death were symbolically buried.

POINTS OF INTEREST

Big Mack Records - This vacant lot was once home to Ed McCoy's label, churning out R&B, soul, and gospel music from the likes of Edd Henry, the Grand Prix's, and Bob and Fred. *7018 W. Warren Ave.*

Dee Gee Records - Formed on this residential block in 1951 by Dizzy Gillespie and Dave Usher, the label put out a number of notable records by Gillespie himself and was bought up by New Jersey's Savoy Records in 1953. *4015 Leslie St.*

Diana Ross Home - After a childhood spent in the Brewster Projects, the singer purchased this modest brick home located on the same street as fellow Supremes Florence Ballard and Mary Wilson. *3762 W. Buena Vista St.*

Ebenezer AME Church - This incredible, ornately constructed English Gothic giant was constructed in 1928 and now functions as an African Methodist Episcopal parish. The sprawling stone sanctuary and building is punctuated by the large square tower at its center. *5151 W. Chicago St.*

Edwin Starr Home - Most famous for the 1970 hit, "War," this singer lived in this modest home with his wife, Annette, in the late 1960s. *20511 Ardmore St.*

First Concrete Mile - In 1909, this mile-long stretch of Woodward Avenue between McNichols Road and 7 Mile Road acted as a test case for the durability of concrete as a road surface. The success of the project changed the way roads were built around the world. *17763 Woodward Ave.*

Francis Ford Coppola Home - Although he spent most of his childhood growing up in Queens, New York, this was the home the famed director was born in. *17540 Kentucky St.*

George C. Scott Home - This lovely brick home in Palmer Woods was the childhood residence of the actor most famous for his leading role in Patton. *18981 Pennington Dr.*

Gilda Radner Home - The famous comedian, a member of the original Saturday Night Live cast, spent large parts of her childhood in this solid brick home in Palmer Woods. *17330 Wildemere Ave.*

Gladys Knight Home - The Motown singer lived in this gorgeous brick home just south of McNichols Road. 16860 La Salle Blvd.

Houdini Death Site / Old Grace Hospital - Demolished in 1979, this hospital was where famed magician Harry Houdini died of a ruptured appendix and peritonitis on Halloween in 1926. *3990 John R.*

Jackie Wilson Home - The singer, known as "Mr. Excitement" and famous for the songs Higher and Higher and Lonely Teardrops, lived in this lovely brick home with his wife. 16522 La Salle Blvd.

James Smith Farm House - The inconspicuous vinyl siding on this residence hides the fact that the home dates from sometime between 1830 and 1850 and is one of two remaining log cabins in the city. *2015 Clements St.*

Jerome Bettis Home - This now-abandoned building was home to the famous Pittsburgh Steelers running back for much of his childhood before he was "The Bus." *10384 Aurora St.*

Magic City Records - This spot once housed the recording studios and office for the label, perhaps most famous for its releases by teen funk outfit Mad Dog and the Pups in the late 1960s and early 1970s. *8912 Grand River Ave.*

Marvin Gaye Home - The singer and his wife, Anna—sister to Motown founder Berry Gordy—lived in this charming brick home on the city's west side in the late 1960s. *19315 Appoline St.*

Michigan-Shaped Lake - Located on the former Michigan State Fairgrounds, this man-made lake is best viewed from the air or in satellite photos. *Woodward Ave. and W. State Fair Rd.*

New Light Baptist Church - Completed in 1929, the sandstone facade of this classical-revival church is dominated by the massive Romanesque columns. The yellow sandstone structure with its bronze entryways seems to almost glow on sunny mornings. *5240 W. Chicago St.*

Old Kronk Gym - Now abandoned, this recreation center was the former headquarters of famous boxing trainer Emanuel Steward, who trained many successful boxers here, including Hilmer Kenty and Thomas "Hitman" Hearns. *5555 McGraw St.*

Orsel and Minnie McGhee House - This unassuming home became the epicenter of a battle over discrimination, when the McGhee family attempted to become the first black homeowners in an all-white neighborhood. They won their case in front of the Supreme Court, which ended legal housing segregation in America, with the help of a promising young lawyer named Thurgood Marshall. *4626 Seebaldt St.*

Philip Levine Home - This pleasant brick house is where the U.S. poet laureate and Wayne State University graduate first began to seriously write poetry. *19360 Santa Rosa Dr.*

Ric-Tic Records - Joanne Bratton and Ed Wingate ran their soul music label on this quiet residential street, recording singers like J.J. Barnes and Edwin Starr, before being bought by their big competitor at Motown Records. *4039 W. Buena Vista St.*

Sidra Records - Now a garage, during the 1960s, this building was home to the mysterious Sidra label, which cut a slew of incredible soul singles that largely went unnoticed at the time. According to rumor, off-duty Motown session musicians and Cass Technical High School music students made up the backing bands for the instrumentally rich recordings. Check out the instrumental Sidra's Theme, credited to Ronnie and Robyn. *18292 Wyoming St.*

Stevie Wonder Home - The singer moved into this home with his family with the help of Motown founder Berry Gordy, who wanted his stars living in desirable neighborhoods. *18074 Greenlawn St.*

Summer in the City Cool Breeze Mural - This geometric mural is painted in jewel tones on the side of the Cool Breeze Ice Cream Shop is the handiwork of the 2011 class of Summer in the City. *10040 W. McNichols Rd.*

Webster Cigars Ghost Sign - Amazingly colorful old mural, including a vibrant commercial portrait, advertising cigars at "2 for 25 cents." *6760 W. Warren Ave.*

CHAPTER 10
FAR WEST SIDE

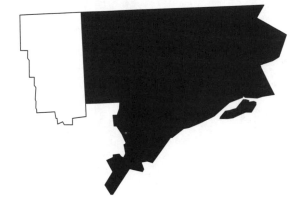

Southfield

8 Mile

Five
Points

Berg
Lahser

7 Mile

Lahser

Telegraph

The Eye

Old
Redford

FAR WEST
SIDE

M-39

Outer Drive

McNichols

Riverdale

Grand River

North
Rosedale
Park

Evergreen

Greenfield

Belmont

Near
Wes
Side

Minock
Park

Rosedale
Park

Brightmoor

Grandmont

Westwood
Park

Eliza
Howell

Grandmont
#1

I-96

Castle
Rouge

Redford

Outer Drive

Weatherby

Grandale

Franklin
Park

Fisk

Herman
Gardens

Parkland

Warrendale

Warren

Dearborn
Heights

Ford

Dearb

N

0   1   2
▭▬▬▬▬▬▬▬▬▬▬▬ Miles

The far west side has a reputation as one of the city's hidden havens for vintage blue-collar bars and restaurants, off-the-beaten-path cultural amenities, and many delightful confectioneries and bakeries. As we've defined it, the far west side is bounded by Greenfield Road to the east and the city's limits to the north, west, and south.

Annexed by the city between 1824 and 1926, and largely built up between 1915 and 1964, the area is among the newest in the city, and developed during the rise of the city's bedroom community suburbs. Like contemporary suburbs, the area was developed subdivision by subdivision by large developers, causing each neighborhood to be distinct from the next, even to this day. The area showcases a spectrum of neighborhood types, from beautiful, dense Depression-era neighborhoods to workers cottages to pre-war duplexes to post-war tract housing. This large, 29-square-mile area is home to many neighborhoods, including Berg Lahser, Brightmoor, Castle Rouge, Eliza Howell, The Eye, Five Points, Franklin Park, Grandale, Grandmont, Grandmont #1, Herman Gardens, Minock Park, North Rosedale Park, Old Redford, Parkland, Riverdale, Rosedale Park, Warrendale, Weatherby, and Westwood Park. Because of their distinct development patterns and social histories, each neighborhood has its own character and draw. Among these, several stand out: Grandmont Rosedale (see separate entry in this chapter), a collection of five beautiful, vibrant 1920s neighborhoods; Brightmoor, a once-dense neighborhood of small wood-frame homes for Appalachian immigrants that is now largely vacant and home to many community gardens; Old Redford, a quaint neighborhood home to a resurgent commercial corridor centered around the gorgeous Redford Theatre; and Warrendale, a tight-knit community welcoming a new Arab-American population that is bringing a host of Middle Eastern eateries and shops to the area.

The far west side offers a bevy of amenities and destinations that make it an attractive, fascinating, and lively destination. A treasure for visitors with a nostalgic eye, the area is home to a host of charming 1940s- and 1950s-era businesses, such as chip shops, slider joints, penny candy stores, and roller rinks. For those looking to admire the city's greenscapes, the far west side offers beautifully manicured lawns and gardens in Grandmont Rosedale, hundreds of urban gardens in Brightmoor, and the city's largest park—the heavily forested Rouge Park. For the traveling sweet tooth, the area has an almost unparalleled concentration of bakeries, cake shops, and doughnut shops. The far west side's artistic and cultural amenities run the gamut, from a small community theater to a civil war center to a spectacular 1920s movie house.

BARS & RESTAURANTS

Auntie Betty's Café - Delicious take-out comfort food is Auntie Betty's specialty. Place your order at the carryout counter and take a seat on the comfy multicolored vinyl chairs overlooking Grand River while you wait. Auntie Betty serves her food fresh and hot, so it's the perfect temperature by the time you make it home. From rib tips to chicken by the piece to fried okra to mac 'n' cheese, Betty has the soul food selection covered. If you have any questions about the menu, Auntie Betty herself will be happy to recommend a dish to fit your tastes. Don't miss the $4.99 lunch specials. Open late. *19601 Grand River Ave., (313) 537-6050.*

Bob's Pizza Palace - A Detroit staple since 1966, Bob's Pizza Palace is a pizzeria in the most classic sense: dough is made fresh daily; sauce is made from scratch using Bob's own secret recipe; mozzarella cheese is browned and bubbly; and the pepperoni is small and crispy, all curled up at the edges. This is a neighborhood family place that is as much a part of the community as the people in it. Order the classic hand-tossed round or the Detroit-style square with some hand-battered fried shrimp, wing dings or ribs. *20510 W. 7 Mile Rd., (313) 538-2742.*

Cafe Gigi - Open since 1973, Cafe Gigi—known by locals as Gigi's—is a gay club renowned for its amazing cabaret shows featuring go-go boys and drag queens. Inside, patrons enter through a narrow hallway before finding the barely lit performance space and a stage packed with characters out of a John Waters movie. Around them are elevated tables and seating, pool tables, and a long bar with cheap, strong pours. Upstairs from the venue is the dance club, which is especially lively on show nights. Mondays and Fridays are often the best nights to enjoy a show and the karaoke on Sundays is exceptional. Obviously, most patrons are men, but Gigi's welcomes everyone. Keep your eyes peeled for local queen of queens Cindy Elmwood. *16920 W. Warren Ave., (313) 584-6525.*

Cardoni's Bar and Grill - More bar than grill, this far west side staple is a laid-back neighborhood watering hole. Built into an old house, Cardoni's has a comfortable, man-cave atmosphere punctuated by an array of old photographs, sports memorabilia, and beer ephemera, and offers a great casual venue to watch the game, shoot pool, or play darts while enjoying a limited menu of tasty pub fare—including burgers, patty melts, steak, chicken fingers, and shrimp. The full bar has a wide array of middle-shelf liquors and domestic and imported bottles. The staff, like the crowd, is friendly and cheerful. Check out their billiards and darts leagues. *6615 Greenfield Rd., (313) 584-1993.*

Chick's Bar - Chick's was opened in Warrendale in the 1950s by a World War II veteran who earned the nickname "Chick" during his military days, and has remained the quintessential neighborhood dive bar with ambience. A regular spot for neighborhood folks, as well as for visitors, the crowd here is relaxed and friendly, and the drinks are cheap and plentiful with draft specials starting at $1.10. The food menu runs the gamut of traditional bar fare, and the bar's legendary fish fries on Fridays are worth the trip—just look for the vintage yellow sign! *18550 W. Warren Ave., (313) 441-6055.*

Crab House - This family-operated shellfish and barbecue restaurant offers affordable surf and turf for carryout or dining in. The main room features a Plexiglas-encased cashier's counter and a few periwinkle booths with small personal TVs, so you can catch your shows while you dine. If the front booths are full, never fear: Just walk toward the back of the room, follow the hallway next door, and you'll find the newly expanded main dining room. Try the barbecue chicken or ribs—rich and smoky in flavor, with a mildly sweet sauce glazed on top—or the popular garlic shrimp, crab leg clusters, turkey neck, or pasta. If you're feeling saucy, try the giant Dump Truck special that includes every seafood item you can imagine. *19721 W. 7 Mile Rd., (313) 535-1400.*

Deangelo's Soul Food, Deli & More - To a jazz soundtrack, this diner-style greasy spoon serves up outstanding soul food to the Old Redford neighborhood. The decor is simple and cozy, but that's because the focus is on the vittles. Slide into one of the old-timey white booths or order to go—you can go a la carte or select an entree, two sides, and a corn muffin. We especially recommend the expertly seasoned fried catfish, the crispy butterfly shrimp, and the collards and green beans which both pack some heat. Though the house specialty is soul satisfying southern food, they also sling a strong selection of soups, salads, sandwiches, and other deli delights. *17425 Telegraph Rd., (313) 535-7157.*

Elias Donuts - More than 30 years ago, the space where Elias Donuts is now was a Dunkin' Donuts. A lot of that old-school DD charm is still present—from the fuchsia facade and awning to the stainless steel and pink formica counters and stools—but this sweet independent doughnut shop is so much more. Every morning at 5am, Elias fries the shop's fresh, delicious, cakey doughnuts—and if you're lucky enough to catch them, you can watch them being made while you order. From traditional flavors like sour cream and chocolate to the more imaginative red velvet, cherry chip, or Froot Loop-encrusted, it's fortunate that when you order a dozen, you get three more free, so you can try them all! If a bag of delicious doughnuts isn't your bag, they also serve other, more savory fare, from bagel sandwiches to burgers to fried fish dinners. Visit on Paczki Day to get your fix. Open 24/7. *19231 Grand River Ave., (313) 535-0070.*

Enjoy Again Family Restaurant - A lower east side staple since the 1960s, Enjoy Again recently migrated to this updated, larger space on the west side—and the generations of loyal customers followed. With large red booths and a cozy, central fireplace, the inviting family-style restaurant slings a wide range of full and hearty American cuisine, with a special flair for barbecue, soul food, and burgers. Early—and not so early—birds can opt to belly up to the counter to dive into the extensive, classic breakfast menu, which features especially yummy grits. Invariably, one of the family owners will greet you at your seat, shake your hand, and remind you to "enjoy again," but you likely won't need much convincing. *24737 W. 8 Mile Rd., www.restaurants-detroit.com, (313) 533-5300.*

Gracie See Pizzeria - This unassuming retro sports bar and restaurant has been serving some of the west side's most popular pizza since opening in 1969. In contrast to the Spartan exterior, the interior oozes character from the Nixon years, including standbys such as wood paneling, period breweriana, and horse-themed, Secretariat-era, figurines, and black velvet paintings. The friendly staff complements this casual atmosphere with its easygoing attentiveness and predilection for terms such as "sweetie" and "doll." Although the menu offers a constellation of American and Italian fare, the house specialty is undoubtedly the pizza. Gracie See specializes in a thin crust type of pie, with a crispy bottom and flakey top, and a perfect balance between crust and pizza. While it's hard to go wrong with their many specialty pies, the Double Deuce—double cheese, double pepperoni—is our favorite. *6889 Greenfield Rd., (313) 581-8070.*

Jamaica Jamaica Restaurant & Bakery - Don't let its size fool you. This small diner in northwest Detroit serves some of the best Jamaican and Caribbean grub around. So good, it's named twice, the service is as warm and friendly as the climate from the restaurant's namesake. While the ambience is lacking, the authentic, incredibly delicious food more than makes up for it. Try the acclaimed tender curry goat, jerk chicken, oxtail, jerk burger, reggae-fried chicken, or chicken curry, along with some of the yummy sides like sweet fried doughy dumplings, roti, plantains, patties, or perfect rice and beans. Wash it all down with one of Jamaica Jamaica's spectacular house-made juices and sodas—try the Irish moss, mango, ginger beer or punch black—and while you're at it, have a slice of homemade cake. If you need the food to come to you, they cater to boot. *17550 W. 7 Mile Rd., (313) 534-3226.*

Kabob Arbeel Restaurant - Though you won't find luxury or quaintness at this hole-in-the-wall eatery named for a citadel in Iraq's Kurdistan region, the place cranks out authentic, delicious renditions of authentic Iraqi food for cheap carryout or dine-in. The $3 sandwiches are served in fresh, fluffy Iraqi samoon bread (more like an envelope than a wrap), and the menu offers customers full dinners of likely familiars: shawarma, falafel, beef or chicken tikka, as well as tilapia or quail. Association football (read soccer) fans will likely enjoy catching a game on Arbeel's flat screen if they show up at the right time. *6551 Greenfield Rd., (313) 582-9209.*

Lady Louisa's Place - Since 1999, Lady Louisa's has offered some of the finest slow-cooked barbecue and comfort food around. Serving up tried and true home cooking, Louisa's was founded by a family of avid cooks and named after their grandmother, whose portrait hangs in the restaurant. The menu highlighting Creole and soul includes celebrated mac and cheese, smothered catfish, fried turkey legs, Memphis-style ribs, and an array of soul sides and desserts. Dine at a booth in the casual dining area or order carryout from the cafeteria-style counter—no matter where you eat it, be prepared to finish your meal satisfied and slightly sleepy. *15535 W. McNichols Rd., www.ladylouisas.com, (313) 273-3663.*

Motor City Java House - The latest addition to a developing block of Lahser Road, over the course of ten years, owner Alicia Marion has collaborated with the local nonprofit Motor City Blight Busters to remodel the vacant space and has realized her dream of opening a coffee shop where neighbors can sip hot beverages, nibble on fresh baked goods and salads, and discuss their vision for the community. With a copper-painted tin ceiling and cheery yellow and green walls, Motor City Java House is a quiet, friendly place, furnished with comfy couches, spacious tables, and free Wi-Fi. Visit Saturdays for an afternoon yoga class or an open mic night, or drop in any old time to order espresso drinks from the rich granite coffee counter, surrounded by serene photography and local artwork. Closed Sunday and Monday. *17336 Lahser Rd., (313) 766-7578.*

Old Fashion Hamburger Company - Don't let the messy appearance dissuade you. This unkempt, Spartan, restaurant serves delicious halal sliders—the best burgers from a bulletproof lazy Susan money can buy. From within the burger workshop, the staff of the Old Fashion Hamburger Company makes outstanding hamburgers that strike the perfect balance of near-gooey bun, grease, caramelized onions, pickle slices, molten cheese, and ground beef. In addition, they use flash-frozen French fries, which offer a brilliant balance of crisp exteriors and starchy interiors. *19533 Warren Ave., (313) 982-3889.*

Omega Coney Island #3 - Though the exterior is reminiscent of a Denny's, the large seating area with green calico booths, wood paneling, vintage photos of Detroit landmarks, and a bakery showcase full of pies seems more reminiscent of a modern neighborhood diner. The parking lot is large, but finding a spot can be difficult when the breakfast crowd rolls in. Although the menu offers a delicious mix of lunch and breakfast options, including omelets, home fries, classic Greek pitas, soups, coney dogs, and burgers, its specialty items—including Daryl's Grill and the South of the Border Fries— are outstanding. Despite being located on one of the city's busiest

thoroughfares, the down-home atmosphere and affable staff give the restaurant a small-town feel. *22501 W. 8 Mile Rd., (313) 533-6000.*

Ozzie's - Ozzie's is everything a visitor would want from a well-worn neighborhood bar—cheap eats—including great burgers, sandwiches, and pub starters—low-priced drinks, and an old-time tavern atmosphere. Illuminated with colored-glass lanterns that provide a red glow, this watering hole offers all the aesthetic touchstones of the best neighborhood dives: wood-paneled walls littered with vintage neon signs and local-interest signage, a line of old-time beer cans perched over the bar, and solid-wood booths that resemble Medieval pews and offer ample table space for dine-in patrons. For entertainment, there are plenty of options: flat-screen TVs, video poker, darts, and a jukebox skewed toward country and classic rock standbys. Lunchtime guests will enjoy a more intimate crowd, but Ozzie's is most popular as an after-work unwind. *6593 Greenfield Rd., (313) 584-9091.*

» Scotty Simpson's Fish and Chips - Founded by James "Scotty" Simpson in 1950, this spot has been an authentic English-style fish-and-chips staple and Brightmoor community anchor since its postwar opening. The simple, vintage yellow-brick exterior features beautiful murals and antique signage, and complements the charming interior's classic patterned carpet, '50s-era wood-lined walls, taxidermy fish mounts, and Happy Days-esque wood tables and chairs. Affable owner Harry Barber and his four friendly staff members have more than 150 collective years of experience at the restaurant and create a laid-back and welcoming atmosphere. Known for its light, crispy, and bubbly batter, the menu is dedicated to all things golden-fried, including its renowned fish and chips, as well as delicious smelt, shrimp, perch, and frog legs. For landlubbers who prefer the bounty of the shore, Scotty's offers scrumptious grilled cheese, hamburgers, and steak. Wash your meal down with an old school ginger beer or orange soda. Scotty's gladly takes call-ahead orders, but beware Barber says, because "once I get them in the door, they're hooked!" *22200 Fenkell Rd., www.scottysfishandchips.com, (313) 533-0950.*

Sonny's Hamburgers - A beautiful example of 1950s White Tower architecture on a quiet strip in Detroit's Brightmoor neighborhood, Sonny's serves some of the city's most delicious and traditional sliders. As an onion-lover's Mecca, Sonny's is not first-date material: the burgers are made of fresh beef from Eastern Market—with onions ground in—cooked on a bed of onions, and served with a healthy dollop of onions. While revered for its sliders, Sonny's also offers delicious shoestring fries, homemade chili, wing dings, and a traditional diner breakfast menu. Although offering carryout, visitors should plan on sitting down to enjoy the original 1950s architecture and decor and the constant stream of entertaining regulars. *20001 Schoolcraft Rd., (313) 535-2278.*

Sweet Potato Sensations - Perched across the street from the Redford Theatre, Sweet Potato Sensations is a cozy pastry and ice cream shop that welcomes customers with the enticing aroma of its fresh pies and friendly staff. Inspired by her husband's love of sweet potatoes, owner Cassandra Thomas sought to create a business centered around this tasty, hearty, and nutritious tuber. With the vintage pumpkin-colored vinyl chairs, orange floor tiles, buttery pecan walls, eclectic antiques in various shades of tangerine, and every sweet potato dessert you could imagine—from ice cream to cookies and cheesecakes—this business warms its customers inside and out with sweet potato goodness. *17337 Lahser Rd., www.sweetpotatosensations.com, (313) 532-7996.*

Tijuana's Mexican Kitchen - For more than 20 years, this restaurant has been serving up Jalisco Mexico specials, including enchiladas, dried peppers, homemade flour tortillas, and salsas. Tijuana's recently expanded from a carryout-only kitchen to a dine-in restaurant, complete with a full bar serving Mexican draft beers, house sangria, and hand-squeezed lime margaritas. Aside from the bar, the addition includes bright orange and yellow walls, warm, glowing stained-glass light fixtures, and Western High School themed

artwork—an homage to the owner's alma mater and Southwest Detroit roots. *18950 Ford Rd., (313) 383-9100.*

Yum Yum Donuts - Though the vintage sign now advertises only "icious Donuts," don't be misled, they are still fully delicious. Offering seating at its fine vinyl, diner-style stools, the shop offers a full line of tasty, fresh-baked standards, from generous apple fritters to classic powdered doughnuts. With its healthy dose of Midwestern appeal and classic Americana, the locale is a welcome alternative to the unmentionable chain competition. And no, Yum Yum is not a chain, it just happens to be a commonly selected name for tempting doughnut shops. *7226 Greenfield Rd.*

SHOPPING & SERVICES

Cakes By Claudette, "The Cake Lady" - Prepare yourself to say several Hail Marys after finishing your cake. Selling her manna by the cake or the slice, Claudette draws customers from far and wide for her incredibly delectable caramel cake. Not a one-hit wonder, she also offers carrot, red velvet, lemon pound, yellow chocolate, double chocolate, coconut pineapple, and German chocolate cakes, all of which are outstanding and trend toward sweet and moist. In addition to selling her relatively inexpensive cakes from her unassuming store, Claudette also dispenses complimentary advice with each purchase, such as, "Cake is cheaper than therapy." *19210 W. McNichols Rd., (313) 537-4782.*

G&R Bike Shop - Offering great deals and bikes to match, this bright yellow shop has been a beacon of hope for Detroiters with two-wheeled trouble for more than 30 years. Although the shop sells many of the season's newest models, G&R is more renowned for its expert repair services and its wide selection of parts and accessories, especially those suited for early model rides. From behind the long counter, the attentive staff helps customers navigate the shop's large inventory and give tips on the finer points of bike maintenance. The veteran staff offers expert, honest, repair services for all types, from commuter to cruiser. Pick up one of the complimentary maintenance primers or Detroit maps on your way out. *21706 Grand River Ave., (313) 531-1146.*

Knudsen's Danish Bakery - A Detroit institution and Rosedale Park staple for more than 60 years, Knudsen's is an adorable, incredibly affordable old-fashioned bakery that bakes a vast selection of classic sweets and other baked goods daily, including—of course—decadent Danishes, popularized in Denmark in the 19th century as a more-indulgent variant of a classic Austrian pastry. From the bakery's pastries to delicious doughnuts, dense egg bread, bread pudding, pie by the slice, and coffee cakes, you can pick up a box crammed with goodies for less than $10. Although its prices are incredibly low to begin with, for the extra budget conscious, it offers day-old goods at a reduced price. Ask about the custom cakes. *18601 W. McNichols Rd., (313) 535-0323.*

Leddy's Wholesale Candy - Hidden behind a sleepy façade, Leddy's Wholesale Candy has been among the city's largest candy stores since it opened in 1926. Leddy's is a candy coliseum—the original hardwood floors, vintage decorations, and historic fixtures are obscured by the overwhelming candy selection. The shop seems to stock every candy ever sold. Saltwater taffy, rock candy, penny candy, candy jewelry, candy cigarettes and exotic candy from around the world—as well as all of the usual suspects—are piled in neat rows from floor to ceiling. Despite being a wholesaler, Leddy's is open to the public, and sells smaller, consumer quantities of most products. Don't spoil your dinner. *15928 Grand River Ave., (313) 272-2218.*

Metro Foodland - Founded by James Hooks in 1984, Metro Foodland is renowned both as a high-quality grocer and as the city's only African-American-owned full-service grocery store. Much like its cheerful owner who welcomes customers into the store, the large shop has a contemporary, welcoming vibe. In addition to the more specialized offerings of the bakery, deli, produce section, and meat and seafood counter, this full-line grocer's spacious aisles are densely stocked with an array of goods, including vegetarian and vegan fare and organic goods. The store is remarkable for its freshness—meat is cut daily, and produce is delivered each morning. Oenophiles will appreciate the large selection of wines from across the state and the world, and the wine pairings offered by the staff chef. *18551 Grand River Ave., www.metrofoodland.com, (313) 838-2754*

Metro Music - For more than 60 years, Metro Music has been a go-to for fledgling musicians on the west side. Specializing in economical rock instruments such as guitars, basses, drum kits, and related equipment, Metro isn't the place for a virtuoso, but it's well-suited for beginners. While the shop is a little rough around the edges, showing signs of wear, it has remained dedicated to providing neophytes places to pick up new instruments, as well as learn them. Mark

Lamonte, the son of the original owner, holds a B.M.E. from Eastern Michigan University and teaches lessons in almost every instrument from woodwinds to strings to percussion for only $5 per half hour—cheap enough to let people keep practicing. *8647 Southfield Fwy., (313) 258-1918.*

Pinky's Shuga Shack - This charming stop-in bakery on the west side has a menu of sugary treats that mirrors its setting: cute, sweet, and homemade. Pinky's is made up in the favorite color of its owner to resemble a pink 1950s bakery counter, where you can take a seat at the chrome stools or at one of the two small tables with matching-colored dishes. The real attraction, however, isn't the ambience—it's the confections. Pinky's serves up homemade cupcakes, brownies, pies (regular or fried), cobblers, cakes, muffins, and cookies, emphasizing quality ingredients (only butter, no oils), and has quickly caught on as a neighborhood favorite for in-and-out treats or special orders. Closed Mondays and Tuesdays, Wi-Fi available. *18929 Schoolcraft Rd., www.pinkysshugashack.com, (313) 837-2253.*

Quvon Tiki's Gifts Galore - Although Tiki's offers a selection of party favors, colorful tablecloths, and greeting cards for all occasions, the real deal here is the balloon arrangements. From custom balloon archways to balloon bouquets numbers and letters to intricate balloon sculptures, Tiki's can add a special touch to any celebration. Drop in to consult with balloon-crafters and see the extensive lookbook, or call ahead to schedule an appointment. And don't be fooled by the name—Tiki's isn't tiki-themed and does balloons for any occasion. *19845 W. McNichols Rd., www.tikiballoons.com, (313) 532-2058.*

Reen's Cakes & Things - There is nothing better than butter, and Reen Jones—owner and baker of Reen's Cakes & Things—knows that better than anyone. In her store in the Grandmont-Rosedale neighborhood, Reen makes "cakes for all occasions," including personal-size mini-cakes. She's been in business in the neighborhood for 18 years, and her cakes are so popular, she'll have lines out the door on weekends. Her cakes are rich, moist, decadent, and flavorful—her signature caramel cake has stovetop-cooked buttery caramel icing, and her 7Up pound cake is lemony with a rich cream cheese frosting. Aside from cakes, she also offers a variety of cookies, pies, and other treats. *17400 Grand River Ave., (313) 836-1940.*

Rosedale Hardware - From hardware to appliance repair, this storied neighborhood shop offers it all. Inside the old-timey brick building, the eclectic showroom displays paints and stains, nails and screws, and even antique key-cutting machines, though the latter are not for sale. Outside of the essentials, homeowners will appreciate the wide selection of remodeling supplies: faucets, fixtures, closet doors. The welcoming owner is eager to offer his mechanical expertise— he'll fix anything from toasters to lawnmowers, living up to the promise of their tagline claiming that Rosedale Hardware is home to "the problem solvers." *19140 Grand River Ave., (313) 532-3848.*

Sisters Cakery - This charming Warrendale classic has been family-owned since the 1950s. The maroon vitrolite tiles still jazz up the facade, just as they did on opening day, and the vintage blade sign and retro awning still beckon to customers. Inherited by the sisters, the children of the original owners and the namesakes of the business, this shop continues to whip up some of the finest baked goods in the area, offering a wide selection of sweets, from cookies to baklava. However, the house specialty is its moist, yummy cakes, which can be skillfully custom-decorated. *15730 W. Warren Ave. (313) 846-4777.*

Strictly Sportswear - Detroit's first hip-hop apparel store, Strictly opened in Highland Park in 1984 but moved to this location in 1989. Take a peek at the photos taped to the counter of owner Kathy Hamlin with LL Cool J, Jay-Z, Eminem, and the many other stars who have visited the shop. Kathy knows the history of the neighborhood, as well as the hip-hop artists and fashion labels that got their start there. Visitors who aren't into hip-hop history can strictly shop the vast selection of men's sportswear: Pelle Pelle jeans, hoodies, Adidas track jackets, 59 Fifty flat-brimmed hats, sport coats, sneakers, boots, and dress shoes, and even colorful Coogi sweaters that Bill Cosby would be proud to wear. A small selection of women's jeans can be found here, but for a fuller selection, just down the road is Strictly Women's, a hip-hop apparel store for women owned by the same family. *17644 W. 7 Mile Rd., (313) 534-5110.*

CULTURAL ATTRACTIONS

Artist Village - Resident artist Chazz Miller owns and operates Artists Village, a community arts space and studio that houses Miller's nonprofit, Detroit Art City. Visit once a month for the Creative Juices open mic nights or drop by one afternoon to tour the artist studio, admire the murals, and explore the urban gardens. Detroit Art City also accepts volunteers to help revitalize the Old Redford area through mural painting, urban gardening, and lot cleanup projects. Call ahead to inquire about the event schedule or to plan a volunteer opportunity. Parking available next door, at the corner of Lahser Road and Orchard Street. *17340 Lahser St., (313) 544-0848.*

Buffalo Soldiers Heritage Center - Opened in 2007, the Buffalo Soldiers Heritage Center educates area youths on the historical significance of the Buffalo Soldiers and exposes children to horses by teaching horseback riding. The beautiful and bucolic center, housed in a former mounted police station within Rouge Park, is home to a large barn, several large, fenced horseback-riding paddocks, and a display area featuring a number of Buffalo Soldier artifacts. The president and resident re-enactor, James H. Mills, prides himself on the center's youth-orientated programming, including re-enactments, educational lessons, and riding sessions on the center's nine horses. Horse and pony rides are available for youths ages four and older. The facility is open year-round, except for when it's raining. If you visit, bring carrots and red apple treats for your equestrian hosts! *21800 Joy Rd., (313) 270-2939.*

ENTERTAINMENT & RECREATION

New Rogell Golf Course - Opened in 1914 as a municipal facility, the historic, par-70 course was purchased by the Greater Grace Temple in 2004, making it the first and only African American-owned course in Michigan, and one of only six in the United States. Designed by famed golf course designer Donald Ross, New Rogell stretches a gorgeous 6,065 yards across the Rouge River. An archetypal Ross design, the greens offer a challenging slope, and accuracy off the tee is a must, with valleys and scenic hazards cutting through the front side, creating narrow fairways. The course is economical, especially if you take advantage of early-bird specials that include cart privileges. The beauty and history of New Rogell makes for a perfect special function or family outing, especially with access to dining facilities. *18601 Berg Rd., www.golfnewrogell.com, (313) 255-4653.*

North Rosedale Park Community House & The Park Players - Opened in 1939, this charming community-owned venue is surrounded by a beautiful six-acre park and located in the heart of the city's historic North Rosedale Park neighborhood. While the community house is a cozy and beautiful space used for community gatherings and private parties much of the year, it comes alive several times a year for Park Players performances. Since its founding in the early 1950s, the Park Players have become renowned for their lively, thought-provoking theatrical productions of comedies, musicals, and dramas including Joseph and the Amazing Technicolor Dreamcoat, Much Ado About Nothing, and One Flew Over the Cuckoo's Nest. The cabaret-style seating and occasional delicious dinner theater performances offer an intimate visitor experience not to be missed. *18445 Scarsdale St., www.northrosedalepark.org, (313) 835-1103.*

Northland Roller Rink - Serving the west side of the city for more than 60 years, Northland is Michigan's largest roller rink and is absolutely packed almost every night of the week with skaters of all ages and abilities. The beautiful rink was recently redone, and the inside has been upgraded substantially. Call ahead or check out the rink's website for its many scheduled nights targeted toward different age groups and musical tastes, including adult skates, dance skating events, laser tag, and classes. Great for private parties (there is a "party room" off to the side—call ahead to reserve it), admission is affordable, the sound system is superior, and there is a snack bar with typical pizza and hot dog fare. Although it offers full rental services, check out Northland's well-stocked skate shop if you're in the market for some new skates or gear of your own. *22311 W. 8 Mile Rd., www.northlandrink.com, (313) 535-1443.*

» Redford Theatre - A Detroit treasure that was once billed as "America's Most Unique Suburban Playhouse," the Redford Theatre is a stunning Japanese-themed movie house that first opened its doors in 1928. With 1,661 seats spread over the first floor and balcony, the theater has been lovingly restored by the Motor City Theater Organ Society, which has been working on the restoration since 1977. Centered around the theater's original Barton organ, the ornate show space is dotted with intricate painted details and fixtures and features a night sky with illuminated stars above the audience and a stage and screen flanked by a two-story Japanese village. Volunteer-run, the theater screens classic films accented by live organ performances, intermissions with live entertainment, and old-timey cartoon preludes. As if the theater's offerings didn't sell themselves, shows are generally just $4, and the concessions are comparably economical. *17360 Lahser Rd., www.redfordtheatre.com, (313) 537-2560.*

Rouge Park - The largest park within the city of Detroit, Rouge Park is a bucolic, serenely forested space that features small programmed areas offering diverse recreational opportunities. Named for the industrial waterway that snakes through it for two miles, Rouge Park was purchased and developed by the city in the 1920s. The park spans more than 1,184 acres—nearly 40% larger than Central Park in New York City. In the face of limited parks spending by the City of Detroit, the Friends of Rouge Park has begun maintaining the space and offering occasional programming since its founding in 2002. Rouge Park features a number of attractions that make it a unique leisure opportunity, including an 18-hole golf course, 14 regulation baseball diamonds, 11 tennis courts, the Brennan pools, more than 200 picnic tables, a driving range, an archery range, playgrounds, eight miles of hiking and mountain bike trails, a model airplane field, a sledding hill, and, in 2012, the largest urban farm in Michigan. Among these amenities, a few stand out:

- **Rouge Park Driving Range** is a full-service driving range adjacent to the Rouge Park Golf Course clubhouse. The range offers yardage flags, target greens, and both turf and natural grass tees, allowing golfers to practice with irons, woods, and drivers.

- Opened in 1923, the **Rouge Park Golf Course** is an 18-hole, par-72, public course stretching 6,325 yards from the black tees. Built on hilly, sloping terrain, the golf course's circuitous fairways and numerous water traps and sandy bunkers make it unforgiving

for those with rusty drivers. The extremely challenging 11th hole still haunts some golfers.

- The **Brennan Pools** is the park's aquatic area. The facility includes a comfortable, paved pool deck, two Olympic-size pools and a smaller diving pool with a diving tower. The pools hosted the trials for the U.S. Olympic Swimming Team in 1948, 1956, and 1960.

- The **Buffalo Soldiers Heritage Center** is an active horse farm and interpretive center dedicated to the Buffalo Soldiers. See separate entry for more details.

- **D-Town Farm**, the largest urban farm in Michigan, is the work of the local nonprofit Detroit Black Community Food Security Network and encompasses seven acres of Rouge Park. The farm offers many, many, organic vegetable plots, mushroom beds, hoop houses, and a compost pile.

Beyond its rich infrastructure, Rouge Park offers hundreds of acres of dense woodlands and scenic prairies, both of which are home to a rich diversity of urban wildlife—including, most notably, raccoons, deer, pheasants, an array of birds, and seasonal butterflies, which flock to the park's fields of milkweed. In the fall months, the park becomes a picturesque landscape as the many trees change color. *Rouge Park runs along W. Outer Drive, between W. Warren Avenue, and Schoolcraft Street, www.rougepark.org.*

SITES

American Concrete Institute Building - Designed by Minoru Yamasaki, a master of modernity, the oft-overlooked American Concrete Institute Building is an underappreciated miniature modern masterpiece. Built in 1959 to house offices for the ACI, a technical and educational society dedicated to all aspects of concrete structures, the one-story building is quintessential Yamasaki, with an airy, sun-laden interior, "floating" pre-cast concrete elements, and triangular flourishes that meld modern minimalism and Japanese traditionalism. ACI sold the property in 1996, and it is now in use by the Starr Commonwealth, a social assistance organization. *22470 W. 7 Mile Rd.*

Grandmont Rosedale - North Rosedale Park, Rosedale Park, Grandmont, Grandmont #1, and Minock Park, the five neighborhoods collectively known as Grandmont Rosedale, form a dense, contiguous historic district defined by its incredible density of architectural beauty and charming oak- and maple-lined streets. Primarily built during the 1920s, the area features custom-built homes in an array of architectural styles, including Prairie, French Renaissance, Tudor Revival, Cape Cod, International, Colonial, and Arts and Crafts. Although the homes in Grandmont Rosedale are more modest than those in some other notable historic districts, such as Indian Village, Palmer Woods, and Boston Edison, the area is unique for its scale. The neighborhood spans more than 5,000 homes and 2.5 square miles, and consequently is home to the state's largest national historic district. The solid, gracious homes were built with unique, custom architectural features and details, with fireplaces, Pewabic tile, and high-end construction materials. Today, the area is a vibrant, diverse community with beautiful parks and landscaped boulevards, making it one of Detroit's neighborhood gems. Although the entire neighborhood has beautiful homes, the area's grandest streets are Bretton Drive, Glastonbury Avenue, and Warwick Street. *Grandmont Rosedale is bounded by Evergreen Ave., McNichols Rd., Southfield Fwy., Grand River Ave., and Asbury Park St., and Schoolcraft Rd., www.grandmontrosedale.com.*

POINTS OF INTEREST

Ford Family Burial Plot - Now located across the street from a derelict gas station and a moderate-income housing development, the small St. Martha's Episcopal Church Cemetery is the final resting place of one of the world's most powerful and wealthy luminaries, Henry Ford, the pioneering industrialist and founder of Ford Motor Company. His wife, Clara, as well as many other members of the Ford family, join Henry in eternal slumber nearby. *15801 Joy Rd.*

Grave of the Lone Ranger - The famous voice of the WXYZ radio show The Lone Ranger, Earle W. Graser, is buried in Grand Lawn Cemetery. Hi-Yo Silver! *23501 Grand River Ave.*

North Rosedale Park Tree Nursery and Outdoor Classroom - Nestled inside of a primarily residential neighborhood, this nursery has transformed an abandoned lot into a gathering place for the community. *16857 Stahelin Ave.*

Obama Gas Station - A unique photo opportunity, some didn't think you could brand a gas station with a presidential theme, but in 2008, the Obama Gas Station said, "Yes we can!" *15800 Joy Rd.*

Son House's Grave - Famous for the songs Death Letter and John the Revelator, legendary Mississippi bluesman Eddie James "Son House" Jr. played with Robert Johnson and idolized by Muddy Waters and Jack White. His gravestone reads, "Go away, Blues; go away and leave poor me alone." *18507 Lahser Rd.*

Ted Nugent Home - "The Motor City Madman" spent his early childhood in this small home on the city's west side. *23251 Florence Ave.*

World War II Memorial - In the median of Outer Drive in Brightmoor stands a small but proud monument to honor the sacrifices of soldiers who served in World War II. *Outer Drive and Lahser Rd.*

CHAPTER 11
HAMTRAMCK/
HIGHLAND PARK

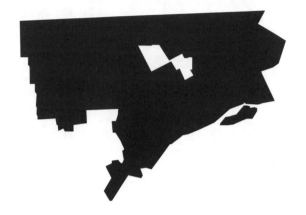

Nestled within Detroit, and surrounded by the city on all sides, are two tiny individual municipalities with distinct histories and cultures—Hamtramck and Highland Park. Because of their small size (2.08 and 2.97 square miles, respectively) and their proximity to and location completely within Detroit, their past and present are intrinsically linked to the city. In many ways, they feel less like separate cities and more like neighborhoods within Detroit. Although very different, the two cities, together, offer visitors a wide range of opportunities to admire the unique character of the region's past, present, and future.

HAMTRAMCK

Named for Colonel Jean Francis Hamtramck—the revolutionary war hero who seized Detroit from British control—Hamtramck is an ethnic enclave with a reputation for diverse international grocers and restaurants, vintage dive bars, popular events, and a storied rock and roll heritage. Although the city has followed its larger neighbor through an ongoing social and physical evolution, the city's distinct waves of Polish, African-American, Yugoslav, Yemeni, Bangladeshi, and Arab residents have continually renewed the city and buoyed its municipal trajectory. Although many of these immigrants have moved to other communities—often only to be replaced by counterparts from other countries—the city's diverse current and past residents have left lasting imprints on the commercial landscape of this cheerful urban hamlet.

Founded in 1798, Hamtramck was a largely agrarian village until the dawn of the industrial revolution; a period marked by remarkable, record-setting growth. In 1910, the Dodge brothers built their Dodge Main plant to build parts for Ford, and ultimately, built Hamtramck. Between 1910 and 1920, the city grew from a population of 3,559 to 48,615, a rate of 1,266%—the nation's fastest growth at the time. The Dodge brothers were far more culturally tolerant than other contemporary magnates, creating one of the most diverse plants and cities at the time. This tolerance and resultant diversity helped lead Dodge Main to become the first plant organized by the UAW, and site of the union's first sit-down strike, in 1937. The city's population peaked in 1930, at 56,268, and has gradually declined since in the wake of plant downsizing and suburban development. Today, 22,423 residents call Hamtramck home.

Despite population loss, Hamtramck remains the densest city in the state, among the most diverse and vibrant, and an exciting place to visit. Generations of the city's increasingly diverse residents have hung their shingle, creating a bustling commercial center, full of neighborhood-scale shops, grocers, restaurants, bars, cultural, and recreational amenities—many of which preserve the flavors of proprietors' home countries. In addition, the city has a rich musical heritage and thriving music scene. The city inherited a host of corner bars from previous generations of autoworkers, and today, Hamtramck, home to the most bars per capita of any city in the U.S., boasts scores of small live music venues as these bars have added stages. The city—the birthplace of Mitch Ryder of Devil in a Blue Dress fame—is home to the nation's largest local music festival—the Metro Times Blowout—and many of the region's favorite rock bands. Once a year, on Fat Tuesday, Hamtramck becomes the center of the region, as thousands of Metro Detroiters descend upon the city to take part in Pączki Day, the Polish tradition of eating doughnut-like pączki before Lent.

HIGHLAND PARK

As a small factory town enclave within Detroit, Highland Park has paralleled its larger neighbor through periods of meteoric growth and tumultuous decline. Despite navigating many chapters of challenging history and bearing the resultant scars of abandonment caused by population decline and plant closures, Highland Park has soldiered on.

The city draws its name from a large ridge once located at Woodward Avenue and Highland Street. In 1818, the feature's natural beauty and strategic location piqued the interest of famed Judge Augustus Woodward, who platted a new community, Woodwardville in 1825. Although the plan was never built, his early work facilitated piecemeal development and eventually led residents to incorporate the area as the Village of Highland Park in 1889. Taking advantage of the low property taxes in this small farming community, Henry Ford purchased 160 acres in 1907 to build what would become the Highland Park Ford Plant and ignited a population explosion. Aspiring autoworkers immigrated in droves, building block after block of Arts and Crafts homes. Between 1900 and 1920, the population increased by 10,815%, from 427 to 46,499. In order to protect its burgeoning tax base, the area incorporated as a city in 1918 to withstand

Detroit's annexation attempts. In 1925, Chrysler Corporation was founded in the city, and Highland Park would remain the site of its world headquarters until the mid-1990s. After Henry Ford moved automotive production to River Rouge in 1927, the city began a sustained population loss. After peaking in 1930 with nearly 53,000 residents, the city's population has continuously declined since, to 11,176 today.

Despite this difficult past, visitors to Highland Park today will find numerous historic automotive heritage sites, a handful of working-class restaurants and shops that remain from the automotive heyday, and a variety of social enterprises. From the historic Ford factory and the original Chrysler headquarters site, to the nation's first freeway and a neighborhood diner once popular with hungry Ford workers, the city is littered with automotive history. With innovative redevelopment examples, such as a nonprofit gourmet restaurant and a community-orientated boutique art gallery, it has a nascent, empowered future.

Some neighborhoods within Highland Park may be unsafe, especially at night. We recommend visitors remain aware of their surroundings and employ common sense safety rules, including avoiding travelling distances on foot.

BARS & RESTAURANTS

7 Brothers Bar - Once upon a time, Macedonian-born George Cvetnovski wanted to open a local theater. It never panned out, but his chosen career probably did more for the local theater community than another black box stage ever could have. The walls in this long, narrow Hamtramck watering hole are adorned with 150 framed headshots of aspiring thespians who have, at one time or another, been regulars at the joint. Some of them have gone on to greatness (most notably Keegan-Michael Key of Mad TV fame), while some have faded into obscurity. And this Friday night, you can bet that some of them will still be sitting at George's bar, chewing the fat on the local theater community. The bar dates to the building's birth in 1924, and 7 Brothers claims to be the oldest bar in Hamtramck (take that boast with a grain of salt: George also says the still-operating refrigerator is original to the building). The ornate tin ceiling carries the traces of decades of pre-ban cigarette smoke. With a great jukebox, a good stash of Polish and American beers and an ever-lively clientele, 7

Brothers is as worthy as any bar in booze-saturated Hamtramck. *11831 Joseph Campau St., Hamtramck, www.7brothersbar.com, (313) 365-6576.*

Aladdin Sweets & Cafe - Interested in enjoying delicious and authentic Bengali and Indian cuisine? Expect to hear Bengali drifting through the air of this neighborhood spot. Since 1998, Aladdin has offered its own delicious (and very inexpensive) takes on all of your favorites: masala, paneer, samosas, naan—especially the naan!—and more. If you can't decide what to order, they offer a bountiful buffet for only $8. Grab some carryout, and take a peek at the selection of decadent desserts in the case at the carryout counter. Take a seat with the locals in the cramped worn booths in the original location, or dine-in at their new "formal" dining room next door. In the summer months, an adjoining patio offers lovely, expanded outdoor seating. *11945 Conant St., Hamtramck, www.aladdinsweet.com, (313) 891-8050.*

Amar Pizza - Within a nondescript storefront without much decor, owner Khurshed Ahmed's Bangladeshi pizzeria offers some of Detroit's most unorthodox pies. Although the pizza has strong fundamentals—fluffy and crunchy crust, flavorful seasonings, a nice cheese-to-sauce balance—the real distinguishing characteristic is the variety of toppings: ghost peppers, naga sauce, cilantro, tandoori chicken, crab, dried shrimp, and eggplant represent only a fraction of the available options. While all the pies are solid, the tandoori pizza and dry fish pizza are exceptional. Lovers of unusual pizza will also enjoy the neighboring Al Qamar Pizza, which offers fine halal pies alongside a stable of tasty subs and sandwiches. *11608 Conant St., Hamtramck, www.amarpizza.biz, (313) 366-0980.*

Amicci's Pizza - Detroit's entrant in the international super-greasy-yet-super-delicious pizza competition, Amicci's is an unassuming neighborhood joint offering all the staples—ribs, wings, grinders, shrimp, burgers, and pizza. This Hamtramck location—like the Southwest Detroit Amicci's Pizza (3849 W. Vernor Hwy.) across town—serves up its tasty, distinctively cheesy and affordable pies until the cows come home. Although Amicci's offers all the usual toppings, it's renowned for its inventive and delicious specialty pizzas, like the Chicken Thai Pie, Pesto Delight, and The Greek. *9841 Joseph Campau St., Hamtramck, www.amiccispizza.com, (313) 875-1992.*

Baker Streetcar Bar - Named for the old streetcar line that once ferried workers from Joseph Campau Street to the Ford plant in Dearborn, this family-friendly, shotgun-style dive bar in downtown Hamtramck isn't much on eye candy but is heavy on charm, comfort, personality, and cheap beer ($1.50 High Life drafts and bottled Tyskie is available). The counter is bookended by TVs and overlooked by a carved Polish Eagle in the middle. There's not much of a kitchen, but there are periodic steak nights on Fridays and live music on a regular basis. The bar is marked only by a small red-and-blue neon sign in the window, so don't miss it. *9817 Joseph Campau St., Hamtramck, (313) 873-8296.*

Bonoful Sweets and Cafe - Since opening in 2011, owners Abu Bokkor, Nazmul Islam, and Mohammed Malik have developed a restaurant and menu worthy of the name Bonoful, which means "bouquet of flowers" in Bengali. The interior of the restaurant is a stark departure from the bright neon lights of the strip-mall exterior. The cozy contemporary space features intimate booths, chandeliers, and high-back leather chairs, offering a dignified environment in which to enjoy your food. Bonoful offers a composite menu of Bengali, Indian, and Pakistani dishes at excellent prices, including a daily lunch buffet. Goat meat, chicken, tandoori, and biryani dishes are the keystones, complemented by several varieties of homemade bread. Bonoful also offers a fine selection of ambrosiac desserts, including gulab jamun—fried milk and flour balls served chilled drenched in sugar syrup—and ras malai, a sweet dairy/paneer concoction, as well as figs and lassi. Bonoful isn't decorated as a fine dining establishment, but the highlights are food, selection, and service. *12085 Conant Ave., Hamtramck, www.bonofulsweetsandcafe.com, (313) 368-8800.*

Burk's Igloo - A seriously one-of-a-kind destination for summertime treats, you can spot Burk's by the nearly 20-foot tall ice cream cone it flaunts from its sidewalk spot in Hamtramck. Offering all the delights you'd expect from a classic roadside ice cream stand, customers can enjoy soft-serve flavors, dipped cones, sundaes, floats, blizzard-type creations, and fried foods galore. After ordering at the walk-up window, plant yourself at one of the nearby picnic tables for some grade-A people watching. Burk's ascribes to a seasonal schedule, so it's generally open spring to fall. *10300 Conant St., Hamtramck, (313) 872-6830.*

Café 1923 - Built in 1923 by Polish immigrants as a corner store and owned by four generations of the same family, this building has been lovingly restored into a beautiful community coffee shop. Enjoy a cup of joe, a tasty treat, comfortable chairs, tons of outlets, and Wi-Fi without the corporate coffeehouse atmosphere. A favorite among locals, this charming spot is the perfect place to dig into a book, a conversation, or some serious work. The gracious front room features an original tin ceiling, counter, and wood floors, and if you're in need of some inspiration, the rear reading room is packed with floor-to-ceiling oak shelves of kitsch and books. Look for frequent exhibits and events from Hamtramck art collective, HATCH. *2287 Holbrook St., Hamtramck, www.cafe1923.com, (313) 319-8766.*

Campau Tower - Once a part of the storied White Tower chain, this castle of carnivorism features the original postwar counter-facing grill, exterior Vitrolite tiles and straightforward menu. Although Campau Tower offers a small variety of items, the fries, sliders, pierogi, and coffee stand out. Whether or not the rumors about the medicinal qualities of Campau's sliders—that they can prevent hangovers—are true, this "medicine" goes down easy. The tiny steam-grilled sliders are renowned for their big taste, caramelized onions, zesty pickles, and gooey buns. A cast of Hamtramck characters contributes to the 1950s diner atmosphere and park themselves on the vinyl stools at the orange laminate countertop, gossiping with the server at the grill. That means customers may have standing room only for this show, which runs through the night at the 24-hour neighborhood classic. *10337 Joseph Campau St., Hamtramck, (313) 873-7330.*

Cornerstone Bistro - Looking for excellent service, delicious food that's easy on your wallet, and a good cause to support? Look no further than Cornerstone Bistro. The restaurant is staffed by chefs, servers, and managers training in culinary arts and business management in an apprenticeship and associates degree program through Detroit Rescue Mission Ministries (DRMM) and Wayne County Community College. Park in the DRMM parking lot and follow the ramp to the restaurant side entrance, where the church building transforms into an elegant bistro offering a five-star dining experience for a very affordable price. The modern interior features granite tabletops wrapped by tall, spacious booth seating, golden walls, and warm, romantic lighting. Attentive and professional servers dressed in sleek black uniforms may suggest anything from Filet Mignon to a classic chicken shawarma sandwich to hearty mac and cheese to a veggie burger—and anything in between! Of the many innovative nonprofit organizations that work to help individuals and positively transform the community, Cornerstone Bistro might very well have the tastiest and most elegant approach. *13130 Woodward Ave., Highland Park, www.drmm.org/restauranthomepage.htm, (313) 993-4700.*

Courage Coffee - Opened in 2012 by the adjoining church and its extraordinarily friendly preacher, the Reverend "Chilly" Chilton, Courage Coffee has quickly built a rabid following thanks to its outstanding coffee and lively atmosphere. Amid a Spartan, dark, industrial aesthetic, the affable staff of coffee aficionados brew Courage's diverse and rotating selection of four fair trade coffees from around the world with drip, French press, and pour-over methods. Courage's pour-overs make for a clean, flavorful, aromatic cup of coffee: the perfect complement to the delicious poppy seed bread. The blazing Wi-Fi, comfortable seating—including former church pews—and plentiful outlets make it popular with local writers and others looking to pore over their work alongside a tasty pour-over. Notably, Courage Coffee does not offer espresso, so those hankering for a latte or a red eye might look elsewhere. *2950 Caniff St., Hamtramck, www.couragecoffee.com, (313) 875-7325.*

Family Donut Shop - As the name suggests, this wood-paneled corner shop on Conant favors the sweet side of the menu, with a cornucopia of tasty, economical cake doughnuts and pączki. However, the neighborhood secret is that the Family Donut Shop is a great place to grab a burek, a delicious, generously portioned Bosnian flake pastry stuffed with meat or feta, served cold or hot, though we suggest the latter. Those looking to sit while they indulge can belly up to the L-shaped vinyl counter and eat under the watchful eye of a framed photograph of Princess Diana. The shop is welcoming and friendly, and gets busy early—weekday hours start at 4:30am. Smoothies, soft serve, and hand-dipped ice cream are also available. *11300 Conant St., Hamtramck, (313) 368-9214.*

Halal Desi Pizza - This place is not your typical demure mom-and-pop Indian, Italian, Chinese, American, and Mexican sandwich and pizza shop. Alongside his more conventional dishes, jolly owner Kazi Miah serves a number of spectacular and unique fusion dishes, including the renowned chicken tikka pizza, malai kebab pizza, chili cheese samosas, and the customizable Hamtramck Sandwich. With only eight always-packed seats, visitors should plan on carryout or free delivery. *2200 Caniff St., Hamtramck, (313) 365-0111.*

Hamtramck Coney Island - Unlike the typical Detroit coney island, Hamtramck Coney Island is known for its locally made sausage and traditional dogs served Polish-style with green peppers, onions, and mustard—just like the hot dog in the restaurant logo. This family-owned business can still do the traditional Detroit coney, as well as other tasty greasy fixtures, like omelets and hash browns that come fast and cheap. You won't find any Greek items on the menu, as is common in Greek-owned coneys, but you will find pierogi. The charming wood paneling, mural of a polish landscape, and counter seating right by the cook's grill make for a cozy breakfast or lunch spot. Sit with a group of friends in one of the brown cushioned booths, or swivel into one of the counter stools next to the boisterous group of regulars. *9741 Joseph Campau St., Hamtramck, (313) 873-4569.*

Kelly's Bar - A lively dive open since 1984, Kelly's is renowned among fans of blues and booze. Set in an old house on a quiet block of Holbrook, the bar is a blithe, dark space full of character, with Christmas-tree lights over the bar, simple wood paneling, and old school breweriana. Although Kelly's offers all the de rigueur mid-shelf liquor and beer options, many guests opt for the Carter administration-era prices on select domestics during the nightly beer deals. The bar's small kitchen offers a small but tasty menu of bar fare, such as coneys, burgers, and fries, but is renowned for the weekly food specials, including the popular Friday night fish fry. Although delightful every night, the bar comes alive on Wednesdays,

Fridays, and Saturdays, when some of the area's finest local blues bands take the stage. *2403 Holbrook St., Hamtramck, (313) 872-0387.*

Nandi's Knowledge Cafe - "Knowledge" is too limited a word for what you'll find at Nandi's. In addition to a cafe set in a used bookstore, Nandi's also has a boutique art gallery one store north. Both are heavily oriented toward illuminating issues in the black community with their selection of literature and artwork, respectively. Whether dining or reading, the bookstore is a comfortable, casual place to browse and relax at a mixture of used tables, spruced up with live plants, and lit by glass lamps hung beneath a tin ceiling. The reasonably priced, satisfying cuisine leans toward vegetarian Southern, with wings and burgers also available. Street side dining is offered. The gallery is decked floor to ceiling with diverse, eye-catching work from local artists, as well as authentic African masks and carvings, aromatically intoned with incense, and decorated with live greenery, which is available for sale. The gallery regularly hosts lectures and open mic poetry nights. Except for events, both the cafe and gallery close early. *12522 Woodward Ave., Highland Park, www.nandiscafe.com, (313) 865-1288.*

New Dodge Lounge - Standing behind the unassuming brown and red neon sign on Hamtramck's main drag is the New Dodge Lounge, perhaps Metro Detroit's most under-appreciated rock and roll bar. Inside, you'll find lofted ceilings with exposed rafters and a balcony that once doubled as a brothel. The well-equipped stage (well, by dive bar standards, at least) is home to local rock, punk, and metal bands on the weekends. The crowd is a mix of townies and tattooed rockers, but the handcrafted bar, wood floors, and tasteful light fixtures give this bar a touch of class that's all-too-absent from most rock 'n' roll havens. Be sure not to miss the New Dodge during Blowout each winter, when the bar regularly hosts a not-to-be missed lineup. Also, see that bright red short bus out front (the one with an "I love roadhead" bumper sticker)? Once Lions season starts, that sucker will ferry you to and from the game for free, with a free post-game buffet. Very nice, New Dodge. *8850 Joseph Campau St., Hamtramck, www.newdodgelounge.com, (313) 874-5963.*

Painted Lady Lounge - A dive bar's dive bar. This is a charmingly grungy Hamtramck joint. Look for the bubblegum pink and mint green facade and enter through the side door to the right of the main front door (that's for bands only). Inside, you'll find an ornate curved wooden bar and a tin ceiling mixed with a punk rock dive bar

aesthetic, including a Pabst Blue Ribbon mirror. The Painted Lady is home to live music every weekend—usually of the punk or rockabilly variety. Take a seat at one of the handful of tables and catch a band, or if you're so inclined, hit the well-loved dance floor. Check the venue's Facebook page for nightly specials and events.
2930 Jacob St., Hamtramck, (313) 874-2991.

Palma Restaurant - Located in an adaptively reused bright yellow duplex, Palma is a casual destination for Bosnian food. The unassuming interior is simple yet beautiful, featuring illustrations of Bosnia, an array of plants, and the unmistakable smells of the mother country emanating from the small kitchen. The pleasant staff is happy to help rookies navigate the menu, which is mostly in Bosnian. Among the constellation of delicious fare, the cevapi (a grilled kebab dish), pileca snicla (chicken schnitzel), and teleca corba (veal noodle soup), stand out. While the menu is solidly Bosnian, fans of Croatian, German, and Mediterranean cuisine will find a handful of nice options. *3028 Caniff St., Hamtramck, (313) 875-2722.*

Paycheck's Lounge - Trying to wrap your head around what a working-class Detroit rock 'n' roll bar feels like? Look no further than the stiff drinks, surly bartenders, and constant thrum of guitars and drums at Paycheck's Lounge. Zbigniew Malkiewicz bought the bar in 1979 (he got his nickname Johnny Paycheck from an exasperated boss who couldn't make sense of his given name) and has been running the place ever since. The bar is characterized by the Christmas lights that dangle from the ceiling and create a moody atmosphere with their blue hues. In the intimate stage area, patrons can catch the true-grit rock (and increasingly, electronic) shows that speckle Paycheck's weekend calendar. *2932 Caniff St., Hamtramck, www.paycheckslounge.com, (313) 874-0909.*

» Polish Village Cafe - Originally established as a basement biergarten in 1925, Polish Village has been an integral part of Hamtramck culture for almost 100 years. The interior, which features Old World accents and an elaborate antique wood and stained-glass bar, has retained every ounce of its aesthetic charm and character. But it's got more than looks. The food here is as authentic as it is reasonably priced: Dinners are less than $10, and most come with vegetables, mashed potatoes, sauerkraut, and a soup or salad. Those craving comfort food would be advised to try the pierogi, crepes, dill pickle soup, or potato pancakes; those with more adventurous tastes might venture to try the duck blood soup or fried chicken livers. Can't decide what to get? Try the Polski Talerz, a Polish sampler plate that includes stuffed cabbage, pierogi, kielbasa, and sauerkraut. Of course, be sure to sample the wide selection of Polish beers and liquors. *2990 Yemans St., Hamtramck, www.thepolishvillagecafe.com, (313) 874-5726.*

» Polonia - Just down the street from Polish Village Cafe lies another of Hamtramck's classic Polish haunts. Beyond the red awning and vintage signage, Polonia is kitschy and comfortable. Sit at a booth or a table under the murals depicting Polish country life and lavish displays of traditional handicraft, and order up some of the exceptional, hearty Old World fare. Of course, there are classics like golabki (stuffed cabbage), dill pickle soup, and the "polish trio" of killer kielbasa, potato pancakes, and your choice of pierogi. But, if you're feeling more adventurous, try the "city chicken" for some Hamtramck flair. Naturally, a meal is best washed down with a bottle of Okocim, Żywiec, or a shot of bison grass vodka. For herbivores, Polonia is the best bet in town for Polish food. The place is very accommodating with substitutions on the "trio," and, unlike some other spots, boasts veg-friendly dill pickle soup and potato pierogi made with fake bacon. *2934 Yemans St., Hamtramck, www.polonia-restaurant.net, (313) 873-8432.*

Royal Kabob - Located next door to sister business Al-Haramain International Foods, this Mediterranean gem is a shawarma- and

falafel-lover's dream. Despite the plain—albeit well-kept—interior, Royal Kabob serves up Middle Eastern food that stacks up to the best in the region (and in Metro Detroit, that's saying something!). Mainly featuring Lebanese food, it dishes up incredible, heaping versions of all the favorites: tabbouleh, hummus, kibbee, fattoush, almond rice salad, lentil soup, mujadara, fluffy warm pita, and—yes—kebabs. Their meat dishes—from lamb to beef to chicken to quail—are perfectly cooked and seasoned and, of course, there are vegetarian options aplenty. It's cheap. It's fast. And the delectable garlic sauce alone is worth a visit. *3236 Caniff St., Hamtramck, www.hroyalkabob.com, (313) 872-9454.*

Sheeba Restaurant - Next door to the controversial "Death to Street Art" mural, this Yemeni restaurant's interior lacks the industrial edge of its surroundings. Sheeba is nearly all kitchen, with a half-dozen shabby booths and two flat-screen TVs broadcasting the latest Middle Eastern news. The menu can be a bit difficult to decipher, and communicating in English with the servers can be a little tricky. But with a bit of patience and some hand signals, you'll be fine. The food shines as the main attraction, with a fan favorite being the hearth-baked tandoor bread that resembles a larger, chewier, and tastier version of the familiar pita. Order this with rice, house-made hummus, and a meat or bean dish, and you'll be glad you came! The Seltah and Fattah stews are popular, but everything is flavorful, filling, and mouthwateringly delicious. Portions are large and good for sharing. *8752 Joseph Campau St., Hamtramck, (313) 874-0299.*

Small's Bar - "They're playing THERE?!" This Hamtramck rock venue has attained a near-mythic status for booking rock bands that could easily sell out much larger venues. The club is an intimate, dark room with killer sound; the bar is a gothic dive (note: not goth) with stained glass and one of the city's best jukeboxes. Keep an eye on the listings to get a chance to tug at the pants of your favorite punk rock legend, and start training now for Pączki Day in February, when Small's brings back its signature pączki bomb: a polish custard doughnut injected with locally produced Hard Candy vodka. Who says you can't have your cake and drink it, too? *10339 Conant St., Hamtramck, www.smallsbardetroit.com, (313) 873-1117.*

Suzy's Bar - Tucked on a little side street just off Joseph Campau Street is Suzy's Bar, a little bar with a lot of old school rock 'n' roll soul. Buzz to enter at the heavy metal door, and step into a jukebox-spinning, well drink-spouting, Polish party place. The walls are decorated with multicolored Christmas lights, 1950s antique trinkets, and Hamtramck T-shirts sporting slogans like: "It's not a party until the kielbasa comes out!" The drinks are cheap, the outdoor smoking patio is cozy, and the bathrooms are cleaner and more cluttered with kitschy antiques than your grandma's sewing room. *2942 Evaline St., Hamtramck, (313) 872-9016.*

Victor Red Hots - Coney dog fanatics who crave the classic diner atmosphere—good manners, good cooks, oldies music, and all—will love Victor Red Hots. The scent of fresh-cooked vinegar fries wafts through this old-style coney diner, complete with red counter stool seating, antique cola signs on the walls, quaint booths, and friendly servers decked out in white aprons and paper cook's caps. Victor Red Hots serves all the traditional diner fare, with one other special menu item: beer! Hurry in for breakfast or lunch, because this pleasant blast from the past closes around 3:30 pm. *12 Victor St., Highland Park, (313) 868-0766.*

Whiskey in the Jar - It's small and dark. The coolers are covered with stickers from long-defunct bands. And its mascot is a stuffed "ratalope" (like a jackalope, but a rat with horns). Ask for a PBR, and they'll want to know whether you want a can, tallboy, or draft. If that doesn't sound like your quintessential neighborhood bar, you must not be from around these parts. Whiskey in the Jar's cheap drinks and affable staff have made this one of the top locals bars for drinkers in both Hamtramck and Detroit. Sit on a barstool, and you'll rub elbows with everyone from the neighborhood drunk to political campaign organizers relaxing after a long day of pounding the pavement. It's hard to explain the easy camaraderie of a true, free-flowing neighborhood joint, but this one has it. You rarely leave without making a new friend, hearing a piece of gossip, and maybe drinking a bit more than you intended. Addcd points: It's possibly the only bar in town that keeps its bottle of Jezy (Hamtramck's ubiquitous Polish blackberry brandy) on ice, should you be looking for a chilled nip of the syrupy booze. *2741 Yemans St., Hamtramck, (313) 873-4154.*

Yemen Cafe - If you've never tried Yemeni cuisine but want to explore some of Detroit's lesser-known culinary delights, stepping into Yemen Café is akin to being transported through a portal to a local dive on the outskirts of Sana'a. The interior and seating are hardly glamorous, and one can easily see into the back kitchen. But the smells coming from within are as enticing as they are exotic, and they make up for any aesthetic deficiencies. Salta, the national dish of Yemen, is brown meat stew spiced with a healthy amount of fenugreek and served in a boiling clay pot. Vegetarian alternatives include fasolia—a white bean stew cooked with eggs and spices—or foul, mashed fava beans with garlic, tomatoes, and onions. Dipping the naan-like bread and sharing over the boiling pots is the custom in Yemen, so don't expect any plates or cutlery unless your request them. *8735 Joseph Campau St., Hamtramck, (313) 871-4349.*

ZamZam Restaurant - The Bangladeshi community of Hamtramck has a jewel in ZamZam. With a unique two-for-the-price-of-one setup, the eatery offers guests a down-and-divey carryout-oriented dining room (favored by Bangladeshi locals) adjoined to a full-service dining room that's easier on the eyes and more date-night friendly (favored by everyone else). The menu features a compendium of succulently prepared and vibrantly flavored Bangladeshi cuisine (which is similar to Indian) including a wide-range of halal meat, fish, and vegetarian dishes served with a choice of fragrant naan or basmati rice and chutneys. Favorite dishes are the lamb and tandoori chicken biryani, though the kormas are also excellent. *11917 Conant St., Hamtramck, www.zamzamcafe.com, (313) 893-9902.*

SHOPPING & SERVICES

Al-Haramain International Foods - A destination for its abundant, high-quality, fresh, CHEAP Middle Eastern and Eastern European groceries, a panoply of olives, organic foods, cage-free eggs, hormone-free milk, bulk grains and nuts, spices, and a vast selection of European chocolates and candy bars, one of Al-Haramain's best features is that it's open till midnight every day of the week! It also stocks a small selection of halal meats and cheeses, quality produce (including some harder-to-find options, like taro root and cactus pears), American pantry staples, and fresh breads and cookies from beloved New Yasmeen bakery in Dearborn. *3306 Caniff St., Hamtramck, (313) 870-9748.*

Barberella - A beauty parlor that's just as quirky, kitschy, and retro-glam as its name implies, Barberella adds a vibrant streak to the Hamtramck community. Tucked away in the corner of a mostly residential neighborhood, it can be difficult to find, but once inside, the place is far from ordinary. Sandy Kramer, the owner and sole stylist of Barberella, is peppy and cute, fitting in perfectly with the decor: bright pink walls, checkered tile floor, and vintage hairdryers, with obscure punk and garage rock tunes coming through the speakers. While the salon pays homage to the past, Kramer's shears are versatile, and she will cut, style, and color your hair based on your needs, whether you're looking for something simple, classic, retro, contemporary, or edgy. *3301 Edwin St., Hamtramck, (313) 871-0070.*

Bozek's Meat and Groceries - Located just a block away from Joseph Campau Street, the highlight of this midsize market is the big walk-in meat cooler featuring cuts from small to massive at affordable prices. Bozek's also features a large selection of Central- and Eastern European-imported and prepared foods (including a broad selection of pierogi), smoked meats, fresh produce, imported candies and chocolates, and a great variety of European soft drinks and juices. Check out the yummy pay-by-the-pound hot-food bar at the back of the market. *3317 Caniff St., Hamtramck, www.bozekmarkets.com, (313) 369-0600.*

CHIIPSS - Detroit skaters have a haven at Chiipss. Recently moved from Plymouth to this bright, beautifully contemporary space in Hamtramck, this shop sells house-machined maple skateboards alongside an array of assertively decked-out boards from local vendors (Anti-Hero, Alien Workshop, and others). It offers skaters competitively priced boards, a range of skate-friendly clothing, including sneakers, pants, jackets, headwear and locally made Detroit-themed T-shirts. Chiipss' most noticeable feature is a four-foot-tall, 16-foot-long skate ramp available for use at no charge, backdropped by an epically sized Old Glory. Don't try to visit in the morning—the shop opens at 2pm most days. *10229 Joseph Campau St., Hamtramck, www.chiipss.com, (313) 874-5336.*

Detroit Threads - Since 1997, Mike Smith has kept Hamtramck pulsing with the sounds of Detroit electronic music. Racks of vintage shoes, clothing, and Detroit-themed apparel (designed by Smith and other local designers) line the perimeter. One of the main attractions of the shop, however, is the vast selection of used and new house, electro, techno, ambient, IDM, drum and bass, synth pop, dubstep, soul, rock, and blues music on vinyl and CD. During the Detroit Electronic Music Festival, internationally known artists are known to stop in to visit Smith, pick up some records and shirts, and even spin for a few hours. *10238 Joseph Campau St., Hamtramck, www.detroitthreadsstore.com, (313) 872-1777.*

Euro Mini Mart - Owner Hane Dreshaj's appealing Albanian market offers an incredible selection in a tiny shop. Euro Mini Mart squeezes in a bakery and deli counter, fresh produce selection, European pastas and packaged goods, and traditional corner store fare. The main floor is stocked with Eastern and Western European sparkling juices, American sodas, and shelves of classic dry goods, imported candies, and canned sauces. Head toward the back into the walk-in cooler, which is stocked with imported beer, wine, and fresh produce. For fresh bread, burek, and baklava, homemade yogurt and sausages, and a decent selection of deli meats, cut through the main floor and head to the deli counter. Try one of the tasty, freshly made sandwiches. *11415 Joseph Campau St., Hamtramck, (313) 365-1371.*

Holbrook Market - This midsize neighborhood Mediterranean market offers all the grocery store staples, but with a great selection of halal products and pre-prepared specialties. Take home delicious salad garnishes from the olive bar, buy a bulk package of hummus with fresh flatbreads, and be sure to try a container of the homemade garlic sauce. In addition to a wide selection of fresh produce, Holbrook Market sells Sharifa Halal packaged lunch meats and boasts a butcher counter that displays such specialties as whole skinned lamb and goat. The newly remodeled space features tile floors and bright red signage, which help shoppers navigate around tightly packed grocery shelves. *3201 Holbrook St., Hamtramck, (313) 972-8001.*

Lo & Behold! Records & Books - This charming, pleasantly cluttered shop is the perfect place to spend an afternoon sifting through plastic milk crates filled with LPs, tables of chapbooks, quirky secondhand reads, and vintage clothing bargains (a vestige from the store's merge with the former Hamtramck Hoard House that was in the same space). LP fans growing their collections will appreciate the build-your own crate options and four-for-a-dollar record deals. The comfortable secondhand vibe thrives in this eclectic space, where friendly owner Richie Wohlfeil often hosts in-store events featuring live music or movie screenings. A musician himself, he may occasionally close up shop for tour dates or gigs, so be sure to check hours on the shop's Facebook page. *10022 Joseph Campau St., Hamtramck, www.lo-behold.net.*

» New Martha Washington Bakery - Though it became "new" about 60 years ago, New Martha Washington has been faithfully serving Hamtramck residents since 1925. With immense Old World, small-town appeal, this compact storefront bakery offers customers a full range of classic indulgences and Polish favorites—such as angel wings, kolaczki (a flaky folded pastry with filling), cakes by the slice or whole, and pączki—which bring lines around the block on Fat Tuesday. Though a 1997 tornado destroyed many of the historic elements of this storied establishment, the charming original display cases and a counter scale remain. Visitors shouldn't leave without a peek in the back to see the room-size oven. Domestic shipping is available. *10335 Joseph Campau St., Hamtramck, (313) 872-1988.*

» **New Palace Bakery -** With its delightful old-timey front window display, this inviting bakery is an institution that has held court in downtown Hamtramck for more than a century. Inside the diet danger zone, patrons can choose from delectable Polish favorites, such as kruschiki, airy fruit kolaczki, sugary angel wings, poppy seed or almond coffee cake, marbled and braided breads, and a cast of other traditional bakery favorites. For pączki lovers, New Palace's "secret" is that pączki are available year-round, including traditional fillings, as well as less common options, such as rosehip or the New Palace's combination of custard, blueberry, and strawberry (patriotically known as the United). All treats are served in a casual counter setting. *9833 Joseph Campau St., Hamtramck, (313) 875-1334.*

» **Polish Art Center -** Founded in 1958 by Polish immigrants, Hamtramck's Polish Art Center is one of the country's premier emporiums of Polish cultural and traditional goods. Spread over two storefronts, it carries every traditional Polish ware you can think of and quite a few that you probably can't! The welcoming, colorful shop is absolutely jam-packed with Polish treasures from amber and crystal, to decorative Boleslawiec Polish Stoneware, Polish food delicacies, Pajaki Paper Chandeliers, Wycinanki Paper Cuts, and a vast array of books, DVDs, and novelties. Family-owned, the proprietors are deeply involved in the community and extremely knowledgeable, welcoming, and helpful. Check the Facebook page to learn about book signings, workshops, and other events. *9539 Joseph Campau St., Hamtramck, www.polartcenter.com, (313) 874-2242.*

Polish Market - Located in the heart of Hamtramck's downtown, Polish Market appropriately offers all the fixings for a hearty Polish meal and the bare necessities to stock your pantry. This store is filled with Polish and European imports—meats, cheeses, spices, candies, drinks, noodles, sauces, and packaged dessert mixes—so don't be surprised if you find yourself asking the friendly staff for label translations! From fresh produce and dairy to smoked meats and frozen pierogi and soups, Polish Market caters to the home cook or the heat-and-eat polish food fanatic. *10200 Joseph Campau St., Hamtramck, www.thepolishmarketinc.com, (313) 873-6110.*

Record Graveyard - Contrary to what the store's name may suggest, vinyl is alive and well at Record Graveyard. Selling LPs, 45s, and even 78 RPM records, the store carries a wide range of music. The shop's 1920s minimalist facade, vintage aesthetic, and original tin ceiling contribute to the store's old-fashioned atmosphere. It's best known for its outstanding jazz collection, although it also carries blues, gospel, and soul. It also has enough obscure rock and punk to keep the leather-jacket-clad set happy. Owner Jeff Garbus is always buying used records, so the store's inventory changes daily. *2610 Carpenter St., Hamtramck, (313) 870-9647.*

Srodek's Campau Quality Sausage Co. - A "modern" classic—by historic Hamtramck standards, at least—Srodek's has been one the city's premier specialty food stores since 1981. This family-owned Polish market is best known as a local destination for its fully stocked deli counter and incredible house-smoked meats, from bacon to kielbasa to hunter's sticks to everything in-between. Offering locally baked (often Polish) breads and sweets—including delectable cakes and tortes—Eastern European beers and wines, and a healthy selection of specialty canned and dry goods, Srodek's also sells more than 30 varieties of house-made pierogi—from potato to fruit—that will preclude you from ever settling for Mrs. T's again. Visitors with more adventurous palates should ask to try the spicy head cheese and jellied pig's feet, two dishes featured in an episode of the Travel Channel's Bizarre Foods America. *9601 Joseph Campau St., Hamtramck, www.srodek.com, (313) 871-8080.*

Stan's Grocery - Located on the main vein of Hamtramck, Stan's Grocery is a small Polish delicatessen and grocery store that boasts fresh pre-prepared Polish food to go. Aside from the traditional selection of kielbasa and stuffed cabbage, Stan's also offers hard-to-find European food brands, including a selection of German Bechtle egg noodles. If you are just dropping in for a quick lunch, be sure to grab a Polish tabloid from the magazine rack by the cash counter or pick up a Bounty Bar from the European candy selection. *11325 Joseph Campau St., Hamtramck, (313) 365-1165.*

Victor Bakery - Long known for preparing delicious baked goods from various ethnic traditions, Victor Bakery carries everything from southern-style caramel cakes, to Armenian flatbreads, Italian bread loaves, rolls, sugar cookies, and pastries. With an old-timey sign and hand-painted windows distinguishing it from the silent, formerly industrial neighborhood around it, this "dessert oasis" lies just down the street from Victor Red Hots. Coney dog fans who saved room for a cup of coffee to-go and a delicious fresh-baked cake should take advantage of Victor Bakery's perfectly portioned to-go slices. *36 Victor St., Highland Park, (313) 869-5322.*

CULTURAL ATTRACTIONS

2739 Edwin - A soaring, singular space inside owner Steve Panton's second-floor Hamtramck loft, 2739 Edwin showcases work by regional, national and international artists in a variety of media. The informal environment sets a conversational tone, and the charismatic hardwood floor and 14-foot ceiling provide a striking backdrop to the work. You'll find thoughtfully curated visual art, as well as installations (the space was made for them), avant-garde jazz concerts, literary readings, political discussions, sound art, and dance performances. Gallery hours are 1pm-6pm on select Saturdays or by appointment. *2739 Edwin St., Floor 2, Hamtramck, www.2739edwin.com.*

Popps Packing - A former meat-packing plant turned cookie factory, Popps Packing has been transformed into a residence/studio/gallery/performance space by artists and husband-and-wife team Graem Whyte and Faina Lerman. The yard to the north of the former plant serves as a space for events and installations, which have included an eight-foot hole filled with fog and light, painted animals, and a "light henge" erected for an expressionistic pinewood derby. The space hosts a broad range of thoughtful, high-quality, and fun exhibitions, artist talks, concerts, performances, and happenings. While some events are held in the Popps Packing building itself, there is an additional commercial property across Carpenter Street now owned by Popps Packing called The Storefront—a unique raw space for exhibitions that is well worth a visit. Check its blog for upcoming events and opportunities; artists are invited to submit ideas or inquire about a possible residency. *12138 St. Aubin St., Hamtramck, www.poppspacking.blogspot.com, (313) 283-5501.*

» Public Pool - Public Pool is a gritty, inviting, and exciting cooperative art space in a Hamtramck storefront that presents the work of a wide range of (mostly) local artists. The single, Spartan room seems endlessly repurposable, hosting installations,

ry light on the wallet. It's most renowned for its $5 Monday night improv show, which is the longest running in Metro Detroit. On weekends, the cozy 40-seat venue runs a seasonal series of full-scale productions that are both intimate and entertaining, but never pretentious. Come an hour early for a chance to share a beer and grill out with the cast members. *2357 Caniff St., Hamtramck, www.planetant.com, (313) 365-4948.*

398 | BELLE ISLE TO 8 MILE

SITES

» **Hamtramck Disneyland** - The magnum opus of a 93-year-old retired General Motors line worker, Hamtramck Disneyland is a curious mechanical folk art carnival that explodes out of mastermind Dmytro Szylak's backyard. A native of Ukraine, Szylak began his masterpiece as a "minor" post-retirement hobby in 1992. While, initially, the project began as a touch of ornamentation atop his garage, the vision and scope grew, and the "hobby" expanded with it: first over and through the artist's 30-foot-wide backyard, then atop the adjoining neighbor's garage, and then two stories into the air. Today, constructed out of brightly colored metal and wood—and hundreds of toys and artifacts that embody kitsch and Americana—the curious and transfixing structure towers over the sea of workers housing around it. From rocket ships to the Statue of Liberty to plastic horses to wind-activated contraptions to photos of American icons, the endearing spectacle is a splendid sight not to be missed. Though Hamtramck Disneyland is best enjoyed during the daytime, it is also a special sight at night, when it is illuminated. *Located in the alley surrounded by Klinger St., Sobieski St., Carpenter St., and Commor St., Hamtramck.*

Highland Park Ford Plant - This unassuming 1910 Albert Kahn-designed complex is significant not for its aesthetics or design, but rather for the technology developed within its walls: the assembly line. Ford Motor Company's former Highland Park Plant is a six-story, 3 million-square-foot utilitarian campus built of reinforced concrete and brick, with spare architectural details and monitored, flat, and saw-tooth roofs. The quilt-like brick façade and patchwork of roofs hint at the fact that the factory was gradually built over time to accommodate Ford's rapidly evolving contemporary assembly approaches. Between 1910 and 1922, Ford continually demolished, built, expanded, and altered parts of the campus as the company developed new methods for mass production. In 1913, the plant employed 60,000 workers and became the first automobile factory in the world to implement the now ubiquitous assembly line. The plant became an unmitigated success and was able to produce a million automobiles a year. Within 10 years, production time for a Model T fell from 728 minutes to 93 minutes, and the cost decreased from $850 to $260. Ultimately, however, the plant was a victim of its own invention. By the early 1920s, the technology developed at the facility favored an even larger factory, and so, Ford began developing the massive River Rouge Complex. In 1927, the final assembly line was moved to River Rouge, and the Highland Park factory was used for tractor assembly for many years. Now it is used for only storage. Although none of the original 1910 structures stand—they were supplanted by the adjacent strip mall—the remaining 1915 portions of the plant stand as a monument to Henry Ford's crowning achievement. *91 Manchester Ave., Highland Park.*

POINTS OF INTEREST

C.F. Smith Ghost Sign - A building demolition revealed this bold mural from the early 20th century, advertising the shop's "Cut Price Grocery." *13843 Woodward Ave., Highland Park.*

Davison Freeway - This stretch of road was the first urban depressed freeway in the country, built to keep heavy traffic off of regular commercial streets. *Davison Fwy. and Woodward Ave., Highland Park.*

Detroit Beautification Project Murals:

- **"The Death of Street Art" Mural** - Cartoonish representations of famous street artists carry a casket labeled "Street Art," in this striking piece by Sever. *Joseph Campau St. and Goodson St., Hamtramck.*

- **American Flag Mural** - This amazing mural, by New Zealand artist Askew, reconfigures the American flag as a whirlpool of symbols, bubbling up toward the sky. *8584 Joseph Campau St. Hamtramck.*

- **Jumble Mural** - This swirling jumble of shapes, painted by Reyes, has a companion piece on the side of the Brooklyn Street Local in Corktown. *2238 Holbrook St., Hamtramck.*

- **Owl Mural** - This gorgeous, flowing mystical creature was painted onto the wall above a dentist's office by Triston Eaton. *11451 Joseph Campau St., Hamtramck.*

- **Welcome to Hamtramck Mural** - This smiling figure, painted by Revok and German artist Flying Fortress, welcomes visitors and residents alike to the city within our city. *8327 Joseph Campau St., Hamtramck.*

Elijah Muhammad Home - From 1923 to 1935, the early leader of the Nation of Islam and mentor to Malcolm X, Louis Farrakhan, and Muhammad Ali, lived in this home, where he started his family while he built the movement. *3059 Yemans St., Hamtramck.*

Hamtown Farms - Although the more common vegetables found growing in gardens around the city can be found here, this massive farm sets itself apart by cultivating more obscure produce, including hazelnuts, rutabagas, and pawpaws. *9100 Lumpkin St., Hamtramck.*

Honor Bright Ghost Sign - Revealed when an adjacent building was demolished, this surprisingly well-preserved sign advertising "Honor Bright" boys clothes, complete with paintings of boys playing in the advertised clothing, is a little window into the not-so-distant past. *16145 Hamilton Ave., Highland Park.*

Kowalski House from Gran Torino - You might want to stay off the lawn of this Highland Park home that was featured in the Clint Eastwood film Gran Torino. *268 Rhode Island St., Highland Park.*

Kowalski Sausage Sign - An iconic symbol of Hamtramck for years, this oversize neon sausage looms over Holbrook and looks especially great at night. *2270 Holbrook St., Hamtramck.*

Pope Park - Created in 1982, a life-size stone statue of Pope John Paul II with wide, welcoming arms, stands 15 feet above this pocket park dedicated in his honor. *Joseph Campau St. and Belmont St., Hamtramck.*

Woodward Tribute Sculpture - With sister installations on Woodward in Ferndale and Pontiac, this 30-foot-tall, solar-powered glass and concrete illuminated sculpture tells the story of Henry Ford and his $5 work day. *Woodward Ave. and Gerald St., Highland Park.*

CHAPTER 12
SUBURBS

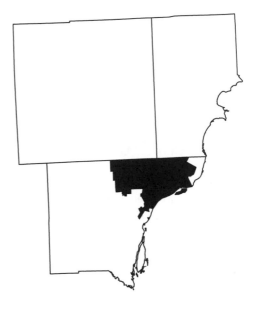

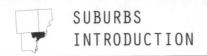

Centered around Detroit, the tri-county Metro Detroit region is the 12th most-populous metropolitan area in the country, home to 133 municipalities and more than 3.8 million people spread across nearly 2,000 square miles. The area is relatively dense, as the majority of the region's residents live just outside the city.

The suburban region's history and geography are inextricably intertwined. As a general pattern, the city's inner ring suburbs nearest the city were built first, while more outlying areas further from the city were developed more recently. With a short drive, visitors can see a century of urban design evolution. While Detroit's innermost suburbs, such as Dearborn and Grosse Pointe Park, were developed along with the city and are rich with historical features, most suburban homes were built during and after the postwar period. Older suburbs often feature the sweeping tree-lined streets and dense blocks of charming brick homes common in the city. In contrast, newer municipalities at the periphery of the tri-county area are defined by winding auto-centric blocks with spacious lawns and recently constructed vinyl-sided homes in newer subdivisions.

The area's older, inner-ring suburbs, especially, are home to well-known cultural enclaves. While suburban Detroit is largely caucasian, some areas are far more diverse, including Dearborn's Arab-American population, Oak Park's Jewish population, Southfield and Inkster's African-American population, and Canton's Asian population.

Like the city that anchors them, the outlying suburban areas collectively offer a diverse culture, rich automotive tradition, and an engaging history. Many of these areas, including Dearborn, Grosse Pointe, and Wyandotte, in Wayne County; as well as Pontiac, Ferndale, Royal Oak, and Birmingham in Oakland County; and St. Clair Shores, Warren, Mount Clemens, and Sterling Heights in Macomb County, are home to a host of popular destinations, including bars, restaurants, and cultural attractions, that showcase the work, flavors, and histories of area residents.

While *Belle Isle to 8 Mile* is focused on the city of Detroit, there are some institutions and sites in the outlying communities that are so extraordinary or unique as to make them a compelling part of a visit to the city. Know that there are many exceptional dining, drinking, and shopping options in the suburbs that were simply beyond the scope of this guide, and we encourage you to explore them if you are visiting the institutions below or other places in Metro Detroit.

CULTURAL ATTRACTIONS

Arab American National Museum - The first—and only—museum in the United States dedicated to the Arab-American experience, the Arab American National Museum brings together stories, artifacts, and exhibits to illustrate the rich history and culture of the Arab people. The only affiliate of the Smithsonian Institution in Michigan, the gargantuan museum, which is architecturally stunning— especially on the inside—is contemporary in its presentation, favoring interactive, multimedia, kid-friendly exhibits that focus their attention on a rich tapestry of stories as much as they do artifacts. Coloring these narratives, the permanent collection includes a fascinating array of art, artifacts, documents, personal papers, and photographs to help visitors relate. In addition to regular and special exhibits, the museum contains a vast resource library through which visitors can browse and hosts a rich calendar of programming, including film screenings, lectures, festivals, classes, readings, and concerts. Check the website for more information. *13624 Michigan Ave., Dearborn, www.arabamericanmuseum.org, (313) 582-2266.*

Cranbrook Art Museum and Institute of Science - The campus of the Cranbrook Educational Community comprises 319 walkable, verdant acres in Bloomfield Hills and features stately academic and public buildings designed in the Arts and Crafts style by renowned architects Albert Kahn and Eliel Saarinen. Cranbrook—home to a top-10 fine arts graduate program and an esteemed K-12 academy—has a great deal to offer visitors. In addition to a wealth of public art—such as the renowned Orpheus Fountain by Swedish sculptor Carl Milles— the campus is home to two major cultural attractions, the Cranbrook Art Museum, and the Cranbrook Institute of Science. The Cranbrook Art Museum, designed by Saarinen and opened in 1942, is devoted to exhibitions of contemporary art, architecture, and design for Cranbrook students to engage with and for the community to witness. The museum provides an intimate, yet spacious, environment for visitors, and the grounds boast sculptures made by Milles, including several fountains throughout the campus. The museum offers regular guided tours of its new wing—including the permanent collection— as well as tours of the Art Deco Saarinen House. Reservations are recommended. The Cranbrook Institute of Science took residence in its current home, also designed by Saarinen, in 1938, and welcomes more than 200,000 visitors each year to its natural history exhibits and programs. The institute features the Acheson Planetarium, as well as an observatory, the Bat Zone (featuring live bats with wingspans of up to six feet), and the Erb Family Science Garden featuring a life study of Michigan plants over different seasons. The institute also offers a variety of family and youth programs. *39221 Woodward Ave., Bloomfield Hills, www.cranbrook.edu, (248) 645-3320.*

» **Detroit Zoo** - Each year, the Detroit Zoo hosts more than 1.1 million visitors to its sprawling, 125-acre campus in Royal Oak, just two miles north of Detroit. One of the great zoos of North America, the zoo is owned by the city but operated by a nonprofit zoological society. Built in 1928, the zoo was the first in the U.S. to use barless exhibits widely. Featuring 3,300 animals of 280 species, here are some of our favorites of the zoo's award-winning exhibits:

- North America's largest polar bear exhibit, **The Arctic Ring of Life**, is a four-acre facility featuring an opportunity to walk through a 70-foot-long clear underwater tunnel amidst swimming polar bears and seals.

- The dreamlike tropical indoor **Butterfly Garden** features hundreds of Central and South American species, and the adjacent free-flight aviary is housed in a stately sanctuary with Pewabic tile peacocks at its entrances.

- **Amphibiville** is two acres of wetlands and a pond featuring diverse frogs, toads, and other amphibians. It was called a "Disneyland for toads" by the Wall Street Journal.

- The zoo is also home to a four-acre ape exhibit featuring a naturalistic habitat filled with gorillas and chimpanzees.

Other attractions include a variety of diverse outdoor habitats, a carousel with 33 hand-carved, hand-painted wooden figures, a small passenger train for intra-zoo transport (for a few bucks extra, kids can even ride with the engineer), movie theaters, a 75,000-gallon fountain with two sculptures of bronze bears, the expansive exhibit of kangaroos and wallabies, an opportunity to feed giraffes, the Penguinarium, many picnic areas, and a spate of regular and seasonal special events, targeted at families and adults alike. *8450 W. 10 Mile Rd., Royal Oak, www.detroitzoo.org, (248) 541-5717.*

Edsel and Eleanor Ford House - Born from a trip Edsel and Eleanor Ford took with architect Albert Kahn to England, the design of the resulting mansion closely resembles the vernacular architecture of

the Cotswold region. Opened in 1929, the Kahn-designed exterior was a masterpiece, including sandstone walls, a slate roof and thick patches of ivy. Kahn's interior was even more elegant and reminiscent of the English countryside, punctuated by a bevy of 14th century stained-glass window medallions, 16th century oak carved linenfold relief paneling, and stone chimneys. The home holds countless treasures of design, furnishings, pieces of Ford family history, and works of art. In addition to the home, visitors will enjoy touring the stunning Jens Jensen-designed grounds on Gaukler Point and the many outbuildings, including the two-third scale Tudor playhouse built for the Ford children. Spanning 87 acres, Jensen's beautifully manicured gardens and meadows use lush flowers, wildlife habitat and fruit to engage all five senses, and make use of his traditional "long view" aesthetic, making them, alone, worth the trip. Visitors can tour the home hourly throughout the week, year-round.
1100 Lake Shore Rd., Grosse Pointe Shores, www.fordhouse.org, (313) 884-4222.

» The Henry Ford - The largest indoor-outdoor museum complex in the country, The Henry Ford is an astonishing, sprawling, must-see history attraction named for its founder, who sought to preserve sites and buildings of historical significance—illustrating and celebrating America's past for future generations. Originally opened as the Edison Institute, the institution was dedicated by President Herbert Hoover to Ford's longtime friend Thomas Edison on October 21, 1929—the 50th anniversary Edison's first successful incandescent light bulb—with several hundred luminaries in attendance, including Marie Curie, George Eastman, John D. Rockefeller, Will Rogers, and Orville Wright. What began as Henry Ford's personal collection of historic objects has become a world-class multifaceted institution crammed with fascinating artifacts, recording and celebrating Americana and history. The complex is made up of three main attractions, detailed below. Check the website for their many fantastic events including unforgettable Hallowe'en at Greenfield Village featuring seemingly endless paths of carved jack-o-lanterns, and the annual holiday lighting ceremony. *20900 Oakwood Blvd., Dearborn, www. thehenryford.org, (800) 835-5237.*

- **Henry Ford Museum:** From the legendary Rosa Parks bus to the chair where Abraham Lincoln was seated that fateful night in the theater to the only remaining prototype of Buckminster Fuller's Dymaxion House to Edison's last breath sealed in a

tube to George Washington's camp bed to the 1961 Lincoln
Continental in which President John F. Kennedy was assassinated
to an Oscar Mayer Wienermobile to a gargantuan, 600-ton steam
locomotive, the mind-blowing attractions bring American history
and innovation alive. Henry Ford Museum is a national Mecca
for history lovers—or the place to go to become one. In addition
to the amazing exhibits and attractions, the museum features
an exceptional IMAX theater with a full program of screenings.
Check the website for further information.

- **Greenfield Village:** Step back in time and explore Greenfield
  Village's 80 acres of the sights and sounds of American history.
  With almost 100 authentic, historic structures punctuated by
  Model Ts, 19th century baseball games, delicious historic dining
  options, a 19th century steam engine, an antique carousel and
  paddle boat, authentic artisans at work (namely blacksmiths,
  glassblowers, tinsmiths, and potters), a working farm, and
  hundreds of historical re-enactors partaking in authentic daily
  tasks like cooking, farming, and sewing, visiting the Village is
  an immersive exploration of the buildings, stories, and people
  of our country's history. Some of our favorite attractions in the
  Village include the Wright brothers' bicycle shop from Ohio,
  Harvey Firestone's family farm, the Illinois courthouse where
  Lincoln practiced law, Henry Ford's prototype garage where he
  built the Ford Quadricycle, Noah Webster's Connecticut home
  where he wrote the first American dictionary, Henry Ford's
  birthplace, Luther Burbank's office, William Holmes McGuffey's
  birthplace, and a replica of Edison's Menlo Park laboratory
  complex from New Jersey. In addition to these relics of American
  innovation, be sure to visit the Hermitage Slave Quarters, two
  1850 brick buildings that were formerly the dwellings of African-
  American families who were enslaved on the 400-acre Hermitage
  Plantation in Georgia—compelling and poignant reminders of
  this painful period in our nation's history.

- **Ford River Rouge Complex and Factory Tour:** After his first
  plants in Detroit and Highland Park, Henry Ford created the River
  Rouge Complex, which at one time was the largest industrial
  complex in the world, producing almost everything necessary
  to build a Model A Ford car, from steel to tires to glass. Visit the
  factory on a self-guided tour and watch Ford F-150 pickups
  being made from an elevated walkway. Additional attractions

include multi-sensory 360-degree theatre experiences, historic manufacturing footage, the largest living roof in the world, and a gallery of five historic vehicles made at the factory. Public tours begin at The Henry Ford's main campus with buses departing for this off-site factory tour every 20 minutes, from 9:20am–3pm. Buses return regularly from the visitor center at the factory, with the last bus returning to The Henry Ford at 5pm.

The Holocaust Memorial Center Zekelman Family Campus - This important institution was the first museum in the United States dedicated to the Holocaust, and as such, many of the excellent exhibits were used as models for the United States Holocaust Memorial Museum in Washington, D.C. Recently expanded, the Holocaust Memorial Center is an extremely moving, impressive, and essential experience. The cutting-edge, thoughtful exhibits tell the story, not only of the incredible evil, but of the courage and strength in the face of it. Often, Holocaust survivors are on the premises to give personal, heart-wrenching testimony about their experiences. Notwithstanding the brutal history and images of the period, the presentations are moving and an eloquent testimony to the power of human spirit. A must-see experience. There is no admission fee, but donations are accepted. *28123 Orchard Lake Rd., Farmington Hills, www.holocaustcenter.org, (248) 553-2400.*

Islamic Center of America - Beautifully housed in modern Islamic architecture within an intricately ornamented, imposing central temple with a 150-foot gilded dome, flanked by two 10-story minarets, the center is an unmistakable embassy for Islam in America. Built at its present location in 2005 to serve Dearborn's vast Muslim population after more than three decades in Highland Park, the center is foremost a Shia mosque—and is the largest mosque in North America. It is also an institute for promoting cultural and religious awareness, including emphasis on resources for learners of Arabic. After the Sept. 11, 2001, attacks, the need for greater dialogue and diplomacy about Islam among Americans has sometimes thrust the center into an unfortunate spotlight as a representative scapegoat for Islamic strife. In 2011, however, a group composed of different religious believers locked arms in solidarity outside the center in rejection of a protest by controversial Florida pastor Terry Jones, showing their support for tolerance rather than divisiveness. E-mail admin@icofa.com to schedule a tour. *19500 Ford Rd., Dearborn, www.icofa.com, (313) 593-0000.*

Marvin's Marvelous Mechanical Museum - Part arcade, part museum, Marvin Yagoda's mechanical repository is a 5,500-square-foot fantasyland packed from floor to ceiling with hundreds of curious and fascinating coin-operated games, animatronic dummies, rides, and other quarter-hungry sights and oddities from throughout the last century. An experience for children and adults alike, the museum is listed in the World Almanac's top 100 most unusual museums in the U.S. Complete with ticket prizes and a concession stand, the collection boasts vintage machines, such as gypsy fortune tellers, "ancient" torture chambers, and mechanical bands, pinball from every decade, and video arcade classics from your childhood. Some of Marvin's collection is extremely rare, some was built specifically for the museum, but everything is playable, so come prepared with a roll of quarters and a couple of hours to spend. *31005 Orchard Lake Rd., Farmington Hills, www.marvin3m.com, (248) 626-5020.*

Selfridge Military Air Museum - Housed in a former hangar, Selfridge Military Air Museum is a museum and air park dedicated to the history and memory of its historic namesake airbase and to the numerous units stationed there over the past century. In addition to a host of informative interpretative displays, the museum is home to 31 antique aircraft and helicopters and an array of military vehicles and missiles. The knowledgeable docents show visitors through the extensive collections of military artifacts and ephemera, scale aircraft models, photographs, cut-away aircraft equipment and engines, an authentic F-16 cockpit, a hands-on air-traffic control system, a hands-on replica link trainer display, and a small gift shop. Don't leave without admiring the World War I airplane. *27333 C St., Selfridge ANG Base, Harrison Twp., (586) 307-5035.*

Yankee Air Museum - Founded in 1981 and based in historic Willow Run Airport, the Yankee Air Museum is an independent nonprofit aviation museum dedicated to celebrating the rich aviation history and tradition of Southeast Michigan. The museum's volunteers and docents have a passion for sharing their unparalleled combat aviation knowledge and passion. In addition to an impressive array of static interpretive displays, the museum's impressive collection of airworthy WWII-era aircraft includes a Douglas C-47, a B-17G Flying Fortress, and a B-25D Mitchell. Visitors looking for a truly unique hands-on experience in an historical aircraft can book a short flight on the museum's B-17G or B-25D. *47884 D St., Belleville, www.yankeeairmuseum.org, (734) 483-4030.*

ENTERTAINMENT & RECREATION

» Ford-Wyoming Drive-In Theater - America's largest drive-in, and a Detroit treasure, the Ford-Wyoming offers a nightly two-movies-for-the price-of-one deal. Showing largely first-run Hollywood blockbusters interspersed with vintage cartoon concession advertisements between pictures, the theater features an original, Art Deco main screen and four ancillary outdoor theaters. Veteran visitors sometimes bring lawn chairs for a laid-back silver-screen experience and are rumored to occasionally bring their own refreshing beverages. For families, several of the theater areas feature swing sets and other playground equipment in front of the screens for that between-film stretch. Though the theater runs year-round—heaters are complimentary—movies are shown only after dark. *10400 Ford Rd. Dearborn, www.fordwyomingdrivein.com, (313) 846-6910.*

Hazel Park Raceway - With 2012 marking the venerable race track's 63rd season, the Hazel Park Raceway is a lovely setting to take part in a Metro Detroit tradition and test your luck on one of the many live races or race simulcasts from around the world. The sprawling and lively campus maintains a number of historical features from its founding in 1949, as well as new state-of-the-art amenities, including three restaurants, several banks of plasma TVs, and a beautifully restored grandstand. As an exclusively Standardbred harness 5/8 mile raceway—in which specially bred horses pull small, lightweight chariots along a short track—Hazel Park is a unique and exciting

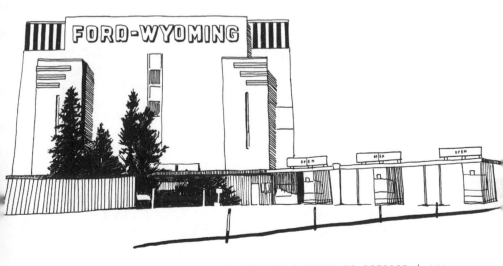

experience even for veteran pony-pickers. For those who don't know a filly from a mutuel clerk, the raceway is accommodating and accessible, offering an array of complimentary primers, glossaries, and quick guides. Don't miss Action on the Apron every Friday for discounted food and live programs. *1650 E. 10 Mile Rd., Hazel Park, www.hazelparkraceway.com, (248) 398-1000.*

Palace of Auburn Hills / Detroit Pistons - One of eight remaining charter members of the National Basketball Association (NBA), the Detroit Pistons have led a storied existence since their founding in 1941. Playing in the NBA's Eastern Conference Central Division, the Pistons have had many successful seasons, including championships in 1989, 1990, and 2004. Perhaps the proudest time in the franchise's history was the late '80s and early '90s, when the Pistons gave Detroit the Bad Boys era of consecutive championships in 1989 and 1990. During this period, the Pistons had one of the most iconic moments in basketball, when guard Isiah Thomas scored 25 points in a single quarter on a badly sprained ankle. Thomas, however, is only one of the city's iconic former stars, which include Joe Dumars, Grant Hill, Ben Wallace, Jerry Stackhouse, Dave Bing (later elected Detroit's mayor), Bill Laimbeer, and Dennis Rodman. The exurban home of the Pistons, the Palace of Auburn Hills, hosts more than NBA games—it is a destination concert venue for popular musicians, traveling shows, and one-time events. Opened in 1988, the Palace offers outstanding sightlines, an energetic crowd, an array of modern amenities, and a seating capacity of more than 24,000, making it the highest capacity arena in the league. *6 Championship Dr., Auburn Hills, www.palacenet. com, (248) 377-0100.*

Yates Cider Mill - An essential autumn tradition for Detroiters, an afternoon spent sipping hot spiced cider while soaking in the fall colors at one of our region's many cider mills, makes the bittersweet end of summer a bit more palatable. One of our favorites, Yates Cider Mill in Rochester Hills has been operating since 1863 and is situated on 1,200 picturesque park-like acres along the Clinton River. The bucolic campus is home to a range of activities beyond the namesake cider mill, including an ice cream shop, a fudge shop, a pony ride pavilion, a petting zoo, a half mile scenic river walk, portrait artists, pumpkin paintings, and stalls selling fall delicacies, like apple cider, apple cider doughnuts, and caramel apples. Since the mill uses seasonal apples, the cider changes as the apple harvest evolves with the season—from Paula reds in August to honeycrisps in the late fall. This unparalleled freshness creates some of the region's finest cider—the perfect complement to the delicious apple cider doughnuts. Aside from the obvious family attractions, the beautiful landscape and river walk make Yates a destination for nature lovers, and the 118-year-old water turbine and cider press make this popular among history buffs, too. Although the mill is open spring through fall, many attractions are open only in September and October. For those looking for a similar experience a little closer to Detroit, try another favorite, the Franklin Cider Mill (7450 Franklin Rd., Bloomfield Hills), which is renowned for its cinnamon spice donuts. *1990 E. Avon Rd., Rochester Hills, www.yatescidermill.com, (248) 651-8300.*

ANNUAL EVENTS

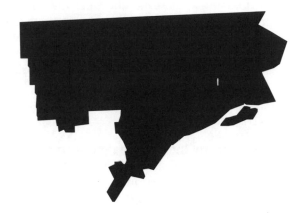

MONTHLY

Critical Mass - A festive monthly ad hoc peloton composed of hundreds of bicyclers, Critical Mass snakes around the city to promote cyclist rights and awareness. Riders meet at the corner of Trumbull Avenue and Warren Avenue on the last Friday of each month starting at 6:30pm.

Detroit SOUP - At these monthly micro-funding dinners, guests enjoy community dialogue and delicious homemade food while hearing pitches from four creative, benevolent, urban agricultural, or social entrepreneurship projects. For $5, guests get soup and a vote, and the most popular project receives the admission proceeds. *www.detroitsoup.com.*

JANUARY

North American International Auto Show - This century-old event, usually hosted each January in Cobo Hall, brings 750,000 visitors to downtown Detroit to inspect hundreds of new car models, custom designs, and prototypes from manufacturers worldwide. A ritzy charity night kicks off the event before it opens to general enthusiasts. *www.naias.com.*

FEBRUARY

Cold Hearted - An annual winter family carnival held around Valentine's Day in southwest Detroit's Clark Park, Cold Hearted features outdoor ice skating, a petting zoo, ice sculpture, marshmallow roasting, and horse-drawn carriage rides.

Hair Wars - A hair stylists' showcase that blends a fashion runway with live performance, Hair Wars features 250–300 outlandish, inspired, and gravity defying hair designs by local stylists. Though it originated in Detroit in 1986, the spectacle has become a national phenomenon, touring cities including L.A., San Diego, Chicago, Las Vegas, and Miami—but it returns to Detroit every spring. *www.hairwarsustour.com.*

Motown Winter Blast - One weekend around Valentine's Day each year, Campus Martius welcomes tens of thousands of visitors to enjoy live outdoor music, ice skating, marshmallow roasting, ice carving, sledding, and pavilions for food and drink in a collective effort to enliven winter. *www.winterblast.com.*

Pączki Day - Every year, Hamtramck rings in the Lenten season with two days of gluttony and good times, centered around music, drinks, and the incredibly tasty pączki—a donut-like filled Polish pastry. Though the best way to celebrate Fat Tuesday is with a booze-filled pączki in downtown Hamtramck, people throughout the region celebrate their real or imagined Polish heritage with a few thousand calories of jam-filled pączki.

Metro Times Blowout - Every winter, downtown Hamtramck plays host to the largest local music festival in the nation. The Metro Times organizes the event, selling multi-day wristbands for ultra-reasonable prices, enabling concertgoers to take in as many shows as they can handle from Detroit's diverse regional talent. *www.blowout.metrotimes.com.*

MARCH

Detroit Bike City - Sponsored by the 501(c)3 of the same name, Detroit Bike City is an annual bicycle trade show and fair that brings 100+ vendors selling and marketing the full spectrum of bikes, bike parts, and gear. The event, which is hosted at Cobo Hall, also features programs and demos for cycling enthusiasts. *www.detroitbikecity.org.*

Detroit Greek Independence Day Parade - Each spring, in the heart of Greektown, marchers in authentic Greek costumes, Greek-American boosters, and lovers of Greek culture and history assemble to commemorate the 1821 uprising by Greece to overthrow the Ottoman occupation—and the impact of Greek cultural on the world. The parade runs a half mile eastbound on Monroe on a Sunday at the end of March. *www.detroitgreekparade.blogspot.com.*

La Marche du Nain Rouge - Based on the French-Detroit legend, the Marche du Nain Rouge is an annual all-day Mardi Gras style costume parade that attracts thousands to the Cass Corridor to banish the impish red dwarf said to have cursed Detroit since 1701. *www.marchedunainrouge.com.*

St. Patrick's Day Parade - Corktown's annual St. Patrick's day parade brings tens of thousands of spectators to the neighborhood as Irish-American organizations, bagpipe brigades, horseman, and others parade Michigan avenue. The parade typically falls before the day, and is preceded by Cork Town Race, a three-decade old 5K that draws more than 6,000 runners. *www.detroitstpatricksparade.com*, *www.corktownrace.com.*

APRIL

Art X - A free multi-day event showcasing work by Kresge Eminent Artists and Art Fellows over a range of media, including dance, visual art, music, literature through public exhibitions, performances, readings, workshops, and seminars. The program is located in several venues throughout Midtown. *www.artxdetroit.com.*

Opening Day - More than 100,000 Tigers fans fill downtown each year for this unofficial holiday to celebrate the Tigers' inaugural game with drinks, food, tailgating, and parties. Fans pack bars, fill parks, and swarm the stadium in anticipation of the game, and the raucous post-game parties.

MAY

Cinco de Mayo - Revelers flock to Mexicantown each May to celebrate Mexican-American food, music, and culture. A parade celebrating Mexicans and Mexican-Americans runs along Vernor Highway starting noon on Sunday of the holiday, and restaurants are packed to the gills all weekend with patrons enjoying margaritas and authentic Mexican cuisine, or just people-watching.

Flower Day - Eastern Market's Saturday crowds are no match for Flower Day. Each May, hundreds of thousands of people flock to the historic outdoor market to choose from 15 acres of plants along Russell Street, soaking up the beginning of summer and a dense array of colors and aromas. *www.detroiteasternmarket.com.*

Movement: Detroit's Electronic Music Festival - Every year, on Memorial Day weekend, tens of thousands of electronic music fans from all over the world descend on Hart Plaza for a three-day celebration of the musical genre Detroit defined. The festival offers scores of performers from many subgenres spread across multiple stages and has featured iconic Detroit-area techno artists like Carl Craig, Kevin Saunderson, Derrick May, and Richie Hawtin, as well as acts like Afrika Bambaataa and The Dirtbombs. *www.movement.us.*

JUNE

Allied Media Conference - An annual conference for independent media activists, the Allied Media Conference employs Wayne State University's campus as its hub and offers informative seminars, meetings, lectures, and roundtables on alternative or grassroots media approaches to the thousands of annual attendees. *www.amc.alliedmedia.org.*

Chevrolet Detroit Belle Isle Grand Prix - On Belle Isle, fans of professional series racing gather to watch widely varied performance racing events over the island's 2.1 mile course. The first day of racing is free to visitors, with a range of reasonable ticket packages for different seating options available thereafter. The racing event attracts 100,000 people annually over the weekend-long event. *www.detroitgp.com.*

Corktown Home & Garden Tour - This annual afternoon strolling tour of the distinct homes and gardens in Detroit's historic Corktown neighborhood takes place each June. The tour provides both architectural and design notes as well as relevant historical background. *www.corktownhistoric.org.*

The Detroit Windsor International Film Festival - Usually held at the campus of Wayne State University, the Detroit Windsor International Film Festival is a festival of short films emphasizing regional filmmakers in different cinematic styles. The festival includes the Challenge event, where filmmakers have 48 hours to script, shoot, and edit a film. *www.dwiff.org.*

Downtown Hoedown - This annual summer country music festival, located around Comerica Park, is regarded as one of the premier country festivals in the industry, having been a career launch pad for Garth Brooks, Rascal Flatts, and many others. The event, hosted by radio station WYCD, switched from a free festival format to charging admission in 2012 but still drew 100,000 people for three days of outdoor music. *wycd.cbslocal.com.*

Indian Village Home & Garden Tour - The historic Indian Village neighborhood hosts a highly anticipated annual summer walking tour of its beautiful and noteworthy mansions and gardens. Participants spend an afternoon viewing different architectural styles and interesting design features, and have the option of lunching at a neighborhood church. *www.historicindianvillage.org.*

Merrick'n Summerfest - Woodbridge Pub hosts an annual day-long block party every summer that's free for all to attend and features two stages of live local music, art, and food and drink for sale from carts outside of the pub. *www.woodbridgepub.com.*

Motor City Pride - A weekend-long festival and parade in Detroit's Hart Plaza, Motor City Pride celebrates members of the Michigan

LGBTQ community with exhibits, live entertainment, community affirmations, and food and drink. The event is more than a quarter century old and draws tens of thousands of attendees. *www.motorcitypride.org.*

River Days - A family-friendly weekend festival designed to show off Detroit's riverfront, River Days boasts carnival rides, live music (local bands with classic rock headliners), sand sculptures, outdoor activities, tall ships, and programming that celebrates the city's cultural and historical legacies. A nominal admission fee applies. *www.detroitriverfront.org.*

Target Fireworks - Timed to coincide with both the American and Canadian Independence Day celebrations, the Target Fireworks, also known as the International Freedom Festival, are a five-decade tradition that boast more than 10,000 pyrotechnic effects. The spectacular display draws more than a million people downtown to watch. Hart Plaza, Belle Isle, and the Riverwalk are the hottest spots for viewing the action, with a small flotilla of personal boats taking in the view from offshore. *www.theparade.org.*

Thunderdrome - Every year, hundreds attend a sporadic summer series of "party racing" competitions for both human-powered and machine-driven bikes at the Dorais Velodrome. Amateur racers compete for prizes, and spectators pay only $5 for each all-day event. *www.thunderdrome.com.*

JULY

APBA Gold Cup Hydroplane Races - These annual races in the Detroit river feature performance racing boats topping out at speeds close to 200 mph. The cup has been awarded since 1904 and draws tens of thousands of spectators to watch the adrenalized speedboats fly around the course from on-shore seating. *www.gold-cup.com.*

Concert of Colors - Detroit's free summer world music concert series, the Concert of Colors grew rapidly from a single outdoor show at Chene Park to a three-day celebration attracting more than 80,000 people. Well-known performers are drawn from Africa, Asia, the Middle East, and the Americas. *www.concertofcolors.com.*

Jazzin' on Jefferson - The Jefferson East Business Association has hosted this free annual weekend summer jazz and blues festival since 2004. Visitors can walk the street festival among prominent local performers, vendors, crafts merchants, and neighbors. *www.jazzinonjefferson.com.*

AUGUST

African World Festival - The African World Festival is a free public street fair offering traditional music, dance performances, a parade of nations, more than 100 different artists, crafts merchants, and vendors of authentic African cuisine. An estimated 300,000 people attend the annual weekend festival, which is sponsored by and held near The Charles H. Wright Museum of African American History. *www.thewright.org.*

Copa Detroit - The Detroit City Futbol League—a municipal soccer league composed of 28 amateur, co-ed neighborhood-based teams—crowns its champion through this hardscrabble day-long bracketed tournament. Free for spectators, the event draws spirited crowds, and local food trucks provide eats. *www.detcityfc.com/dcfl.*

Detroit Agriculture Network Tour of Urban Gardens and Farms - Organized by the Detroit Agriculture Network to showcase some of the city's 1,400 urban gardens by bus and bike, the tour of new alternative food sources in the city draws hundreds of attendees, who pay admission on a sliding scale. *www.detroitagriculture.net.*

Detroit Caribbean Cultural Festival - This annual summer festival celebrating Caribbean culture, cuisine, music, and artwork is three-day family friendly event held in New Center Park each August. Admission is free and open to all. *www.myccco.org.*

Fash Bash - An annual fundraiser fashion show for the DIA, Fash Bash celebrates Detroit art and fashion, including a cocktail reception, runway show, and an afterglow party to wind down the evening. Held at the DIA, Fash Bash attracts a "who's who" crowd and invites guests to show off their own fashion sensibilities. *www.dia.org.*

Sweetest Heart of Mary Pierogi Festival - A weekend-long pierogi festival to celebrate Polish cultural heritage takes place at the historic Sweetest Heart of Mary Church north of Eastern Market. In addition to Polish dinners for sale, there are Polka masses, live music, traditional Polish dance performances, and activities for children. *www.sweetestheart.org.*

People's Art Fest - The Russell Industrial Center hosts a weekend-long festival showcasing more than 100 local artists who offer work for sale, as well as filmmakers, fashion designers, live music acts, and food and drink vendors. Visitors can attend for free, though a small fee for parking on-site applies. Check out the People's Art Fest Facebook page for details.

Praise Fest - Inaugurated in the summer of 2012, Praise Fest is a free, all-day concert at Detroit's Chene Park featuring modern gospel acts, with an emphasis on local talent. Food and beverages available. *www.cp4g.org.*

Ribs R&B Jazz Festival - A three-day outdoor live soul, R & B, and contemporary jazz showcase, this festival attracts tens of thousands of fans and is held in Hart Plaza. In addition to classic tunes, the festival features a (delicious) rib cook-off competition that draws barbecue talent from around country. *www.ribsrnbjazzfest.com.*

Noise Camp - Since 1994, experimental, noise, and other music acts have performed at this kitschy, nomadic grown-up summer camp party—crafts tent, staff nurses, and bonfire included. *www.timestereo.com.*

SEPTEMBER

Cornhole Tournament - A day of revelry centered around Detroit's favorite yard game, this annual tradition is at once a competitive tournament, outdoor party, and fundraiser for the maintenance of the venue, Roosevelt Park. In part thanks to the live bands, local food, and craft beers on tap, hundreds of teams participate in this highly anticipated festival. Check out the tournament's Facebook page for scheduling.

Dally in the Alley - Since its christening more than three decades ago, the Dally has been a growing all-day music and art festival in the Cass Corridor. Local bands, independent craftspeople, and food and drink vendors attract thousands of attendees annually on the first Saturday after Labor Day. *www.dallyinthealley.com.*

Detroit Design Festival - This event hosted by the Detroit Creative Corridor Center features hundreds of designers—showcasing their work at dozens of design happenings over a multiday period in Downtown, Midtown, and New Center. During the event, art, architecture, furniture, fashion, interior design, and illustration are given a collective forum to interact with the public, the city, and one another. *www.detroitdesignfestival.com.*

Detroit Fashion Week - Since 2005, for a week in the fall, Detroit hosts a select group of designers for a show at a rotating location. Women's spring/summer, bridal, formal, and ready-to-wear clothing is shown, and related events, including a trunk show, enhance and diversify the appeal. *www.detroitfashionweek.com.*

Detroit International Jazz Festival - This annual Labor Day weekend festival in downtown Detroit is one of the most visible free jazz concerts in America, having hosted iconic jazz performers like Sonny Rollins, Dave Brubeck, Pat Metheny, and Wynton Marsalis as well as local jazz legends like Curtis Fuller and Marcus Belgrave. Hundreds of thousands of concertgoers trek to Detroit over its three days for a diverse array of jazz. Food and drinks available. *www.detroitjazzfest.com.*

Detroit Marathon - Each fall, tens of thousands of runners lace up for the Detroit marathon, which features a route that crosses the Ambassador Bridge and the tunnel to Canada, making it both an international event and the only marathon with an underwater mile. Team marathons, half marathons, and 5K races are also offered. *www.freepmarathon.com.*

Hamtramck Labor Day Festival - Hamtramck responded to the closing of Dodge Main in 1980 by throwing a festival around which the city could rally. The three-day festival was so successful that it endured and expanded in the decades since, growing to include live music, street canoe races, kielbasa eating contests, a carnival, an art fair, and plenty of food and drink. *www.hamtownfest.com.*

North Rosedale Park Home and Garden Tour - Each fall, the Rosedale Park neighborhood hosts an annual day-long tour of the architecturally diverse homes and gardens in its community for visitors. Attendees have the option of purchasing a buffet lunch with an advance ticket. *www.northrosedalehometour.org.*

Tour De Troit - A gargantuan one-day organized ride for bicyclists that snakes through the city, Tour De Troit draws thousands of riders of all ages for either a 35- or 60-mile route at a modest pace on a closed course enforced by police escorts. The after party in Roosevelt Park features a festival atmosphere and ample food and drink. *www.tour-de-troit.org.*

Detroit Restaurant Week - An annual 10-day soiree every spring and fall, Detroit Restaurant Week features reduced-price three-course prix-fixe menus at more than a dozen high-end eateries throughout the city's core. The event invites new and familiar diners to explore the city's fine dining options. *www.detroitrestaurantweek.com.*

OCTOBER

Art Detroit Now / Detroit Gallery Week - Detroit Gallery Week is a collaborative regional effort for art spaces in Detroit and across the metro region, prompting hundreds of events at dozens of galleries, museums, and nonprofit art centers, and drawing tens of thousands of art aficionados to Midtown and communities throughout the tri-county area. *www.artdetroitnow.com.*

Dlectricity - Inaugurated in 2012, this two-night spectacle captivates Midtown with dozens of free public light art exhibits that run the gamut from entertaining to thought provoking, including projected films that interact with their architectural backdrops, kinetic animation, and curious light displays. *www.dlectricity.com.*

Eastern Market Beer Festival - Autumn in Detroit is rung in each year in Eastern Market by thousands of beer lovers who sample from hundreds of available brews made by Michigan craft breweries. Drinks—and live music—are included with admission, but purchase your tickets in advance as the event sells out early. *www.mbgmash.org.*

Theatre Bizarre and Associated Events - Detroit's carnival of darkness, running from dusk 'til dawn one night every October, Theatre Bizarre boasts hundreds of creatively macabre performers including musicians, burlesque dancers, ghouls, sideshow acts, and performance artists throughout seven floors of the Masonic Temple. Advanced tickets and costumes are required to attend this unparalleled interactive spectacle. *www.theatrebizarre.com.*

NOVEMBER

America's Thanksgiving Day Parade - Bringing cheer and Thanksgiving revelry to Detroit since 1924, America's Thanksgiving Day Parade attracts more than 1,000,000 spectators who line the route down Woodward Avenue to see hundreds of floats, balloons, marching bands, and other favorites. The 10,000 seats available in the grandstand make for in-demand tickets each year. *www.theparade.org.*

Dia de Los Muertos - A multi-day celebration in honor of Day of the Dead on All Saints' Day, Dia de Los Muertos festivities, which are centralized in Southwest Detroit, include a Run of the Dead race, packed bars, and incredible street food.

Turkey Trot - As a token of healthfulness to offset some of Thanksgiving's indulgence, the Turkey Trot ushers in the holiday with a set of short (timed) 10K, 5K, and one-mile fun runs in the morning before the parade. Participants—numbering in the tens of thousands—are known to wear holiday-themed costumes, and cheering crowds at "cheer stations" along the downtown routes provide encouragement for runners. *www.theparade.org.*

DECEMBER

Detroit Holiday Food Bazaar - A celebratory evening-long pop-up market featuring Detroit's myriad small-batch, independent craft food vendors, the Detroit Holiday Food Bazaar moved from Eastern Market to the Jam Handy Building in New Center in 2012. Check out the Facebook fan page for schedule and details.

Detroit Urban Craft Fair - Held annually at the labyrinthine Masonic Temple, the DUCF is a two-day DIY craft fair featuring 100+ crafters and artists that represent some of the region's best maker talent. Fair entrance is $1. *www.detroiturbancraftfair.com.*

Noel Night - This celebration of Detroit's cultural center draws tens of thousands of visitors each year to venerable institutions such as the DIA, the Scarab Club, the Detroit Historical Museum, and the Main Library, as well as dozens of smaller venues, each of which hosts appropriately themed events. Look for live music, readings, food and drink, Santa sightings, and horse drawn carriage rides throughout the neighborhood. *www.midtowndetroitinc.org/events/noel-night/noel-night.*

Santarchy - Santarchy is a national movement of December pub crawls for citizens costumed in Santa garb. Detroit's Santarchy busses more than a thousand appropriately cheered revelers to bars in Detroit from pick-up points throughout the Metro area. *www.detroitsantarchy.net.*

1515 Broadway & Magenta Giraffe Theatre, 26
1701 Cigar Bar, 27
1917 American Bistro, 332
234 Winder Street Inn, 14
24grille, 27
2739 Edwin, 397
555 Non-Profit Gallery and Studio, 223
5e Gallery, 188
7 Brothers Bar, 381
8 Mile Pancake House, 306

A&L Restaurant, 205
Abick's Bar, 198
Abraham Lincoln Statue, 82
Abreact Performance Space, 190
African Amalgamation of Ubiquity Mural, The, 327
African Bead Museum, 242
African World Festival, 421
Akbar's Restaurant, 332
Al-Haramain International Foods, 392
Al's Fish, Seafood & Chicken, 155
Al's Paradise Cafe, 28
Aladdin Sweets & Cafe, 382
Alex Manoogian Grave, 350
Alfred Fisher Mansion (Palmer Woods), 348
Alfred J. Fisher Mansion (Boston Edison), 252
Algo Especial Super Mercado, 216
All Star Books, 316
Allemon's Landscape Center, 316
Alley Deck, 137
Allied Media Conference, 418
Amar Pizza, 382
Ambassador Bridge, 227
America's Thanksgiving Day Parade, 424
American Concrete Institute Building, 372
American Coney Island, 28
Amicci's Pizza, 382

Amphibiville, 406
Anchor Bar, 28
Andiamo Detroit Riverfront, 28
Andrews on the Corner, 266
Angel's Place, 198
Angelina Italian Bistro, 29
Anna Scripps Whitcomb Conservatory, 277
Another Time Antiques, 316
Ant T Bettie OK Puppets Museum, 342
APBA Gold Cup Hydroplane Races, 420
Apex Bar, 238
Arab American National Museum, 405
Archer Record Pressing, 317
Architectural Salvage Warehouse of Detroit, 110
Arctic Ring of Life, The, 406
Arden Park, 252
Aretha Franklin Home, 258
Armando's Mexican Restaurant, 199
Art Center Community Garden, 146
Art Detroit Now, 424
Art X, 418
Arthur and Clara Buhl House, 293
Artist Village, 368
Arts & Scraps, 317
Asian Corned Beef Deli, 306
Assembly Line Buffet, 191
Astoria Bakery, 29
Astro Coffee, 176
ATAC International Records, 83
Athletic Field & Field House, 282
Atlas Global Bistro, 94
Atwater Brewery Tap Room, 266
Auntie Betty's Café, 358
Automotive Mural, 146
Avalon International Breads, 95

Back Alley Bikes, 114
Bagley Fountain, 83
Bagley Pedestrian Bridge, 227
Bagley Vision, 184
Bai Mai Thai, 267

Baker Streetcar Bar, 383
Baker's Keyboard Lounge, 344
Balduck Park, 321
Baltimore Bar & Grill, 29
Bangkok Crossing, 30
Barberella, 392
Basrah Store Fixtures, 338
Bayview Yacht Club, 267
Be Nice Yoga, 133
Beach & Water Slide, 282
Bel Air 10 Theater, 322
Belle Isle, 280
Belle Isle Aquarium, 278
Belle Isle Casino, 282
Belle Isle Nature Zoo, 278
Belle Isle Practice Center, The, 282
Ben & Jerry's, 30
Bernhard Stroh Grave, 291
Berry & Sons Islamic Slaughter, 167
Berry Gordy, Jr. Mansion, 252
Bert's Market Place, 155
Best Deals Market, 258
Beth El Cemetery, 291
Better Made Potato Chip Factory &
    Store, 317
Big Book Store, 243
Big Mack Records., 351
Bike Tech, 318
Bill's Recreation, 133
Bingley Fales House, 293
Birdie Records, 298
Birthplace of Kiwanis, 83
Birwood Wall, The, 346
Bishop Gallagher Residence, 348
Bishr Poultry and Food Center, 318
Bistro 555, 69
Black Bottom and Paradise Valley, 83
Black Dress, The, 110
Blessed Hands Hair and Nail Salon
    Sign, 325
Bloomtown Detroit, 258
Blue Bird Inn, The, 347
Blue Cross Blue Shield Campus Art, 84

Blue Pointe Restaurant, 306
Blumz, 54
Boatyard, 289
Bob's Classic Kicks, 110
Bob's Pizza Palace, 358
Bogart'z Cafe, 307
Boggs Center, 278
Boll Family YMCA, 64
Bonoful Sweets and Cafe, 383
Bonstelle Theater, 133
Book Cadillac Hotel (Architecture), 72
Book Tower, 73
Borreal Wetlands Forest., 282
Bosco Fish Market, 338
Boston-Edison, 252
Bottom Line Coffee House, The, 95
Bozek's Meat and Groceries, 393
Bread Basket Deli, 308
Brennan Pools, The, 370
Brewster-Douglass Housing Projects,
    146
Brixel Murals, 170
Broadway, The, 54
Bronx Bar, The, 96
Brooklyn Street Local, 176
Brooks Barron Home, 348
Brooks Lumber, 184
Brooksey's, 333
Brother Nature Farm, 193
Brush Park, 139
Brush Park Community Garden, 146
Bucharest Grill, 30
Buddy's Rendezvous Pizzeria, 308
Buffalo Bill Train Crash Site, 258
Buffalo Soldiers Heritage Center, 369
Buhl Bar, The, 31
Burk's Igloo, 383
Burns Room, The, 72
Bust of MLK, 258
Busy Bee Hardware, 160
Butterfly Garden, 406
Byblos Cafe and Grill, 97

C.C.C. Club, 325
C.F. Smith Ghost Sign, 400
Cadieux Cafe, 309
Cadillac Place, 253
Cadillac Urban Gardens, 232
Café 1923, 384
Café con Leche, 199
Cafe D'Mongo's Speakeasy, 31
Cafe Gigi, 358
Cakes By Claudette, "The Cake Lady", 365
California Wine Grape Co., 217
Calihan Hall, 346
Campau Tower, 384
Campus Martius Park, 64
Canine to Five, 111
Capers, 309
Capital Poultry, 161
Capitol Park, 73
Capuchin Soup Kitchen, 275
Cardoni's Bar and Grill, 358
Caribbean Citchen, 333
Carmine's Pizza Kitchen, 32
Cas Bar, 199
Casey Kasem Home, 146
Casey's Pub, 177
Cass Cafe, 97
Cass City Cinema, 134
Cass Farms Green Alley, 142
Cathedral Church of St. Paul, 139
Cathedral of the Most Blessed
    Sacrament, 254
Catherine Ferguson Academy, 193
Cave Gallery, 248
Centaur Bar, 32
Center Galleries, 122
Central United Methodist Church, 74
Chandler Park Golf Course, 285
Charles Brady King Auto, 258
Charles H. Wright Museum of African
    American History, 122
Charles Lang Freer House, The, 140
Charles Lindbergh Home, 146
Charles T. Fisher Mansion, 252

Charles Trowbridge House, 298
Charlie's Bar, 200
Chase Scene from Beverly Hills, 146
Cheap Charlies, 161
Checker Bar, 32
Chene Park Amphitheater, 286
Chevrolet Detroit Belle Isle Grand Prix,
    419
Chicago's Pizza, 200
Chick's Bar, 359
CHIIPSS, 393
Chilango's Bakery, 217
Christ Church of Detroit, 298
Christopher Columbus, 84
Cinco de Mayo, 418
Circa 1890 Saloon, 97
City Bird, 111
City Slicker Shoes, 55
City Sports Center, 286
City Wings, 239
CK Mediterranean Grille & Catering, 32
Clairmont and 12th: 1967 Riots Site,
    254
Clark Park, 224
Cleopatra Mediterranean Grill, 309
Cliff Bell's, 33
Clique, The, 267
Cloud Bridge, 232
Coach Insignia, 33
Cobo Center, 74
Col. Frank J. Hecker House, The, 140
Cold Hearted, 416
Coleman A. Young Grave, 291
Coleman A. Young International
    Airport, 325
College for Creative Studies, 123
College of Education Building, 145
Collingwood Manor Massacre, 259
Colombo's Coney, 200
Color Cubes, 84
COLORS, 34
Comerica Park, 65
Comet Bar, 98

ALPHABETICAL INDEX

Concert of Colors, 420
Connie & Barbara Soul Food, 333
Contemporary Art Institute of Detroit, The, 121
Context Furniture, 189
Copa Detroit, 421
Corktown Cinema, 190
Corktown Home & Garden Tour, 419
Corktown Mural, 193
Corktown Tavern, 177
Cornerstone Bistro, 385
Cornhole Tournament, 422
Cost Plus Wine Shoppe, 162
Courage Coffee, 385
Cow Head, 298
Crab House, 359
Cranbrook Art Museum, 405
Cranbrook Institute of Science, 405
Critical Mass, 416
Cuisine, 239
Curl Up & Dye, 111
Curtis Museum at the House of Beauty Hair Mall, 343
Cutter's Bar & Grille, 155

D-Town Farm, 372
D-Town Records, 259
D:hive, 55
Da Edoardo Foxtown Grille, 34
Da Kitchen II, 333
Dago Joe's, 36
Dairy World Food and Treats, 310
Dakota Inn Rathskeller, The, 310
Dally in the Alley, 422
Dangerously Delicious Pies, 98
Daniel Burnham Architecture, 75
David Broderick Tower, 84
David Dunbar Buick Grave, 230
David Ruffin Grave, 350
David Whitney Building, 75
David Whitney Grave, 230
Davison Freeway, 400
Deangelo's Soul Food, Deli & More, 359

Death of Street Art Mural American Flag Mural, The, 400
Dee Gee Records, 351
Del Ray Crib in The Hood, 232
Dell Pryor Gallery, 119
Dequindre Cut, 286
Design on the Prairie House, 298
Detroit Agriculture Network Tour of Urban Gardens and Farms, 421
Detroit Antique Mall, 112
Detroit Artists Market, 123
Detroit Athletic Club, 66
Detroit Athletic Company, 184
Detroit Beautification Project - Fat Captain America Mural, 193
Detroit Beautification Project Murals, 400
Detroit Beer Company, 34
Detroit Bike City, 417
Detroit Boat Club, 282
Detroit Caribbean Cultural Festival, 421
Detroit Center for Contemporary Photography, 248
Detroit City Football Club, 134
Detroit City Futbol League, 287
Detroit Community Acupuncture, 112
Detroit Denim Co., 189
Detroit Derby Girls, 134
Detroit Design Festival, 422
Detroit Farm and Garden, 217
Detroit Fashion Week, 423
Detroit Film Theatre, 135
Detroit Flyhouse, The, 169
Detroit Gallery of Contemporary Crafts, 243
Detroit Gallery Week, 424
Detroit Golf Club, 345
Detroit Greek Independence Day Parade, 417
Detroit Hardware Company, 243
Detroit Heritage Tours, 18
Detroit Historical Museum, 123
Detroit Holiday Food Bazaar, 425

Detroit Hot Air Balloons, 18
Detroit Industrial Projects, 248
Detroit Institute of Arts, 124
Detroit International Jazz Festival, 423
Detroit Lions, 68
Detroit Main Library, 127
Detroit Marathon, 423
Detroit Marriott at the Renaissance
   Center, 15
Detroit Masonic Temple, 135
Detroit Massage and Wellness, 185
Detroit Mercantile Co., The, 162
Detroit Opera House, The, 61
Detroit Pistons, 412
Detroit Police Auctions, 338
Detroit Princess Riverboat, 66
Detroit Red Wings, 70
Detroit Repertory Theatre, 343
Detroit Restaurant Week, 423
Detroit RiverWalk, 66
Detroit Rugby Football Club, 322
Detroit Sail Club, 289
Detroit Seafood Market, 34
Detroit SOUP, 416
Detroit Store Fixture Company, 338
Detroit Symphony Orchestra, 136
Detroit Theater Organ Society, 226
Detroit Threads, 393
Detroit Tigers, 66
Detroit Tour Connections, 18
Detroit Urban Craft Fair, 425
Detroit Waldorf School, 293
Detroit Wholesale Produce, 162
Detroit Windsor International Film
   Festival, The, 419
Detroit Yacht Club, 287
Detroit Zoo, 406
Detroit's Cheesecake Bistro, 35
Detroit's Last Lustron Home, 290
Detroiter Bar, 34
DeVries & Co. 1887, 162
Dia de Los Muertos, 425
Diamond Jack's River Tours, 18

Diana Ross Home, 351
Diana's Bakery, 218
Dime Building, 75
Discount Candles, 163
Dish, 311
Dittrich Furs, 243
Diversity Is Our Strength, 232
Division Street Boutique, 163
Djenne Beads & Art, 55
Dlectricity, 424
Doll's Go Kart Track, 345
Dome Home, 228
Donovan's Pub, 200
Donut Villa, 201
Dorais Velodrome, 322
Dorothy S. Turkel House, 347
Dossin Great Lakes Museum, 279
DoubleTree Suites by Hilton Hotel
   Detroit Downtown - Fort Shelby, 15
Downtown Hoedown, 419
DSE @ Grand, 56
Duly's Place Coney Island, 201
DuMouchelle's Art Galleries, 56
Dutch Girl Donuts, 311
Dyer's Bar and Grill, 311

E&L Supermercado, 218
Earthworks Urban Farm, 298
East Bar, 311
East Ferry Street Historic District, 140
East Side Parks, 288
Eastern Market Antiques, 163
Eastern Market Beer Festival, 424
Eastern Market Cold Storage Mural,
   170
Eastern Market Seafood Co, 156
Eastern Market Welcome Mural, 170
Eastern Market, 154
Eastside Check Cashing Mural, 326
Eastside Locksmiths, 319
Ebenezer AME, 351
Edsel and Eleanor Ford Honeymoon
   House, 293

Edsel and Eleanor Ford House, 406
Edsel B. Ford Grave, 350
Edward F. Fisher Mansion, 253
Edwin Starr Home, 351
El Barzon, 201
El Club Lounge & Mexicantown Fiesta Center, 202
El Guapo Grill, 36
El Papa de los Pollitos, 202
El Primo, 212
El Rancho Restaurant, 203
El Rincon Taraxco, 203
El Taco Veloz, 212
El Taquito, 212
El Zocalo, 203
El-Lynn's Soul Kitchen, 334
Elaine L. Jacob Gallery, 127
Elias Donuts, 360
Elijah Muhammad Home, 400
Elizabeth Theater, 47
Elmer's Hamburgers, 334
Elmwood Cemetery, 291
Elwood Bar & Grill, 36
Embassy Foods, 164
Emily's Across the Street, 84
Empowerment Plan, 189
En Garde! Detroit, 189
Energy 4 Life Health Food Store, 319
Enjoy Again Family Restaurant, 360
Entertainment & Recreation, 249
Eric's I've Been Framed, 339
Ernie Harwell Memorial Park, 192
Euro Mini Mart, 393
Evie's Tamales & Family Restaurant, 204
Exodus, 38

Family Aquatic Center at Chandler Park, 288
Family Donut Shop, 385
Family Treat, 204
Farmer's Restaurant, 156
Farnsworth Neighborhood, 298

Fash Bash, 421
Father Bernard "Solanus" Casey Grave, 299
Father Gabriel Richard Sculpture, 299
Father Gomidas Armenian Memorial, 84
Faygo Factory, 299
Faygo Ghost Sign, 326
Feedom Freedom Garden, 299
Fender Bender, 114
Fillmore Detroit, The, 67
Finney Barn Site Historic Marker, 85
Firewater II Bar and Grill, 239
First Concrete Mile, 351
First Congregational Church, 141
First National Building, 85
Fishbone's Rhythm Kitchen Cafe, 37
Fisher Body 21, 255
Fisher Building, 255
Fisher Theatre, 249
Fishing Piers and Bulkheads, 283
Flo Boutique, 112
Flood's Bar and Grille, 37
Flower Day, 418
Flynn Pavilion, 283
Food Field Garden, 259
Foran's Grand Trunk Pub, 37
Ford Building, 75
Ford Family Burial Plot, 373
Ford Field, 67
Ford Hunger March Site, 232
Ford Hunger March Victim Graves, 230
Ford River Rouge Complex and Factory Tour, 407
Ford-Wyoming Drive-In Theater, 411
Former Translove Energies Site, 146
Fort Street Presbyterian Church, 68
Fortune Records, 147
Fountain Bistro, 37
Fourteen East, 98
Fourth Street, 259
Fourth Street Garden, 147
Fowling Warehouse, 322
Fox Creek, 291

Fox Theatre, 68
Francis Ford Coppola Home, 351
Franklin Cider Mill, 412
Franklin Furniture, 274
Fred "Sonic" Smith Grave, 291
Fred's Key Shop & Locksmith, 113
Frederick J. Fisher House, 253
Frederick K. Stearns House, 293
Ftoni Wholesale Meats, 164

G. R. N'Namdi Gallery, 128
G&R Bike Shop, 365
Gabriel Importing Co., 164
Gabriel Richard Grave at Saint Anne's
    Church, 232
Gaelic League and Irish-American Club
    of Detroit, 177
Gardella Furniture, 274
Garden Bowl, 136
Garrick Theater Site, 85
Gateway to Freedom International
    Memorial to the Underground
    Railroad, 85
Gazelle, 285
Gem and Century Theatres, 68
General Alexander Macomb Statue, 85
General George S. Patton P.L.A.V. Post
    11, 204
General Thaddeus Kosciuszko Statue, 85
Gents By D'Mongo's Salon, 57
George C. Scott Home, 351
George Washington Statue, 85
Georgia Cafe, 312
Georgia Street Community Collective,
    324
Germack Coffee and Tea Shop, 156
Germack Pistachio Company, 164
Ghetto Recorders, 86
Giant Slide, 283
Gilda Radner Home, 351
Giovanni's Ristorante, 205
Gladys Knight Home, 351
GM Poletown Plant, 326

Goatyard, The, 289
Gold Dollar, 147
Golden Fleece Restaurant, 38
Golden Gate Cafe, 312
Golden World Records, 259
Gonella's Italian Foods, 205
Good Girls Go to Paris Crepes, 98
Good People Popcorn, 57
Goodrich Tire Ghost Sign, 86
Goods, 113
Goodwells Natural Foods Market, 98
Gordon L. Grosscup Museum of
    Anthropology, 128
Gospel Hands Car Wash, 299
Grace Harper Florist, 113
Gracie See Pizzeria, 360
Grand Army of the Republic Building, 76
Grand Circus Park, 76
Grande Ballroom, The, 348
Grandmont #1, 372
Grandmont Rosedale, 372
Grandmont, 372
Gratiot Central Market, 165
Grave of the Lone Ranger, 373
Great Lakes Coffee, 99
Greektown Casino, 69
Green Dot Stables, 178
Green Garage, The, 142
Greenfield Village, 407
Greening of Detroit, The, 185
Greenroom Salads, 38
Greensafe Store, 245
Greenwich Time Pub, 38
Gregg's Pizza & Bar-B-Que, 334
Grobbel's, 167
Guardian Building, 77
Hacienda Mexican Foods, 218
Hair Wars, 416
Halal Desi Pizza, 386
Ham Palace, 205
Ham Shop Cafe, 39
Hamilton Carhartt Grave, 230
Hamtown Farms, 401

Hamtramck Coney Island, 386
Hamtramck Disneyland, 399
Hamtramck Labor Day Festival, 423
Hand of God, Memorial to Frank
  Murphy, The, 86
Harbor House, 39
Harbor Island Canal Area, 291
Harbor Island, 291
Harbortown Market, 274
Harmonie Garden, 99
Harmonie Park, 86
Harpos Concert Theatre, 323
Harry's Detroit Bar and Restaurant, 100
Hart Plaza, 69
Hashbrown Cafe, 312
Hastings Street Ballroom, 249
Hazel Park Raceway, 411
Hazen S. Pingree Grave, 350
Hazen S. Pingree Memorial, 76
Hector's Men's Wear, 219
Heidelberg Project, The, 279
Helen L. DeRoy Auditorium, 145
Hellenic Museum of Michigan, 129
Hello Records, 185
Henry Ford Mansion, 253
Henry Ford Museum, 407
Henry Ford Workshop Site, 86
Henry Ford, The, 407
Henry Leland House, 293
Henry the Hatter, 57
High Lift Building, 297
Highland Park Ford Plant, 399
Hilberry Theater, 136
Hipster Beach, 283
Hiram Walker Grave, 291
Historic Fort Wayne, 228
Holbrook Market, 394
Holocaust Memorial Center Zekelman
  Family Campus, The, 409
Honest John's Bar and No Grill, 100
Honey Bee La Colmena, 219
Honor & Folly, 15
Honor Bright Ghost Sign, 401

Hope Takes Root Garden, 193
Horace Dodge Grave, 350
Hostel Detroit, 15
Hot Sam's, 58
Hot Spokes, 100
Hot Taco, 39
Hotel Yorba, 233
Houdini Death Site, 352
Hub, The, 114
Hubbard Farms, 229
Hudson Cafe, The, 40
Hugh, 114
Hurlbut Memorial Gate, 297
Hurlbut Memorial Gate, 297
Hygienic Dress League Wheat Pastes,
  147
Hygrade Deli, 206

Ice Tree, 283
Illuminated Mural, The, 260
Imagination Station, 188
Indian Village, 293
Indian Village Centennial Garden, 299
Indian Village Home & Garden Tour,
  419
Indian Village Tennis Club, 300
Inn on Ferry Street, The (Hotel
  Amenities), 15
Inn on Ferry Street, The (Architecture),
  140
International Institute of Metropolitan
  Detroit, 100
Invictus Records, 86
Iridescence, 178
Isaac Agree Downtown Synagogue, 62
ISKCON Temple of Detroit at the Fisher
  Mansion, 279
Islamic Center of America, 409
Ivanhoe Cafe, 268

J L Stone Co., 55
J.L. Hudson Grave, 350
J.L. Hudson Mansion, 253

J.W. Westcott Co., 229
Jack White Home, 233
Jackie Wilson Home, 352
Jacoby's German Biergarten, 40
Jam Handy Building, 250
Jamaica Jamaica Restaurant & Bakery, 361
James Couzens Grave, 350
James E. Scripps Grave, 230
James Hamilton House, 293
James J. Brady Memorial, 285
James Jamerson Grave, 350
James Scott Memorial Fountain, 284
James Smith Farm House, 352
James Vernor, Sr Grave, 230
Jamison Social Club, 250
Jazzin' on Jefferson, 420
Jefferson Avenue Presbyterian Church, 293
Jerome Bettis Home, 352
Jimmy Hoffa Home, 233
Jo's Gallery, 339
Joe Louis Arena, 70
Joe Louis Fist Sculpture, 77
Joe Louis Home, 253
Joe Muer Seafood, 40
Joe Randazzo's, 319
Joe's Auto Truck Welding Perforated Metal Installation, 193
Johann Friedrich von Schiller Sculpture, 285
John DeLorean Home., 326
John Dodge Grave, 350
John Dodge Mansion, 253
John Judson Bagley Grave, 230
John K. King Used & Rare Books, 186
John's Carpet House, 289
Johnny's Ham King, 207
Joseph Berry Subdivision, 294
Josephine F. Ford Sculpture Garden, 129
Jumble Mural, 400
Jumbo's Bar, 101

Kabob Arbeel Restaurant, 361
Kap's Wholesale Meats, 165
Kay Foods, 165
Kelly's Bar, 386
Kern's Clock, 86
Kids Kingdom Playscape, 284
Kingpin Airbrushing Academy, 339
Kita Pita, 268
Klenk Street, 291
Knudsen's Danish Bakery, 365
Korash Florists, 275
Kowalski House from Gran Torino, 401
Kowalski Sausage Sign, 401
Krakus Restaurant and Bar, 312
Kunsthalle Detroit, 188

La Carreta, 221
La Casa De La Habana, 41
La Dolce Vita, 313
La Gloria Bakery, 219
La Marche du Nain Rouge, 417
La Mexicana Supermercado, 213
La Michocana Tortilla Factory, 219
La Terraza, 207
Lady Louisa's Place, 361
Ladybug Studios, 224
Lafayette Coney Island, 41
Lafayette Greens, 77
Lafayette Park, 295
Laid in Detroit, 326
Las Brisas, 207
Latino Mission Society, 225
Lawndale Market, 229
Le Petit Zinc, 179
Leddy's Wholesale Candy, 366
Lee Plaza, The, 256
Lefty's Lounge, 101
Leland City Club, 70
Levi L. Barbour Memorial Fountain, 285
Levi Stubbs Grave, 350
Lewis Cass Grave, 291
Lewis College of Business, The, 141
Lewis Trade Center, 339

Liberty Motor Car Company Headquarters, 295
Library Street Collective, 62
Life Style Soccer, 219
Lincoln Street Art Park, 245
Little Asia Mart, 114
Little Foxes Fine Gifts, 58
LJ's Lounge, 179
Lo & Behold! Records & Books, 394
Lobster Pot, The, 320
Loco's Tex-Mex Grille, 42
Loncheria el Parian, 213
London Chop House, 42
London Luggage, 244
Los Altos Restaurant, 207
Los Corrales, 208
Los Galanes, 208
Lots O' Greens Farm, 259
Lott Anter Tailoring and Cleaning, 58
Lou's Deli, 335
Louie's Ham and Corned, 157
Louie's Ham and Corned Beef, 313
Louis Kamper House, 293
Louisiana Creole Gumbo, 268
Luci & Ethel's Diner, 43
Lucki's Gourmet Cheesecakes, 339
Luna's Bakery II, 220
Lunchtime Global, 43
Lupita Laundromat, 220

Mac Shack, 36
MacArthur Bridge, 284
Magic City Records, 352
Magic Stick, 137
Majestic Café, 102
Majestic Theater, 137
Malcolm X Home, 326
Malice Green Memorial, 233
Maltese American Benevolent Society, 179
Manoogian Mansion, 300
Manoogian Visual Resource Center Library, 122

Mantra, 115
Marcus Hamburgers Restaurant, 313
Mariner and Riverfront-Lakewood Parks, 291
Mariners' Church of Detroit, 78
Mario's Italian Restaurant, 102
Market, The, 154
Markowycz's European Homestyle Sausage, 220
Marquette, LaSalle, Cadillac, and Richard Sculptures, 147
Marshall Mathers Home, 326
Marshall's Bar, 269
Martha Reeves Home, 300
Marvin Gaye Home, 352
Marvin's Marvelous Mechanical Museum, 410
Marwil Bookstore, 115
Mary S. Smith House, 293
Marygrove College Campus Architecture, 349
Matrix Theatre Company, 226
Max M. Fisher Music Center, 136
McGregor Memorial Conference Center, The, 145
McShane's Irish Pub and Whiskey Bar, 180
Mercury Burger & Bar, 180
Merrick'n Summerfest, 419
Metro Foodland, 366
Metro Music, 366
Metro Times Blowout, 417
Metropolitan United Methodist Church, 259
Mexican Village Restaurant, 208
Mexicantown Bakery, 221
MGM Grand Detroit, 71
Michael Jackson Death and Obama Inauguration Commemorative Murals, 300
Michael Jackson Memorial, 350
Michigan Central Station, 191
Michigan Hot Glass Workshop, 248

Michigan Opera Theatre, 62
Michigan Science Center, 129
Michigan Theatre Parking Garage, 78
Michigan-Shaped Lake, 352
Midland Steel Strike, 326
Midtown Yoga Shelter, 138
Mike Wallace Home, 147
Mike's Fresh Market, 340
Mike's Pita & Grill, 157
Mike's Antiques, 320
Mike's Famous Ham Place, 209
Milano Bakery & Cafe, 157
Millan Theatre Company, 343
Millenium Bell, 77
Milt's Gourmet Barbecue, 314
Minock Park, 372
Mitch's On The River, 102
Model T Automotive Heritage
    Complex, 246
Mondrian Building, 326
Monroe St. Steakhouse, 44
Monumental Kitty, 193
Mootown Creamery and More, 157
Moses W. Field House, 300
Motor Bar, 44
Motor City Brewing Works, 103
Motor City Java House, 361
Motor City Party Supply, 115
Motor City Pride, 419
Motor City Soul Food, 335
Motor City Wine, 44
MotorCity Casino, 190
Motown Historical Museum, 247
Motown Records Original Site, 259
Motown Winter Blast, 416
Motz's Hamburgers, 210
Movement: Detroit's Electronic Music
    Festival, 418
Mr. Lovely Williams & Sons Ice Cream,
    269
Mr. Mike's, 240
Ms. Lottie's Ice Cream and Candy
    Factory, 244

Mt. Elliott Cemetery, 291
Mudgie's Deli, 181
Murray Lighting and Electrical, 340
Museum of Contemporary Art Detroit,
    130
Music Hall Center for the Performing
    Arts, 71
My Dad's Bar, 269

Nancy Brown Peace Carillon, 284
Nancy Whiskey, 181
Nandi's Knowledge Cafe, 387
National Dry Goods Co., 186
Natural Hair Market, The, 59
Nemo's, 181
Nest, 115
Neveria La Michoacana, 210
New Center Eatery, 240
New Center Park, 250
New Dodge Lounge, 387
New Light Baptist Church, 352
New Martha Washington Bakery, 394
New Palace Bakery, 394
New Parthenon, 45
New Rogell Golf Course, 369
New World Antique Gallery, 340
Nick's Gaslight, 45
Niki's Pizza, 45
Noel Night, 425
Noise Camp, 422
Nora, 116
North American International Auto
    Show, 416
North Cass Community Garden, 147
North End Studios, 189
North Rosedale Park Community
    House & The Park Players, 369
North Rosedale Park Home and
    Garden Tour, 423
North Rosedale Park Tree Nursery and
    Outdoor Classroom, 373
North Rosedale Park, 372
Northern Lights Lounge, 240

Northland Roller Rink, 370
Northwood-Hunter House, 144
Nunn's Barbeque, 314

Oakland Sugar House, 259
Obama Gas Station, 373
Old Boblo Docks, 233
Old Fashion Hamburger Company, 362
Old Grace Hospital, 352
Old Kronk Gym, 352
Old Main of Wayne State University, 142
Old Miami, The, 103
Old Plum Street, 86
Old Shillelagh, The, 46
Old St. Mary's Church, 86
Olympia Stadium Site, 260
Olympic Grill, 103
Omega Coney Island #3, 362
Omega Psi Phi Fraternity, 141
OMNICORPDETROIT, 167
On The Rise Bakery, 275
One Detroit Center, 79
One Woodward Avenue, 79
Opening Day, 418
Orchestra Hall, 136
Orchid Thai, 46
Ornela's Bakery, 221
Orsel and Minnie McGhee House, 353
Ossian H. Sweet House, 290
Other Side Lounge, 314
Owl Mural, 400
Ozzie's, 363

Packard Motor Car Company, 296
Pączki Day, 417
Painted Lady Lounge, 387
Palace of Auburn Hills, 412
Pallister Street, 256
Palma Restaurant, 388
Palmer Park, 345
Palmer Woods, 348
Panini Grill & Juice Bar, 335

Parade Company Tours, 321
Park Antiques, 320
Park Bar, 46
Parks Old Style Bar-B-Q, 241
Pauline's Closet, 116
Paycheck's Lounge, 388
Peacock Room, The, 116
Peck Park, 147
Pegasus Taverna, 47
Penobscot Building, 80
PenzDetroiT, 59
People for Palmer Park, 345
People Mover Station Art, 80
People's Art Fest, 421
People's Records, 117
People's Restaurant Equipment Company, 275
Peoples Brothers Bakery, 221
Pete's Barber Shop, 59
Pewabic Pottery, 276
Philip Levine Home, 353
Phoenix Group Building, The, 144
Pinky's Shuga Shack, 367
Pit Stop, 191
Pizza Papalis, 47
PJ's Lager House, 182
Plaka Cafe, 48
Planet Ant Theatre, 398
Plantation House, 343
Players Club, The, 289
Plum Street Greenhouse, 86
Polish Art Center, 395
Polish Market, 395
Polish Village Cafe, 388
Polish Yacht Club, 268
Pollo Chapin, 210
Pollo los Gallos, 213
Polonia, 389
Ponyride, 189
Pope Park, 401
Popps Packing, 397
Potato Place, The, 104
Power House Productions, 324

Praise Fest, 422
Prentis Hall, 145
Presto Gourmet Deli, 48
Prince Valley Gigante Supermercado, 222
Professional Racquet Services, 341
Public Pool, 397
PuppetART, 71
Pupusaría y Restaurante Salvedoreño, 211
Pure Detroit Downtown, 59
Pure Detroit New Center, 244
Pure Michigan Detroit Welcome Center, 13

Quvon Tiki's Gifts Galore, 367

R&R Saloon, 211
Rachel's Place, 187
RAGS, 60
Rattlesnake Club, 270
Raven Lounge, 270
Re:View Contemporary Gallery, 130
Record Graveyard, 396
Recycle Here!, 245
Red Bull House of Art, 168
Red Smoke, 48
Red's Park-In Bar, 211
Redford Theatre, 370
Reen's Cakes & Things, 367
Reinvented Detroit Flag Mural, 260
Ren Cen 4, 72
Renaissance Bowling Center, 323
Renaissance Center, 81
Ribs R&B Jazz Festival, 422
Ric-Tic Records, 353
Rivard Plaza, 67
River Days, 420
Roast, 49
Robert Burns Sculpture, 148
Rocky Peanut Company, 166
Rodin, 104
Rodriguez Vaquerita, 222

Roma Café, 158
Romanowski Park, 233
Rono's Family Dining, 335
Roosevelt Park, 192
Rosa Parks Final Resting Place, 350
Rose and Robert Skillman Branch, Detroit Public Library, 63
Rosedale Hardware, 367
Rosedale Park, 372
Rouge Park, 370
Rouge Park Driving Range, 370
Rouge Park Golf Course, 370
Rowland Cafe, 49
Royal Barbecue, 270
Royal Kabob, 389
RunJit, 189
Russell A. Alger Memorial Fountain, 77
Russell Bazaar, 248
Russell Industrial Center, 248
Russell Street Deli, 158

Saad Wholesale, 166
Sacred Heart Major Seminary, 257
Saint Andrew's Hall, 72
Saints Peter and Paul Jesuit Church, 87
Sala Thai, 159
Salad 101, 104
Salt and Cedar, 168
Salt Mines, 233
Salvation Army, 187
Sam's Barber Shop, 222
Sam's Barbershop, 63
Sandwich Shop, The, 314
Santarchy, 425
Santorini Estiatorio, 49
Savvy Chic, 167
Scarab Club, 131
Schvitz Health, The, 251
Scotty Simpson's Fish and Chips, 363
Scripps Park Sensory Garden, 148
Sebastian S. Kresge Mansion, 253
Second Baptist Church of Detroit, 81
Second Baptist Church, 87

Segways2u, 19
Selfridge Military Air Museum, 410
Senate Resale, 112
Senate Theatre, 226
Señor López Mexican Restaurant, 212
Serman's, 60
Seva Detroit, 105
Sgt. Pepperoni's Pizzeria & Deli, 105
Shangri-La, 106
Sheeba Restaurant, 390
Sheila's Bakery, 222
Shelter, The, 72
Shorecrest Motor Inn, The, 16
Shotz, 69
Show me Detroit Tours, 19
Showcase Collectables, 117
Showtime Detroit, 118
Shrine of the Black Madonna Cultural Center and Bookstore, 341
Sidra Records, 353
Signal-Return Press, 168
Silver Fox Furs, 244
Silverbolt, 260
Simmons & Clark Jewelers, 60
Simply Casual, 341
Sindbads, 271
Sippie Wallace Grave, 300
Sisters Cakery, 368
Site of 1805 Fire, 87
Slows Bar B Q, 182
Slows To Go, 106
Small Plates, 50
Small Ville Learning Farm, 300
Small's Bar, 390
Smokey Robinson Home, 260
Socra Tea, 106
Sole Sisters, 118
Son House's Grave, 374
Sonny Bono Home, 300
Sonny's Hamburgers, 363
Source Booksellers, 119
Southern Fires, 271
Southwest Detroit Outdoor Mercado, 223

Southwest Detroit Taco Trucks & Grills, 212
Spanish-American War Monument, 285
Spectacles, 61
Spiral Collective, 118
Spirit of Detroit, 82
Spirit of Hope Farm, 193
Srodek's Campau Quality Sausage Co., 396
St. Albertus Church, 296
St. Aloysius Church, 87
St. Cece's, 183
St. Francis D'Assisi Parish, 233
St. John's Church, 88
St. Josaphat Catholic Church, 143
St. Patrick's Day Parade, 417
Stan's Grocery, 396
Stanley's Other Place, 336
START Gallery, 63
State Bar & Grill, 67
Ste. Anne de Detroit, 230
Steak Hut Restaurant, 183
Stearns Telephone Plaque, 88
Stella International Cafe Downtown, 49
Stella International Cafe New Center, 241
Steve's Place, 50
Steve's Soul Food and The Key Club, 271
Stevie Wonder Home, 353
Stone House Bar, The, 315
Strictly Sportswear, 368
Stukenborg, 189
Submerge Records, 249
Sugar Hill Clay, 131
Sugar House, The, 183
Summer in the City Cool Breeze Mural, 353
Summer in the City Jefferson East Mural, 300
Sunday Dinner Company, 272
Sunnyside Bakery & Deli, 321
Supino Pizzeria, 159
Suzy's Bar, 390

Sweet Potato Sensations, 364
Sweetest Heart of Mary, 297
Sweetest Heart of Mary Pierogi
    Festival, 421
Sweetwater Tavern, 51
Swords Into Plowshares, 74

Tacos el Toro, 213
Tamaleria Nuevo Leon, 213
Tangent Gallery, 249
Taqueria El Naciemento, 213
Taqueria El Rey, 214
Taqueria Lupita's, 214
Taqueria Mi Pueblo, 214
Taqueria Nuestra Familia, 215
Target Fireworks, 420
Target Mural, 233
Tashmoo Biergarten, 272
Ted Nugent Home, 374
Telway Hamburgers, 215
Temple Bar, 107
Teresa's Place, 336
Terry's Enchanted Garden, 342
Textures by Nefertiti, 119
Theatre Bizarre and Associated
    Events, 424
Theatre Bizarre, 327
They Say, 272
Third Avenue Hardware, 120
Third Street Bar, 108
Thunderdrome, 420
Tiger Stadium Field, 192
Tijuana's Mexican Kitchen, 364
Tip Toe Shoe Repair, 61
Tom Selleck Home, 327
Tom's Oyster Bar, 51
Tom's Tavern, 336
Tommy T's Pub, 215
Tommy's Detroit Bar & Grill, 51
Tour De Troit, 423
Town Pump Tavern, The, 52
Tradewinds Liquor & Wine Shop, 342
Traffic Jam & Snug, 108

Transmat Records, 170
Trinosophes, 169
Trolleys, 273
Trumbullplex, The, 138
Tuba Records, 327
Tulani Rose, 119
Turkey Grill, 241
Turkey Trot, 425
Tuskegee Airmen National Museum, 224
Two Way Inn, 315
Ty Cobb Duplex, The, 144
Ty Cobb Home, 253
Ty Cobb Home, 260

UDetroit Cafe, 52
Ukrainian American Archives &
    Museum of Detroit, 398
Ulysses S. Grant Home, 325
Union Street, 108
United Sound Systems, 257
United States District Court 7th Floor
    Marble, 88
University Club, 300
University Foods, 120
University of Detroit Mercy Campus
    Architecture, 349
University of Detroit Mercy Titans
    Men's Basketball, 346
Uptown BBQ, 337
Utrecht Art Supplies, 120

Value World, 245
Vergote's, 315
Vicente's Cuban Cuisine, 52
Vicki's Barbecue & Shrimp, 215
Victor Bakery, 396
Victor Red Hots, 391
Vince's Italian Restaurant & Pizzeria, 216
Virgil H. Carr Cultural Center, 64
Vivio's, 159
Wah-Hoo, 53
WaLa, 53
Walt's Spirits & So Much More, 273

Walter Briggs Mansion, 253
Walter P. Reuther Home, 260
Walter P. Reuther Library, 131
Warrior Demonstration Garden and St. Andrew's Allotment Garden, 148
Wasabi Korean & Japanese Cuisine, 109
Water Works Park, 297
Waterfront Ziggurat, 88
Wayne County Building, 82
Wayne State University Art Department Gallery, 132
Wayne State University Farmers Market, 121
Wayne State University Planetarium, 132
Wayne State Warriors Football, 138
Webster Cigars Ghost Sign, 353
Welcome to Hamtramck Mural, 400
Welcome to Woodbridge Mural, 148
Well, The, 53
West Canfield Historic District, 143
West Village, 293
Westbound Records, 260
Westin Book Cadillac Detroit, The (Hotel Amenities), 16
Wheelhouse Detroit, 277
Whiskey in the Jar, 391
Whitdel Arts, 122
Whitdel Arts, 224
Whitney, The, 109
Wigley's Meats and Produce, 167
William A. Fisher Mansion, 253
William Cotter Maybury Monument, 76
William Fisher Mansion, 348
William G. Milliken State Park and Harbor, 290
William Livingstone Memorial Light, 285
William Woodbridge Grave, 291
Wish Tree for Detroit, 88
Wolfgang Puck Pizzeria & Cucina, 54
Woodbridge, 144
Woodbridge Bikes Art Installation, 148
Woodbridge Community Garden, 148
Woodbridge Pub, 109

Woodlawn Cemetery, 350
Woodmere Cemetery, 230
Woodward Cocktail Bar, 242
Woodward Tribute Sculpture, 401
Woodward Windows, 88
Woofbridge Feed and Supply, 111
Work: Detroit, 132
Worker's Row House, 192
World War II Memorial, 374
Wurlitzer Building, 88
Xavier's 20th Century Furniture, 187
Xochi's Gift Shop, 223
Xochimilco, 216

Yamasaki Architecture on the WSU Campus, 145
Yankee Air Museum, 410
Yates Cider Mill, 412
Ye Olde Butcher Shoppe, 121
Ye Olde Tap Room, 273
Yemen Cafe, 391
Yondotega, 301
Yum Yum Donuts, 365

Z's Villa, 242
Zachariah Chandler Grave, 291
ZamZam Restaurant, 392
Ze Mound, 301
Zeff's Coney Island, 160
Zug Island, 231